Representation

REPRESENTATION
The Case of Women

Edited by
Maria C. Escobar-Lemmon
and
Michelle M. Taylor-Robinson

OXFORD
UNIVERSITY PRESS

OXFORD

UNIVERSITY PRESS

Oxford University Press is a department of the University of Oxford.
It furthers the University's objective of excellence in research, scholarship,
and education by publishing worldwide.

Oxford   New York
Auckland   Cape Town   Dar es Salaam   Hong Kong   Karachi
Kuala Lumpur   Madrid   Melbourne   Mexico City   Nairobi
New Delhi   Shanghai   Taipei   Toronto

With offices in
Argentina   Austria   Brazil   Chile   Czech Republic   France   Greece
Guatemala   Hungary   Italy   Japan   Poland   Portugal   Singapore
South Korea   Switzerland   Thailand   Turkey   Ukraine   Vietnam

Oxford is a registered trademark of Oxford University Press
in the UK and certain other countries.

Published in the United States of America by
Oxford University Press
198 Madison Avenue, New York, NY 10016

Cataloging in Publication data on file with the Library of Congress

ISBN: 978-0-19-934010-1 (hbk); 978-0-19-934011-8 (pbk)

To Phoebe, Zachary, and Mark

To Forest

CONTENTS

ACKNOWLEDGMENTS

This volume grew out of a troubling interest we both had with how to measure women's interests so that we could empirically (and in particularly statistically) examine the link between descriptive and substantive representation. Many fine works of political theory about representation of women indicate that there *should* be a link between descriptive and substantive representation. But as with so many topics in social science, it is important to test whether reality meets the expectations of theory. As long-time students of institutions in Latin American politics, where descriptive representation of women has increased in many countries to notable numbers, we thought the opportunity was ripe for empirical investigation of this theorized link with a comparative cross-national research design. However, implementing such a test meant grappling with the problem of how to measure women's interests, which led to discussions of what women's interests are.

Some scholars studying substantive representation have chosen to focus on one issue that obviously matters to women broadly and to feminists (e.g., adoption of laws to stop violence against women or abortion rights laws). For the research we wanted to do, however, that strategy was not feasible because it would have required us to determine ex ante what type of interests elected or appointed officials saw as their representational job, or as their legislative agenda. Moreover, we struggled with the different salience of issues given different cultural contexts and levels of development (e.g., while women in the United States fight for equal pay for equal work, women in other parts of the world may be fighting for the right to inherit property). Because we wanted to be able to evaluate and compare the representational activities of officials in multiple countries, who would be affiliated with an ideologically diverse array of parties, and who could hail from different socioeconomic backgrounds and possibly different ethnic groups and religious groups, it was not feasible to select one issue—even if that issue was clearly an important and fundamental right for women—that would be a valid measure across space and time.

This concern led to organization of a round table titled "The Meaning and Measurement of Women's Interests" held at the 2010 Midwest Political Science Association conference. The panel produced a wealth of ideas and showed the depth of interest in this topic in the women and politics field. The latter was clear when the 8 A.M. Sunday morning panel was packed with attendees and the discussion continued until we absolutely had to leave the room to allow the next panel to enter. The success of the panel and the multitude of requests as we were leaving the room led to a proposal for a *Critical Perspectives* section in *Politics & Gender* about the meaning and measurement of women's interests. Thankfully, all the conference panelists contributed essays, and the *CP* was published by editor Jennifer Lawless in 2011.

Still, our questions and discussions continued as we worked on our cross-national study of the representation of women in presidential cabinets. In summer 2011 the College of Liberal Arts at Texas A&M University put out a call for proposals offering funding for projects that could include mini-conferences, and this appeared to be an opportunity to again bring together a group of scholars to further discuss this issue. Ultimately, our mini-conference was funded as part of a much bigger multi-conference proposal developed by our colleague Ken Meier, and in February 2012 the authors of all the chapters in this volume came to College Station to present papers at a conference about "Identity, Gender and Representation: Empirical Analysis of Representation of Women's Interests." Important additional funding for the conference came from Texas A&M's European Union Center. We also benefited from sponsorship by and logistical support from the Program in Equity, Representation & Governance, the Program in the Cross-National Study of Politics, the Department of Political Science, and the Women's and Gender Studies Program. The conference discussion was greatly enriched by four discussants from outside the field of women and politics whose job was to push us all to think broadly. We owe a big debt of thanks to Eduardo Alemán, Ken Meier, Vicki Wilkins, and Rick Wilson for their thoughtful "outside the box" insights, for prodding for greater breadth, and for being such great colleagues. They gave selflessly of their time and "entered the lion's den" when they pushed a group of women and politics scholars to think beyond the case of women. This project benefited from their suggestions at the conference and afterward, and also from their encouragement to pursue publishing the conference papers as a book! The conference also benefited from the support of Judy Baer, Sarah Fulton, and Jane Sell, who served as panel chairs, and from the comments and suggestions of the many faculty and graduate students who attended the mini-conference. In addition, we must thank Bethany Shockley and Samantha Chiu, two hard-working graduate students who provided much-needed logistical support throughout the conference.

That conference was the beginning of what has been an amazingly rapid and gratifying book production process—first, working with all the conference participants to revise papers into chapters and to write introduction and conclusion chapters. Then, with the incredible support of Angela Chnapko of Oxford University Press, the volume sped through the review process and the manuscript as a whole benefited from the comments of the anonymous reviewers. We want to thank all the participants in this project for being awesome scholars and team players and for their helpful comments on the introductory and concluding chapters. It has been an incredibly positive experience to work with and to get to know people whose work we had read and admired, but did not know personally. Without their hard work this volume would not have been possible. We hope that bringing together these diverse scholars, with different global and theoretical areas of expertise, has produced a volume that will help to take the study of representation—not only of women, but of other historically under-represented groups more broadly—to the next level.

Finally, we want to thank our families for their support of this project from mini-conference to final manuscript and their patience while we talked about it with them (and each other). Without their understanding of the long hours this project would require, this volume would still be waiting to be submitted for initial review. Thank you for your ongoing support of both of us, for our research about representation of women, and for understanding why sometimes there were no chips or chocolate left in the house.

College Station, Texas, October 2013

LIST OF CONTRIBUTORS

Karen Beckwith is the Flora Stone Mather Professor in the Department of Political Science at Case Western Reserve University.

Elizabeth Andrews Bond is a PhD Candidate in the Department of History at the University of California, Irvine.

Drude Dahlerup is Professor Emerita in the Department of Political Science at Stockholm University.

Maria C. Escobar-Lemmon is Associate Professor of Political Science at Texas A&M University.

Ange-Marie Hancock is Associate Professor of Political Science and Gender Studies at the University of Southern California.

Kerry L. Haynie is Associate Professor of Political Science and African and African American Studies at Duke University.

Valerie Hoekstra is Associate Professor in the School of Politics and Global Studies at Arizona State University.

Mala Htun is Associate Professor of Political Science at the University of New Mexico.

Alice J. Kang is Assistant Professor of Political Science and Ethnic Studies at the University of Nebraska-Lincoln.

Miki Caul Kittilson is Associate Professor in the School of Politics and Global Studies at Arizona State University.

Emelie Lilliefeldt is a researcher at the Swedish Confederation of Professional Organizations.

Richard E. Matland is Professor and Helen Houlahan Rigali Chair in Political Science at the Loyola University Chicago.

Beth Reingold is Associate Professor of Political Science and Women's, Gender, and Sexuality Studies at Emory University.

Leslie A. Schwindt-Bayer is Associate Professor of Political Science at Rice University.

Michele L. Swers is Associate Professor in the Department of Government at Georgetown University.

Michelle M. Taylor-Robinson is Professor of Political Science at Texas A&M University.

Representation

CHAPTER 1

Dilemmas in the Meaning and Measurement of Representation

MARIA C. ESCOBAR-LEMMON AND
MICHELLE M. TAYLOR-ROBINSON

Since the inception of representative democracy, scholars, theorists, and politicians have struggled with what it means to provide good representation. Representation and "good representation" in particular are viewed as normatively desirable outcomes. Yet saying that representation is desirable is distinct from observing, measuring, and assessing it, which require a clear standard by which representation can be observed and metrics by which it can be judged.

The problem is further complicated when we consider the interests of groups traditionally excluded from power. Especially if institutions have been structured to deliberately under-represent, exclude, or marginalize a group, what representation "means" and what it looks like may be very different from representation of majority interests or of groups with political power. Or it may not. In part, we do not know the answer to this fundamental question because of difficulties in systematically studying representation—chief among those being the challenges inherent in translating our ideas about what representation means into systematic and empirical measures that we can use to study it.

That citizens want their interests to be represented in government is a basic assumption in democratic regimes, and research about democratic institutions explores how the design of institutions creates or limits officials' incentives to do so. Yet how can we study the degree of representation of specific categories of people unless we can define their interests? How can we study representation of historically under-represented groups if institutions are biased against them? In spite of (or because of) institutional structures, who represents those groups, and about what, when, where, and how? These questions, raised in a 2008 article by Celis, Childs, Kantola and Krook, and efforts to develop research strategies to address them underpin this volume.

In this volume we examine representation of women's interests, but the studies presented here are applicable to other groups as well. Women constitute one of many historically under-represented groups in societies across the world. There are traits of women as a group that make women different from other historically under-represented groups—in particular, that women are found in all groups within a society (i.e., geographically dispersed, all social classes, ethnic, racial, religious, and linguistic groups), and the ubiquitousness of women affects political strategies for incorporating women (see Htun 2004). At the same time, the size and geographic spread of women as a group also means that women should be a group that is politically important, particularly in democracies, because women represent at least half of the potential voters, which creates an incentive for politicians and parties to appeal to women.[1]

Women are a strong case for exploring how to study representation of a group that historically has been under-represented because numerical representation in government of women is on the rise. In a few countries women now hold about half of the seats in the national legislature, and in a growing number of countries women now occupy more than a "token" seat in the cabinet, often filling a quarter or more of cabinet posts, and women also populate the bureaucracy at all levels in increasing numbers. Women have obtained positions of power and prominence in many governments, including the highest post of president or prime minister in some countries, leader of the parliament, the most prestigious cabinet posts, seats on high courts, and party leadership posts. In sum, women are more frequently seen in government and politics in many societies, and that may mean that women are becoming *accepted* and *successful* players in policy debates. The capacity of women to make demands, both from outside and from within government, is growing, and that would be expected to positively impact representation of women, making women an ideal test for addressing representational concerns.

In order to systematically study representation, we need to identify interests of the group under study. We must also be able to measure representation of those interests in order to discover which types of government officials

---

1. For other historically under-represented groups, the incentive to appeal to group members for votes may be geographically limited to the areas where group members live—both facilitating representation of the group's interests on a local scale and impeding representation on a national scale. Also, as Htun (2004) and Hughes (2011) explain, electoral incentives may result in group-specific parties reaching out to group members, instead of incentivizing parties from across the ideological spectrum to advocate for issues that appeal to group members.

are providing representation. These same needs apply to the study of representation of smaller, or geographically concentrated, but still historically under-represented groups as well. This volume addresses the topics of defining and measuring women's interests. It then explores how our knowledge about *who* represents women, on *which issues, where, when*, and *how* varies across research questions, research venues, and the breadth or narrowness of the definition of women's interests that the researcher applies.

REPRESENTATION: WHAT DOES IT MEAN THROUGHOUT THE POLICY PROCESS?

A key issue in representation, and specifically representation of historically under-represented groups, is *whose interests* receive representation in government, as even in democratic governments some groups are often excluded, or their interests are ignorable at the policy bargaining table (Bachrach and Baratz 1970; Lukes 1974). If a group is not present in the deliberation of policy, will surrogate representation benefit/protect them (Mansbridge 2003; Rubenstein 2007)? Does presence constitute representation (Phillips 1995), or must officials who can be said to descriptively represent a group also have the ability to get their group's concerns on the policy agenda and to successfully press for the group's interests in policy deliberation (see Mansbridge 2003; Franceschet and Piscopo 2008; Htun, Chapter 7 of this volume), and obtain some of their group's desired policy outcomes for there to be representation (Dahlerup, Chapter 4 of this volume)? And what of symbolic representation (Pitkin 1967)?

Representation of historically under-represented groups has long been a rallying cry for improving the quality of democracy, and a vast literature, including an important feminist theory literature, speaks to this topic.[2] But what constitutes representation? Women and minority groups first pressed for the right to vote and to run for office and later pushed for the ability to exercise those rights. That battle slowly began to produce some electoral successes, prompting extensive scholarly study of descriptive representation. Descriptive representation means representatives who "stand for" their group (Pitkin 1967), and in the case of a legislature it means an assembly whose membership mirrors the makeup of the nation as a whole. Descriptive

2. Certainly women are not the only identifiable group that has been excluded from access to power. Thus, we see the volume as contributing to a broader, cross-national literature on representation of minority interests, including studies of representation of racial, ethnic, and religious minorities, encompassing those with territorially defined interests (and those without) as well as intersectionally defined groups, including groups whose minority status may be empowering in some contexts (see Hancock, Chapter 3 of this volume).

representation is significant because getting group members *into* government increases the chances that the group will have a seat at the policy-making table, and because descriptive representation "symbolizes who is legitimated to make decisions in society" (Paxton and Hughes 2007: 3).

A related question is whether elected officials who are descriptively representative of a broad group that historically was excluded from government can serve as surrogate representatives for sub-groups still lacking their own representatives. Put another way, can upper middle class white women in government serve as representatives for women of color, or for poor women? Mansbridge (2003: 522) defines surrogate representation as "representation by a representative with whom one has no electoral relationship." It is "a noninstitutional, informal, and chance arrangement" (2003: 523). Rubenstein (2007: 627–28) theorizes about the challenges for surrogate accountability to fully represent the interests of another group, particularly when the surrogates do not fully understand the other group's interests, or when the surrogates' interests conflict with the interests of the group that lacks its own direct representatives. Htun (Chapter 7 of this volume), echoing Mansbridge's "anticipatory representation," considers the challenges electoral institutions create for minority women legislators to serve as symbolic representatives of their group throughout their country's territory when they are elected from only one district; she also considers whether by representing minority women they are neglecting the interests of minority men, or of all people of their district. If, by representing the interests of ethnic minority women, they will not represent the interests of a majority of voters in their district, in the next election they can anticipate that they will be sanctioned or defeated (Mansbridge 2003: 516–17). But Htun also argues that by their very presence minority women legislators educate other legislators and maybe even voters, again echoing Mansbridge on anticipatory representation (2003: 518). Htun thus seems to concur with Mansbridge (1999) that those who share a descriptive characteristic are needed to represent that group in a deliberative sense by bringing forward their issues.

The above discussion illustrates the challenges—and the importance—of how one defines representation. How symbolic representation impacts the meaning and measurement of women's interests, and where/how representation occurs is complex. Symbolic representation, like descriptive representation, is also "standing for," but in the sense of being the object of feelings, not as an actor (Pitkin 1967: 103). "[N]ot an acting for others but a 'standing for'; so long as people accept or believe, the political leader represents them, by definition" (Pitkin 1967: 102).

As descriptive representation of women increased, scholars began to study whether descriptive representation led to substantive representation of the group—"acting for" the interests of the represented (Pitkin 1967). But note that Pitkin (1967: Chapter 6) refers to representing as "acting for" and does not actually use the label "substantive representation," though she does use "descriptive" and "symbolic representation." The implication of this is discussed extensively by Dahlerup (see Chapter 4 of this volume). Pitkin does, however, write about "the substantive activity of representing another...substantive activity is going on, as distinct from mere presence..." (1967: 141). Yet Pitkin cautions that the fact that an official "is a very good descriptive representative does not automatically guarantee that they will be good representatives in the sense of acting for..." (1967: 142).

Scholars have asked questions such as: Do female officials have different policy preferences from men? Do women bring different topics to the party platform, the legislative agenda, the court docket, or agency decisions about regulation and implementation than men? And does the existence of a women's agency change policy? Yet results have varied regarding whether descriptive representation leads to increased substantive representation. The accumulation of knowledge is hampered, we argue, by the need to confront and the lack of agreement around some basic questions: (1) What are women's interests? (2) Are *all issues* women's interests? (3) Do all women have the same interests? (4) How should we reconcile, in theory, conflicting interests of different groups of women—how should we handle intersectionality in the study of representation of women? (5) How can we measure women's interests? (6) Is interest articulation, or getting bills on the legislature's agenda, enough to constitute substantive representation, or do the bills need to be passed or even policy outcomes change?

Change in policy outcomes is a particularly high bar for representation because politics is about compromise, so no group gets what it wants all the time. Additionally, the policy *process* (moving from interest articulation all the way to policy implementation) has many stages, and a victory at one stage can be lost or overridden at a later stage. Many conceptions of representation are linked to voters holding elected officials accountable (e.g., policy congruence, promissory representation via mandate, or trustee conceptualizations), but how does accountability affect representation of women's interests when women are only half the potential voters in a district, or when different women have different policy preferences (see Beckwith, Chapter 2 of this volume; Hancock, Chapter 3 of this volume)? Do voters reward and/or punish individual officials or parties? If a party represents women (descriptively or substantively), will that help the party to win the next election? What if voters reward elected officials for providing particularistic benefits, or community resources and infrastructure; is that representation of women's interests? It could qualify for Pitkin's (1967) representation as "acting in the interest of" a voter or community, and if said particularistic benefit ameliorated a situation that was disproportionately affecting women it might also fit into Smooth's (2011) broadened conceptualization of "women's interest."

Figure 1.1 illustrates the complexity of the process of representation. Many groups in society—some with compatible interests or in coalition, and others

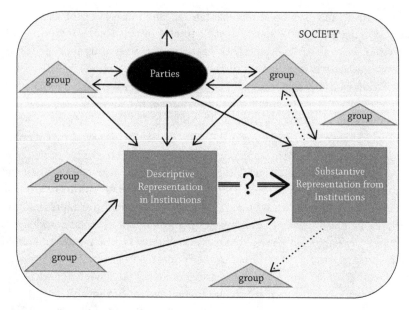

Figure 1.1
The Complex Process of Representation

with conflicting interests—attempt to obtain representation. Parties respond to groups and voters, so some groups find themselves having influence upon parties. Some groups do not find their interests taken up by parties, and some will seek to directly influence government institutions. But, parties can also educate or shape society's preferences (recall Mansbridge's anticipatory representation) by the types of people they place in government and the policies they work for. Descriptive representation in government institutions (conceived broadly as various institutions at all levels of government) *is expected to* influence the types of policies that government institutions produce, but the questions of whether it does, when, and in what institutions (see Celis et al. 2008: 103, 105) are subjects for empirical research, including some in this volume. Policy outputs (substantive representation) generate feedback loops, with the possibility of mobilizing (new or old) groups, which can increase or decrease support for parties in the next election, and influence the next iteration in the policy-making debate. In sum, representation of a historically under-represented group is a contingent and multipart process.

STUDYING REPRESENTATION: PROPOSITIONS AND TESTABLE IMPLICATIONS

Representation is a contingent process. Representation can occur in various venues or by various actors, but it may not occur or it may start (interests are articulated) but not be finished (policy outcomes are not forthcoming) due to power imbalances across groups (see Beckwith, Chapter 2 of this volume). For example, a group may demand representation of their group or representation on specific issues. There may, however, be disagreement within the group about the specific nature of their policy preferences, leading to competing policy demands. Other groups may oppose the first group's inclusion in government or the group's policy preferences. The group demanding entrance may obtain positions in government—providing descriptive and possibly symbolic representation—but they might not achieve substantive representation. Due to diversity within the group, only some privileged sub-groups may be represented in actuality, though as Hancock (Chapter 3 of this volume) reminds us, who those privileged sub-groups are can vary across issues and venues.

Representation (descriptive, symbolic, substantive) can occur in diverse local to national government institutions: elected (legislature), appointed (cabinet, court), bureaucratic agencies (with women's agencies being of particular interest for their potential influence on all venues for representation). However, some venues for representation may be more likely to change policy, while others may bring attention to the issue or policy preference, but not go beyond that (Beckwith, Chapter 2 of this volume). Differences in the effectiveness of venues for bringing about changes in policy outcomes point to the need to consider the meaning of substantive representation: Is articulating an issue in government substantive representation, or must there also be policy change, or is the latter stretching the concept of substantive representation (see Beckwith, Chapter 2 of this volume; Dahlerup, Chapter 4 of this volume)?

The policy process generates feedback loops. The dynamic component to representation may enhance or constrain representation of historically under-represented groups, or intersectionally defined sub-groups (see Hancock, Chapter 3 of this volume). For example, if more women are elected to the legislature and they produce laws that appeal to voters (possibly voters who previously perceived their interests to be under-represented), then parties may receive signals from voters to continue nominating women or to nominate more women. However, if the group's representatives articulate issues that produce strong and organized opposition, making them seem like electorally weaker candidates, they may find their issues obstructed by representatives of other groups within their institution, obstructed in other parts of government, or parties may not nominate group representatives.

The contingent nature of representation and the policy process depicted in Figure 1.1 suggests three propositions. While each proposition is not necessarily directly testable, they generate observable implications that could be tested. Support for a testable implication provides a way to triangulate on whether the proposition is correct or not. For each proposition we offer two implications which are evaluated in the volume's empirical chapters.

Proposition 1

Incentives to incorporate a new group into politics ebb and flow due to fluctuating organizational strength and unity of the group demanding representation, or in response to feedback loops prompted by policy battles that threaten or compliment the interests of groups with long-established power. As a result, the capacity of a historically under-represented group to obtain presence in government may vary over time, and across institutions. The quest for descriptive representation is about seeking a venue in which interests, issues, and preferences can be articulated and have a chance to be realized.

Implication 1.1

Women's access to decision-making venues increases as women as a group become organized and demand voice and participation.

Implication 1.2

Women's access to decision-making venues will decrease if women's issues or preferences threaten the power of groups with long-established power.

Proposition 2

People elect representatives to articulate their interests. Even when people have a common interest, they often disagree about issues or have different preferences. Similarly, groups in society may have contradictory interests or preferences. Consequently, even if a group articulates an interest and there are descriptive representatives of that group in government, the group (or some subsets of the group) may not obtain substantive representation.

Implication 2.1

Women in government (regardless of venue) will articulate women's issues more than men.

Implication 2.2

As the visibility of women as a politically relevant group and women's access to government venues expand, more divergent preferences around the same issues will be articulated.

2.2A

More women in government leads to more women's interests being articulated.

2.2B

Women being present in more venues leads to articulation of more women's interests.

Proposition 3

Policy preferences can be articulated in one government venue, made into laws or regulations in another, and implemented in a third (see Celis et al. 2008: 105). Where a group has descriptive representation will influence which institutions, agencies, or levels of government respond to their demands for representation by articulating the group's interests and preferences or by acting on them to change policy. Because some government venues may be more effective for getting a policy preference heard than for actually changing policy, a group's success at obtaining its policy preferences may be limited if it has access in only some venues. Equally important, though, is that policy articulation, adoption, and implementation is a multistage process (recall Figure 1.1). Policy opponents can organize and attempt to stifle policy promoted by new groups (or sub-groups) by either preventing their selection or by blocking adoption and/or implementation at later stages in the policy process if the new group obtains policy victories at early stages. Groups seeking representation must strategize dynamically to navigate this process and maximize their chances of success.

Implication 3.1

Access to the right venue is critical for the ability of representatives of women's interests to change policy.

Implication 3.2

Success in realizing the transformation of preferences into policy is more likely when women have an influential voice in multiple venues.

We expect the definition of women's interests will matter for who the players (supporters and opponents) are regarding a policy topic, their strategy, the venue(s) where the policy will be made and implemented, and whether the policy is politically useful or harmful for politicians or parties. Definitions of representation, what counts as fair representation of women, and how expectations have changed over time and may differ across venues in government are themes that this book grapples with. How we define "women's interests" and how we move from the definition of this contentious concept to indicators of representation *should be expected* to produce different empirical findings about whether representation of women's interests is occurring.

DEFINING WOMEN'S INTERESTS

A major challenge to the empirical study of whether representation of women *in* government produces representation *of* women is defining what are women's interests.[3] Women are half of the population in almost every electoral unit of the world's democracies, so women's interests should be part of the political agenda for parties, politicians, and governments everywhere. Yet women are a diverse group, and not surprisingly there are disagreements among women. In addition, the concerns of women—even when women agree—vary across time and space. For example, when women did not have the right to vote, suffrage was a major women's interest (though even on that interest there was disagreement among women). Having obtained the right to vote and run for office, women's interests have shifted to how to exercise those rights. Even today, we cannot say that women worldwide have the same interests. In advanced industrialized democracies, women have the right to vote and hold office, and they have education levels similar to, or greater than, men. Women participate in the workforce, and equal treatment is stipulated by law. Yet even in those "advantaged" settings, where women have achieved some semblance of legal equality, the interests of women differ across countries. For example, in Scandinavian countries, maternity and child care are accepted and guaranteed rights, and women's interests have moved to other topics; in the United States, however, maternity and child care policies remain contentious and are a still a women's interest, though there is disagreement about how this interest should be addressed by government policy. Not all scholars agree with equating family issues and women's issues. Baldez (2011: 421) argues that doing so "essentializes traditional norms about women, and discourages men from embracing them. Defining family issues as consonant with women's interests precludes defining them as issues that men and women increasingly share (or should share). . . ." Meanwhile, in less developed countries, women often have interests they are still trying to get on the policy agenda, such as

3. As Dahlerup (Chapter 4 of this volume) explains, even within feminist research there is disagreement about what constitutes women's interests.

protection against violence in the home or the right to inherit property. Here again, women have different preferences, even when there is agreement on the interest that needs to be addressed.

Further compounding the research challenge, scholars have disagreed about how to define and measure these interests. For instance, comments from distinguished panelists at a 2010 Midwest Political Science Association conference roundtable, "The Meaning and Measurement of Women's Interests," highlighted some of the challenges of this enterprise. Lisa Baldez (2011) offered a narrower measurement, suggesting that what women share is really an interest in not being discriminated against because they are women (something Beckwith, Chapter 2 of this volume and 2011, refers to as a "meta-interest"). For Baldez, other definitions run the risk of reinforcing stereotypical thinking about male and female roles, but by ending discrimination women can pursue other interests, whatever they are, and thus she recommends using the United Nations Convention on the Elimination of All Forms of Discrimination Against Women (CEDAW) to measure interests. Reingold and Swers (2011) eschew predefined lists of women's interests and prefer to define them endogenously, focusing on the contentious political process that often surrounds the articulation of these issues (also see Celis et al. 2008: 106). Weldon (2011a) challenges the entire enterprise of defining women's interests, suggesting a social perspective that allows us to think of women as able to organize in solidarity because of collective experiences of inequalities, without positing that there is a shared interest. When we add in challenges posed by women's intersectional identities, the problem of which women are doing the representing becomes even thornier (Smooth 2011).

In the face of this challenge, how can we define women's interests in order to study whether women's interests are being represented, by whom, when, where, and how? Part I of this volume, "Representation: Theoretical Aspects," focuses on building theory for studying representation of women's interests.

Karen Beckwith, in Chapter 2, provides a thoughtful explication of the difference between *interests, issues,* and *preferences.* She explains that "[w]omen have similar experiences and share similar circumstances that give rise to political interests." Yet she underscores that women's interests are not essentialist, but are "socially constructed within specific contexts, coalitions, and organizations" (Beckwith, Chapter 2 of this volume, quoting Vickers 2006: 22). As a way to identify a women's interest, she suggests that "[i]f women are the major disputants in an issue contest, this is probably a strong signal that a women's *interest* is involved; in fact, that the interest of concern is a women's interest," and that finding intersectional disputes among women also indicates that a women's interest is at stake.

For Beckwith and the other contributors to this volume, an "interest" is a fundamental substantive value about which people (or a sub-group of the population) are concerned and want to change or wish to defend, and thus want government to address.[4] Under this definition there can be *societal interests* that are matters of concern for all the people of a community, or there can be *group interests* that matter to some segment of the population (e.g., women, environmentalists, native peoples). "In contrast to interests, issues are strategic choices that emphasize components of interest as a point of mobilization and policy initiative. Derived from interests, issues are more specific, immediate, and limited" (Beckwith, Chapter 2 of this volume). Even if (and it is an if) there is agreement about the need to address an issue, women may still disagree about the specific policies they would like to see enacted, which reflect different "preferences."

Ange-Marie Hancock, in Chapter 3, confronts the challenges of fully operationalizing intersectionality. It has become accepted in women and politics scholarship that women are a varied group, and that many women in government wear multiple identity "hats." But Hancock argues that existing work about how multiple identities affect representation of women tends to use an additive research design, possibly including interaction terms, which comports with conventional statistical methods, but is incomplete because it views race/ethnicity as a static category. Hancock argues that this strategy does not account for much of the important nuance in intersectional identity. She proposes "paradigm intersectionality" that "considers intersectionality to be an analytical framework...that corrects the imbalances of both the intersectionality embodied and intersectionality as testable explanation approaches to empirically operationalizing intersectionality," and then offers examples of how this strategy might change our findings about who represents women's interests and how.

In Chapter 4, Drude Dahlerup argues that the literature suffers from conceptual stretching with respect to the meaning of substantive representation, and that this lack of clarity is an explanation for disparate findings about representation of women, as well as the negative conclusions of many feminists about the effectiveness of women in government at representing women. Contrary to some authors in this volume, she emphatically states that "[t]he concept of 'substantive representation of women'...only makes sense when embedded in feminist theory about changing male dominance." Her chapter proposes research strategies that do not require an a priori definition of "women's interests." She proposes an empirical approach in which researchers seek to identify issues where multiple women's organizations work together, suggesting that broad alliances are a sign of a women's interest. Her chapter indicates that part of the frustration feminists feel about women politicians is

---

4. As political scientists we are concerned with the public side of interests—topics that people want to get onto the government's policy agenda. There may also be private interests that concern people, but which they do not view as matters that government should address and attempt to regulate.

that they do not view articulation of women's interests, even feminist women's interests, as enough; they want changes in policy (outputs and outcomes) before they will conclude that getting women into government has produced substantive representation of women.

ENGAGING IN REPRESENTING WOMEN: WHO, WHEN, WHERE, HOW, AND WHICH INTERESTS?

Part II of the volume, "Representation: Gaining Presence in Politics," primarily focuses on descriptive and symbolic representation of women. This first empirical section of the volume illustrates ways in which groups in society and parties are able to influence women's presence in government, as highlighted in Figure 1.1, connecting in particular to the first two propositions developed above.

Richard Matland and Emelie Lilliefeldt in Chapter 5 explore how preferential voting rules affect election of women, taking into account the preferences of parties and the sectors of the electorate who are the parties' supporters. Studying Norway and Latvia, they show that the effect of preferential voting is impacted by the previous success of women in institutionalizing representation. When parties have adopted highly equalitarian rules for candidate nominations, party voters may decrease descriptive representation of women by using their preference votes to promote men, while in situations where the party leadership has completely stymied the advance of women, voters can serve as a corrective mechanism. In some cases, party supporters vote for women because they are identified with another group with which the voter identifies. Their analysis provides evidence in support of implications 1.1 and 1.2. This chapter also invites consideration of whether intersectional candidates who happen to be female will have an incentive to represent women's interests once they are in office. Should women who have reason to believe they won voter support because of, for example, their ethnicity, labor union connections, or affiliation with some region of the electoral district represent women's interests or the interests of other groups supporting their election?

In Chapter 6, Valerie Hoekstra, Miki Kittilson, and Elizabeth Andrews Bond analyze the appointment of women to constitutional courts in western European countries, an institution where descriptive representation of women is still very limited. They explore how types of appointment mechanisms, leftist governments, and the percent of women in the legislature relate to increased descriptive representation of women on the high court. They find that more women in the legislature influences appointment of women to the court, even when formal appointment procedures remain the same, thus illustrating the dynamic and contingent nature of representation, which indicates support for implication 1.1.

Mala Htun examines surrogate and descriptive representation of Afrodescendant women in Latin American legislatures in Chapter 7. She presents qualitative analysis that indicates that despite their extremely small numbers of seats, most Afrodescendant women do work in the legislature to promote the rights of women, blacks, and sometimes also of black women—they play an important role as surrogate representatives. By studying a group that still has only minimal representation, Htun shows that inclusion can have an impact on *which* interests at least get voiced in the legislature. In addition, she argues that the political presence of Afrodescendant women improves the quality of deliberation, because "[m]erely by being present in power, they prevent people from ignoring or denying this inescapable reality of a diverse society and compel them to take it into account." This chapter connects to implications 2.1 and 2.2A, contradicting the former and providing evidence in support of the latter.

Part III, "Representation: Securing Women's Interests in Policy" is the volume's second empirical section, and it moves the focus to substantive representation. The chapters in this section often highlight the "?" in the arrow from descriptive to substantive representation shown in Figure 1.1 by exploring *which* women (or men) are providing representation of women's interests and of *which* interests and *where*. They provide evidence generally in support of, but in some cases contradicting, the propositions presented above. These chapters also highlight the strategic aspect of obtaining representation (who does the work, where to lobby), how the political opportunity structure faced by politicians can enhance or limit representation of women's interests, and how broad or narrow definitions of women's interests influence the results of empirical study of substantive representation. As Swers writes, "Aggregate indexes of women's issues tend to obscure differences in policy focus among women and the varying incentives provided by the political opportunity structure" (Chapter 9 of this volume).

In Chapter 8, Alice Kang examines factors that help explain which African countries adopted the Maputo Protocol on the Rights of Women. She explores the role that women's rights activists played in the ratification decision of states. Including both liberal groups and conservative religious groups in her study, Kang illustrates the aspect of Figure 1.1 that highlights how groups in society can have contradictory preferences that impact substantive representation (the *who* question). The policy issue (the *which issues* question) for her chapter is not the Maputo Protocol in general, but specifically the clause about protecting abortion rights. She focuses on how different types of groups strategized to obtain their policy preference in different institutional settings and how their actions impacted the probability of ratification, finding that advocacy by women's groups positively impacts the chances of a country ratifying the Protocol. Her research offers evidence in support of implications 3.1 and 3.2.

Michele Swers, in Chapter 9, uses data from the US Senate to study whether the legislative activity of women and men differs on three types of issues typically thought to fit under the heading "women's interests": health policy, education policy, and women's health. She argues that party is an important control when studying the legislative activity of women and men in the United States because the parties have different stances on welfare issues that raise the cost for Republican women of representing women, while Democratic women may be rewarded by their party for representing women, indicating that party interests may trump gender differences. The political opportunity structure shapes the incentives that both female and male senators have in pursuing some topics over others (e.g., because health care is a higher profile topic than education, all senators are more likely to engage in legislative activity about health issues). She illustrates how the political opportunity structure can enhance or obstruct the connection between descriptive representation of women in a chamber and representation of women's interests. Her findings support implication 1.2, provide positive and negative evidence regarding implication 2.1, and support implications 2.2A and 3.1.

In Chapter 10, Beth Reingold and Kerry Haynie utilize data from six US state legislatures to examine *which* women legislate for women on *which topics*, and whether women in different race/ethnic categories behave differently from their co-ethnic male colleagues. They code bills into categories ranging from the narrowest "women-specific issues" to broader categories for health, education, or welfare/poverty bills, and a category including all these types of bills, which permits a finely grained analysis of how gender and race/ethnicity are related to legislative agenda setting. They expect that women of color will be more active legislators on the more broadly defined categories of women's interests that overlap with racial/ethnic group interests. Interestingly, they find that *who* legislates on different topics related to women's interests is complex, and answers differ by both gender and race across each of the measures of "women's interest" legislation. Connecting to Figure 1.1, they show that descriptive representation is linked to substantive representation, but the link is subtle and complex. Women legislators from all racial/ethnic groups are engaged in substantive representation of women, but depending on the definition of women's interests and the measure of representational advocacy, legislative women of color frequently stand out as agenda-setting leaders. Their empirical tests indicate support for implications 2.1 and 2.2A.

Maria Escobar-Lemmon, Leslie Schwindt-Bayer, and Michelle Taylor-Robinson in Chapter 11 study agenda setting with data from Colombia and Costa Rica, by examining the legislative agendas of men and women in both the cabinet and the congress, where the two cases permit an explicit comparison of two distinctive legislative venues within two countries. They explore whether answers to *who* represents women vary depending on *which* types of legislation are included under the rubric of women's interests (women's equality, children/family, pro-poor bills). Women in the Colombian legislature are frequently advocates for women's interests, across most definitions, but in the Costa Rican legislature, gender differences are only apparent for women's equality bills. In contrast, women ministers in Colombia are not active representatives of women's interests regardless of the measure used, and in Costa Rica women ministers are no more active than men—particularly remarkable findings in Latin America, where policy is generally expected to come from the executive branch. The intra-country and cross-national comparisons of legislatures and cabinets speak to the *where* question concerning the venues that are most auspicious for substantive representation of women. Their empirical tests indicate support for implication 2.1 with regard to women in the legislature, but, particularly with regard to the cabinet, the evidence contradicts the expectation of implications 2.1, 2.2B, and 3.2.

CONCLUSIONS AND DIRECTIONS FOR FUTURE RESEARCH

Part IV, "Representation: Women and Beyond," draws conclusions about how the meaning and measurement of women's interests impact the accumulation of knowledge and shape how we study representation. In Chapter 12, Maria Escobar-Lemmon and Michelle Taylor-Robinson return to the topics outlined here: multiple meanings of representation; representation as a contingent and multipart process that can be derailed, as illustrated in Figure 1.1; and the three propositions about representation. This concluding chapter reminds us about the challenging question of whether all action on women's interest topics constitutes representation—does it include "acting for" by conservative women, or just feminist perspectives? This chapter also suggests directions for future research that move beyond simply comparing what women and men do in government: how questions of *who, where, how, when*, and *which issues* shape the political strategies of groups in civil society that are lobbying to improve the quality of life of women, or of other historically under-represented groups. Building on the experience of studying representation of women, the conclusions prompt us to think generally about how research design decisions and even the questions asked can influence our conclusions about (a) what representation looks like; (b) who does the representing, where, when and how they do so; and, (c) if representation is happening. The concluding chapter synthesizes these findings to extract general lessons for studying representation of under-represented groups. In concluding the book we propose an agenda for research that will move forward academic understanding about how and when the representation of historically under-represented groups occurs. Understanding the *who, what, where, when*, and *which issues* dimensions of representation (Celis et al. 2008: 104) is critical for informing policy and for giving groups seeking representation the information they need to gain political voice, thereby improving the quality of democracy.

PART ONE

Representation: Theoretical Aspects

CHAPTER 2

Plotting the Path from One to the Other

Women's Interests and Political Representation

KAREN BECKWITH

INTRODUCTION

Women have shared political interests, and these constitute the foundation of women's political representation. What are women's interests? Who advances these interests? How and where might those interests be represented? This chapter defines women's interests as the basis for women's representation, and distinguishes women's "interests" from women's policy "issues" and "preferences." Differentiating among "interests," "issues," and "preferences" offers distinct analytical advantages for understanding women's political representation; these include the disaggregation of competing and/or overlapping intersectional interests (see Hancock, Chapter 3 of this volume), the identification of multiple strategies for advancing (or opposing) women's interests in different political contexts (including national legislatures and governments), and a recognition and empirical appreciation of issue contests among women.

This chapter employs two women's interests—full equal political inclusion and rights to reproduction—to explore how women's interests can be understood in terms of women's political representation. It demonstrates that shared interests nonetheless produce differences across gender lines, complicating how such interests might be represented in policy terms, and raising questions about which women work to advance women's interests. Finally, it considers representational venues for women's interests: social movements, political parties, and national governmental institutions. As a result, this chapter asserts a comprehensive ambition: to speak of women's representation for women in all their diversity, including across class, race, and country, that is, to join the "dialogue about the parameters of a truly international feminist theory and practice that represents the interests of gender in cross-cultural and historical perspective (Jónasdóttir and Jones 2009: 1).[1]

DEFINING WOMEN'S INTERESTS

Women have similar experiences and share similar circumstances that give rise to political interests.[2] By "interest," I mean the fundamental "substantive values 'that politics puts into effect and distributes'" (Jónasdóttir 1988: 40 in Hill and Chappell 2006: 1).[3] Women's lives are constructed in specific instances by political, economic, and social arrangements that (1) shape their life histories and life options, and (2) differ substantially from the shaping forces and trajectories of men's lives. This does not mean that all women experience exactly the same lives or are subject to the same constraints or benefit from the same advantages, but it does recognize that, within specific contexts, similar shaping forces exist and have similar consequences for women in a wide range of countries. These similarities of women's experiences, deriving from socially constructed gendered constraints and exclusions, provide the foundation for the emergence of similar interests among women.

Because women experience lives shaped by similar political, economic, and social forces, their experiences are constructed by human agency, and hence cannot be treated as essentialist. Women's experiences as mothers are constructed, for example, by public policies providing (or failing to provide) prenatal care, birthing services, child and maternal subsidies, and paid parental leave, and by the availability of and access to legal contraception and abortion. Women's experiences as spouses are shaped by legislation defining marriage, partner legal responsibilities within marriage, spousal protections within marriage, and property and parental rights within marriage and in divorce. Finally, women's experiences as workers are influenced by laws regulating access to and conditions of employment, legal protections against

1. For the importance of feminist theory in identifying women's interests, see Dahlerup, Chapter 4 of this volume.

2. Htun (2005a: 157) identifies three dimensions defining women's interests: "the sexual division of labor, normative heterosexuality, and war and militarism." Iris Marion Young, on whose work Htun builds, identifies "large-scale [gendered] social structures that differentially position [women] in relations of privilege and disadvantage" as including the sexual division of labor, normative heterosexuality and "hierarchies of power" (2002: 410).

3. See also Truman (1951: 33–34) for a similar definition. For Truman, interests are "one or more shared attitudes" that create a "kind of common response," and are evidenced by group voice, claims-making, and interaction.

discrimination and violence against women in the workplace (Baker 2008), cultural willingness to employ women for pay, and family obligations and responsibilities that impinge upon or support women's paid employment, among others. These examples constitute a subset of women's shared experiences and a subset of the factors that construct them, but should suffice to demonstrate how women's lives, in their similarities across countries and cultures, derive from human agency and the institutions and practices that human beings construct and develop.

Circumstances and experiences do not immediately give rise to interests. Interests, like the forces and circumstances that undergird them, are socially and politically constructed. *Interest*, therefore, involves politics and power, and hence conflict, which is not always recognized in the assessment of women's interests. Power shapes the recognition of interests and the individual's understanding of her interests. Identification of *interests* is related to deliberative democracy, where interests are articulated by participating citizens in a context of inclusion, where "all those [likely to be] affected by [decision making] are included in the process," and where those participants would be affected by the resulting "decisions and policies [that would] significantly condition [their] options for action" (Young 2000: 23). Inclusion of affected persons in deliberative democracy also requires "inclusion on equal terms," free "from domination" in the deliberative process (Young 2000: 23). In short, women's interests are evidenced by women's visible assertion of those interests in a context of political presence, freedom, and equality.

In contexts where women are not present, where the power dynamic silences women or requires them to refrain from full expression and articulation, differences in political power are evident and the identification of women's interests is difficult at best, if not ultimately impossible. The identification and shaping of interests are political acts and expressions of power:

> Power is...exercised when [a more powerful actor] devotes his energies to creating or reinforcing social and political values and institutional practices that limit the scope of the political process to public consideration of only those issues which are comparatively innocuous to [him]. To the extent that [the more powerful actor] succeeds in doing this, [less powerful actors are] prevented, for all practical purposes, from bringing to the fore any issues that might in their resolution be seriously detrimental to [the more powerful actor's] set of preferences. (Lukes 1984: 16)

Such conflict is not always visible, but exercise of power that silences women or results in their absence from decision-making venues constitutes a bias in the political system that, again, fails to furnish the conditions under which women's interests are publicly identifiable.[4] Nonetheless, as I argue below, women share an identifiable meta-interest in access to political power and voice.

"Understanding 'interests' as substantially socially constructed within specific contexts, coalitions and organizations is less likely to lead to false claims of objective or common interests" (Vickers 2006: 22). Are there, however, "objective" women's interests that can be conceptualized, or are we limited to considering only what are more accurately identified as issues or preferences? How do we bring women's interests to the fore in a political context in which such interests may be considered, free from domination and inclusive of those whose "options for action" or "life chances" are likely to be affected by the resulting decisions and policies (Young 2000: 23; Giele and Smock 1977)?

We have to take into account the context in which interests are developed and expressed—or fail to develop or are repressed. "The bias of the system can be mobilized, recreated and reinforced in ways that are neither consciously chosen nor the intended result of particular individuals' choices" (Lukes 1984: 21). Because, first, nearly all political offices are held by men, in every political system, and, second, because the presence of women in public office enhances women's mass-level political participation and involvement (Burns et al. 2001), where women are not included across the range of public offices, we might conclude that the *absence* of women in public office functions to suppress women's political participation and the factors that inform and enrich it. That is, the dominance of men in all political institutions, such that women's likely participation is dampened, constitutes a context of *political drag* on the identification of women's interests (see Hoekstra et al., Chapter 6; Htun, Chapter 7; Matland and Lilliefeldt, Chapter 5; all in this volume).

If, therefore, the development and expression of women's political *interests* depends upon women's inclusion in political deliberation as equals, free from domination, the preponderance of men in public office—elective and appointive—makes the identification of such interests problematic. This does not mean that men in office necessarily fail to reflect (some of) women's *policy preferences*, but rather that an identification of women's *interests* is highly problematic in a context where women are not fully included in democratic political deliberation. Women's interests are unlikely to develop or to find articulation in a context of their overwhelming exclusion from governing institutions,[5] despite the range of women's organizing outside those institutions. Moreover, because women also

4. Truman (1951: 34) similarly claims that interests can be identified as the basis "of various potential as well as existing interest groups... [inviting] examination of an interest whether or not it is found at the moment as one of the characteristics of a particular organized group... [I]t is possible to examine interests that are not at a particular point in time the basis of interactions among individuals but that may become such."

5. Note that I do not argue here that parity of women in public office will increase the substantive representation of women; rather, I argue that the identification of

differ along class lines—in terms of what we might expect in regard to the identification of their interests (rather than simply their preferences), and because women are present in all racial and ethnic groups—we need to consider the context of race and class in terms of those who govern, beyond simply the presence of "men" as a group with overwhelming power of governance.[6] That is, how can "women's interests" be conceptualized in a political context of government where, e.g., in the United States, almost all those who rule are white[7] and whose economic circumstances are so much better than is the case for most women (and most men)?[8]

Differences *among* women also require us to consider how women might identify common and/or competing interests in a context of intersectionality. Such identification of *interests* requires *"self-organization ... '* and [assertion of] the importance of women's organizations to democratic politics in order to make women equal to other social interests, class interests, groups interests, and private interests, in all of which individual women also may have an interest" (Vickers 2006: 24; see also Weldon 2011b). Furthermore, Vickers claims, "we can make it a rule of methodology to assume that women will have *both* interests in common and interests in conflict unless there is persuasive evidence to the contrary" (Vickers 2006: 22).

Interests, Issues, and Preferences

Interests differ from issues. Interests are more fundamental, related to major gendered cleavages, social structures, and institutions (Htun 2005a: 157). Interests emerge from constant contexts of women's life circumstances, and from women's opportunities for autonomous organizing and democratic deliberation, free from exclusion and domination. Women's movements' activism locates women's interests in women's lived circumstances (Diamond and Hartsock 1981; Young 2002), in relations to state power that attempts to constrain women's life chances and options for action, and in women's

women's interests will not be possible by examining legislative behavior until there are sufficient numbers of women in public life to construct continuing opportunities for their own relatively autonomous democratic deliberation, independent of the constraining power of others. The equitable presence of women in public office is a necessary but not sufficient condition for identifying women's interests. For a more detailed discussion, see Karpowitz et al. 2012.

6. Diamond and Hartsock identify "sex, race, and class" as "three of the most significant factors that structure social relations" (1981: 719–20).

7. At least 457 members of the 112th Congress can be identified as white (85.4%).

8. In 2010, 261 members of the US Congress (or 48.8%) were millionaires, placing them in the top 1% of individual income holders in the US (Condon 2010; Lichtblau 2011).

persistent mobilization around these issues. How interests are met is a separate consideration.

Most of the scholarship on women's substantive representation turns not on women's interests but on women's issues. In contrast to interests, issues are strategic choices that emphasize components of interest as a point of mobilization and policy initiative. Derived from interests, issues are more specific, immediate, and limited. For example, women have an interest in being free from violence, in not being subjected to beatings by husbands, fathers, mothers-in-law, and vigilantes.[9] How women organize around this *interest*—freedom from violence against women—is by *identifying an issue* deriving from this interest, such as legislation that criminalizes spousal assault. The selection of this particular issue, from among a range of possible issues, is a strategic choice made in the context of political opportunity and women's autonomous organizing and strategic deliberations. In addition, lack of political opportunity—in contexts of political threat, women's oppression and their inability to organize, state hostility to women and women's interests—means that absence of women's organizing around women's issues (let alone women's interests) cannot serve as evidence of lack of interest.

Finally, *preferences* constitute a range of discrete, limited alternatives in relation to a specific issue. Once an issue is identified (and advanced and promoted), the range of possible positions on the issue will both diminish and consolidate. For example, in regard to criminalizing spousal assault, preference alternatives will be constructed in regard to, e.g., the role of the state, level of criminalization, target of criminalization, and funding. Activists, elected officials, voters and others involved in the issue resolution will focus debate on their preferences (including opposition). Debate and deliberation on the issue are more likely to turn on possible preferences and less on the fundamental interest from which the issue has emerged (although this is, clearly, an empirical question).

The distinction among interests, issues, and preferences is illustrated in Figure 2.1. Using the interest of women's freedom from violence against women as an initial example for purposes of illustration,[10] Figure 2.1 maps issues and preferences to that interest. For example, issues related to the larger women's interest of freedom from violence against women include rape and violent sexual assault, sexual harassment, wife-beating, and "honor" killings, among others. These issues have been identified by organized women as those to address at the level of policy initiatives in state venues. The selection

9. "[V]iolence against women, rape and wife-beating are concepts used by activist groups and governments in all stable democracies" (Weldon 2002a: 10).

10. It is beyond the scope of this chapter to provide a full justification of freedom from violence against women as a women's interest; see, however, Kantola 2006; Elman 2003; Htun and Weldon 2012; Weldon 2002a.

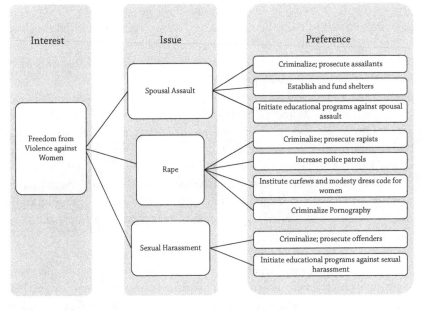

Interest	Issue	Preference

Interest: Freedom from Violence against Women

Issue: Spousal Assault
- Criminalize; prosecute assailants
- Establish and fund shelters
- Initiate educational programs against spousal assault

Issue: Rape
- Criminalize; prosecute rapists
- Increase police patrols
- Institute curfews and modesty dress code for women
- Criminalize Pornography

Issue: Sexual Harassment
- Criminalize; prosecute offenders
- Initiate educational programs against sexual harassment

Figure 2.1
Women's Interest, Issues, Preferences in Freedom from Violence Against Women

of a specific issue—e.g., rape—is a strategic choice, and issue selection leads to a range of potential preferences deriving from that issue. For example, rape as an issue can produce a range of policy preferences, including criminalizing rape and prosecuting rapists, criminalizing pornography and prosecuting pornographers, increasing security and police patrols to diminish the incidence of rape, establishing curfews for women to foreclose opportunities for rape, and/or imposing public dress codes for women—including support for and opposition to these preferences.

It is at the level of women's *issues* that conflict among women, advocating around the same *interest*, is likely to become visible. Shared interests among women do not mean uniform agreement about women's issues. Because women are uniquely positioned as a distinctive politically relevant demographic group, identification of women's interests and organizing these interests for eventual policy representation require appreciation of diversity among women and women's full agency in advancing their specific and diverse (and often conflicting) issues.

Women constitute a distinctive politically relevant group in at least three ways. First, for most nations, women constitute the majority of the population, and, where women are free to vote and participate in politics, their majority status should empower them in political representation and policy outcomes. Second, women are territorially dispersed; that is, unlike religious adherents or racial minorities, women (like men) are not geographically concentrated. For racial or religious minorities, geographical concentration has often served to reinforce the linkage between descriptive and substantive political representation. Shared location—whether for good or ill—can provide a foundation for shared experience, linking individuals' politically relevant demographic characteristics with collective identities, serving to develop shared political interests, and promoting collective action and electoral mobilization. With territorial dispersion, women lack the structural advantages of geographic concentration, and must find alternative routes to developing collective identities as women and to mobilizing for political action. Uniformity of women's interests do not emerge from territorial location; hence, in political systems where governmental institutions are structured in territorial terms, groups (like women) that are not geographically concentrated face disadvantages in mobilizing for national representation and public policy influence.

Third, women are present in all politically relevant demographic groups. Any political cleavage that would serve to define women's interests compared to men's is potentially cross-cut by all other interest-based cleavages, including those based on class, ethnicity, ideology, race, region, and religion. The resulting fragmentation of women's political interests along cross-cutting cleavages makes identification of women's interests more challenging, but does not obviate women's shared interests. Such fragmentation further highlights the need for an intersectional analysis of women's interests (see Hancock, Chapter 3 of this volume).

Women share political interests but do not necessarily hold the same issue positions.[11] If women are the major disputants in an issue contest, this is probably a strong signal that a women's *interest* is involved—in fact, that the interest of concern is a women's interest. Moreover, disputes among women are those most likely to concern women's interests; at the level of issue position, women will be most invested in these interests, but intersectional differences among women, along, e.g., lines of race and class, will cause them to diverge at the level of *issue*.[12] As Weldon (2011b: 35) observes, "[I]nteraction among women often involves conflict, and subordinated sets of women often have difficulty getting their issues recognized as issues of importance by women who are more privileged. But debate among women makes these divisions themselves the topic of discussion."

11. "There may be more than one discourse relevant to ... women's interests, which a unitary framing of that group's interests will not capture" (Dryzek and Niemeyer 2008: 483).

12. For example, women's political equality and rights are women's *interests*; the ERA and women's suffrage are women's *issues* deriving from these interests; and women contest around those issues based on their *preferences*, where we see intersectionality.

IDENTIFYING WOMEN'S INTERESTS

Political Voice and Inclusion

One persistent shared political interest among women emerges from women's self-organizing: direct access to political power to articulate and express women's interests.[13] This interest is evidenced by its assertion across time and space; women in different time periods, in different nations and localities, have asserted their desire for political voice, even as "women as a group have remained excluded from public authority" (Diamond and Hartsock 1981: 719). In 1995, the United Nations Fourth World Conference on Women identified "women in power and decision-making" as a key concern,[14] and stated two explicit strategic objectives: "Take measures to ensure women's equal access to and full participation in power structures and decision-making" and "Increase women's capacity to participate in decision-making and leadership" ("Platform for Action"), a strong claim of women's interest in public voice and political inclusion. Women's interest in political inclusion has been evidenced across a range of issues, including voting rights, constitutionalized equal rights under the law, and access to political office, and across all possible venues. The distinctions among women's interests, issues and preferences in regard to political inclusion are illustrated in Figure 2.2.

Across the nineteenth and early twentieth centuries, a major democratization wave involving women's political inclusion was the result of independent women's movements, nationally based and internationally linked, demanding women's full voting rights (see Caraway 2004; see also "Women's Suffrage").[15] Between 1848 and 1950, women's movements militated for women's voting and citizen rights (among others) in 29 countries across Asia, Europe, the Middle East, and the Americas (Chafetz et al. 1990; Banaszak 1996: 4). In the United States, African American women have long militated for voting rights and inclusion in state and national electorates (Smooth 2006a; 2006b: 118–22). As recently as 1990, following a long series of failed campaigns and a constitutional amendment in 1971, the Swiss women's movement secured voting rights for women in the remaining cantons that had excluded women from their electorates (Banaszak 1996: 3–4).

In the United States, a long, slow campaign for women's equal constitutional rights was manifested in 1972 in a congressional proposal of an Equal Rights

---

13. Sen (1999) provides a more comprehensive discussion of inclusion and voice as "political freedom."

14. See http://www.un.org/womenwatch/daw/beijing/platform/decision.htm (accessed January 5, 2012).

15. Organized women in the US (in various state-level organizations) and in the UK (the National Women's Anti-Suffrage League), for example, also opposed extension of full voting rights to women.

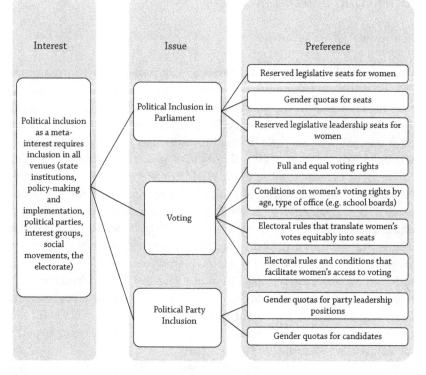

Interest	Issue	Preference

Political inclusion as a meta-interest requires inclusion in all venues (state institutions, policy-making and implementation, political parties, interest groups, social movements, the electorate)

Political Inclusion in Parliament
- Reserved legislative seats for women
- Gender quotas for seats
- Reserved legislative leadership seats for women

Voting
- Full and equal voting rights
- Conditions on women's voting rights by age, type of office (e.g. school boards)
- Electoral rules that translate women's votes equitably into seats
- Electoral rules and conditions that facilitate women's access to voting

Political Party Inclusion
- Gender quotas for party leadership positions
- Gender quotas for candidates

Figure 2.2
Women's Interest, Issues, Preferences in Political Inclusion

Amendment (ERA) to the Constitution, which was followed by a decade-long campaign to secure ratification by three-fourths of the US states, a campaign that ultimately failed. More recently, organized women have sought women's full access to national and subnational legislatures and other governing bodies by advocating gender quotas for nomination, appointment, and election to office.[16] The international Institute for Democracy and Electoral Assistance (IDEA) lists 118 countries where gender quotas have been implemented through constitutions or legislation, or voluntarily by individual political parties (http://www.quotaproject.org/country.cfm); gender quotas now operate in countries on every continent. The earliest gender quotas were adopted in India under the 1935 Government of India Act (as reserved seats), with 10 countries employing formal gender quotas between 1935 and 1980 (Krook

---

16. Gender quotas include "reserved seats, party quotas, and legislative quotas" (Krook 2009: 6). Some quota and reserved seat provisions appear to have been initiated by governments and parties in the absence of an organized women's movement or visible women's advocacy, although, as Krook writes (2009: 21), "efforts to nominate more female candidates rarely occur in the absence of women's mobilization."

2009: 27).[17] Major evidence of the universality of women's interest in political voice and formal inclusion was the proposal of gender quotas in several countries following mass protests and removal of political leaders in the "Arab spring" democratization movements.

As has been the case for the Equal Rights Amendment and women's voting rights, advocates of gender quotas (and the debate around gender quotas) have involved both feminist and non-feminist actors, including women (Krook 2009: 32). Women of different ideologies and with cross-cutting interests have joined to support initiatives around women's interests in citizen rights (see, e.g., Lépinard 2007), but have also fought against them (Krook 2009: 21–22), perhaps most bitterly during the US ERA campaign.

Lisa Baldez (2002: 15) claims that "what unites women is 'exclusion from the political process and their collective status as political outsiders.'" As a result, women share a real interest, *as women*, in access to political power and voice. Women's interest in access to political power and voice is a *meta-interest*: it constitutes both an interest in and of itself; that is, women organizing autonomously and with full agency have asserted such an interest, again in multiple time periods, across numerous political systems and in a wide range of contexts. Moreover, this meta-interest is in fact an assertion of the necessity of access to the context within which articulation of women's interests becomes fully possible; indeed, it is the only context within which recognition of women's interests can be realized.[18] In this regard, interest understood as "form," or "the demand for involvement and control over politics and public affairs" (Hill and Chappell 2006: 1; Jónasdóttir and Jones 2009: 9) is, for women, a substantive claim for inclusion, around which women clearly have long organized and asserted as a fundamental value requiring response from the state and other authoritative institutions, and which would constitute a redistribution of power across gender lines. For purposes of empirical analyses of women's representation, women's political voice and inclusion is a substantive women's interest that can be evaluated in terms of specific issue proposals, the venue where the proposals are advanced, the actors who advocate for them, and how they do so.

Women's Reproductive Interests

Like women's political voice and inclusion, women's reproductive rights in law and policy involve fundamental, substantive values that "'politics puts into effect

17. Thanks to Marcela Rios Tobar and Mona Lena Krook for information about the earliest gender quotas. For a table listing gender quota adoption by decade, see Krook 2006: 312–13; for a listing by year, see Krook 2009: 227–38.

18. To paraphrase Amartya Sen (1999: 10), women's interest in access to political power is not only a primary end; it is its principal means of achieving that end.

and distributes'" (Jónasdóttir and Jones 1988: 40 in Hill and Chappell 2006: 1). These include, for example, the termination of pregnancy, continuation of pregnancy, access to maternal health care, prenatal and postnatal care, conditions of birth and labor, support for infant health and nutrition, access to safe and free contraception, "occupational health and safety" in regard to women's (and men's) reproductive health and state-subsidized high quality child-care" (Nelson 2003: 134), and government funding to support child education. This broad definition is similar to that advocated by the reproductive justice campaign in the United States.[19] Although women may disagree about the elements and content of women's reproductive interests, they do not disagree about reproductive rights as a fundamental women's interest.

Women's reproductive experience and interests intersect with their locations and experience in class and race (Nelson 2003; see also Hancock, Chapter 3 of this volume). The unhappy history of exploitation of the reproductive capacities of poor women and of women of color in the United States provides ample evidence of how reproductive policies vary across subsets of women.[20] In the United States, the initial development of safe oral contraceptives for women involved testing of birth control pills on Puerto Rican women and on US women in psychiatric hospitals in the 1950s and 1960s (Quintanilla 2004; "The Boston Pill Trials"). For poor women of color, Native American women and First Nations women, social welfare support in Canada and the United States was often conditioned on sterilization (Lopez 1993; Nikoukari 2001).[21] Limitation of access to contraception only to married persons[22] and the criminalization of contraceptive use and abortion have had different impacts upon different women, depending upon their age, marital status, geographical location, and nationality.[23] Limitations to access to contraception and abortion include, for example, the Republic of Ireland's constitutional debates and amendments concerning prohibitions against women's access to

19. The reproductive justice movement addresses concerns of women of color with reproductive rights. See http://reproductivejustice.org/emerj; and http://www.protectchoice.org/section.php?id=17.

20. That the intersection of sex, race, and class has often been cynically exploited to undermine women's access to contraception and abortion does not refute the claim that reproductive rights is a crucial women's interest.

21. See http://library.duke.edu/rubenstein/scriptorium/wlm/poor/ for documents concerning Black poor women in the US and access to contraception and abortion; see also http://www.libertadlatina.org/Crisis_Forced_Sterilization.htm, for discussion of forced sterilization policies across North and South America.

22. For the US, married couples' rights to access to contraception were secured in the Supreme Court case of *Griswold v. Connecticut* (1965), a case that did not extend such rights to non-married persons.

23. Abortion is illegal under any circumstances in Chile, El Salvador, Malta, and Nicaragua. See "Summary of Abortion Laws Around the World." Abortion in Latin America is still criminalized, with the exceptions of Cuba, Uruguay, and the Yucatan in Mexico (Htun 2003a: 142).

abortion services, information about abortion services, and travel for purposes of obtaining an abortion;[24] and Portugal's 1984 legislation that criminalized abortion and exacted prison sentences for women convicted of violating the law (de Queiroz 2007).

Activist women have engaged in political struggle on all sides of their reproductive interests. Around abortion, women have been advocates for full rights and access to abortion services, as well as concerted opponents to any liberalization of abortion. In Portugal, women were active on both sides of the two national referenda on liberalization of abortion, in 1998 and in 2007 ("Portugal Ratifies Law Allowing Abortions"). Italy liberalized its abortion law by national referendum in 1981 (Beckwith 1987); in the campaign, women had organized on both sides of the abortion issue. In the United States, nationwide legalization of abortion resulted from the Supreme Court's 1973 decision in *Roe v. Wade*, provoking mobilization against the decision and access to abortion, in what became known as the "pro-life" movement.[25] Women in the United States have been active, on both sides, in the opposing "pro-choice" and "pro-life" campaigns around abortion and reproductive rights. The activism and advocacy of women around reproductive rights issues support a claim that reproductive rights constitute a crucial women's interest. Across time and space, women have persisted in organizing around reproductive interests, however broadly or narrowly defined, under conditions of free association and free speech, and they have done so explicitly as women.

Conclusion: Women's Interests

Women's interests are fundamental, substantive values, which enhance women's life chances, support development of their full human capabilities, and underscore their social dignity. Women articulate and organize around these interests, which are expressed when women have political presence in a context of political freedom and equality. Moreover, the fundamental nature of women's interests is evidenced by their persistence across other politically relevant categories, such as race, class and nationality. Although they are manifested differently as issues of public policy debate, women's interests nonetheless are identifiable, representable, and empirically measurable.

24. Ireland held three national referenda that amended the Irish Constitution concerning abortion rights. See Amendments 8, 13, and 14. Additional amendments limiting access to legal abortion were attempted in 1992 and 2002, but were unsuccessful.
25. For a thoughtful analysis of women's understandings of abortion and their support of or opposition to abortion rights, see Luker 1984; see also Staggenborg 1991 on women's organizing in the pro-choice movement.

INTERESTS, ISSUES AND WOMEN'S REPRESENTATION

For purposes of empirical analyses of women's representation, women's interests can be evaluated along three dimensions: (1) as specific issue proposals deriving from those interests, (2) by the venues in which the proposals are advanced, and (3) by the actors who advocate for them. These dimensions can be expressed as four questions. *Which* women's interests are articulated as issues for women's representation? *Where* does representation take place; that is, in which venues? Third, *who* represents women by advancing preferences on issues that derive from women's interests; that is, who are the explicit actors? Fourth, *how* do actors work to advance their preferences on policy proposals (that is, on issues embedded in women's interests)?[26]

These questions, and the identification of issues for representation of women's interests, do not encompass issues or interests that might be gendered but that are not, strictly speaking, women's interests (or that, at the least, require detailed explanation and justification as women's interests). Gendered interests that are not women's interests as defined in this chapter include foreign policy, environmental concerns, and national military defense. This is not to say that these issues do not have consequence or meaning for women, but rather that their consequences are gendered, even as such interests are not women's interests. Such a distinction spares scholars from having to defend a position that "every issue is a women's issue," and it brings to the forefront those interests that are specific to women and have fundamental, unique consequences for women that are beyond (or tangential to) men's experience.

What are the conditions under which women's interests receive representation? Representation is defined as "claims-making through...governmental institutions" (Truman 1951: 37).[27] Claims-making involves identifiable actions by citizens, either individually or collectively, directed toward government actors and agencies[28] that have the capacity to respond with authoritative public policy decisions. As a result, representation includes a range of principal actors (e.g., citizens, voters, voluntary associations and interest groups, and social movements) and institutional agents (e.g., legislatures, courts, and cabinet ministries).

26. Celis et al. (2008: 99) pose a similar question in regard to the substantive representation of women, which they define as "attention to women's policy concerns," asking "Who claims to act for women?" and "Where, how, and why does the substantive representation of women occur?"

27. The meaning of representation is the subject of a current and lively debate in political science, in empirical research, and in democratic political theorizing (Disch 2011; Dryzek and Niemeyer 2008; Mansbridge 2011; Powell 2009; Rehfeld 2011, 2009).

28. Consistent with the empirical and theoretical scholarship, representation is defined in relation to the state and state entities, and excludes representation through non-state entities and social movement targets, such as universities, religious institutions, and economic institutions. The emphasis on the state is consistent with mobilization models of representation (Disch 2011: 108; Weldon 2011b).

Representation occurs when citizen preferences are evidenced through governmental institutions in public policy initiatives.[29]

The focus on public policy *initiatives* is intentional. Multiple interests are expressed and advocated as specific issue preferences in a range of state venues, and multiple actors, within and outside states, assert those preferences and struggle to achieve them. By focusing on initiatives rather than outcomes, representation (claims-making) encompasses policy *attempts* and is differentiated from policy *outcomes*. Policy success depends upon a range of factors, including political opportunity structures and configuration of party power within, for example, a legislature. Dodson (2006: 49) reminds us of the representational constraints facing female members of the US Congress, worth quoting at length:

> Women office-holders: are ostensibly charged with representing both women and men...; are members of a masculine institution with deeply entrenched traditions that change only slowly; operate within a partisan structure that creates intersecting (but not identical) pressures and incentives for Democratic and Republican women members; are drawn from a culture whose awareness of the gendered stakes of policy continues to evolve...; and negotiate the political ladder within a society and an institution that disagree over what it means to represent women, what women's needs and interests are, and whether they matter....

A focus on public policy *initiatives* recognizes these constraints and allows scholars to locate where women's interests have been advocated in state venues (and hence where women have received representation) and where women's interests have succeeded in being enacted as policy (or not). Moreover, this distinction allows researchers to identify who represents women (by advancing policy proposals that derive from women's interests) and where (that is, which venues) representation is most likely to be successful, and under which conditions. In sum, there is a difference between *representing* interests and *securing* interests.

Venues of Women's Representation

Representation of women's interests can be achieved in a range of state venues. Most of the research on representation of women's interests focuses on national legislatures and legislative behavior (Dodson 2006; Htun 2003a;

29. For the difficulties of assessing representational effects (that is, citizen influence on policy outcomes), given the "multiple and complex interactions" which they entail, see Franzese 2009: 48–53.

Kantola 2006; Mateo Dias 2005; Schwindt-Bayer 2010; Swers 2002) and on state legislatures (Reingold 2000; Thomas 1994). Legislatures, by definition, have the power to enact laws that shape public policy and, in the absence of other state institutions with authoritative policy-making powers, are the locus of legislation. Furthermore, in democratic political systems, representational claims are most clearly tied, in political theoretical terms (Mansbridge 2003; Pitkin 1967; Rehfeld 2011), to citizen and constituency representation through legislatures. It is unsurprising that research focusing on representation of women's interests would identify national (and subnational) legislatures as prime venues for assessing representation of women's policy issues.

National legislatures are not, however, the only state arenas in which representation of women's interests occurs. Annesley (2010: 50–51) makes a strong claim that

> [f]or studies trying to explain...policy outcomes, this focus [on parliaments] is in the wrong place. It is important to put women's political activity in the context of the institutional configuration of a particular political system. This is especially the case in the Westminster model, where policy-making is dominated by the core executive and policy networks, but it also applies to traditionally corporatist decision-making systems such as those in Sweden or Germany, where decisions are traditionally thrashed out between social partners before they reach parliament.

A growing body of research emphasizes the importance of cabinet ministries and the national bureaucracy in representing women's interests and in advancing women's policy issues. Celis et al. identify women's policy agencies as locations for advancing women's issues, separately if not independently of a national legislature (2008: 103; see also Atchison and Down 2009; Banaszak 2010; Stetson and Mazur 1995). Annesley (2010: 70) found that "welfare policy reform in the UK under New Labour was not driven by women in parliament or in a women's policy agency such as the [Equal Opportunity Commission]. Rather, it was framed, developed and pushed through by a core coalition of MPs, ministers, political advisers and special advisers." National executive agencies, the core executive, and women's policy agencies are all non-legislative venues where women's interests may be represented and that may "reflect women's movement demands [by advancing] social and economic policies that may be beneficial to women as a group" (Celis et al. 2008: 103, but see also Escobar-Lemmon et al., Chapter 11 of this volume).

Courts have been venues of representation, where claims-making through lawsuits have evidenced efforts by organized women to exact policy response from the judiciary. For the United States, abortion-rights cases are perhaps the best known in recent history, where feminist activists established constitutionally based rights to abortion through the Supreme Court decision in *Roe v. Wade* (1973), a decision which overturned abortion law in 46 US states.[30] In the United States, activist women have used the courts to challenge women's exclusion from employment, rights to children, rights to property, voting rights, jury duty, and right to a trial by a jury of one's peers, as well as defense of protective labor laws for women.[31] In France and in Italy, women's access to candidacy for public office was both denied and eventually secured after legal battles involving the constitutional courts, where parity in party nominations was legislated, and eventually was secured through constitutional amendment, in response to claims brought by activist-organized women; similar struggles have involved the Spanish constitution regarding parity legislation (see Rodríguez Ruiz and Rubio-Marin 2008; Threlfall 2007; see Hoekstra et al., Chapter 6 of this volume, for analysis of women's inclusion on constitutional courts, potentially expanding venues for representation).

Women's interest representation involves women's movements and organized women in both identifying and advocating women's interests and in identifying appropriate and receptive venues for advancing interests as policy issues. Not every policy issue will find a favorable reception, not only because specific actors within a venue at a specific period of time may themselves be unreceptive, but because different institutional venues are structured for different purposes. The nature of the issue itself may result in its advocacy in one state venue (for example, an executive branch agency) rather than another (for example, a constitutional court). Women's movements, like social movements generally, engage in venue-shopping, focusing on the most likely receptive venue for advancing policy issues, and shifting to a new state location when policy advocacy is unsuccessful (see Kang, Chapter 8 of this volume).

Asking *where* women's interests are represented is a key question for women's movements, allowing activist women to discern where they have their best opportunities for advancing policy demands, how they can coordinate across multiple venues, and where the actors most sympathetic to their cause are located. Venues for women's representation extend beyond the legislative, as developing scholarship is demonstrating. Being specific in asking about multiple venues will be key to understanding the full range and process of the representation of women's interests.

---

30. For a discussion of state legislative battles over abortion rights preceding *Roe v. Wade*, see Baer and Goldstein (2006: 368–69).

31. See Vickers (2006: 29) for trenchant comments regarding the changed political opportunity structure of the US Supreme Court in regard to women's interests.

Who represents women's interests? Actors in representation include voluntary associations and interest groups, social movements, and political parties. Identifying *who* represents women's interests allows us to identify pressure points and pathways to women's policy successes, and to evaluate decisions about strategy in advancing policy issues. Women's movements' identification of who might best be positioned to represent women's interests is implicated in the selection of venues for such representation. Beyond the structural differences of various state institutions and agencies, the presence of potential allies within those institutions is key both to venue selection and to the political opportunity context for advancing policy issues.

Most of the scholarship on women's political representation focuses on *women* as representatives of women's interests, primarily but not exclusively, for theoretical reasons. First, women within the state, like women generally, are subject to a range of life experiences, *as women*, which shape their perspectives and understandings of their interests as women (although female state elites are likely to hold different preferences among themselves, based on these interests).[32] Second, women within the state, like women outside the state, organize around their interests to advance women's issues (although not in every instance and not in a uniform direction). Third, women within the state, unlike women outside the state, are positioned to produce representation, that is, to make claims within the state on behalf of women's policy issues and to implement them.

For practical reasons, the scholarship on women as actors representing women's issues has focused primarily on women elected to national legislatures,[33] and hence has conflated *who* the actors are (women) with *where* representation might take place (parliament).

Asking about representation of women's interests requires that scholars ask about women's role in their own representation, including within legislatures as legislators themselves. Although much of the scholarship on women in parliaments focuses on the relationship between women's descriptive and substantive representation (Childs 2004; Dodson 2006; Krook 2010; Mateo

---

32. If this were not the case, we would have to accept, in theory, that elected women have no interests of their own and/or that they are unable to recognize their own interests—unlike women generally. We would have to make an argument for the exceptionalism (in this example, exceptional ignorance) of women holding office, compared to women in the mass public.

33. Until recently, the numbers of women in state institutions other than parliaments were so small that generalization at the level of disciplinary standards was impossible. In addition, widely accessible data on women as cabinet members, and as judges and justices, have only recently been available; national legislative data on women's and men's descriptive representation within national legislatures are available through the Inter-Parliamentary Union from 1997 to the present.

Diaz 2005), investigating the claims-making of female members of parliaments is not limited to "[asking] whether an increase in the number of female representatives...results in an increase in attention to women's policy concerns" and need not "[ignore] important differences among women, at the same time that it overlooks men as potential actors on behalf of women as a group" (Celis et al. 2008: 99). Instead, women in legislatures constitute one set of women who are potential actors for articulating as well as asserting (multiple and conflicting) issue claims based on women's interests. It is reasonable to ask whether and under what conditions women in legislatures seek to advance their interests as women within the state venue in which they are situated,[34] as well as to ask about their willingness to advance women's interests articulated by those outside the state.

More recently, scholars have turned to extra-institutional groups as the locus for representation of interests, beyond the simple articulation of interests (Disch 2011; Strolovitch 2007, 2006; Weldon 2011b). Weldon argues that intra-legislative representation is not the most useful venue for all citizens in advancing policy demands, and that social movements are primary actors for representing women's interests, particularly the interests of women of color. "[T]he more marginalized and disadvantaged [the group], the more important civil society avenues appear to be, and the less it appears that intralegislative representation (parties, descriptive representation in legislatures) offers a feasible and effective avenue of change" (Weldon 2011b: 108; see also Table 3, 68–69).

Women's movements are particularly important actors in advancing women's interests, even in the absence of women's full inclusion in the state. Clearly, women's movements were key to women achieving suffrage rights across a wide range of countries, that is, achieving political rights in the absence of political rights. Weldon (2011b: 64–66) identifies paid maternal leave in Norway as a women's issue implemented in 1909, with the mobilization of organized activist women, four years before their enfranchisement.

Both women's movements and women's interests, by definition, depend upon women as key political actors, in experiential terms (life options, political status) and in organizational and mobilization terms (as women). Because scholars define women's movements in part by who the actors are, that is, women (Beckwith 2005: 129–30), this both heightens and complicates the question of whether women represent women's interests. Nonetheless, who the actors are and which interests they advance are conceptually separate questions that require careful disentanglement to clarify *which* women are

---

34. Moreover, women organize as women within the state, in caucuses and other groups, although a full discussion of these collectivities is not possible here. Note, as US examples, the Congressional Women's Caucus and Federally Employed Women.

analyzed and *which specific interests* they articulate.[35] Intersectional analysis is crucial for answering these questions, particularly in regard to conflicts among women in the same interest area.[36]

Political parties also serve to make claims upon, and within, the state, and such claims include those advancing women's interests. Women's collective organizing is distinctive for its rare use of women's political parties as structures for claims-making around women's interests. Because women constitute a group "whose boundaries crosscut partisan divisions" (Htun 2004b: 439), with multiple, reinforcing, and conflicting identities, dispersed rather than concentrated geographically, organized women rarely mobilize in women's political parties (Fidler 2005; Htun 2004b), and the few attempts that scholars have studied have been short-lived (e.g., Icelandic Women's Alliance, Women of Russia). If, as Schattschneider claimed (2009 and 1942: 1), "political parties created democracy and . . . modern democracy is unthinkable save in terms of . . . parties," it is not yet clear what democracy means for organized women in the absence of women's political parties or what the implications of such absence are for women's interests and public policy initiatives.

In the absence of women's parties, political parties of the Left appear to be the most likely to advance women's interests (see, however, Htun 2003a) and have the strongest records, compared to parties of the Right, of nominating and electing women to national legislatures, even in defeat. Nonetheless, parties of the Right assert policy positions in regard to women's interests, including policies regarding women's employment, child care, and reproductive rights. Political parties articulate issue positions within and outside the state; the identification of political party activism in advancing women's interests should, in theory, be visible in party directives and documents, in campaign platforms and party manifestos, and in policy proposals within state institutions.

CONCLUSION

The questions we ask constrain the type of answers we are likely to find. Asking what women's interests are and how they can be measured systematically, which women's interests are being considered, which women advance these interests, where and how, expands our focus on women's representation.

35. For a stellar example of the careful articulation of which women might advance specific components of welfare polices for women and children, see Reingold and Smith 2012: 131–39.
36. See, for example, the conflict among political women in the post–World War II era in the US over the issue of protective labor laws for women, which involved conflicts across and within class lines.

This leads us beyond (although not necessarily away from) questions of policy outcome to consider questions of policy demands and claims-making around women's interests, expressed as discrete issues—which may then be addressed more specifically (if less directly or completely) by actors within the state, some of whom will be women.

This expanded focus complicates our understandings of representing women by its requirement that we consider women in all their complexity: as members of racial and ethnic groups, as actors with class identities and commitments, as makers as well as subjects of government policy. It allows us to identify conflict *among* women as they struggle for representation, as well as to identify points of solidarity where representation of women's interests is more cohesive, more targeted, and presumably, more successful—although this is an empirical question.

Asking where women's interests might find representation that leads to policy innovation and successful implementation encourages additional questions:

- With which women's interests are we concerned?
- How are those interests manifested as issues for policy initiatives?
- Where could those interests best be advanced? Which state venue is most appropriate for advancing the specific issue as a policy initiative, and in which state venue does the policy initiative have its greatest chances of success?
- By whom could these interests be advanced? Which actors are positioned to advocate for the issue within the specific state venue?

The conundrum of women's representation and women's interests is this: (1) women have interests, and (2) women are both inside and outside the state. This means, first, that women inside the state are positioned to represent their own intersectional interests; that is, they are located in a state policy-making institution that allows them to advance their specific interests as women of specific race, class, and other salient, politically relevant identities. Within legislatures, this means that women are likely both to work in concert with and in opposition to each other, as they differ intersectionally and as these differences produce different fundamental interests.

Second, this conundrum means that scholars must disentangle the descriptive and substantive representation of women when they analyze women's elite political behavior. Representing, at some level, their own fundamental interests as women, women in the state embody the conflation of descriptive and substantive representation of women. As *numbers of women* increase in the political elite, *diversity among women* in the state is also likely to increase, in demographic terms, producing increased diversity in the resulting women's interests seeking representation. Diversity of women's interests—along intersectional lines and, almost certainly, partisan and ideological lines—is likely to produce a range of cooperation and conflict among women within the state. A careful plotting of women's interests, in their full range, will help us find the path, or paths, to their political representation.

CHAPTER 3

Intersectional Representation or Representing Intersectionality?

Reshaping Empirical Analysis of Intersectionality

ANGE-MARIE HANCOCK

INTRODUCTION

For most Americans, the Susan G. Komen for the Cure Foundation is the signature organization fighting breast cancer. In defining themselves as a "breast cancer movement," Komen's vision is simple: "a world without breast cancer." In the 30 years since the foundation began, it has raised and awarded over $1.9 billion for cancer research and screenings across the United States.

Planned Parenthood is likewise one of the most prominent advocacy organizations for reproductive health care access, most associated with the provision of what they define as safe, legal abortions. Despite this reputation, abortions constitute just 3% of Planned Parenthood's health care services. Their Komen-funded cancer prevention services, on the other hand, constitute 14.3% of their services, which translated into over 170,000 clinical breast exams and 6,000 low- or no-cost mammograms.[1]

The explosion of controversy in January 2012 between the two ardent advocates of what Beckwith might term women's "interest" in health care access came as a surprise. Most Americans were unaware of the year-long chain of events that preceded a stunning Associated Press report. In January 2011 the

---

1. According to their 2009–2010 annual report, sexually transmitted diseases (38%) and contraceptive care (33.5%) represent the bulk of the health care they provide.

Komen Foundation hired former Georgia state representative Karen Handel, who had run unsuccessfully for governor on a platform that included an end to all funding for Planned Parenthood. Soon after hiring Handel as a senior vice president for public policy, a three-person committee of Komen board members formed a committee to specifically analyze Komen's financial support of Planned Parenthood. In November 2011 they voted to transform funding policies in a way that would bar all future support of Planned Parenthood. Ostensibly, the board voted to bar organizations under investigation from applying for funds, but did so after a review that singled out one grantee organization and after Planned Parenthood's notification in September by House member Cliff Stearns (R-FL) that they faced a federal investigation.

The Komen Foundation informed Planned Parenthood in December 2011 that they would no longer be eligible for Komen community grants that supported free or subsidized mammograms for low-income women, many of whom are also women of color. What transpired between January 31 and February 3, 2012 (when Komen changed its policy and restored Planned Parenthood's eligibility) provides a widely accessible case study regarding the challenges of women's interests, issues, and preferences (Beckwith, Chapter 2 of this volume). Moreover, the standoff and fallout among women about women's health and provision of women's health care illustrates the challenge of empirically operationalizing intersectionality theory to answer questions of women's representation.

The shocked response of the public occurred largely because Komen was previously assumed to substantively represent women's health interest in a way that transcended cross-cutting categories of race, class, and religion. However, we can see that their process, while largely legal, failed to meet Beckwith's condition for the assertion of interests: deliberative democracy, where those who are most affected by decisions get to participate in the process of deciding about them. Without this deliberative process, which Dahlerup (Chapter 4 of this volume) might characterize as one that could produce substantive representation, Komen's removal and subsequent restoration of funding for Planned Parenthood was doomed to substantially damage Komen's reputation.

In this chapter, I use the Komen-Planned Parenthood controversy as an ongoing example for an argument that centers on the challenge of empirically operationalizing intersectionality to answer questions of representation. To do so, I establish two typical approaches to operationalizing intersectionality in the representation literature, and suggest a third way designed to overcome prior flaws in research design and methodology.

THE REPRESENTATIONAL CHALLENGE

Dara Strolovitch (2007) articulates the precise challenge facing groups like Komen, who share a common interest in women's health care provision with groups like Planned Parenthood but, as Beckwith reminds us, operate in historically contingent political and power contexts. Strolovitch introduces the term "intersectional stigma" to describe how groups with values and visions end up representing only an elite, more advantaged portion of their constituency. Building on the work of Strolovitch and Cathy Cohen's analysis of African American communities' response to the HIV/AIDS crisis during the 1980s and 1990s, I contend that multiple responses to the challenge of representing diverse populations with a shared interest like access to health care or "a world without breast cancer" issue can emerge, often surprising the very constituents they purport to represent.

In 1991 Kimberle Williams Crenshaw introduced the term "political intersectionality" to describe how the representational failure created by using an elite or privileged group member as a prototype for policy remedies prevents the comprehensive representation, and by extension, remedy of the obstacles created by the drivers of racial, gender, class and sexuality disparities. Following Crenshaw, Cohen (1999) demonstrated that black lesbian, gay, bisexual, and transgender (LGBT) people who sought action from black political elites regarding the HIV/AIDS epidemic ravaging their communities were targets of secondary marginalization—overt discrimination and oversight based on common perceptions that HIV/AIDS was not part of a broad black political agenda because it did not affect most or all black people—and therefore did not deserve a significant amount of black political capital or attention. The approach of black elites to representation in this vein could easily be formulated quantitatively, in terms of focusing only on issues that affect most or all blacks. However Cohen thoughtfully explains that the lack of representation was far more than a numbers game. It was couched, in fact, in a set of middle-class racial uplift norms regarding black sexual behavior. This understanding that the intersectional representational challenge has both *quantitative and qualitative dimensions* will play a large role in the discussion of extant intersectionality scholarship below.

Writing eight years later, Strolovitch found that the representational failure deemed "political intersectionality" persisted across a vast range of interest groups (including labor unions, women's organizations, environmental, and civil rights organizations), though the explanations were more apologetic: organizations claimed a lack of resources or expertise to explain why they did not fully represent the populations considered to be parts of their key constituencies. Outside political science, the social movements literature uncovered fears that giving attention to additional identity categories/inegalitarian traditions would divide the movement (see also Pastor et al. 2009).

Strolovitch and Cohen both used a variety of standard empirical methods to ostensibly conduct examinations that illustrate the ongoing impact of Crenshaw's political intersectionality: surveys, in-depth interviews, and content analysis. They took Crenshaw's articulation as a "frame" for their research questions, which were grounded in the standard questions of political science.

In a similar vein, those who study women and politics have also operationalized intersectionality in a manner that emphasizes the traditional questions that women and politics scholars ask. Mary Hawkesworth (2003), Wendy Smooth (2001), Nadia Brown (2012), and others have produced important work that interrogates the challenges that women of color legislators have faced. Their operationalization of intersectionality has occurred primarily as a subject identity—that is, the representational challenge is assumed to be one located in each legislator's intersecting identities—that they are female and people of color, for example. This qualitative research has shown, perhaps unsurprisingly, resonances with the larger women and politics literature: that navigating legislative contexts can be tricky under any circumstances, but as a woman of color, invisibility and exclusion are common obstacles they must overcome (see Htun, Chapter 7 of this volume). Quantitative research by Bratton et al. (2006), also responds to this general interpretation of Crenshaw's clarion call: to place women of color at the center of the analysis. Fraga et al. (2007) similarly center women of color with a different finding regarding representational challenge. They coin the term *strategic intersectionality* to suggest that Latina legislators deploy their multiple identities severally and strategically for the benefit of their careers and their constituents.

If we focus on the deliberative democracy and dynamic representation standards set by Beckwith and Dahlerup, Komen's three-person committee, while legal, clearly fails. The events also fail Crenshaw's test of acknowledging the complexity of intersecting categories of privilege and disadvantage that Planned Parenthood's patients navigate. Thus, Komen stood on the right side of the law, but the wrong side of politics and public opinion. The trust in the Komen brand as politically transcendent has been severely damaged: 50% of their previously scheduled three-day walks in 2014 have been canceled.

INTERSECTIONALITY EMBODIED

We might call all of these identity politics operationalizations of intersectionality—among elites, interest groups, and constituents—the *intersectionality embodied* operationalization. Subjects for the study are selected based on the identities that intersect, and processes of stigmatization or strategic deployment are traced directly to the intersectional identities of the research subjects. This approach to intersectionality is not just common in political science; sociologists Choo and Ferree term this approach an "inclusion" operationalization of intersectionality: "Part of the utility of an intersectional analysis, therefore, was to give voice to the particularity of the perspectives and needs of women of color who often remained invisible..." (2010: 132). The *intersectionality embodied* approach, perhaps due to its grounding in identity politics, has usually focused on that general spirit of Crenshaw's original articulation.

As it has been conducted, this research's intent has mostly been to reveal the invisible. Unfortunately, there are several gaps in this operationalization that merit concern. First, such research is usually limited to political intersectionality, which ignores the two additional formulations of intersectionality articulated by Crenshaw in 1991: *structural intersectionality,* which highlights the contextual factors that produce an inability to obtain legal remedies that are presumed to be available to legal subjects; and *representational intersectionality,* which addresses the ways that people who straddle multiple social locations are culturally constructed. For example the intersectionality embodied literature generally has led to a conceptualization of individuals as frozen in time, which is inattentive to historical context (Reed 2002). This myopia might have been corrected by sufficient attention to structural intersectionality. Second, the mobilization of multiple categories has been incomplete. Prior intersectionality research is criticized for presumptions of some categories' relevance (e.g., race-class-gender) over others (see Wadsworth 2011) and an incomplete treatment of social locations by focusing solely on disadvantage without concomitant attention to sources of agency or privilege (see Fogg-Davis 2008; Hancock 2011).

Moreover, this approach makes it difficult to develop policy solutions that are scalable beyond an extremely localized level. The relevant question here is whether such research can be sufficiently attentive to the structural intersectionality domain, and can offer the critical eye on the social movements and nongovernmental organizations (NGOs) who purport to represent populations who lack access, like the women whose similar experiences of what Beckwith (Chapter 2 of this volume) calls "socially constructed gendered constraints and exclusions" that would purportedly provide a foundation for the emergence of similar interests.

For the Komen Foundation, failing to attend not simply to intersectionality embodied, but their own representational intersectionality, left them reeling. In just a week their position as a "global leader" to end breast cancer for all women was severely threatened by their attempt to exclude a segment of the female population (the low-income women served by Planned Parenthood) from access to breast cancer diagnosis, education, and prevention. Focusing on Planned Parenthood as solely a provider of abortions, instead of an organization that many women view as a women's health care provider for predominantly low-income women of color, produced massive drops in foundation income, and declining participation in the signature Komen Race for the Cure program. Many individual supporters of the foundation have, in the immediate aftermath, expressed disappointment that near-universal agreement with the value of a world without breast cancer has been so deeply threatened by abortion politics, which are perceived to affect so many fewer women.[2] Attention to intersectionality writ large, as well as the three domains identified by Crenshaw, could assist the Komen Foundation going forward to prevent the destruction of a global interest group for women's health. Unfortunately, the intersectionality embodied operationalization does not facilitate a fully comprehensive intersectional analysis.

The intersectionality embodied operationalization thus has three central limitations: (1) it has not comprehensively attended to all three domains of intersectionality (structural, political, representational); (2) its focus on only marginal dimensions of identities fails to sufficiently plumb the delicate balance between marginalization and agency (or disadvantage and privilege); and (3) its lack of attention to historical context. The final trouble for this operationalization is the lack of space for solidarity and non-identity-based intersectional representation. This approach would not be able to explore or explain President Barack Obama's support for the Lily Ledbetter Act, or then Senator Joe Biden's leadership on the Violence Against Women Act, or former Senator George Voinovich (R-OH)'s leadership on an administrative law change that granted the exact kind of relief that Crenshaw said often goes missing: a change in customs policy that reduced the excessive number of strip searches of black women by U.S. Customs agents upon reentry across the border, which stands as the only federal remedy for "racial profiling" that has managed to be codified. Beyond "strategic intersectionality" mobilized by those with intersecting marginalized identities, experimental research has demonstrated that an "intersectional political consciousness" can be cultivated by those who have intersecting privileged identities (Greenwood 2008; Greenwood and Christian 2008). The prime, as described by psychologist Ronnie Greenwood, emerges from a structural intersectionality analysis.

Some would define Obama, Biden and Voinovich's acts as substantive representation (but see Dahlerup, Chapter 4 of this volume, regarding conceptual stretching of this term); nevertheless, the intersectionality embodied approach to representation has largely ignored this area. If we model intersectionality as (a) only applicable along the marginalized poles of various identity axes and (b) presume that substantive representation cannot emerge from other identity combinations, we miss a lot of what Mazur and Goertz call the "gray zone" between binary alternatives. My point does not undermine the claim that women should be representing themselves in greater numbers and shares of legislatures throughout the United States; I suspect none of the three male leaders expended political capital without women's interest groups, policy scholars, and lobbyists articulating the desired change for them. Nevertheless the Beckwith definition of interests rightly creates space that has been left

2. However, this perception is itself flawed. By the age of 45, one out of three US women will have had an unintended pregnancy and been forced to consider their options.

uninterrogated by embodied intersectionality-type scholars of representation. That said, this approach has provided key analytical insights (e.g., the idea of racing-gendering as a process rather than a static moment in time) and, as Choo and Ferree rightly note, a wider view of the landscape, one that is more inclusive of women of color legislators as not simply the polar opposite of the default (translation: white, androcentric standard) legislator, but as legislators with discrete sets of key experiences that are part of the process of democratic representation, and, who, at times, can get issues on the agenda and resolved in solidarity with other women. That said, when framed as an "analysis," or "approach," intersectionality necessitates attention to all three domains in order to comprehensively explain a causal outcome of interest. This alternative formulation expands the intersectionality embodied strategy and speaks directly to the challenge articulated in Proposition 2 of Chapter 1. Increased articulation does not guarantee increased consensus.

INTERSECTIONALITY AS TESTABLE EXPLANATION

Most large-N empirical interrogations of intersectionality and representation in political science formulate intersectionality as one possible explanation of the data among several. This approach has broad appeal beyond representation scholars in political science (see Hughes 2011; Bratton et al. 2006; Simien and Clawson 2004) and sociology (McCall 2001; Dubrow 2008). The *intersectionality as testable explanation* approach takes that same general interpretation of Crenshaw to place women of color at the center of study as both *women* and *as people of color, inserting* it into a largely uncritically executed net effects analysis (see Alexander-Floyd 2012 for a trenchant critique of this approach). Empirical scholarship in this vein usually claims to empirically investigate or operationalize intersectionality by leaning heavily on the literature of the scholar's main research interest (e.g., gender), and superficially mobilizing the second category by introducing a dummy variable (1 = female, 0 = male) and an interaction term (race x gender).

In a manner similar to the intersectionality embodied method, this operationalization strategy represents a well-intentioned merging of standard women and politics questions with intersectional claims, following the examples of large-N studies of race and large-N studies of gender. For example, most quantitative empirical approaches to identifying causal mechanisms for disparities of race or gender or class have clumsily or myopically attended to race and ethnicity this way, most often fitting them as one or two variables into preexisting models, despite cautions against incorporating gender and race as static categorical variables (see Chae et al. 2011; Choo and Ferree 2010; Lee 2007; Omi and Winant 1994). Though Dubrow (2008) suggests that multi-measure variables for ethnicity can address this matter in his analysis of the European Social Survey, it (a) leaves gender untouched, and (b) does not address the core problem of this approach.

Usually the argument for such an inclusion is couched in the assumptions of quantitative modeling, which privileges the generalizability and broader statistical power associated with such methodologies as particularly helpful for "scaling-up" local solutions to the state or the federal level. However, this approach usually decontextualizes gender and the sexism associated with it. This move has been severely critiqued in the legal literature (Chang and Culp 2002: 489), feminist theory (Knapp 2005; Alexander-Floyd 2012), and sociology (Choo and Ferree 2010). This operational logic has also affected operationalizations of intersectional claims, extending to modeling of intersections of race, gender, and class variables as interaction terms. This strategy usually constitutes the primary or sole method of capturing the force of intersectional claims made by theorists, depending on the author. As with the problematic operationalization of race or gender, the assumptions of standard net effects regression analysis do not match up with intersectionality's claims.

The racing-gendering processes described by Crenshaw, for example, do not equal race x gender effects. Net effects analysis requires the assumption that each independent variable (race, gender, sexual orientation) compete with each other, holding everything else equal. Not only does this not happen in the real world, it is tied to an assumption that there is a single causal combination—a single equation's solution—that can explain the most variation. Most of the policy challenges raised by intersectionality theory address social problems that are causally complex.[3] Causal complexity in the policy world signifies that there are multiple causal recipes that sets of individuals can pursue to the same outcome of interest. Whether the relevant outcome is the Violence Against Women Act, funding for Planned Parenthood's free and subsidized mammogram program, or a reversal of *Ledbetter v. Goodyear*, the case that led to the Lily Ledbetter Equal Pay Act, understanding that interests may be universal (e.g., access to preventive care, equal pay) but that policy preferences to achieve the goal may vary (see Beckwith this volume) based on different populations, based on their intersecting locations, is an important and relevant consideration for policy makers.

As with the intersectionality embodied approach, intersectionality as testable explanation does not comprehensively address the multiple domains of intersectionality (structural, political, and representational) whereas, according to Crenshaw, an intersectional analysis provides greater clarity about marginalized women's constrained sociopolitical location. This is particularly problematic for large-N explanatory studies of intersectionality as testable explanation, however, because they seek, more

3. See Ragin (2000, 2008) for a definition of complex causality.

frequently as a matter of course, to draw quasi-causal conclusions. Using an "include-variables-and-interaction-terms" approach, though valid as a social science methodology, does not match up with the logical changes that intersectionality requires (Carbado and Gulati 2013, Hancock 2013).

Table 3.1 is instructive in understanding this limitation. Hancock (2007) identified three distinct ways in which scholarship in political science, sociology, ethnic studies, and gender studies has conceptualized categories of difference like race, gender, class, and sexuality across methodological operationalizations as variables (e.g., self-report race or sex); longitudinal formations or historical processes (e.g., racial formations, gendered political development), and multilevel drivers of disparate outcomes (e.g., individual or structural heterosexism). Each conceptualization strategy in Table 3.1—unitary, multiple, intersectional—has important ramifications for research design and methodology that have not been systematically interrogated in the intersectionality literature, including the scholarship on intersectionality and representation.

Though empirical intersectionality research has used the terms "multiple" and "intersectional" interchangeably, Table 3.1 illustrates key differences (in all caps) that non-empirical intersectionality theorists have criticized. For

Table 3.1. THREE EMPIRICAL APPROACHES TO CONCEPTUALIZING
CATEGORIES OF DIFFERENCE

	Unitary Approach	Multiple Approach	Intersectional Approach
Number of Relevant Categories/Processes	One	More than one	More than one
Posited Relationship Between Categories/ Processes	None	PREDETERMINED & CONCEPTUALLY DISTINGUISHABLE RELATIONSHIPS	RELATIONSHIPS ARE OPEN EMPIRICAL QUESTIONS TO BE TESTED
Conceptualization of Each Category	Static at individual OR institutional level	Static at individual OR institutional level	Dynamic interaction between individual and institutional factors
Case Makeup of Category/Class	Uniform	UNIFORM	DIVERSE; MEMBERS OFTEN DIFFER IN POLITICALLY SIGNIFICANT WAYS
Approach to Intersectionality	Lip Service or Dismissal	INTERSECTIONALITY AS TESTABLE EXPLANATION	INTERSECTIONALITY AS PARADIGM/ RESEARCH DESIGN

Adapted from Hancock (2007).

example, the idea that there is a predetermined, posited relationship between each pair of categories, and that effects of categories themselves are distinguishable, is commonly considered within the boundaries of intersectional analysis (see, e.g. Weldon 2008; McCall, 2005). A standard women and politics research study regarding representation would similarly find no fault with first-order research questions stemming from the unitary or the multiple modes, suggesting distinct possible formulations of an empirical research question:

Unitary Quantitative Formulation:
Did the lawmaker's gender (or some other single category) have the
    strongest net effect on male versus female legislators' advocacy of a
    particular policy in women's interest?
Unitary Qualitative Formulation:
What role did the lawmaker's gender (or some other single category)
    play in his or her advocacy of a particular policy in women's
    interest?
Multiple Quantitative Formulation:
Did the lawmaker's (a) gender, (b) race, or (c) gender and race together
    have the strongest net effect on male versus female legislators'
    advocacy of a particular policy in women's interest?
Multiple Qualitative Formulation:
How did gender and race play roles in a lawmaker's advocacy of a par-
    ticular policy in women's interest?

My point in enumerating the formulations is to illustrate that all four formulations can be worthy ways to interrogate the same substantive issues often discussed by intersectionality theory, including questions of descriptive and substantive representation, opportunities for remedy, or successful institutional reform.[4] However, these formulations are not intersectional, largely because they inaccurately translate theoretical claims regarding the indivisibility of identities and claims (Alexander-Floyd 2012, Carbado and Gulati 2013, Hancock 2013).

IMPROVING THE STUDY OF INTERSECTIONALITY AND REPRESENTATION: PARADIGM INTERSECTIONALITY

Though international organizations and governing bodies like the United Nations and the European Union have incorporated intersectional logic

---

4. Bratton et al. (2006) is a deservedly well-respected example of this scholarship.

further into their agencies and regulations than the United States (Yuval-Davis 2006), the United States remains a site ripe for the incorporation of improved empirical intersectional approaches. The paradigm intersectionality approach to empirical policy research has emerged from over 20 years of scholarship around the world, inspired by the landmark logic and scholarship of racialized women in the United States. In this section I outline paradigm intersectionality's tenets, in order to illustrate the distinct design and data demands of a paradigm intersectional approach, noting where relevant its distinctions from prior operationalizations of intersectionality in empirical research.

The Komen for the Cure controversy is an excellent illustration of the need for a more comprehensive marriage of the intersectionality and representation literatures. Paradigm intersectionality builds upon multimethod research designs like the one used by sociologist Mignon Moore (2011) and methodological recommendations by Choo and Ferree (2010). Though Choo and Ferree make three distinct recommendations, they present them as alternatives: (1) mixed methods to analyze interactions; (2) denaturalize power relationships by attending equally to "unmarked categories of power and privilege" and (3) use more dynamic, process-oriented models (2010: 147). Paradigm intersectionality, by contrast, suggests a research design that can accommodate all three recommendations into a single study using a large-N, narrative-friendly method, fuzzy-set qualitative comparative analysis (fs(QCA)).

Paradigm intersectionality, as its name suggests, considers intersectionality to be an analytical framework—an approach to conducting research— that corrects the imbalances of both the intersectionality embodied and intersectionality as testable explanation approaches to empirically operationalizing intersectionality. First, it draws the mobilization of intersectionality further upstream in the research process, ahead of the post-design, post-data collection, and methodological selection stage typical of the intersectionality as testable explanation approach.[5] This move will enable scholars to collect data that can fully leverage newer methodologies like fs(QCA). Second, paradigm intersectionality proposes a standard for the more qualitatively driven intersectionality embodied approach that pushes scholars to reflectively and comprehensively plumb the richness and depth of their analyses beyond unbalanced attention to disadvantage and agency, or uninterrogated relevant categories (Choo and Ferree 2010; Trahan 2011; Winker and Degele 2011). As well, paradigm intersectionality responds to prior critiques of intersectionality research (see Reed 2002) and connects to the political dynamics identified by Proposition 1 in Chapter 1. Specifically,

---

5. Though far less common in the intersectionality embodied literature, Hawkesworth (2003) is one example of the post-data collection and methodological selection stage approach.

it includes injunctions to historically situate analyses and to conceptualize dynamic interactions among individuals navigating structural contexts (individual institutional relationships).

The first dimension, *Categorical Multiplicity*, pushes scholars to engage in a formal thought process of which categories are worthy of inclusion in the research design according to transparent standards (see Dhamoon 2011), rather than simply assuming that race and gender, for example, are the only relevant categories for women of color. This may admittedly pose a challenge to women and politics scholars who by definition seek to analyze gendered processes of interest formation and representation. However, the formal process exists to remedy the problematic implications that stem from such assumptions: first, assuming that race and gender are *a priori* the only relevant categories (ignoring, for example, class, sexual orientation, national status, (dis)ability, religion, among others), and second, assuming that these categories are only important on their marginalized sides of the spectrum, rather than worthy of interrogation as dynamic sites of marginalization, privilege, and agency (see Fogg-Davis, 2008; Choo and Ferree 2010; Winker and Degele 2011). Indeed, as the Komen Foundation controversy reveals, even among demographically similar and/or similarly situated women, there are power dynamics (here, of grant funder and grantee) that can be daunting. Moreover, the stakes are higher precisely because, as Beckwith notes, women are underrepresented on nearly every metric of women's equality and empowerment.

If we think of intersectionality as a theory with potential utility in other nation-states and regional political institutions, this three-step process is even more important, for the US triumvirate of race-class-gender is not necessarily the approach for all other states, or for comparisons between nation-states. Indeed, Knapp (2005) notes the distinct lack of applicability of race (Rasse) and class (Klasse) in Germany based on its uniquely tragic history of the Holocaust, and how feminists who seek to utilize intersectionality as a tool render themselves irrelevant to discourse and scholarship in social theory and politics if they remain wedded to this *a priori* selection of categories (256–57). Dhamoon (2009) has discussed indigeneity as a category of analysis distinct from race or ethnicity. It is critical to note that the idea here is not to consider every category in every investigation, which would violate empirical standards of feasibility (qualitative research) and parsimony (quantitative research). The selection process is, however, designed to step away from the aforementioned problematic assumptions and ramifications of *not* engaging in a systematic process.

Three criteria have been presented in the literature (see Dhamoon 2011) to guide category selection. First, what signs of injury, social stigma, or lack of access are present? Returning to our Komen Foundation example, clearly the lack of access to affordable health care—specifically mammograms for early diagnosis of breast cancer—is the specific question, with the initial move to "defund" Planned Parenthood a key sign of injury, because the program would likely end in the absence of Komen funds. If our interest is women's health in general, the Millennium Development Goals set by the United Nations and its agencies have articulated several "issue indicators" on which progress through 2015 is measured, but this is a separate piece of data from the signs of injury themselves—women remain underrepresented, undereducated, underemployed, and disempowered throughout many parts of the Global South. However, a paradigm intersectional analysis would cast a critical eye upon the Global North as well, instead of leaving the so-called "Developed World" as an invisible normative standard.

The second criterion provides further opportunities to confirm the categories indicated by the marker of stigma, and preserves attention to the critical theory aspects of intersectionality theory: What is the substantive issue of social justice? Has the person or group of people been denied certain constitutional rights that may indicate attention to another category not yet identified? Here the question is not simply whether rights have been denied, but the legislative, judicial, or policy history associated with the interpretation of such rights, which may indicate attention to an additional category of disparity (this also reflects the interactive influence of the Time Dynamics dimension, which I discuss below). For example, the year-long history of Komen's study of prior Planned Parenthood grants and the personal history of Karen Handel and her hostility to Planned Parenthood based on 3% of the services it provides are all part of the interrogation here. While it may not be clear from the introductory paragraphs that started this chapter, another key factor in the push for Komen's policy change was the National Conference of Catholic Bishops. Comprehensively attending to the substantive issue of social justice in this way suggests that gender, class, and religion/religiosity are all relevant analytical categories for an empirical investigation (Kang, Chapter 8 of this volume, also interrogates the role of religion).

The last criterion, the scope and target of critique, is more dynamic. While the recent history might indicate certain categories' inclusion, thinking through the scope and target of critique is a more dynamic process that proceeds more like grounded theory analysis, particularly in the context like that of the Komen for the Cure debacle. Planned Parenthood's response was not simply to "go public" to the media. They mobilized their grassroots supporters to pressure corporate sponsors, who raise hundreds of millions of dollars for Komen through the pink ribbon logo, to walk away. Moreover, thinking through the scope and target of critique, depending on shifting politics, can also be broader than just the Komen Foundation itself. Part of why Komen has emerged as the leader of a global movement is the same evidence that helped inspire Millennium Development Goals 3 (Enhance Gender Equality and Empowerment) and 5 (Improve Maternal

Health), which is to say that women's health is a worldwide women's interest (again using Beckwith's definition), which could lead us to ensuring that any form of so-called reform of the health care system include provision of free preventive care, which would include mammograms and perhaps other strategies (e.g., medically supervised breast self-examination). In the United States this preventive care coverage is part of the Affordable Care Act (ACA) of 2009, recently upheld by the US Supreme Court. These recent facts may shift our analysis, reaffirming class as a category, because the ACA obligates insurance companies to cover preventive costs like mammograms. However, the Supreme Court struck down the federally mandated expansion of Medicaid to cover uninsured women, which reinforces the degree to which class relations still shape this debate.

The second dimension, *Categorical Intersections*, also suggests a standard of engagement beyond the net-effects solution of an interaction term. Net effects analysis (i.e., bivariate, multivariate regression and methods building upon their assumptions and premises) assumes that the net impact of a given independent variable (such as gender) functions the same way across all the values of the other variables (such as race/ethnicity) and in all their different combinations (Ragin 2008: 178). Intersectionality theory's arguments regarding Categorical Intersections directly contradict this assumption. Racing-gendering processes are not often productively decomposed into race effects x gender effects precisely because such intersections are sites of critically relevant qualitative difference (Crenshaw 1991; Hawkesworth 2003; Hancock 2013). It is a theory that explicitly articulates wide within-group variation. In other words, the combinations of processes and disparities faced by Latinas, white females, and Asian American males, as Laurel Weldon (2008) and Taeku Lee (2007) suggest separately, may not simply feature quantitatively different roles for race and gender on the same question, but qualitatively different roles as well. Intersectionality's central arguments likewise suggest that interaction relationships can vary within a single population sample, not simply between samples. Categorical Intersections facilitates comprehensive attention to what subsets share in common *without* the assumptions of within group homogeneity.

Diversity Within facilitates comprehensive attention to the systematic variation within groups, contingently conceptualized. For example, if one seeks to understand the racing-gendering processes of women of color in Congress, the common processes affecting all of them are part of Categorical Intersections. Any systematic variation in such processes, whether attributable to individual orientations (like personality or prior career background) or group orientations (like political party or district characteristics) are classified as Diversity Within. This decomposition of intersectional analysis into Categorical Intersections and Diversity Within pushes even qualitative researchers to more fully engage with their rich data for potentially generalizable Categorical Intersections without sacrificing the uniqueness contained in Diversity Within aspects of their data. This dual-dimension framework can also more faithfully account for the roles of agency and collective action among populations who may choose to pursue different strategies or have different resources available to them for utilization, including those defined as "strategic intersectionality." The framework also more faithfully attends to the reality of organized opposition at multiple stages of the policy process (see Proposition 3, Chapter 1 of this volume).

As described above, Categorical Multiplicity mandates commensurate conceptualizations across categories. The final two dimensions of paradigm intersectionality flesh out precisely how the multiple categories go beyond conceptualizations as self-reported dummy variables. Time Dynamics focuses on the relevance of sociopolitical development across time and within a particular sociohistorical context, an important way to incorporate the notion that interests, issues, and preferences are all socially constructed. Individual-Institutional Relationships join with Categorical Intersection and Diversity Within to more fully engage with agency and collective action by analyzing outcomes as products of ongoing, dynamic interactions between and among individuals, groups, social movements, and institutions.

It is important to note that the five dimensions—Categorical Multiplicity, Categorical Intersections, Diversity Within, Time Dynamics, and Individual-Institutional Relationships—are interrelated and thus are designed to serve as parts of a single comprehensive research design. A skeptic might question whether this is too comprehensive—that paradigm intersectionality is an unreachable ideal. Previous studies have been conducted using this framework explicitly (Hancock 2011) and implicitly (Moore 2011), demonstrating its feasibility.

The data demands of paradigm intersectionality are simultaneously logical and daunting. Both McCall's (2005) and Hancock's prior work (2007) have been cited as exemplars of intersectionality work that insufficiently privileges narratives (Alexander-Floyd 2012). In addition to placing women of color at the center, attention to narrative is the second shift that legal theorists demanded in their original push for intersectional analysis. While certainly archives of previous interviews with political elites, intersectionally identified or not, are a trove of information about representation, original data collection must extend beyond the intersectionality embodied/multiple approach framework that seeks to draw a causal link between identities while continuing to consider them conceptually distinguishable and therefore rank-orderable. Future scholars of intersectionality and representation will continue to vet empirical research designs that can systematically privilege narratives and attend to issues of scalability.

CONCLUSION

Over the past 20 years a number of strategies—qualitative and quantitative—have emerged to empirically operationalize intersectionality for questions of representation. They have traditionally taken questions, research designs, and methodologies as formulated within political science and have applied them to questions of women and representation. For example, work in the intersectionality embodied vein has been conceptualized as a site of inclusion—intended to reveal that which unitary approaches continued to render invisible and silent. Similarly, the intersectionality as testable explanation approach has brought large-N quantitative strategies to studies of new populations of legislators and representational schemes (see, e.g., Hughes 2011). Neither approach, unfortunately, fully incorporates the logical shifts in the first order question demanded by the original interlocutors of intersectionality.

For many women and politics scholars, this less than comprehensive operationalization is unproblematic, for the questions they seek to ask remain grounded in a framework that is seeking inclusion of intersectionality into women and politics' preexisting epistemological framework, rather than to shift the terms of the very framework itself. In a similar vein, those who are familiar with the philosophy of social science recognize that the "traveling" of concepts and theories often results in transformations of the concept itself into something unrecognizable by its originators. In their well-regarded book, *Politics, Gender and Concepts*, Gary Goertz and Amy Mazur (2008) contend that expansion of a concept (like intersectionality) is often the result of its travels across time and space, where modifiers emerge to point out previously missing dimensions of a more quotidian concept like stigma or praxis. Indeed, the aforementioned "strategic intersectionality" and "intersectional stigma," as well as Erica Townsend-Bell's (2011) "intersectional praxis," to describe women of color activism in Uruguay, are three modulations of intersectionality theory that tie directly to questions of political representation. Goertz and Mazur, like most scholars in the age of Web 2.0, have no meaningful way to restrict the growth of a new lexicon. However, they do propose their own set of options for "naming:" "1) keep the name but change the substance; 2) choose a new name; or 3) hyphenate or 'adjectivize' that concept" (2008: 22). As with the emergence of the gendering representation literature (Celis 2008), in the 23 years since Crenshaw and Collins coined the intersectional metaphor, many more modifiers may yet still emerge.

What if we were to rename the intersectionality embodied and intersectionality as testable explanation as "multiple identity" research? What if we were to fully operationalize intersectionality in such a way as to change the first order question to one where gender is assumed to be a relevant consideration unless the three-step Categorical Multiplicity selection process indicates otherwise, rather than assuming either (a) that every interest is a women's interest or (b) that no interest is a women's interest until proven otherwise? I contend that paradigm intersectionality provides a wealth of ways to ask questions regarding the ever-more complicated challenge of democratic representation. In a nation like the United States, which is facing demographic changes that are currently causing sincere anxiety among those who have been in power, there is no better time to think through how the first order question could be different if only we knew how important it was to change it. One brief case in point shall suffice: the anti-immigrant elements of the American populace have sought to restrict the rights of undocumented women by proposing an end to birthright citizenship enshrined in our Constitution.

The Komen Foundation continues for now to be led by Roberta Brinker, the sister of Susan G. Komen, whose death from breast cancer inspired its creation. However, the questions of women's health as women's interest face a number of concerns as we continue to use the same approaches that assume it is only the marginalized who need to change and are responsible for making the change. Incorporating a paradigm intersectionality approach can expand substantive representation for women and create solidarity across other categories of difference that can truly lift all boats. The changes that paradigm intersectionality poses to the first order question and beyond might one day serve to render the Komen for the Cure's vision of a world free of breast cancer a reality, without doing so at Planned Parenthood's expense.

CHAPTER 4

Representing Women

Defining Substantive Representation of Women

DRUDE DAHLERUP

INTRODUCTION

Most campaigns for enhancing women's political representation have made use of the argument that women will make a difference in politics. Politics has for too long been male dominated and consequently, it is argued, politics is mainly made in the interest of men, neglecting women's interests. For feminist research this expectation represents a challenge. Theoretically it is a challenge, since there is no agreement among feminist researchers about what constitutes "women's interests" and thus when women politicians can be said to represent women citizens. Empirically it is a challenge, since both feminist activists and feminist researchers differ considerably in their evaluation of the effect of having more women in elected assemblies. What do we expect from the growing number of women politicians? Here it is important to keep in mind that obviously, not all women politicians want or are able to "represent women."

And what do women want? The following quotations show two opposite positions in this discussion, one arguing that women say "we" too seldom, and the other that they do it too often:

Simone de Beauvoir in *Le Deuxième Sexe* from 1949:

But women do not say "We," except at some congress for feminists or similar formal demonstration; men say "women," and women use the same word in referring to themselves. They do not authentically assume a subjective attitude. (Beauvoir 1953: 11)

Judith Butler in the first sentences of her book *Gender Trouble* from 1990:

> For the most part, feminist theory has assumed that there is some existing identity, understood through the category of women, who not only initiates feminist interests and goals within discourse, but constitutes the subject for whom political representation is sought. (Butler 1990: 3)

I will argue that Simone de Beauvoir was right that women in general do not position themselves as a political subject, a "we," even if they are constructed as a group by men and even by themselves: women are talkative; women belong in the home; women do not understand mathematics; or the more recent, women are from Venus. Beauvoir's statement was, of course, more appropriate in the 1940s, before the modern feminist mobilization starting in the 1960s and 1970s, but it holds true even today.

Judith Butler is right, that there is no unified women's identity. But I will argue that she is wrong when she criticizes the feminist movement for seeking political representation for some assumed essentialist common identity of women. From in-depth studies of first and second wave feminist movements, including my own studies, it becomes clear that the feminist movements were always well aware of the fact that there is no unitary women's "we" and that, consequently, the movement had to work hard to try to construct a common political cause, a *political* identification among women across social and political cleavages, in order to change male dominance. Butler later modified her critique of women acting as a group (Butler 1999: preface), but her initially strong criticism of what she and other critics label "identity politics" has become highly influential in the present individualistic era.

Concepts of different "interests" are central to most thinking about representative democracy, yes, even in earlier conceptions—since systems of representation predate democracy (Dahlerup 2011). In this chapter I will discuss the contested concepts of "women's interests" and "substantive representation of women" from a theoretical point of view (in feminist theory), as well as from a perspective of how to make these concepts relevant in empirical analyses.

Following this introduction, in the second section I discuss various definitions of "women's substantive representation," a widely used term in contemporary research on women in politics. The third section discusses variations in scope of the *who, what, how,* and *where* of representation from a gender perspective. Do we see a tendency toward concept stretching here, since most research on "women's substantive representation" seems to start out from Hanna Pitkin? In the fourth and fifth sections, the theoretical foundations of the concepts of women's interest and the representation of women are discussed. It is argued (in contrast to Beckwith, Chapter 2 of this volume) that at the most fundamental level a concept of women's interest can only be derived from feminist theories about male dominance and patriarchy, which is why a parallel concept of "the substantive representation of men" does not make sense. Further, various feminisms might give different answers. To give an example: whether militarism (war and peace) is seen as a fundamental "women's interest" (see Beckwith, Chapter 2 of this volume) will be answered differently by liberal and radical feminists. This leads to an outline in the sixth section about possible approaches to the study of women's representation, none of which requires an *a priori* definition of women's interests. Rather, we pose empirical questions. From a social movement research perspective, we ask: *How* have various actors defined what women's interests are, and *when* and on *which issues* has it been possible to form broad alliances among a diversity of women politicians, women's organizations, and movements? Prior to the conclusion, the seventh section points to the fact that all political decision making, also on feminist policy issues, is the result of political bargaining with mixed motives.

REPRESENTING WOMEN: THE CONCEPT OF "SUBSTANTIVE REPRESENTATION"

With the global focus on increasing women's political representation, e.g., through the use of gender quotas and with the actual growing number of women in elected assemblies (Dahlerup 2006a; Krook 2009; Dahlerup and Freidenvall 2010), the subject of women politicians representing or not representing women voters has become more salient. In the public debate, the connection between number and policies is discussed, for instance in the debate over the scholarly contested, but publicly widespread, theory of a critical mass (Dahlerup 2006b; Beckwith 2007). But what are women politicians supposed to represent?

New concepts, such as "gender perspective," "gender sensitivity," and "gender mainstreaming," have found their way into national as well as international documents during the last decades, adding to or replacing older terms, such as "equality perspective," and "women's issues," and even older ones, such as "women and family matters."

There is, however, no general agreement about what concepts like "gender perspective" or "gender mainstreaming" imply in terms of policy goals and policy outcomes. Of course, such vague terms may be applied for strategic reasons—avoiding conflict over their exact meaning and even hiding more radical goals, like the concept of "reproductive health," which often hide radical demands (e.g., free access to abortion). However, such terms can, of course, also cover very limited ambitions. Today, a bureaucrat in a local, national, or international institution can safely talk about "gender perspective" or "gender mainstreaming" without being asked what that implies, whereas labels like "women's interests" or "feminist goals" would lead to various objections.

In contemporary feminist research, the term women's "substantive representation" is used increasingly, and the number-policy connection is being discussed in terms of the relation between descriptive and substantive representation, terms hardly used a few years ago (see. e.g., Wängnerud 2000; Mackay 2001; Goetz and Hassim 2003; Lovenduski 2005; Dahlerup 2006b). The concept of substantive representation has no doubt opened up new perspectives for research. However, different evaluations of the effects of increases in women's representation, the effects of various quota systems, as well as disagreements in the evaluation of the performance and effectiveness of women politicians in the scientific literature derives often, Dahlerup and Freidenvall argue (2010), from lack of clear criteria for evaluation, including criteria for what constitutes "substantive representation of women"?

From the feminist movement critique is often made that women politicians are "token" women, "proxies," and primarily party loyalists—in general, *not sufficiently feminist* in their work in parliament or local assemblies. But as researchers we need to develop evaluation criteria independently of the feminist movements, even if we personally may share feminist goals. Let's take a critical example: Is a non-feminist, right-wing woman politician who opposes free abortion because she, like many of her voters, believes that abortion undermines the traditional family (which is supposed to protect women and children) engaged in "substantive representation" of women? In a way she is, if she is representing her conservative constituents, but the answer totally depends on how we define women's interests and thus what constitutes women's substantive representation.

Stretching Hanna Pitkin

In the following we can see some nominal definitions of what women's substantive representation is.

> ...women's substantive representation (the promotion of women's interests). (Franceschet and Piscopo 2008: 394)
> ...attention to women's policy concerns (women's substantive representation). (Celis et al. 2008: 99)
> While descriptive representation functions somewhat by default (because there are women in parliament, women are therefore said to be represented), substantive representation requires consciousness and deliberate actions: a woman MP must speak and act in favor of the expectations, needs and interests of women. (Tremblay 2007: 283)

In the conclusion of the book *Representing Women in Parliament* (Sawer et al. 2006), Jennifer Curtin defines the question of substantive representation as the contentious issue "of whether we can expect women, once elected, to act on behalf of women." (Curtin 2006: 244)

These basic definitions are, as one can see, not uniform, but they do point in the same direction. All of the definitions mentioned above evolved around being a representative of women, around the issue of "women's interests," or "on behalf of women." However, many problems remain unsolved by these definitions.

Studies that make use of the term "women's substantive representation" often take as their point of departure Hanna Pitkin's concept of "representing as acting for...in the interest of" (Pitkin 1967: 111–13, 209). This concept was developed in Pitkin's text as one of four different concepts of representation, the others being formalistic, symbolic, and descriptive representation. Pitkin, however, does not use the exact term "substantive representation," even if she does talk about "substantive acting for others" (115). She wanted to identify conceptually "[t]he view of representation centered on the activity of representing, the role of a representative..." (112).

It has been argued that Hanna Pitkin never explained how these four different views of representation fit together (Dovi 2006). Consequently, the focus on the relation between descriptive and substantive representation, so central to the study of gender and politics today, is in fact, neither in the exact term, nor in the focus on the relationship, a perspective of Hanna Pitkin's.

Further, Pitkin's main interest is the relation between the represented and the representatives in political assemblies, not policy outcomes as such. Attaching the discussion of women's substantive representation to Pitkin's purely conceptual analysis is an example of concept stretching. However, whether or not based on Hanna Pitkin, exploring the connection between the *who*, the *what*, the *how*, and the *where* of representation is an important theoretical and empirical task (Diaz 2005; Galligan 2007; Dahlerup 2011).

THE *WHO*, THE *WHAT*, THE *HOW*, AND THE *WHERE* OF REPRESENTATION

In an attempt at "gendering" Pitkin's categories, Yvonne Galligan defines three distinct but interrelated dimensions: *who* represents, *what* is represented, and *how* it is represented, the latter implying the political structures (Galligan 2007: 557). It was, among others, the feminist movements and the black movements that vehemently argued for the importance of adding the *who* to the liberal notion of democracy, criticizing its limited focus on the *how*, i.e., the procedures of democracy. Even newer theories of democracy, such as deliberation theories, have to be reminded of the importance of who participates (Phillips 1995; Dahlerup 2011). In the literature on substantive representation, the importance of the *what* is further stressed, i.e., the substance or content of representation, the actual policies and policy outcomes. One may add a further dimension to Galligan's list, the question of *where* such representation takes place, thereby widening the scope to include forms of representation outside the formal political institutions, even non-elected representation (Saward 2010). In Part II of this book, all four dimensions of representation will be discussed.

From recent empirical studies the following three approaches reveal a substantial expansion of the scope of investigations into the substantive representation of women: from the relation between voters and their representatives (a), to studies of legislative processes and policy outcomes (b), to a very broad study of actors, sites, goals and means (c), all under the heading of the substantive representation of women, the case of representing women.

The Classic Focus on the Relation Between Voters and Representatives: Adding the *Who* to the *How*

This is the classic narrow understanding as found in Pitkin's work. Under this approach, the themes are *mandates* (When do women parliamentarians see themselves as representatives of women?); *accountability* (Do the voters expect female and perhaps even male politicians to be accountable to women and women's issues?); *issue congruence* among voters and representatives; and *the legislative autonomy* of women politicians under various party and quota systems (Wängnerud 2000; Diaz 2005; Rai et al. 2006; Childs and Krook 2009; Threlfall et al. 2012; Zetterberg 2009). Jane Mansbridge's influential article "Rethinking Representation" (2003) also has the voters-representative relation as its focus.[1]

---

1. Of her four forms of representation—"promissory," "anticipatory," "gyroscopic," and "surrogate"—Jane Mansbridge, and others after her, place responsibility for gender along with race, sexual preferences, disability, etc., under the fourth category, surrogate representation, i.e., a situation in which the representative feels responsible to surrogate constituents in other districts. However, for party-dominated political systems using the proportional representation electoral system (PR), the category "surrogate representation" seems less relevant, since most representatives do work across district lines in representing the political ideas of their party in parliament, not to the same extent as in plurality/majoritarian electoral systems, limiting their work as representatives to the electoral district where they were elected.

A Wider Perspective That Includes Policy Outcomes: Adding the *What*

In our view, much of the existing literature conflates two distinct aspects of substantive representation: the process of acting for women and the fact of changing policy outcomes.

(Franceschet and Piscopo 2008: 395)

Under this broader perspective, the policy formation process and the policy outcome are added to the voter-representative perspective, thus adding the *what* to the *who* and the *how*. At the center are questions of institutional barriers to and opportunities for women in their tasks as representatives. In their study of the effect of quotas on women's substantive representation with empirical data from Argentina, the first Latin American country to introduce electoral gender quotas by law, Franceschet and Piscopo (2008) "disaggregate" substantive representation into, first, the study of the processes of agenda building—whether and when female legislators advance women's interests and issues, to use Karen Beckwith's concepts—and, second, the outcome—how and why female legislators succeed or fail in advancing women's issues. In the Argentine case, women politicians mostly succeeded in representing women in the first sense; however, they failed, the authors argue, in the second sense, that of actually influencing legislation (2008). In the growing research field on the effects of electoral gender quotas, this broader definition of substantive representation is common, and attention is directed toward the effects of various institutional arrangements, different electoral systems and different quota systems on policy outcomes (Goetz and Hassim 2003; Diaz 2005; Sawer *et al.* 2006; Temblay 2007; Childs 2008; Dahlerup and Freidenvall 2010).

Anne Marie Goetz and Shireen Hassim are critical of the distinction between descriptive and substantive (or strategic) representation, since it may overstate the role of political agency and downplay the impact of the political institutions, encouraging, they say, a focus on the failures of female politicians (2003: 5). This is an important point, and today most researchers in the field do take up studies of the importance of the institutional context. It seems crucial to shift the focus from women politicians per se to the institutional and discursive constraints—as well as the opportunities—under which they work. These aspects of political opportunity structure are considered in Chapters 9, 10, and 11 (by Swers, Reingold and Haynie, and Escobar-Lemmon et al.) in this volume.

An Ever Broader Definition, Including Extra-Parliamentary Activities (NGOs): Adding the *Where*

Celis et al. suggest a shift in the terms of the debate away from the traditional questions of "Do women represent women?" or "Do women in politics make a difference?" to questions such as "Who claims to act for women?" and "Where, why, and how does substantive representation of women (SRW) occur?" (Celis et al. 2008: 99). Following Michael Saward (2010), Celis et al. argue that representation takes place everywhere in society, not only in political assemblies. In this way, studying women's substantive representation involves studying "a wide range of actors, sites, goal, and means" (2008: 99). Such aspects of representation are studied in Chapter 6 (by Hoekstra et al.) and Chapter 8 (by Kang) in this volume.

This last perspective adds the *where* to the *who*, the *what*, and the *how*. To look at who claims to act for women, inside or outside the formal political assemblies, is a very interesting perspective, which involves studying, among other themes, the acts and influence of national and transnational women's organizations and agencies. We are back to studying women's diverse organizations, feminist as well as non-feminist women's groupings, trade unions working on behalf of their women members, feminist bureaucrats, etc., etc. Naming this much broader perspective a study of women's substantive representation is no doubt an obvious example of concept stretching. Yet, who acts for women, or who says that they act for women are interesting questions per se. It might, however, be more appropriate to continue studying women's movements from a social movement research perspective and develop other, special tools for the study of women politicians working within political institutions characterized by different degrees of male dominance (Dahlerup and Leyenaar 2013). However, we still have not solved the fundamental problem of what it is that should be represented in various settings: What is "women's interest"?

"WOMEN'S INTEREST" EMBEDDED IN FEMINIST THEORY

We will now return to the question of defining *substantive representation* of women and *women's interests*. First, some formal problems of definition should be raised. Can we talk about varying degrees of substantive representation? Can "substantive representation" be defined in gender neutral terms—"the substantive representation of men"? Why must this last question probably be answered in the negative?

Substantive representation is sometimes defined dichotomously as something that is either achieved or not achieved, as when a researcher is analyzing "the parliamentary practices affecting the likelihood of women's substantive representation" (Zetterberg 2009: 85). Other researchers use a language or an approach that explicitly or implicitly indicates a scale of more or less substantive representation, as when concepts like "enhanced" or "improved" substantive representation are used (Bauer 2008: 365; Franceschet and Piscopo

2008: 421). Further, are "women's interests" per definition *common* interests, shared by all women?

Second, and most important, even Karen Beckwith's excellent distinction between the more fundamental women's interests and issues and preferences (see Chapter 2 of this volume) leaves some questions unanswered. Apart from universal claims of autonomy and self-determination, on what ground are some problems defined as fundamental interests of women, while others are not? At the beginning of this chapter, I mentioned the example of the military, war and conflicts, dimensions of society which by radical feminists are seen as an integrated part of patriarchy, while liberal feminism may fight for equality for women in the military.

Today, the Marxian concept of objective interests is in general dismissed, partly because it seems to imply that diverging opinions are just expressions of "false consciousness." However, a definition of "women's interests" has to be based on a structural understanding of the causes of the subjection of women and gender inequality. This, however, implies that there will be only a limited and partial common understanding of women's interests, even within feminism.

Consequently, I will argue that a theoretical definition of women's interests has to be derived from and embedded in feminist theory about the structural foundations of male dominance and patriarchal society at large. Such concepts are born out of feminist scholarship dealing with how to change male dominance, and some common grounds can be found. This, however, implies that a term like the "substantive representation of men," in contrast to "women's substantive representation," is meaningless. The concept "substantive representation of women," in my opinion, only makes sense when embedded in feminist theory about changing male dominance.

In an original attempt to identify some common interests of women, Anna Jónasdóttir points out that the term "interest" comes from the Latin *inter esse*, meaning "to be among" (1991: 156). Women across the political spectrum first and foremost have a common interest in being part of political assemblies, being part of the deliberations (see also Phillips 1995). In contrast, based on her distinction between "actual" and "principal" women's interests, Beatrice Halsaa argues that it should be possible to define common principal interests for women in relation to motherhood and labor, work that is performed only by women (1987: 52). This argument has its parallel in Anne Phillips's statement that even if some women do not have children, pregnancy is not a gender-neutral event (Phillips 1995: 68). All such definitions are highly contested and constantly discussed, as is the genesis of women's oppression in general. Depending on our understanding of what representation implies, it may, however, not be necessary to have solved these fundamental theoretical questions in order to study women's representation.

REPRESENTATION SEEN AS A PROCESS

The subject of women's representation touches upon central themes in representation theory and in feminist theory.[2] In the following, our understanding of representation is discussed in its relevance to the study of women's substantive representation.

Diaz asks if we should, in the discussion, see women's representation in terms of individual rights (opening access for individual women), in terms of group rights, or as general representation (2005: 16)? The answer is related to the debate over our understanding of representation. Do we see representation, not as an act of giving voice to fixed and well-defined interests or identities, but as a demand to be included in a dynamic process and interaction between the represented and the representatives?

Iris Marion Young's theory is useful in this discussion, when she argues against viewing the notion of inclusiveness of women or minorities as a kind of interest representation. Rather, her model "emphasizes the ideals of inclusion, political equality, reasonableness, and publicity" (2000: 17). According to Young, the arguments against such inclusiveness, for instance through the use of quotas for women and for other groups, derive from a misunderstanding of the nature of representation more generally. Representation is not about a relation of substitution or identification, but a dynamic, "differentiated relationship" among political actors (2000: 123).

The idea of a dynamic concept of representation also responds to the concern over "essentialism" in the meaning of biologism or universalism. It opens up a discussion of women, not as a fixed, but as a historically and socially or culturally changing, category. Such a dynamic concept of representation points to empirical analyses of when, where, around which issues, and how women are mobilized on account of gender.

In the literature on women's substantive representation, there seems to be a growing agreement to disassociate this field of research from any notion of a fixed, static ("essentialist") notion of women and women's interests.[3] However, this point of departure gives rise to new questions: which feminism and for which women is representation sought in order to call it "substantive representation" of women?

2. While this chapter is written within the framework of women's representation in liberal democracies, many of the discussions here are also relevant for semi-democratic and even those non-democratic political systems that have parliamentary assemblies based on elections.

3. I confine the term "essentialism" to biological arguments. While biological essentialism is counter-productive in feminist research, gender categorization is a necessary research tool and should not be labeled "essentialist."

Which Feminism?

Contrary to Judith Butler's statement, mentioned at the start of this chapter, the feminist movements have always been very well aware of the many disagreements among women and between various women's organizations, even between different feminist circles. In a minimalistic definition, covering all feminisms, feminism is an ideology, which has as its basic goal to fight against male dominance, and against the discrimination and degradation of women and of the tasks predominantly performed by women (Cott 1987; Dahlerup 2013a). Feminism is more easily defined by what one is against than by a common goal. In general, I argue, that there is no common feminist utopia, only partial feminist utopias, and, consequently, the question of what constitutes good substantive representation of women can ultimately be answered differently with reference to the different goals of liberal feminism, radical feminism, socialist feminism, post-structuralist feminism, post-colonial feminism, queer feminism, etc. Consequently, we may have to give up trying to find a common understanding of what constitutes "women's interests," outside abstract, theoretical understandings of women's oppression and male dominance. Ultimately, the transformative potential of increased women's representation will have to be judged in relation to the different and perhaps contrasting goals of various feminisms, or even broader goals including non-feminist or "right-wing feminist" claims.

Which Women?

An important criterion of success for the efforts to change women's historical under-representation is whether increasing the number of women in political institutions leads to the representation of a diversity of women and that different voices of women are being heard (Celis 2006; The FEMCIT Project). The present discussion of intersectionality is highly relevant to any discussion about improving women's representation. Which women get represented?

We may speak about *intersectionalizing representation*. This implies that multiple or integrated structures of disfavoring—and of favoring—must be considered in the discussion about women's representation. Do electoral gender quotas tend to favor representation of majority women? Are minority women even less represented than men from minority groups (not always the case, for instance not in Scandinavia)? How do various minority women's groups define their ideal representation (Freidenvall and Dahlerup 2011, see www.femcit.org)? On this topic, see Chapter 3 (by Hancock) and Chapter 7 (by Htun) in this volume.

There are reasons to warn against double standards: representing diversity is a problem for the representation of men as well as of women, and should not just be discussed as a problem concerning only women's representation. Further, women's under-representation and even to a large extent conflicts among women are to be interpreted within the context of women's historical exclusion from political power.

The many problems described above concerning defining women's interests and the substantive representation of women do not imply that we should not engage in empirical investigations about women's substantive representation. But it requires that we as researchers are open about our approach and our criteria of evaluation.

EMPIRICAL RESEARCH ABOUT REPRESENTING WOMEN

Compared to research on women's descriptive representation, research on substantive representation, according to Lena Wängnerud, is "less mature" (2009: 52). Franceschet and Piscopo also focus on the absence of common operationalizations that would make comparative research possible (2008: 495). Dahlerup and Freidenvall make the claim that differences in research results on the effect of women in politics often derive not just from different cases or historical periods, but also from the use of disparate criteria of evaluation (2010: 407; see also Dahlerup and Leyenaar 2013: 8).

Having identified various problems related to the use of the concepts of women's interests or "substantive representation of women," I will now turn to a discussion of possible approaches and strategies in empirical research on women in politics, none of which requires an *a priori* all-encompassing definition of women's interests—that is turned into an empirical question.

Using Certain Indicators

A relevant research strategy is to identify some key indicators of women's position and gender (in)equality, known from the debate, and then go on to test them using a comparative research strategy—looking for differences between countries, between municipalities, possibly at several points in time, all in relation to different levels of women's representation.

In this way the researcher avoids getting involved in the theoretically complex attempt to define women's interests. Instead, a number of key dimensions, *a priori* indicators, are selected for empirical study, for instance, violence against women, marriage laws, child care, income and pay equity, pensions, parental leave, or equality laws. The research interest could be the processes of agenda setting, actual legislation and regulations, or outcomes in the form of changes in women's and men's actual positions. The increasing number of global gender indexes rests on the use of such outcome indicators: Gender-Related

Development Index (UNDP), Gender Index (OECD), and Global Gender Gap (World Economic Forum).

In their ambitious project, Mala Htun and S. Laurel Weldon want to explore when and why governments promote women's rights through a comparative analysis of the experiences of 70 countries between 1975 and 2005 (see framework article 2010). Many more studies of this kind are needed.

Focus on the Claims of Women's Organizations

Indeed, women's organizations used to be the main source of any discourse on women's interests and substantive representation of women. Women's organizations are here understood as organizations with predominantly women as members and leaders. Not all women's organizations are feminist, and not all declared feminist organizations have only women as members. Within the group of women's organizations, feminist organizations or movements are distinguished by their explicit feminist ideology (for definition of the core of feminism, see above).

What is interesting to study empirically is how, when, and on what issues women's organizations—such as housewives' organizations, women's sections within political parties, or associations of women university teachers, to mention just a few—have acted together with declared feminist organizations for common aims.

Thus, in contrast to Judith Butler's ontological approach, my recommendation for research on women's substantive representation is to approach the issue by empirical research. Which issues have mobilized the broadest coalitions of women's organizations to act together? When have we seen alliances of women from ideologically different parties, classes, and ethnic background, and when did they succeed? When have men as feminist actors joined in? In sum, instead of trying to define what women's interests are *a priori*, this approach points to empirical studies of historical coalition formations among women's organizations and groups.

From research in the area we know that some of the *broadest alliances* of women in the Western world have been established around the issues of women's suffrage and later changing women's historical under-representation, women's education, support for single mothers, combating violence against women, and in more secular countries also around women's reproductive health. Much more research is needed following this approach.

Studying Changing Positions, Attitudes of and Actions by Women Politicians

This is an expanding research field within the overall theme of gender and politics. With the increasing number of women in elected assemblies, internationally, nationally, and locally, it is highly relevant to study the positions, attitudes and actions of women politicians (over time, across countries, across municipalities). Two sub-themes will be mentioned in the following.

The Position of Women Politicians

In many countries around the world today, we see a significant increase in the number and share of women in leadership positions in government and within elected assemblies, even if politics is still heavily dominated by men. At the end of 2013, 21% of the world's parliamentarians were women (www.ipu. org); only around ten women were serving as prime ministers and less than ten women as presidents (www.guide2womenleaders.com). A prerequisite for women's ability to make policy change, if they so wish, is a stronger position within the hierarchies of political parties, parliaments, and other important political institutions. We see a new tendency that women are represented and function as parliamentary committee chairs and hold government portfolios in all types of issue areas, not as previously restricted to social and educational affairs. In general, labeling social and educational portfolios "soft," which even feminist researchers tend to do, seems to be a result, not of any characteristics of the actual policy areas (the social and educational areas do have some of the largest budgets), but a tautological way of reasoning based on the fact that many women politicians are found working in these policy areas, based on their previous professions and political interests (Dahlerup and Leyenaar 2013).

Attitudes and Actions

Studies from all corners of the world show that it is predominantly female politicians, sometimes together with a few male colleagues, who have placed issues like child care provisions, violence against women, equal pay, gender equality legislation, and women's under-representation on the political agenda, and have tried to push them through their own party groups and the legislative process at large, though not always with success. In strong party systems, it is, however, seldom seen that women politicians across party cleavages act together as one block against male politicians. Rather they will try to persuade male colleagues in each party fraction. Further, attitude surveys among politicians have also demonstrated that female politicians do not constitute one unified group, but that within each party, on the other hand, women tend to be somewhat more interested in social affairs and gender equality issues than their male colleagues, although a generational divide seems to be emerging. The picture is highly context dependent. To give an example: in the Scandinavian countries, differences in attitudes and behavior between women and men members of parliament seem to be diminishing, while women politicians from the Global South, with South Africa as the outstanding example, today tend to speak more openly about women politicians working together for women's interests and "sisterhood." Dahlerup and Leyenaar ask (2013) to what extent such variations are linked to the differences between the *incremental track change* in women's political representation in old democracies versus the *fast track change* experienced especially in many post-conflict countries, not least by their use of electoral gender quotas.[4]

GENDER POLICIES ARE ALSO THE RESULT OF POLITICAL BARGAINING AND MIXED MOTIVES

Tokenism, "proxy women," "being too dependent on their political party or political leader"—these are among the accusations that women politicians meet, not least from the feminist movement from all over the world (Dahlerup and Freidenvall 2010). The criteria that such evaluations are based on, however, are not always explicit. To give an example: some researchers find that the female majority in the Rwandan parliament, the first in the world, has been a failure, while others point to the new land reforms and laws against violence against women. In Sweden, with a parliament of 45% women, the evaluation of the effect of having an almost gender balanced parliament differs considerably, in the public as well as among researchers.

Three different sources of this widespread discontent with women politicians can be identified. First, I would argue, that research in this field, including my own, has sometimes followed the judgments of the feminist movements too closely. All throughout history, the feminist movements have been critical of women politicians. One may argue that criticism of legislators and legislation is a normal task of any social movement or lobby group. Nevertheless, based on an expectation of common interests, there has often been a strong sense of 'betrayal' hanging in the air between women politicians and feminist movements.

Second, women politicians are being met with contradictory expectations. They are accused by feminist movements of being too dependent on their parties and not sufficiently supportive of feminist demands. However, when they seek to create cross-party alliances on women's issues, they often experience

---

4. In relation to Implication 2.1 in Chapter 1, it is important to avoid what has been called "the difference fallacy" (Dahlerup 2006a). A lack of difference between male and female politicians in terms of attitudes and parliamentary actions may derive from the fact that the large number of women politicians have successfully influenced the political agenda and the attitudes on women's issues among male colleagues and party leaderships.

criticism from the party leadership for betraying the party line. In strong party systems, it is a victory when an issue, perhaps initiated as a "women's issue," is transformed into a party issue, supported by men as well as women. To document this kind of informal women's network, interviews and policy tracing are needed—a time-consuming research strategy.

Third, because of the lack of a common understanding of women's interests and women's issues, women politicians who support the demands of some women's groups will expose themselves to criticism by other women's groups, as laid out in Proposition 2 in Chapter 1. In the Scandinavian countries, the right-wing women's organizations attack left-wing and Social Democratic women's organizations for trying to monopolize feminism. Yet, in spite of these controversies, from time to time throughout Scandinavian history, grand coalitions of 'right wing feminism' and 'left wing feminism' have been formed, especially on the issues of changing women's under-representation, improving the position of single mothers, equal pay, and combating violence against women. Women's groups tend to be successful when they have cooperated across all cleavages in grand coalition (Dahlerup 2013b; Freidenvall 2013).

In a remarkable new discourse, xenophobic parties now represented in many European parliaments, and also in Scandinavian parliaments, argue that gender equality is a Danish, Norwegian, Dutch, or Austrian value that immigrants are not capable of learning. It is an amazing discourse, since these parties used to vote against almost all gender equality legislation in the past. Now they try to use gender equality to stress their distinctions between "us" and "them." The basis of this new discourse is, one should notice, that gender equality *has already been achieved* by the "natives," while no further gender equality interventions are needed, except toward immigrant groups!

The institutional frames for women's representation and the possibility for gender equality policies to succeed are important research themes. Do the feminist movement and sometimes even feminist researchers tend to base their analyses of women's substantive representation on unrealistic or idealistic assumptions about the political process? Do we only accept "pure" feminist motives behind a piece of legislation, be it quotas, legislation on violence against women, or money for shelters? Otherwise, our judgment will be predominantly negative: "They only do this because of..."

But political life is a game of bargains, compromises, and mixed motives. That is the case in equality policies as well as environmental policies, educational policies, and in fact all other policy areas. I would like to see studies that compare the adoption of equality policy with the adoption of environmental policy during the same historical period. What are the similarities and differences between the adoption of these contested new policy areas? It is a general methodological problem that researchers tend to study policies issue by issue, perhaps *diachronically*, neglecting the fact that political decisions are made *synchronically*: "If your party votes for my budget, we will vote for your quota law" (Dahlerup 2008; Dahlerup and Freidenvall 2010).

To sum up: there is an urgent need for developing a set of standard definitions and indicators that enable cross-country comparative research on the performance and effectiveness of women (and male) politicians in furthering gender equality policies (Franceschet and Piscopo 2008; Wängnerud 2009). In general, cross-national studies are fruitful in that they require uniform criteria.

CONCLUSION

"Women" is no doubt an ambiguous category, as Simone de Beauvoir stated. For women's organizations, and especially for the feminist movements, this fact has complicated their advocacy on behalf of women. But this fluidity constitutes a challenge for feminist research as well.

The concern in this chapter is not primarily with the lack of universal definitions of what women's interests, gender sensitivity, and other similar notions imply—concepts that the idea of substantive representation are usually based on. A theoretical definition of women's interests is a matter for Feminist Theory, since, it is argued in this chapter, such definitions have to be embedded in abstract theories of male dominance and gender inequality. This, however, should not prevent empirical research on women's descriptive and substantive representation. This chapter has discussed various approaches and research strategies in this field, for which an *a priori* definition of women's interests is not necessary. What is needed are clearly stated criteria of evaluation, which is not always the case today. Interesting research themes for empirical studies of women's political representation and of the relation between elected women and women citizens are studies of how concepts of women's interests and women's issues have been used and defined by various actors and movements at various points in history, on what grounds mobilization has taken place, and when and on what issues larger coalitions of women's organizations have been formed in order to change policies and the structure of political decision making, and when they have been successful.

The use of the concept of "identity" in this regard, in my opinion, constitutes a major problem. The present trend of speaking of social movements in terms of "identity movements" is unfortunate, since it downplays the political aspect of these movements—their attempt to mobilize against discrimination and inequality. Should we similarly refer to the working class movement as an "identity movement"? Of course not. From a social movement perspective, common ideology and solidarity within a group—be it workers, blacks, women, immigrants, or LGBT persons—is clearly a result of organizational effort, not something instinctive or inherent (Dahlerup 2011, 2013a).

Changing women's historical under-representation is one of the political issues, which has gathered the largest coalition of diverse women's organizations. Research from many countries has shown that transforming male dominant political institutions into open and inclusive ones is a widely shared common goal. As during the suffrage movement, today we are seeing large national and international coalitions formed behind the claim for gender balanced political institutions—partly because such joint actions against male dominance in politics do not require any common agreement as to what this increased political influence should be used for.

PART TWO

Representation: Gaining Presence in Politics

CHAPTER 5

The Effect of Preferential Voting on Women's Representation

RICHARD E. MATLAND AND EMELIE LILLIEFELDT

The wave of democracy that has washed over the world over the past three decades brought with it predictions of greater access as the political process opened up. Yet adopting more democratic rules has not automatically led to greater access for women. There has been significant progress, however, in understanding the factors influencing women's access to national legislatures in democracies (Darcy et al. 1994; Matland 1993, 1998; Matland and Montgomery 2003a; Matland and Studlar 1996; Norris 1997; Rule 1987). A central explanatory variable identified in this work is the electoral system used to select representatives. Representation is improved by the adoption of a proportional representation system. A crucial distinction across proportional representation systems is closed versus open lists (Katz 1986; Karvonen 2004). In closed list systems, parties promulgate candidate lists and candidates are elected in the order that parties predetermine. In open list systems, parties present lists of candidates, but voters decide which candidates are elected.

Research looking at how preferential voting impacts women's representation has produced mixed results. Rule and Shugart (1995) argue open lists advantage women, because supporters can be mobilized to vote for women (see also Schmidt and Saunders 2004; Kittelson 2006). Other researchers argue open list systems hurt women, because they allow voter bias against women to influence outcomes (Thames and Williams 2010). Valdini (2012) notes that if parties are concerned about voter skepticism to female candidates, this can affect party strategy and may lead to fewer women being nominated. Empirically, Kunovich (2012) presents empirical evidence that women are helped by preferential voting in Poland, while Hellevik and Bjørklund (1995) provide explicit evidence that women are hurt by the preferential vote in Norway.

These inconsistent findings leave a gap in the literature. Our theoretical model bridges that gap. Further, we test the model by analyzing the effects of preferential voting on women's representation in two very different settings: local elections in Norway and national elections in Latvia. These analyses are designed to broaden our understanding of when women obtain representation and which women gain representation. Chapter 1 of this volume suggests women's access to decision-making venues increases as women become organized and demand the right to participate (Implication 1.1), but can decrease if women's issues threaten the power of other groups (Implication 1.2). Often this is couched in terms of intraparty competition over nominations. In proportional representation systems, when the voters have the final say over who in the party is elected, success within the party nominating caucus risks being upended by the voters or, alternatively, individual voters can provide the ability to work around a roadblock caused by patriarchal dominance within the party. This chapter considers the impact of voters in affecting women's ability to gain such access.

THEORETICAL MODEL

We believe the confusion regarding the impact of preferential voting comes from not considering the rest of the system in which electoral institutions are embedded. There has been a desire to provide an unambiguous answer to the question "Does letting voters choose among the listed candidates help or hurt women?" This electoral rule, however, does not operate in a vacuum. A preferential voting system interacts with other factors prior to voters having their input. Especially important is the role that parties play. We believe insufficient emphasis has been placed on parties and the process of list production.

Individual parties develop norms and promulgate rules to deal with many internal and external issues when determining which candidates to nominate (Hazan and Rahat 2010). Equal representation may be a dormant issue in some parties but quite active in others. There are significant differences across parties, even in the same country, in how well organized and successful women are at getting nominated. Therefore voters face lists with substantial variation in women's presence. Because parties produce radically different lists, this must be taken into consideration when estimating the impact of preferential voting on women's representation.

Furthermore, party voters can have different perspectives on the importance of women's representation and in their desire to vote for better representation of women. For some party members the issue of women's representation is highly salient; for many, however, it is of limited importance. These voters are more worried about specific issues, the candidates' occupational background, or political experience. Representation of women does not factor into their evaluation when deciding which candidates get their preferential votes. The proportion of those engaged by women's representation, those indifferent, and those aggressively anti-women varies across parties. In some parties most voters will be supportive of promoting women; in most parties women's representation is unlikely to influence the bulk of party voters; while in a final set there can be a negative impact. These differences have implications for individual women candidates.

Being blind to candidate sex need not mean preferential voting has no impact on women's representation. There may be a relationship between how individuals vote and women's representation, but it may be spurious. For example, consider a farmer who votes for the Center Party in Norway. This voter may vote for any farmer he finds on his party's list. This person will vote primarily for male candidates but he is voting for them *not because they are male,* but because they are farmers.

Our model estimates the salience of women's representation for the party and for the party's voters. While these variables are theoretically continuous, our ability to detect the level of concern is not sophisticated enough to merit such a fine-grained level of measurement. Instead, we have identified three levels of concern about women's representation for parties and voters producing the 3 x 3 matrix in Table 5.1.

By estimating the salience of women's representation for parties and their voters we can identify which cell the case belongs in and predict the effect of preference voting. Effects can vary from strongly positive to strongly negative. Voters' and their parties' positions are unlikely to be entirely independent. Parties do not have a long-term interest in having policies strongly opposed by their voters, and over time voters adjust their viewpoints to be consistent with their party (Gerber and Jackson 1993). Therefore, in the long run we suspect that actions move toward equilibrium at cells A, E, and I. Yet at any point in time an imbalance may exist as the issue's salience for a party and its voters can differ.

For some parties equal rights is a central plank, while others hew to a more traditional view of the proper role for women in society and politics. Furthermore, while some consciously adopt rules guaranteeing women equal representation (quotas), many parties recruit through "old boys" networks, which exclude women. Therefore we expect each of the three conditions on the X axis in Table 5.1 will appear across a diverse set of parties.

We believe the bulk of voters fall into the middle row—neither proactively supporting nor actively voting against women candidates. The literature suggests candidate sex is not a major determinant of voting behavior (LeDuc et al. 2010). Even in countries with majoritarian electoral systems, where parties

Table 5.1. PREDICTED IMPACT OF PREFERENTIAL VOTING ON WOMEN'S REPRESENTATION

VOTERS \ PARTIES	Party strongly committed to gender equality, has adopted positive action policies, and strongly promotes women	Party not hostile to women, yet has not adopted strong positive action policies nor aggressively promotes women	Party is skeptical to women, seen as outsiders and inferior candidates, women are impeded by the party
Party Voters strongly committed to gender equality; consciously vote for women	LIMITED (A)	POSITIVE (B)	STRONG POSITIVE (C)
Party Voters not hostile to women, yet not actively concerned about representation	NEGATIVE (D)	LIMITED (E)	POSITIVE (F)
Party Voters skeptical to women, seen as inferior representatives	STRONG NEGATIVE (G)	NEGATIVE (H)	LIMITED (I)

nominate a single candidate, female candidates do as well as their male counterparts (Black and Erickson 2003; McElroy and Marsh 2010; Rekkas 2008; Seltzer et al. 1997; Welch and Studlar 1986). Studies in Eastern Europe also find that women do as well as men at the polls, or that voters express no bias in polling data (Birch 2003; Moser 2003; Sieminenska 2003). In experiments designed to test the impact of candidate sex, sex is consistently overwhelmed by more powerful cues such as party labels or policy proposals, even in highly patriarchal societies (Matland and Tezcur 2011). If these cues are unavailable, however—often the situation when a voter is casting a preferential vote—then sex may have a greater impact.

NORWEGIAN LOCAL ELECTIONS

Local Party System

Norwegian municipal elections are held every four years, most recently in 2011. Municipalities range from Oslo with 620,000 inhabitants to 25 municipalities with fewer than 1,000 citizens. Most municipalities are sparsely populated (median about 4,500). In 2011, 59,496 candidates vied for 10,785 positions on local councils across 430 municipalities (*kommuner*) in this country of 5 million people.

The party system varies across municipalities but largely reflects the picture at the national level. Ideologically, the Socialist Left (SV) is to the Left of the Labor Party and is concentrated in urban areas. The Labor Party (A) is the largest party at the national and local level and elects representatives in virtually every municipality. The traditional parties of the Center [Center Party (Sp), Christian's People's Party (KrF) and the Liberals (V)] are all stronger at the local than the national level and dominate many rural municipalities. The traditional party of the Right, the Conservative Party (Høyre) has a broad presence throughout the country and the second largest number of elected representatives. The Progress Party (FrP), initially a tax protest party on the Right, has grown from a base in Oslo and Bergen to become established in many communities. Municipal elections, especially in smaller municipalities, also produce local lists pushing local concerns or expressing a desire to keep local politics free of party politics (e.g., Anti-Toll Road List, Islands List, Non-partisan List). Especially in rural communities, local lists can dominate local politics.

Preferential Voting in Local Elections

Initially, parties at the local level have nomination meetings to develop a list of candidates ordered from 1 to N.[1] Voters can cast a ballot for their party without using their personal vote. They have the right, however, to also vote for specific candidates on the party lists. Voters may add a plus as a positive vote for as many individuals as they wish on the party's list. After all the votes have been cast, ballots are first counted to determine the number of seats each party wins based on a party's proportion of the total vote. Which candidates on the party list are elected is decided by counting the individual pluses that each candidate receives.

While preference votes matter, parties strongly influence who is elected. Through placing candidates in a specific order parties signal their preferences. In addition, parties can select a set of candidates to receive a "party preference" designation. These candidates receive a preference vote bonus equivalent to 25% of the total party vote.[2] This designation effectively sets up a

---

1. A party list must have a minimum of seven names, but can have as many names as there are members of the local councils; local councils vary from 11 to 78 members.

2. If the municipal council has 11–23 members the party can identify up to four candidates who receive the preferential bonus, in 25–53 member councils up to six candidates can receive the bonus, and in councils with greater than 55 members up to ten candidates.

two-tier system; those candidates with bonuses compete against each other, and those without bonuses compete against each other.

Below we compare the actual outcome to what would have occurred had the parties' lists been followed exactly in the order proposed. In effect, we compare the results from the existing open list system with a hypothetical closed list system. Of the 10,785 local counselors elected, 23.4% (2,525) were elected because of the personal votes they received. These individuals would have been replaced by a different candidate had party lists been the only basis on which councilors were selected. Because we have a data set with almost 60,000 candidates of which more than 2,500 either lost or won because of personal voting, we can test for consistent effects across the individual parties and their voters.

Expectations for Norwegian Parties

Parties on the Left, especially the Socialist Left (SV), have actively tried to draw support from feminists. SV was one of the first two parties to adopt quotas and has been strongly committed to gender equality as a bedrock principle. The Labor Party (A), after both internal pressure from its women's wing and external pressure from SV and Liberals, adopted formal quotas for parliamentary candidates in the mid-1980s. Just prior to the 2003 local elections, the Labor Party raised their local quota from 40% to 50% and adopted a rule that the two top names in each community must include a man and a woman (Christiansen et al. 2008).

The parties of the Center have all adopted 40% quotas for parliamentary and local council lists. The Liberals (V) were the first party in Norway to adopt quotas in 1972, while the Christian People's Party (KrF) was the last in the 1990s. Both KrF and the Center Party (SP) are strongest in rural areas with many elderly voters who have a more traditional perspective on the role of women. When these parties adopted 40% quotas for local nominations they were ahead of their voters. It is quite possible the parties remain more engaged on this issue than their voters.

On the Right, both the Conservatives (H) and the Progress Party (FrP) have argued that quotas are an anathema to choosing the most qualified candidate. Both parties claim to evaluate candidates only on their merits. While lagging behind the other parties, the Conservative Party has been susceptible to a contagion effect and has increased the proportion of women nominated when the other parties did (Matland and Studlar 1996). The Progress Party (FrP) has been vocal in its desire to identify itself as different from the other parties. While equal access is important, FrP consciously rejects the idea that equal representation is an important goal. FrP insists, however, that it is not biased against women and nominates qualified women. There are, however, no policies to increase women's participation.

All parties face the reality of having to recruit a very large number of candidates. On election day 2011 more than 1% of the country's population appeared on electoral ballots. Academic accounts of nomination meetings occasionally describe local party officials pleading with people to stand, with some agreeing to be nominated only if they were guaranteed to not get elected (Hellevik and Skard 1985; Aars 2001; Christiansen et al. 2008). Therefore, while many parties profess support for equal representation, they occasionally see it as a luxury when putting together their lists. After a certain amount of competition for the top positions, they need bodies, male or female, to complete the party's list.

Our discussion identifies the Socialist Left, Labor, and the Liberals as parties strongly committed to gender equality. The Center Party and Christian People's Party are also in agreement with gender equality policy, but equality plays a less central role in the ideology of these parties. The Conservatives have been quite willing to nominate women but have limited policies to insure greater representation. The Progress Party has not adopted any positive action policies to promote women. It is going too far to say that FrP is officially skeptical of women, but they do not engage in active outreach.

Table 5.2 shows the female proportion of candidates each party fielded for the 2011 municipal elections. An impressive 41.8% of all candidates were women; only the Conservatives at 36.0% and the Progress Party at 28.9% are below 40%. The parties largely fit the pattern we predict.

Expectations for Norwegian Voters

To estimate the importance of women's representation to the voters of the various parties, we use national survey responses.[3] We use a question concerning equality policies from the 2005 national election study done during the parliamentary election and a question concerning women's participation in local politics from the 2003 and 2007 local election studies (see Table 5.3 for full text of questions).

There is little support for the idea that equal rights for women have gone too far, only 6.3% of the public concurs, 33.3% believe policies have gone far enough, while 60.4% say these policies should be expanded. Table 5.3 presents the means among voters for the seven major parties. The voters of the Socialist Left are the most ardent supporters, while both Labor and the Liberals also provide strong support for increased equality. Support is more limited in the Center among Christian People's Party (Krf) and Center Party (Sp) voters. In fact, Krf is the most negative of the seven parties. We should be

3. Thanks to Atle Alvheim and Christopher Tønnesen at the Norwegian Social Science Data Services for their prompt replies and help in procuring these data.

Table 5.2. SEX OF CANDIDATES BY PARTY LISTS, NORWEGIAN MUNICIPAL ELECTIONS, 2011

Party Sex	Socialist Left (SV)	Labor (A)	Liberals (V)	Center Party (Sp)	Christian People's Party (Krf)	Conservatives (H)	Progress Party (FrP)	Other Parties and Local Lists	TOTALS
Female	2,922 (53.0%)	4,830 (47.6%)	2,835 (42.7%)	3,383 (40.1%)	2,311 (45.1%)	3,244 (36.0%)	1,822 (28.9%)	3,496 (42.0%)	24,843 (41.8%)
Male	2,594 (47.0%)	5,310 (52.4%)	3,800 (57.3%)	5,047 (59.9%)	2,819 (54.9%)	5,756 (64.0%)	4,492 (71.1%)	4,835 (58.0%)	34,653 (58.2%)
Total	5,516	10,140	6,635	8,430	5,130	9,000	6,314	8,331	59,496

Table 5.3. SUPPORT FOR EQUAL RIGHTS AND INCREASING WOMEN'S PARTICIPATION IN LOCAL POLITICS ACROSS PARTIES

Party Survey Question	Socialist Left (SV)	Labor (A)	Liberals (V)	Center Party (Sp)	Christian People's Party (Krf)	Conservatives (H)	Progress Party (FrP)	Other Parties and Local Lists	TOTALS
Q1: Equal Rights Policy (2005)	1.21 (.04)	1.37 (.02)	1.37 (.06)	1.59 (.06)	1.66 (.06)	1.45 (.04)	1.56 (.04)		
Q2 (2003): More Women in Local Politics	64.2%	55.7%	61.3%	50.2%	40.2%	49.7%	52.9%	55.9%	52.1%
Q2 (2007): More Women in Local Politics	65.7%	53.2%	51.8%	53.6%	39.5%	43.9%	48.7%	48.4%	50.3%
Average Q2 (2003 and 2007)	65.0%	54.5%	56.6%	51.9%	39.9%	46.8%	50.8%	52.2%	51.2%

Question #1: "When thinking about equality between the sexes, would you say these activities need to be expanded (1), that we now are at a point where equality policies have gone far enough (2), or would you say equality policies have reached a point where they have gone too far (3)?" Table shows mean and standard deviations for each party. (2005, N=1,503).
Question #2 (2003 and 2007): "Do you believe women should participate to a greater degree than they do presently in municipal decision making and local political work, are things just fine the way they are, or should women participate less in local political work?" Table shows proportion who answer "Women should participate more." (2003, N=1,986) (2007, N=1,991).

cautious, as this may be because of the tie between sexual equality and abortion rights, which is a red flag issue in KrF. Nevertheless, the Conservatives are surprisingly more supportive than either of the two Center parties.

The second question asked whether respondents thought more women should get involved in municipal governance and local political work. In both years only 1.5% suggested women should become less involved, but a fair number said things were fine the way they were (44.0% in 2003 and 46.2% in 2007). A bare majority said women should be more active (52.1% in 2003 and 50.3% in 2007). Socialist Left voters are the strongest supporters of more women participating. Labor and Liberal voters also provide above average support for women's participation. The Christian People's Party is again the least enthusiastic. This may be due to traditional values, but it may also be in reaction to the party adopting quotas for candidates at the local level. The Conservatives and the Progress Party, who have not adopted quotas and who nominate fewer women than the other parties, show only marginally lower support than the Center Party and higher support than the Christian People's Party for women becoming further involved.

Further analysis shows the Socialist Left and the Christian People's Party voters are disproportionately women (58% and 60%), while Conservatives and Progress Party voters are overwhelmingly male (57% and 60%). This replicates results concerning the gender gap in party support found in earlier work and is a stable feature of the Norwegian polity (Listhaug et al. 1995). If voters prefer to vote for someone like themselves (i.e., of the same sex), these skewed ratios may affect preferential voting.

Even when voters do not vote for or against candidates because of their sex, they can use a candidate's sex as a heuristic to evaluate the candidate by making ideological inferences based on the candidate's sex. A consistent finding in US studies is that when voters have limited information, they assume a female candidate is more liberal than a similar male candidate (McDermott 1997; Koch 2000, 2002; Matland and King 2002; Dolan 2004). This may happen in Norway as well. In particular, voters on the Right may be skeptical of female candidates, not because they believe women are unqualified, but because they believe women may be too moderate. While women who are visible and are able to present a clear message consistent with the party program are supported, for women farther down the lists who are relatively unknown, we suspect the impact is negative because of skepticism about their willingness to stand for "true conservative values." This effect is likely to be especially acute among Progress Party voters.

Theoretical Predictions of the Preferential Vote Effect

Based on the data mapping the preferences of parties and voters we make the following estimations:

- Cell A: Strong support from party and voters for women candidates: Socialist Left (SV), Labor (A), Liberals (V). Personal vote is predicted to have limited impact.
- Cell D: Strong support from party, modest support/indifference from voters: Center Party (Sp), Christian People's Party (Krf). Personal vote is predicted to have a negative impact.
- Cell E: Modest support from party, modest support from voters: Conservatives (Høyre). Personal vote is predicted to have a limited impact.
- Cell H: Modest support from party, skepticism among voters: Progress Party (FrP). Personal vote is predicted to have a negative impact.

Results in Norwegian Local Elections

We can compare the female proportion among local councilors who would be elected under either a closed or an open list system, and those elected exclusively via preferential voting, i.e., those who would not have been elected had there been a closed list but who are elected because voters used their personal vote to raise the candidate's ranking. The bottom row of Table 5.4 shows a noticeable drop-off in women's success among those elected by personal vote. Women are 40.1% of municipal councilors elected under both closed and open list systems, but only 31.7% of those elected via preferential voting. For the Liberals and Socialist Left, where we predicted the party and the voters would both strongly support women's representation, the differences are not statistically significant, and women actually do better at winning preferential vote-seats than list-seats. For all other parties women win about 10% fewer seats among preferential vote winners. While these results are suggestive, they do not measure the precise impact of preferential voting.

It is important to use the right counterfactual. To estimate the impact of preferential voting we should not compare the 2,525 councilors elected based on preferential votes with the 8,260 municipal councilors who would be elected whether there was a closed or open list system. Instead we should compare the 2,525 candidates who *would have been* elected if the results had fully followed the parties' lists and compare them with the 2,525 candidates who *were* elected because of their ability to garner more personal votes. Table 5.5 reports across parties the female percent of Personal Vote Winners (those elected because of the personal vote) and Personal Vote Losers (those who, despite being higher on the party list, were bumped down by someone with more personal votes).

We predicted the three parties on the Left (SV, Labor, Liberals) were in equilibrium at high levels of support for women and therefore the personal vote should have little impact. Table 5.5 shows this is only true for the Liberals,

Table 5.4. SEX OF LOCAL COUNCILORS BY SEAT TYPE, NORWEGIAN MUNICIPAL ELECTIONS, 2011

Party	Sex	Total seats		Winners only under open system		Winners under both closed and open		Chi²	Prob.
		N	Pct.	N	Pct.	N	Pct.		
Socialist Left	Women	185	51.1	35	54.7	150	50.3		
(SV)	Men	177	48.9	29	45.3	148	49.7	0.4	.53
Labor (A)	Women	1,482	43.9	326	38.3	1,156	45.8	14.3	.00
	Men	1,896	56.1	525	61.7	1,371	54.2		
Liberal (V)	Women	251	39.2	49	41.5	202	38.7	0.3	.57
	Men	389	60.8	69	58.5	320	61.3		
Center Party	Women	557	39.2	99	31.0	458	41.6	11.6	.00
(Sp)	Men	863	60.8	220	69.0	643	58.4		
Christian	Women	237	36.3	39	30.0	198	37.9	2.8	.10
People's Party (KrF)	Men	416	63.7	91	70.0	325	62.1		
Conservatives	Women	828	35.3	161	26.4	667	38.4	28.5	.00
(H)	Men	1,519	64.7	449	73.6	1,070	61.6		
Progress Party	Women	306	26.8	41	19.3	265	28.5	7.3	.01
(FrP)	Men	837	73.2	171	80.7	666	71.5		
Local and	Women	269	32.0%	51	23.1	218	35.1	10.9	.00
other parties	Men	573	68.0%	170	76.9	403	64.9		
Complete	Women	4,115	38.2	801	31.7	3,314	40.1	57.8	.00
sample	Men	6,670	61.8	1,724	68.3	4,946	59.9		

where a large proportion of those losing seats because of the personal vote were women, but a large proportion of those winning seats because of the personal vote were also women. The difference is -6%, smaller than all other parties and the only difference that is not statistically significant.

The Socialist Left (SV), despite nominating the highest number of women, is the only party where the personal vote advantages women and where men are disproportionately represented among those who lost their seats because of the personal vote. There is an 18.8% gap in the female proportion among winners and losers. The Labor Party shows a surprisingly large drop-off: 54.8% of the Personal Vote Losers are women, but only 38.3% of the Personal Vote Winners are women. This 16.5% gap translates into 140 fewer Labor women on local councils. Quite unexpectedly, we find the personal vote consistently hurts women on Labor lists.

As predicted, for the two centrist parties there is a significant gap between personal vote losers and winners; 53.9% of the Christian People's Party's Personal Vote Losers are women while only 30.0% of the Personal Vote

Table 5.5. FEMALE PERCENT AMONG PERSONAL VOTE LOSERS AND WINNERS, NORWEGIAN MUNICIPAL ELECTIONS, 2011

Party	Socialist Left (SV)	Labor (A)	Liberals (V)	Center Party (Sp)	Kristian People's Party (KrF)	Conservatives (H)	Progress Party (FrP)	Other Parties and Local Lists	TOTALS
Personal Vote									
Winners	54.7%	38.3%	41.5%	31.0%	30.0%	26.4%	19.3%	23.1%	31.8%
Personal Vote Losers	35.9%	54.8%	47.5%	52.4%	53.9%	48.7%	50.0%	56.4%	51.9%
Difference	18.8%**	-16.5%***	-6.0%	-21.4%***	-23.9%***	-22.3%***	-30.7%***	-33.3%***	-20.1%***
N	64	851	118	319	130	610	212	221	2,525

= sig. at .05 level, *= sig. at .01 level, two-tailed tests.

Winners were women. The Center Party numbers are 52.4% and 31.0%, respectively. For these two parties there are formidable 23.9% and 21.4% gaps in the sex of the winners and losers. It appears the parties' push for almost equal representation, often causing them to nominate women who are not well-known in the local community, generates a negative reaction among their parties' voters.

Finally, for the parties on the Right, we find significant negative effects. We had expected the Conservative Party to show a small gap but they produce a pattern similar to the parties of the Center. Even though the party has not adopted formal quotas, local party affiliates have been pressured to increase representation on local lists by the central party machinery. They do not want to be seen as sexist when compared to parties that have adopted quotas. While women were a respectable 36% of the Conservative Party lists, women are far more likely to be among those who lose because of the personal vote (48.7%) and less likely to be among those who win (26.4%). This results in 135 fewer female Conservative councilors. Perhaps the most striking results are for the Progress Party. While women were a modest 28.9% of the Progress Party candidates, they were 50% of Personal Vote Losers but only 19.3% of Personal Vote Winners, producing a cavernous 30.7 point gap. Finally, on lists for other and local parties women do especially poorly, with a 33.3% gap between losers and winners.

We hypothesized the salience of equal representation for the party and the party's voters, and their interaction, is crucial in determining the impact of the electoral rule. We see this especially well at the periphery of the political spectrum. The Socialist Left is the only party where the party lists have more women than men. Nevertheless, this is the only party where the impact of the personal vote *increases* the representation of women. On the right, the Progress Party produced the largest gap between Personal Vote Winners and Losers, despite nominating fewer women than any other party. These findings indicate quite strongly that open list systems enable voters to correct their party if it nominates candidates out of line with their preferences. In Norway organized women have successfully made demands within their respective parties to participate. Parties have reacted, as five of the seven major parties have adopted and implemented quotas. But, because the institutional system allows voters to also influence the process, the voters can and do react to their party's behavior and can further increase or decrease descriptive representation of women, as predicted by Implications 1.1 and 1.2.

In reviewing our hypotheses, the predicted result of modest differences for the Liberal Party, because the party and the voters were in equilibrium, is confirmed. The expectation of large differences for the Center Party and Christian People's Party and for the Progress Party, all cases where we argued the parties and the voters were in disequilibrium, also confirm the model.

The three cases where the predictions were wrong were the Socialist Left and the Labor Party, where we expected both party and voters to strongly support women, and the Conservative Party, where we expected modest support for women among both party and voters. Our theory may be incorrect, but an alternative explanation is that our interpretations of the underlying cases were inaccurate, leading us to generate incorrect hypotheses. Our description of equal representation as highly salient for Labor Party voters may be incorrect. Certainly a number of feminists have argued that Labor has a strong strain of male dominance going back to its roots as a party tied to industrial trade unions, an extremely masculine and patriarchal base. Many working-class Labor voters may not see women's representation as highly salient. Our description of the Conservative Party as indifferent or failing to support women may also be faulty. The Conservative Party nominates 36% women. Outside Norway this is a strong record and it may actually represent a reasonably aggressive party campaign to recruit and support women. The Conservatives claim they find high-quality women candidates without using quotas. Perhaps party recruitment is more active than we gave them credit for.

The final anomaly is the Socialist Left, where the party strongly supports equality, but the voters demand even greater representation of women. One reaction is to reconsider the original model. In Table 5.1 the lower right corner cell is where the party and their voters reject women and prefer men, the upper left corner cell is not the logical opposite, which would be the party and voters rejecting men and preferring women. Instead the initial model has equality in the upper left. A theoretically complete model should be a 4 x 4 rather than a 3 x 3 matrix. Party leadership strongly supports *equal* representation, but Socialist Left voters strongly support *female* representation. This disequilibrium would lead to exactly the effect we find.

Why would SV voters promote women in this manner? One explanation is that the most strident feminists among Socialist Left voters really do believe that men do not understand what is needed and only women can be effective representatives. Another plausible explanation was described in discussions with a small sample of Socialist Left local leaders and voters. They claim that Socialist Left voters believe in equality; not the superiority of women. The institutions to which they are electing representatives, however, are overwhelmingly male. The Socialist Left is a small party that is contributing only a small portion to a city council that will be majority male. It makes sense to counterbalance the male dominance on the council by overweighting the SV delegation with women. If the party dominated a city council, SV voters might be more concerned about making sure the SV bench was equal, but when providing only three or four of 67 councilors, as they do in Trondheim and Bergen, aggressively promoting women over men, even within their own party, makes sense. The party formally rejects this argument, but sufficient numbers of SV voters may apply this thinking, resulting in the outcome we find.

Individual Voter Behavior

The consequences of the preferential vote in Norway are unambiguous. More than 500 *fewer* women are elected to local councils because of voters use of the personal vote. While the outcome is clearly negative for descriptive representation, we do not have proof that voters are being sexist in their voting behavior. Women are not necessarily hurt because they are women, they may be hurt because of other factors correlated with sex.

Responses to surveys done in conjunction with the local elections in 2003 and 2007 find that when asked what factors were important in using their personal vote, voters emphasized specific policies a candidate promoted, previous experience on the council, the geographical locality an individual was from, and personal knowledge of the candidate (Christiansen et al. 2004, 2008). Only 10.7% in 2003 and 6.8% in 2007 said the sex of the candidate played a large role in their personal voting decision. Over 80% of the voters in each year said candidate sex played no role at all in their personal voting decision. Furthermore, many of the voters saying sex played a role were supporting women, as Liberal and SV partisans scored highest on this question in 2003 and SV supporters were highest in 2007.

Voters may extrapolate from candidate sex to policy positions, especially when they cannot use party labels to distinguish among candidates. There is evidence that voters in Norway do draw ties between candidate sex and policy positions and competency (Matland 1994). In the Christian People's Party and in the Progress Party, voters may be concerned about issues where they believe a female candidate may be more moderate than male candidates. For example, the Progress Party is particularly strident on immigration policy. It is easy to imagine a Progress Party voter might fear a woman would be "too soft" on this policy and therefore might vote for a male candidate. Within the Christian People's Party, younger and female candidates are often suspected of being more sympathetic to gay marriage and are opposed for these reasons. In short, the preferential vote system allows voters to correct course if they believe the party is too aggressively promoting women (note this is consistent with Implication 1.2).

Finally, there is a strong correlation between sex and being a local notable. People, especially in smaller communities, have a tendency to vote for individuals who they know; 42% of the voters in the smallest municipalities, i.e., where the town center was under 2,000 people, stated personal knowledge of a candidate was very important in casting their preferential vote. Most prominent individuals in the community are male. Because they are well-known, they are recruited heavily by the political parties. To insure gender equality on their party lists, the parties also must recruit women, but these women are often party regulars, not prominent citizens. When voters enter the voting booth they may simply recognize more of the male candidate names, leading to these candidates getting more personal votes. Support based on personal acquaintanceship is available to female candidates, but it is likely there will be fewer recognizable women on the ballot.

PREFERENTIAL VOTING IN LATVIA

Latvia is also a small (2.2 million people) European democracy but quite different from Norway. Election results have been volatile with major new parties in every election since re-establishment of democracy (Rose and Munro 2009). There has been little convergence in the party system. Parties start to establish an identity but then are rocked by corruption scandals and disappear from the electoral map. In addition, ethnicity has been a strong electoral cleavage increasing party diversity as parties explicitly catering to the Russian population or the nationalist strain among native Latvians have maintained strong positions in Latvian politics.

Gender representation and equality have not been topics of political debate, save during EU accession (Novikova 2006; Lilliefeldt 2011). None of the parliamentary parties has argued strongly for guaranteed representation. In the four national elections since 2000, women comprised between 25% and 28% of candidates fielded by parties winning seats in the national parliament, the Saeima. The share of women MPs elected has fluctuated between 18% and 21% (CSB 2011). In comparison to Norway, Latvian parties field fewer women candidates and elect even fewer.

One hundred Saeima representatives are elected in five multimember constituencies with a 5% national electoral threshold. Voters select a party ballot and on the ballot they can add positive or negative preferential votes to as many candidates as they wish. The proportion of ballots with preference markings has grown from 23% in 1993 to 64% by 2010 (Ikstens 2013). The preferential vote system does not allow a party to protect candidates. One single preferential ballot changes the rank ordering of candidates and would determine who is elected. Until 2010, candidates could run in several constituencies simultaneously; it was normal for the most prominent candidates to run in all districts. When they won in several, they were elected where they got the most votes and gave up their seat in the other districts. From 2010 forward, candidates have had to choose one single constituency in which to run.[4]

4. There are significant differences in the impact of preferential voting pre- and post-2010. Parties were forced to expand their recruitment, and changes occur in how preferential voting impacts representation. The story is complex. For this chapter we concentrate on the existing conditions, i.e., the rules that have been in place since 2010.

Expectations for Latvian Parties

Dealing with citizenry questions concerning Russian immigrants who arrived during Soviet times, Latvia's interest in joining the EU and NATO, and economic development issues, including a huge economic contraction after 2008, have crowded out concerns about greater representation of women. Furthermore, as many Latvian parties are built around prominent individuals, with little party membership, there has been limited pressure from inside the parties to ensure greater representation. Party decision making has been highly centralized and candidate selection has been dominated by a few people.

Nevertheless, Latvian parties can be identified as belonging to specific party families (Rose and Munro 2009; Ikstens 2013), and these provide cues as to the likely openness toward women candidates. Harmony Centre (SC) draws votes overwhelmingly from the Russian minority (Lublin 2013) and has historical links back to the Latvian Communists. Despite these roots and party platforms with social democratic planks, SC has rejected quotas and has been overwhelmingly male in terms of leadership. Typical of nationalist parties, Harmony Centre is highly patriarchal and is considered unfriendly to women. The National Alliance is a nationalist party emphasizing the rights of the Latvian majority. It, too, has a very traditional view of the role of women. The ZZS, the People's Party, and Latvian Way (the last two merged to form Party for a Good Latvia) have been broadly pro-market but with ties to strong political interests (ZZS has strong ties to agricultural interests). These parties show little interest in promoting women but are not aggressively anti-women. They are perceived primarily as tools of their benefactors and have been associated with corruption. A third set of parties, New Era, Unity, and Reform, also are built around a small number of people, but these parties have emphasized a liberal message, pro-Europe, pro-markets, and anti-corruption. They have been especially open to women who were prominently known outside politics. These parties have nominated significant numbers of women, not to push women's issues but to emphasize these women as competent technocrats and as less corrupt than the average Latvian politician.

Expectations for Latvian Voters

Latvia is 36th on the UNDP's Gender Inequality Index behind its Baltic neighbors Lithuania and Estonia but ahead of other Eastern European countries (UNDP, 2011). Latvia was at the median (31st of 62 nations) on the Gender Equality Scale developed by Inglehart and Norris (2003) from the World Values Survey. This places Latvia well ahead of Russia, Ukraine, and Poland but behind the Czech Republic, Slovenia, and Lithuania. Unfortunately, the detailed public opinion data for individual party voters available in Norway are not available for Latvia. Nevertheless, we predict, based on previous literature on voting for women in Eastern Europe (Matland and Montgomery 2003b), that most voters fall primarily in the middle column of neither supporting nor opposing women as candidates. We expect considerable divergence with some progressive voters and others skeptical of women.

A cautious set of predictions follow: for the nationalist parties (SC and National Alliance) we expect a disequilibrium, with voters being largely indifferent to candidate sex but with a party hierarchy that is unsympathetic holding qualified women back, therefore preferential voting should help women (cell F of Table 5.1); for the parties representing the power brokers, including ZZS and the Party for a Good Latvia, indifference from both voters and the party hierarchy toward women should lead to cell E, with the personal vote having only a limited impact. New Era, Unity, and Reform, who have been very willing to nominate women, are closer to cell D, so we expect preferential voting to have a negative impact as there would be a disequilibrium with the parties being more supportive of women than their voters.

Latvian National Elections Results

Table 5.6 presents outcomes across parties in terms of nominations and seats. Among parties winning parliamentary representation, women make up approximately one-quarter of the candidates and one-fifth of the MPs. Looking across parties, we see the Russian ethnic party, SC, shows a consistent pattern of skepticism toward women nominating fewer women than any other party. Furthermore, until 2011 SC had never elected a woman MP. The Latvian nationalist party (National Alliance) has also been slow to nominate and elect women. The oligarchs, as the leader of the Reform Party derisively labels the ZZS and the Party for a Good Latvia, have been willing to nominate women, but have been neither leaders nor laggards on the issue. Finally, New Era, later running as Unity, has been at the forefront both in terms of nominating and electing women. The Reform Party, trying to distance itself from other parties, strongly supported women nominating female candidates without previous strong ties to politics.

To evaluate the personal vote we start, as in Norway, by comparing MPs who would have been elected under either closed-list or open-list systems with those who were elected exclusively because of preferential votes. In 2010 women were 15.9% (10 of 63) of those who would have been elected under both systems but 24.3% (9 of 37) of those elected because of their preferential votes. In 2011 they were 17.1% (12 of 70) of those who would be elected under both systems but 30% (9 of 30) of those elected via preferential votes. While women are a higher proportion of those elected via preferential votes, this does not guarantee that women are advantaged by the preferential voting system. This comparison is deceiving, because it compares very prominent

Table 5.6. CANDIDACIES AND REPRESENTATION AMONG PARLIAMENTARY PARTIES, 2010–2011

Election Year	Party	Party Group	# of Female Candidates/Total # of Candidates	Percent of Candidates Who Are Female	# of Female MPs / Total # of MPs	Percent of MPs Who Are Female	Ratio: MPs to Candidates
2010	SC	Slavic Nationalist	19/115	16.5%	0/29	0.0%	.00
	Nat. Alliance	Latvian Nationalist	24/115	20.9%	1/8	12.5%	.60
	ZZS	Agrarian	31/115	27.0%	4/22	18.2%	.67
	For a Good Latvia	Conservative-Centrist	25/115	21.7%	2/8	25.0%	1.15
	UNITY	Liberal	43/115	37.4%	12/33	36.4%	.97
	TOTAL		**142/575**	**24.7%**	**19/100**	**19.0%**	**.77**
2011	SC	Slavic Nationalist	25/115	21.7%	3/31	9.7%	.45
	Nat. Alliance	Latvian Nationalist	28/115	24.4%	3/14	21.4%	.88
	ZZS	Agrarian	28/115	24.4%	3/13	23.1%	.95
	UNITY	Liberal	33/115	28.7%	6/20	30.0%	1.05
	Reform	Liberal	36/114	31.6%	6/22	27.3%	.86
	TOTAL		**150/574**	**26.1%**	**21/100**	**21.0%**	**.80**

Party labels: SC: Harmony Centre, National Alliance: Coalition between TB/LNNK and All For Latvia, ZZS: Union of Greens and Farmers, Party for a Good Latvia: Coalition between People's Party (LPP), Latvia First and Latvian Way, UNITY: coalition between New Era, Civic Union, and Society for Other Politics.
Source: Data from the Latvian Election Authorities CVK.

Table **5.7.** GENDER IMPACT OF PREFERENTIAL VOTE, LATVIAN NATIONAL ELECTIONS, 2010–2011

Party	Party Group	Actual Election Results (Preferential Vote Winners)		If List Position Determined (Preferential Vote Losers)		Change in outcome (women)
		Women Won	Men Won	Women Would Have Won	Men Would Have Won	
2010 ELECTIONS						
SC (Centre for Harmony)	Slavic Nationalist	0	11	1	10	–1
VL1-TB/LNNK (National Alliance)	Latvian Nationalist	1	1	0	2	+1
ZZS (Union of Greens & Farmers)	Agrarian	3	5	5	3	–2
LPP-LC	Conservative-Centrist	1	3	1	3	0
Unity	Liberal	4	8	8	4	–4
TOTAL, 2010		9 (24.3%)	28	15(40.5%)	22	–6
2011 ELECTIONS						
SC (Centre for Harmony)	Slavic Nationalist	3	4	0	7	+3
VL1-TB/LNNK (National Alliance)	Latvian Nationalist	0	4	1	3	–1
ZZS (Union of Greens & Farmers)	Agrarian	1	1	0	2	+1
Unity	Liberal	3	3	2	4	+1
Reform Party	Liberal	2	9	6	5	–4
TOTAL, 2011		9 (30%)	21	9 (30%)	21	0

Analysis only includes seats where preferential votes result in changes in outcomes: 37 seats in 2010, 30 seats in 2011.
Source: Data from the Latvian Election Authorities CVK, 2010, 2011, and Lilliefeldt (2011).

candidates who were both at the top of party lists and popular, i.e., those elected under both systems, with those who were ranked initially at the middle level but were able to win some of the last seats a party won through personal popularity. The correct comparison is to look at those who would have won those seats if personal vote winners had not been elected. These are rarely candidates at the very top of the list, who usually are disproportionately men; rather, they are slightly farther down the party lists. These mid-level nominees already may include a number of women. In Table 5.7 we use the party lists to establish the counterfactual, as if there are no preferential votes. We assume voters vote the same with respect to party but cannot cast preferential votes.

We see that women would have picked up six additional seats in 2010 had there been no preferential vote. Representation in parliament would have been a record 25% rather than 19%. In 2011, on the other hand, preferential voting had no impact on the number of women elected. Of the 30 seats won through preferential voting, nine went to women. Without preferential voting, 30 different representatives would have been elected, but the gender balance would have been the same, nine women elected.

Looking at the individual party results in Table 5.7, we see they are largely supportive of our model of preferential voting.[5] Harmony Centre (SC) lists are overwhelmingly male. In the 2011 elections, we see women getting elected by party voters over the heads of the party leadership. When the party leadership refused to nominate well-qualified women in strong positions voters reacted and the net impact was an increase of three women elected to parliament. These three were the *only* women Harmony Centre elected in 2011. The net effect of the preferential vote for the National Alliance for 2010 and 2011 was no gender change. Fourteen seats switched in 2010 and 2011 because of the preferential vote for the Centrist parties ZZS and the LPP/LC. These resulted in a small change of one less woman in parliament. The Unity and Reform parties have been most aggressive in nominating women, and several women who were nominated in strong positions failed to get elected. The net effect of preferential voting for these two parties was that women lost four seats in 2010 and three seats in 2011.

These results are consistent with our model, which predicts the preferential vote has an impact when there is a disequilibrium between the party and its voters. In the case of Harmony Centre in 2011, voters reacted to a party actively undervaluing well-qualified women by supporting those women. For centrist parties, who are open to women but do not promote them aggressively, we expect an equilibrium between the voters and their party, and the preferential vote will have little impact. Finally, both Unity and Reform show that if the party aggressively promotes women, there can be a reaction as

5. As the numbers are so small, statistical testing is not possible; any findings can only be described as suggestive.

voters end up preferring candidates who they are more familiar with, candidates who are coincidentally male. The experience of women in Latvia again indicates that when voters have the opportunity they will "correct" party lists, if top nominees do not reflect their interests; in some cases this increases representation (SC), in others it decreases descriptive representation of women (New Era, Unity, and Reform).

THE IMPACT OF PREFERENTIAL VOTING ON SUBSTANTIVE AND DESCRIPTIVE REPRESENTATION

What are the implications of our finding for representation? Representatives of SV and the Liberals in Norway have an uncomplicated decision process. Both their party and voters believe that women's representation is important and they are free to work on issues of importance to women. While there might appear to be greater dissonance for other parties, we do not see a dilemma. In most parties candidates faced voters who were largely indifferent about women's representation. Negative effects appear when parties generated lists close to equality, while their voters end up promoting a limited number of male candidates over female candidates. In Norway these male candidates have traits beyond sex that make them more attractive to voters (Christiansen et al. 2008). The parties are ahead of their voters in emphasizing the importance of equal representation. Over time there is reason to hope parties can convince the citizenry that equal representation is an important goal. Furthermore, as the proportion of women increases, more women are likely to have the characteristics (e.g., political experience, being a local notable) that presently make some male candidates more attractive.

A second concern with respect to representation is that while women are getting elected, they are not getting elected *as women*; rather, other characteristics lead to their election such as party experience or endorsements. As noted earlier, Norwegian surveys find over 80% of voters said candidate sex had no influence on their preferential vote. The concern is that if "being female" is not part of a politician's political identity, it may not influence her political actions. The issue of whether electing any woman automatically promotes women's interests is a central concern in the debate concerning women's representation (see Beckwith, Chapter 2, and Dahlerup, Chapter 4, in this volume).

On this issue, while we freely admit the impact of presence is likely to vary from venue to venue, we believe presence can be sufficient by itself to ensure both interest articulation and substantive representation. While we are less certain this is true in the Latvian case, in the case of Norwegian local councils, we believe a number of factors suggest presence alone is sufficient. Partially this is because presence is likely to be more important when the political role is less demanding and encompassing. Many women who reach positions of power in their national assembly have a long career as a politician behind them. Unlike these professional politicians who, after many years, have been socialized to see things from a political and party perspective, municipal councilors bring far more of their non-political self into their roles. Councilors are political amateurs. They rarely have a full-time job in politics, and local councils are invariably their first elected position. Being female may not be a central part of their political identity, i.e., they were not elected as women, but it is central to their personal identity and we suspect it especially influences perspectives and activities as a local councilor.

In local council decision making, much of local council action deals with trade-offs between goods that all value. It is not that men are positive to transportation projects while women are negative, or that women are positive to expansion of day care while men are negative. Both men and women prefer better roads and day care coverage. The problem occurs when they must allocate between desired goods. Even if representing women was not part of the political platform leading to their presence, when deciding how to allocate limited resources women are likely to have a different preference ordering than men because of their life experiences, and this is likely to be especially important in a role as citizen legislator and amateur politician. Furthermore, political parties are less dominant at the local level allowing other factors, such as biography, to have a greater impact.

This is precisely what Bratton and Ray (2002) find in their study on expenditures for day care in Norwegian municipalities. Even after a broad series of relevant factors are controlled for, such as ideology, demand, and resources, local municipal councils with greater women's representation were quicker to spend scarce resources on day care construction. Interestingly, the impact of presence was most important at the very start of the move toward greater day care coverage. By the time the movement truly gathered steam, all municipalities were supportive, but the place where greater coverage first broke through was where women's representation, independent of party, was greatest.

While our estimate of the net impact of preferential voting on substantive representation must be speculative, the effect on descriptive representation for the cases we considered is largely negative. Nevertheless, the impact varies considerably across parties and years (and we suspect countries). In both Norway and Latvia, there are parties where women benefit from the preferential vote and where women are hurt. In short, this electoral institution does not have a monolithic effect. The literature finds inconsistent outcomes because the impact is inconsistent. Nevertheless, by carefully analyzing the context we find predictable patterns. Crucial to those patterns are the interaction between the voters' perspective and the party's perspective on women's representation. When there is a serious imbalance between a party and its voters, the institution has a strong impact. When the two are in equilibrium, the impact is much smaller.

CHAPTER 6

Gender, High Courts, and Ideas about Representation in Western Europe

VALERIE HOEKSTRA, MIKI CAUL KITTILSON, AND
ELIZABETH ANDREWS BOND

Saint Paul said: 'Women shall be silent in the Church.' If Saint Paul were still alive, he would say 'Women shall also be silent in the courts'... Because administering the judicial system is a rational and logical problem, which has to be set out and solved with strong emotionality, not with that superficial emotion peculiar to the female gender.
——Guiseppe Bettiol, member of Italian Parliament (1946)[1]

Although the quote above dates back over six decades, very little has changed in regard to women's voices in the judiciary across the globe.[2] Women's share of seats on national high courts remains staggeringly low. Even across Europe, where legislative gender quotas have been adopted, and women have

1. We draw this quote from Palici di Suni (2012). In her paper, she provides the original and her own translation as: Bettiol said: "San Paolo diceva: 'Tacciano le donne nella Chiesa.' Se San Paolo fosse vivo direbbe 'Facciano silenzio le donne anche nei tribunali'... Perché il problema dell'amministrazione della giustizia è un problema razionale, è un problema logico, chedeve essere impostato e risolto in termini di forte emotività, non già di quella commozione puramente superficiale che è propria del genere femminile" ("Saint Paul said: 'Shall women be silent in the Church.' If Saint Paul were still alive, he would say 'Shall women be silent also in the courts'... Because administering the judicial system is a rational and logical problem, which has to be set out and solved with strong emotionality, not with that superficial emotion peculiar to the female gender)" (391). We believe our translation better captures the intended meaning.
2. This project is funded by a grant from the Institute for Social Science Research (ISSR) at Arizona State University. The authors wish to thank Patrick Kenney for comments on earlier versions of this manuscript and Jill Carle and Patrick Roe for help with data collection.

made great strides in electoral politics, women remain under-represented on most high courts. Only a handful of countries have enacted or even considered enacting judicial quotas for women (e.g., Ecuador, India, South Africa, Kenya, Britain; see Hoekstra 2010).

Gender equality on high courts matters for judicial decision-making. In Chapter 2, Karen Beckwith suggests that women share a meta-interest in full and equal political inclusion. Further, in Chapter 4, Drude Dahlerup contends that we need an understanding of representation, not as "giving voice to fixed and well-defined interests or identities, but as a demand to be included in a dynamic process" (p. 93). Given that both legal and legislative institutions have been traditionally dominated by men, the lack of women's voice in the debate may give short shrift to the gendered nature of policies or circumstances. Women judges may offer a unique social perspective to the process of judicial decision making that similarly situated men may not share. Women's unique shared backgrounds, based upon a gendered division of labor in both the private and public spheres, and women's newcomer status to high courts, may enhance the likelihood that women on the judiciary will lead to outcomes that promote gender equality. Further, as alluded to in Proposition 3 offered in Chapter 1, women's interests are best represented if considered at multiple stages in the policy-making process. If women's representation in legislatures matters for the introduction of new policies, especially those regarding gender justice and equality, it follows then that woman judges could be allies in the application and interpretation of those policies. For example, in countries where women legislators promote and secure candidate gender quotas, these new policies may be challenged in courts. In turn, women on the courts may be more likely to accept these cases and ultimately to affect the deliberation over how these cases are decided.

In this chapter we ask: How do women get appointed to high courts? A comparative study is necessary to examine how political institutions shape men's and women's presence on high courts. In addition, we believe a longitudinal approach will enhance our ability to understand the changing dynamics within nations as well. We discuss some clues to identifying the mechanisms behind increasing women's presence on high courts by examining gender equality trends on national high courts over time. Rather than offering cross-national snapshots, we suggest that sequence and timing are important to the appointment of women to high courts. We examine cross-temporal patterns in women's advancement on high courts, and identify the confluence of factors that led to the appointment of women on some of the most gender-egalitarian high courts. Therefore, this chapter provides evidence useful for examining Implication 1.1 proposed in Chapter 1 regarding how women's access to decision-making venues can increase depending on women becoming organized and demanding representation.

The empirical puzzle of cross-national variation in the gender balance of high courts must not be viewed in isolation from other formal political venues. Specifically, we contend that gender equality in other venues matters for whether there may be a conscious effort to appoint more women to high courts. As women make strides in parliaments and government cabinets, advocates for more women on courts can leverage their claims by comparison. Ideas about political representation and what constitutes fair representation evolve over time and may diffuse across branches of domestic political institutions and across countries. Rising attention toward and actual increases in women's presence among elected officials creates a source of legitimacy with which advocates can justify their claims for women on high courts. If fair representation in national legislatures invokes questions about who sits among the elected representatives, then so too does fair representation on high courts call for the inclusion of a wide range of social groups, including women. In this way, formal political institutions and societal norms of gender equality shape incentives for those appointing justices to high courts.

And why might greater gender equality emerge in national legislatures before high courts? Scholars have long suggested that the more powerful the political body, the fewer the women. Indeed, national legislatures often number several hundred members, while high courts often range between 10 and 20. Justices on high courts, especially those charged with the power of judicial review, wield substantial leverage over important national decisions, and their tenure is often set for decades. The smaller size of these courts also inhibits turnover, providing newcomers with fewer opportunities for appointment. We also contend that as women make up a greater share of the elite strata that have the authority to appoint justices or even forward and discuss names of potential appointees, norms surrounding gender equality become more pervasive and women in elite positions may actively push for women on the bench. In effect, women in legislatures are an important agent for heightening gender equality on courts, but not as much the other way around. Moreover, since advancement to service on high courts often includes a career that begins in political and government service, greater representation of women in those positions will increase the pool of women to serve on high courts. In other words, if political and/or governmental service is thought to be critical to appointment to high courts, then having more women obtain this experience will enhance the number of women considered eligible for appointment.

EXPLAINING GENDER EQUALITY ON HIGH COURTS

Although the bulk of research on women and judiciaries focus on the United States, a few important pieces investigate this topic from a cross-national perspective (especially Williams and Thames 2008). Taken together, past research on gender equality within courts suggests four sets of explanation for gender inclusiveness on high courts: (1) the gender balance in national legislatures; (2) the presence of gender quotas; (3) method of appointment; and (4) appointer ideology. Although the latter two sets of explanations have dominated previous research, we argue that the first two explanations also are important because they set the foundations for expectations regarding gender and representation, thus structuring the incentives for "selectors" to favor women. We focus on the authority of appointment, rather than nomination. In most of our sample, the power of appointment is more critical since nomination, in our cases, is not a formal gatekeeping process. The individual/group charged with selecting the appointee is not bound by choices offered by any other actors in the selection process.

First, a few previous studies suggest that a higher percentage of women in the national legislature may be associated with higher shares of women on the high court (Williams and Thames 2008; Hoekstra and Andrews 2009). Theoretically, gender equality in one political arena may "spill over" into another (Escobar-Lemmon and Taylor-Robinson 2005). This diffusive process is rooted in Kingdon's (1995) work on policy change, in which he asserts that ideas spill over from one sphere to another. In a case study of Britain, Kenney (2008) draws out connections between women's increased representation in parliament and pressure for more women on high courts. The absence of women on the British high court called into question its very legitimacy among the British electorate as women made strides in parliament in the late 1990s. Within Britain, as discourse surrounding women's representation shifted, these new expectations permeated ideas about the importance of who sits on high courts. In short, as gender equality became commonly expected in the legislative branch, so too followed pressures to heighten gender equality on high courts.

Similarly, women's presence in cabinets and as heads of state can create a climate of gender equality where the lack of women's presence on high courts becomes more salient. Culturally, positive attitudes and norms of gender equality may advance women's full inclusion in a variety of arenas, including the judicial.

Past literature emphasizes the role of the method of selection of justices in impacting the likelihood that women will be appointed to the bench. Appointments may be made by a single individual, or by a group. We distinguish between executive and legislative appointment. The person with the responsibility for appointment may be an elected official, such as a president (or a member of her cabinet), or appointment may be by a group of elected officials, such as a parliamentary committee. In their cross-national study, Williams and Thames (2008) find some evidence to support the connection between executive appointment and higher numbers of women on the high court. This finding is consistent with some research on the advancement of women to state high courts in the United States (Bratton and Spill 2002). Elected officials may perceive greater pressure to prioritize women's advancement to high courts. When appointment is by one person accountable to the electorate, such as a president or her agent, direct electoral pressure may spur women's nomination. Electoral pressures may stem from efforts to secure votes, or from pressure groups (Kenney 2008). An individual is more easily held accountable for outcomes than a group that is collectively charged with the power to appoint. Therefore, legislative or multiple layers of appointment make it easier to diffuse criticism by shifting blame to others involved in the process. On the other hand, some recent research suggests that the larger the number of people involved in appointing a justice, the greater the likelihood that a woman will be nominated (Gill 2012). The argument is that a larger group is likely to be more diverse itself and therefore more likely to consider a diverse pool of potential nominees.

An appointer's ideology also appears to play a key role. Because leftist parties have been associated with candidate gender quotas and greater gender equality within their parliamentary delegations and cabinets (Duverger 1955; Lovenduski and Norris 1993; Htun 2003a; Escobar-Lemmon and Taylor-Robinson 2005; Kittilson 2006; Davis 1997), so too might we expect leftist governments to appoint more women to the bench. Leftists may hold a more egalitarian ethos generally, and/or perceive greater pressures from women's organizations inside and outside their parties to advance women to high courts.

In the United States, at the federal level where all judges are appointed by the president, the tendency to nominate women has been stronger among Democratic presidents (Segal 2000; Diascro and Solberg 2009). Similarly, at the US state level, gubernatorial appointment, particularly when a Democrat occupies the governorship, increases women's advancement (Bratton and Spill 2002). From a cross-national perspective, leftist presidents are more likely to appoint women to governmental cabinets (Escobar-Lemmon and Taylor-Robinson 2005). However, it is important to keep in mind that the explanatory power of ideology may wane over time. Clearly, women voters and activists are important sources of support for centrist and rightist parties. It was, after all, Republican President Ronald Reagan who appointed the first woman, Sandra Day O'Connor, to the United States Supreme Court. In recent years rightist parties have often made strides in promoting women for office. In Europe, both the British Conservative and German Christian Democratic parties have made great effort to advance women within their ranks (Childs 2008; Childs and Webb 2012; Wiliarty 2010). Across Latin America, Htun (2005b) suggests a similar trend, as major right-wing parties have gained ground in promoting women for office.

Among these sets of explanations, we contend that gender equality in national legislatures is the most fundamental and direct. Figure 6.1 depicts

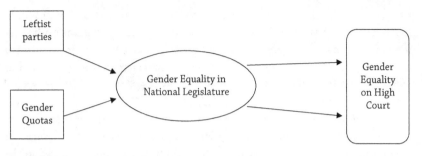

Figure 6.1
Modeling Increases in Women's Presence on High Courts

the causal flow of mechanisms to increase women's presence on high courts. At the center of the figure is our main explanatory factor, gender equality in national parliaments. We theorize the link between gender equality in national parliaments and on high courts flows through two pathways. First, as women become increasingly present and visible in national legislatures, norms and expectations shift surrounding women's presence in positions of power and authority in the arena of government. This may also signal appointers of the importance of women's presence. Second, the link flows through active strategies to appoint more women. Efforts to nominate women may be pushed by those seeking electoral support, or by those with a feminist ethos.

Leftist ideology and quotas may be important influences, but we believe prior research has not captured the more subtle influence they may exert. As such, in Figure 6.1 these two factors are depicted to the left, as indirect influences. In the first place, leftist parties and parties with gender quotas send more women to the national legislature (Kittilson 2006). Indeed, leftist ideology among appointers to high courts appears important. Not only may leftists be more likely to hold gender egalitarian attitudes, they also come from the political parties that send more women to parliament. Further, party-level quotas are most often adopted in leftist parties (Kittilson 2006). In this way, party-level quotas may be associated with more justices on high courts, but not through a direct causal mechanism. Party gender quotas are often not visible enough to the electorate to raise shared expectations for either legislatures or executives to appoint women with greater frequency. As Chapter 5 by Matland and Lilliefeldt in this volume shows, gender quotas may even be adopted by party leaders before gender is a salient issue among voters.

These linkages from national legislatures to high courts may hold whether nomination is by the executive or legislative branch. Growth in common expectations for women's faces among judges on the bench may flow from having high shares of women among parliamentarians. These expectations for women's presence in top-level political positions will be conveyed to prime ministers and presidents by the electorate and pressure groups. At the same time, appointments made by legislatures may also be conducive to women's appointment—when there are more women in the legislature itself. Conversely, appointments made by legislatures with few women may not lead to dramatic increases in women's representation among justices. In short, although most prior studies point to the importance of the appointment process for women's presence on high courts, we contend that executive, legislative, or mixed processes can be equally conducive to improving gender equality when women have already achieved greater equality in national legislatures. Moreover, we also contend that where women's representation in the legislature is low, the appointment mechanism also matters little.

CROSS-NATIONAL DYNAMICS IN THE NUMBER OF WOMEN HIGH COURT JUDGES

Currently, there is little systematic information about the distribution of women on high courts across the globe (but see Williams and Thames 2008; Gill 2012) or longitudinal studies within countries or regions. Most of the research conducted so far examines a single country, and even these case studies are few. Our sample includes the constitutional courts of 12 Western European nations: Austria, Belgium, Denmark, Finland, France, Germany, Ireland, Italy, Norway, Portugal, Spain, and Sweden.[3] The courts in our sample, along with the method of selection, number of justices, and type of court (constitutional or combined appellate/constitutional) are included in Table 6.1. Where nations have both a court of last resort *and* a court empowered with judicial review (a constitutional court) we select the constitutional court because of the importance of these courts in reviewing (and potentially overturning) laws rather than simply reviewing the actions of lower courts. It is these institutions that exert the greatest influence over policy considered and enacted in the other branches of government, even if these courts do not exercise this power frequently. Courts of last resort without the power of judicial review are important judicial institutions, but since they mostly review lower court actions, their effect on larger political and legal questions is more limited. Moreover, constitutional courts are generally considered more prestigious institutions and therefore women's presence on these courts is of greater political importance. Thus, the appointment of women on those courts represents greater achievement of women in all aspects of governance.

Denmark, Finland, Ireland, Norway, and Sweden have courts that serve both as appellate courts of last resort and also have the power of judicial review (much like the Supreme Court of the United States). Austria, Belgium,

---

3. All of these courts are in civil law nations except for Ireland, which comes from the common law tradition. We include Ireland in order to include one non-Scandinavian nation that uses executive appointment.

Table 6.1. DESCRIPTION OF THE CONSTITUTIONAL COURTS

Country	Method of Appointment	Number of Judges	Type of Court
Norway	Minister of Justice	19	Combined
Denmark	Minister of Justice Upon advice from committee	19	Combined
Sweden	Cabinet	16	Combined
Ireland	President	8	Combined
Austria	President	14	Constitutional
Finland	President	18*	Combined
Spain	Mixed 4 by Congress of Deputies (lower chamber) 4 by Senate (upper chamber) 2 by President 2 by General Council of Judges	12	Constitutional
France	Mixed 1/3 by President 1/3 by President of National Assembly 1/3 by President of Senate	9	Constitutional
Italy	Mixed 1/3 by Members of Superior Courts 1/3 by Parliament in joint session 1/3 by President	15	Constitutional
Portugal	Mixed 10 Legislative 3 by the Justices	13	Constitutional
Belgium	Appointment by King (formally) From a list of two sent alternately from House and Senate	12	Constitutional
Germany	Legislative Appointment ½ upper chamber ½ lower chamber	16	Constitutional

Notes: By law, the Finnish court is required to have at least 15 members. It currently has 18. We list courts that serve as the courts of last resort as well as having the power of judicial review as "combined" courts. In those countries that separate these functions, we include those with the power of judicial review (i.e., constitutional courts).

France, Germany, Italy, Portugal, and Spain have chosen to vest this power in a separate constitutional court.

These 12 courts are set within countries that share similar trajectories of economic development, values, history of democratic institutions, and institutionalized party systems. Given that the supply of women with the traditional qualifications for justice positions is both ample and fairly consistent across

Western Europe (Shaw and Schultz 2003; Label and Lewis 1996; Nousiainen and Pylkkanen 1997), we can focus our attention on the forces that shape the demand for women's representation (Norris and Lovenduski 1995).

At the same time, these courts vary on our key explanatory variables. Since much of the prior work emphasized the importance of the method of selection, we include courts where the method differs. Thus, we include five nations where the method of selection is appointment by an individual, either the minister of justice or the prime minister: Austria, Denmark, Ireland, Norway, and Finland. High court justices in Belgium, Germany, and Portugal are appointed primarily by the legislatures. Spain, France, Sweden, and Italy use a mixed method. In Sweden, appointments are made collectively by the cabinet. In the remainder of the mixed method systems, some members of the high court are appointed one way, while other members are appointed by a different process.

Table 6.2 displays the number and percentage of women selected to serve on the high courts of these 12 nations, by decade, from 1980 to 2009. In terms of absolute numbers, many countries remain quite stagnant from the 1980s to 2009. When we consider percentages, the percentage of women remains at or below 30% in the most recent decade for all but two countries. This under-representation occurs despite rapidly increasing numbers of women obtaining legal educations and serving in positions that traditionally serve as springboards to appointment to the high courts (Kenney 2008; Shaw and Schultz 2003).

Although women are under-represented on each of these high courts in every decade, we observe some considerable jumps in the percentage of women over time. The addition of just a few women on a small court leads to a much greater proportion. Further, the countries vary greatly in the gender balance. For example, Italy has only had one woman serve on their 15-member Corte Costituzionale della Repubblica Italiana in the three decades in our study (one more woman was appointed in 2011), and the numbers in Spain, Portugal, and Ireland are only marginally higher. In France, however, nearly 30% of the appointments to the Conseil Constitutionnel in the last decade have been women. In Norway and Sweden, close to 45% of the appointees to these high courts have been women, whereas comparatively fewer were appointed in Denmark during the same period (see also Hoekstra and Andrews 2010).

Given that our primary interest is in explaining the timing and confluence of events that enhance the likelihood of the appointment of a woman to the high court, we first trace the dynamics in the number of women appointed over time. Two countries stand out for steady progress in the addition of women to their high courts—Norway and Sweden. In the 1980s both countries appointed one woman to the high court, and by the 1990s this number had risen to three. For the first decade of the 2000s, Norway's appointments rose to four and Sweden's to five. Similarly, France witnessed gains for women on its high court, rising from no women in the 1980s to two appointed in the

Table 6.2. GENDER BALANCE ON HIGH COURTS AND NATIONAL
LEGISLATURES, BY COUNTRY AND DECADE

Country	Decade	Number of Women Appointed	% Women Appointed High Court	% Women National Legislature	Quota for National Legislature
Austria	1980–1989	0	0	11	No
	1990–1999	1	38	25	
	2000–2009	1	22	31	
Belgium	1980–1989	1	8	7	Yes, 1994
	1990–1999	1	14	12	
	2000–2009	1	10	32	
Denmark	1980–1989	2	25	26	No
	1990–1999	2	13	34	
	2000–2009	2	25	36	
Finland	1980–1989	2	22	31	No
	1990–1999	3	20	36	
	2000–2009	3	20	40	
France	1980–1989	0	0	5	Yes, 2009
	1990–1999	2	18	7	
	2000–2009	3	30	14	
Germany	1980–1989	2	12	11	No
	1990–1999	6	43	25	
	2000–2009	2	11	31	
Ireland	1980–1989	0	0	7	Yes, 2012
	1990–1999	0	0	12	
	2000–2009	1	25	14	
Italy	1980–1989	0	0	13	No
	1990–1999	0	0	12	
	2000–2009	1	7	14	
Norway	1980–1989	1	13	32	No
	1990–1999	3	20	38	
	2000–2009	4	44	37	
Portugal	1980–1989	2	7	8	Yes, 2006
	1990–1999	2	17	11	
	2000–2009	2	10	21	
Spain	1980–1989	1	5	6	Yes, 2007
	1990–1999	1	7	17	
	2000–2009	1	11	33	
Sweden	1980–1989	1	6	31	No
	1990–1999	3	38	39	
	2000–2009	5	45	46	

1990s and three by the 2000s. Germany presents a puzzle, bucking the trend of linear gains for women. German women made great strides on the high court in the 1980s, rising from just two to six women appointed. However, by the 2000s the number was down to two again. This, however, could be driven by the relatively small number of opportunities in each decade, and evidence does not indicate a backlash against women.

By contrast, Austria, Belgium, Denmark, Finland, Ireland, Italy, Portugal, and Spain are characterized by lower and largely stagnant numbers of women appointed to the high court. By 2009, this set either hovered at the same numbers as in the 1980s or added just one woman over a 30-year period. Although stagnant over time, it is important to note that Denmark and Finland leveled off at a higher number of women than, say, Italy or Belgium.

Within Europe, our data provide only weak support for the dominant hypothesis that method of selection influences increases in women's representation on high courts. Among the three leaders in women on high courts, Sweden, Norway, and France, Norway's justices are in effect appointed by one person, the Minister of Justice, while in Sweden appointment is via the cabinet, and in France the method is mixed, with the president, and presidents of the National Assembly and Senate involved. At the same time, Denmark and Ireland employ appointment by one person, yet the number of women appointed to those high courts remains at only two in Denmark and one in Ireland from the 1980s to present. Importantly, the method of appointment has remained unchanged in these countries, while we have witnessed gains for women only in recent decades.

In addition, we find mixed support for the idea that the initial push for increasing gender diversity would be led by leftist parties. On the one hand, evidence from Norway bolsters the importance of appointer ideology (Shaffer et al. 2011). For Supreme Court justices who were still sitting during the 2000–2007 period of their study, among the women, only one of seven is a non-socialist government appointee (14%), while among the men, 9 of 21 were non-socialist government appointees (43%). On the other hand, when we look across the countries in our study at the political party ideology of the individual/group that was responsible for selecting the first woman justice, we actually observe greater emphasis for women among parties to the right of center. In Belgium, Italy, Portugal, Germany, Ireland, Norway, and Austria, the first women appointed (during our time span) were nominated by members of parties on the right. In Finland, the first woman was selected by a president in the political center. Only in Denmark, Sweden, Spain, and France were the first women selected by parties on the left of the political spectrum.

Given the mixed support for method of appointment and for the ideology of the selector, we turn to our main explanatory variable of interest—the gender balance in the national legislature. We are interested in connecting this mechanism for change to increases in women's presence on high courts.

The penultimate column of Table 6.2 presents the percentage of women in the national legislature by decade for each country in our study. The final column of Table 6.2 tells whether or not a country has a national-level gender quota for the legislature.

A snapshot glance at the relationship between the gender balance on high courts and national legislatures in the early 2000s lends some support to our hypothesis. We divided our set of countries into two groups: high (30% women or higher in the most recent decade) and low (under 30%) shares of women in the national legislature. We do not suggest that 30% is any sort of "critical mass," but rather for simplicity's sake suggest that more than one-third of parliament composed of women sets a country at a relatively higher level than its peers. So, eight cases fall into the "high" shares of women, and four cases in the "low" shares group. The four cases in the "low" group have considerably less than 30% women, and we observe a clear break in the data. Countries with 30% or more women in the national legislature average 23.5% women on the high court in the first decade of the 2000s. By contrast, countries with low percentages of women in the legislature during this decade average only 18% women on the high court.

To further investigate the dynamics of this relationship, we examine how the gender balance in the legislature in one decade affects the gender balance of the court in the subsequent decade. For the 12 countries in our study for each decade (N = 36), the simple bivariate correlation between the percentage of women on the high court and lagged percentage of women in national legislature (prior decade) is .58**. This is a fairly strong, positive relationship.

In fact, women's presence in the legislature back in the 1970s does a fairly good job of predicting how well women will fare on high courts in the most recent decade. Figure 6.2 presents the relationship between the average percentage of women in the national legislature during the 1970s and the average percentage of women nominated to the high court in the early 2000s. Not only do the "rich get richer," but greater gender equality in the elected arena appears to precede greater gender equality on courts. France and Ireland stand out somewhat as outliers, with their low share of women in legislatures out of step with relatively high shares of women on the high court.

How then does change in women's presence in national legislatures stack up with change in women's presence on high courts? Recall our three leaders in steady gains for women on high courts, Sweden, Norway, and France. In both Sweden and Norway, women have been a visible contingent in the legislatures since the 1980s. Neither Sweden nor Norway has adopted national-level gender quotas. Still, women have made steady gains over the past three decades in both countries. In Norway, "serious effort has been made to create gender balance on the court" (Shaffer et al. 2011: 3). In other words, women's gains on the court did not spontaneously arise from women's educational or occupational advances or from conducive appointment procedures, but rather were the product of deliberate, concerted efforts to nominate and appoint more

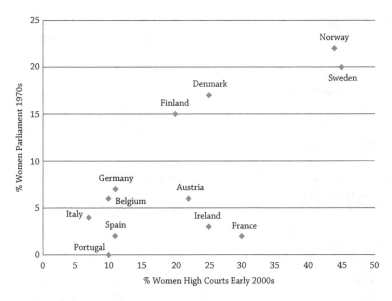

Figure 6.2
Women in Legislatures (1970s) and Women on High Courts (Early 2000s)

women. Further confirmation of Norway's commitment to gender equality is evidenced by its decision to establish gender quotas for board positions on publicly listed companies, which, like high courts, remain vastly unrepresentative of women. The Norwegian experience indicates support for the expectation of Implication 1.1 regarding the importance of women's organizing and demanding voice and participation.

France has a lower percentage of women in its legislature, but the percentage doubled from the 1990s to 2000s. Moreover, we observe that the first woman appointed to the French constitutional court, Noelle Lenoir, was nominated by Socialist Party member Henri Emmanuelli (chairman of the National Assembly), shortly after the party adopted the first party-level quota in France in 1990—more evidence supporting Implication 1.1. The first woman was nominated in 1992, while women were still vastly underrepresented in the legislature (less than 4% of the National Assembly between 1988 and 1993). However, France adopted a very strict national-level gender quota in 2000, requiring that 50% of seats in both chambers be reserved for women. Since then there has been a noticeable increase in the number of women in the National Assembly. In France, at least, it appears as though women's presence in both the legislature and the constitutional court is happening simultaneously.

As early leaders in gender equality in national legislatures, Sweden and Norway have similarly been early leaders on the high court front. Gains for women on high courts in these two countries have been steady, but have come after gains in the legislature. We believe this sequence of gains speaks to something fundamental to women's presence among political elites: women's heightened presence in one formal institution of government can spur increases in other institutions. In Norway and Sweden alike, fair representation has come to mean the visibility of women's faces among power holders. We also note that in both Norway and Sweden, the national legislatures have been dominated by left-leaning parties throughout this time period. While we center our theory on the role of women in the legislature as the proximal cause to increases in women's presence on high courts, we are also keenly aware of how support for left of center parties and gender quotas increase women's share of legislative seats.

CONCLUSIONS

This chapter focuses on the *how* question—how women gain representation on high courts, which, as we discuss briefly here, can also influence *where* women's interests are represented. We theorize that the empirical connection between greater gender equality in national legislatures and high courts is important on three levels. First, and more broadly, through the diffusion of ideas, norms, and standards of gender equality, women's presence comes to be expected among public positions of power. Ideas about what constitutes fair or effective representation may shift over time. With more women in elected positions, and calls for gender quotas to institutionalize gender equality, the inclusion of women has become more integral to the quality of political representation. We believe this is related not only to the advancement of women to high courts, but to other prominent positions of power more broadly, including the recent push to enact quotas on boards of corporations. Norway, a leader in terms of the number of women serving in parliament, enacted the first corporate quota laws in 2004, and they are now being adopted and debated across Europe.

Second, women in legislatures may lobby for more women on high courts. As women's representation in legislatures increases, so too does the number of policies that address gender justice or issues previously considered "private" (O'Regan 2000; Bratton and Ray 2002; Schwindt-Bayer and Mishler 2005; Kittilson 2008). When we look to the background of the women who have been appointed to the high courts in our sample, we find that while their pathways to appointment were similar to men's—if male judges are typically selected from elite governing/political/academic positions, so too were women—the women who were appointed often had some experience with these "private" issues: women, marriage, family, and mental health. While this was not universally true, and we do not here address the complicated topic of substantive representation, the implications seem clear: as women's representation in legislatures increases, and an interest in policies relating to what had previously been considered "private" issues flows from that, it would be wise to include more women who will ultimately rule on these issues. As suggested in Proposition 3 in Chapter 1, legislators understand that policy does not end with the passage of legislation: it must also withstand scrutiny by judges. Thus, legislators might also understand the value of increasing women's presence on courts in order to increase the chances that judges may share perspectives with the legislators.

Third, serving in political and governing positions, such as in the legislature and in cabinet positions, provides women with the kind of experience beneficial to serving on a high court. Indeed, in many cases, members of constitutional courts—both male and female—had prior government and political leadership positions. It follows then, that the greater the number of women to be elected to office and appointed to important cabinet positions, the greater the pool of visible candidates from which to select.

CHAPTER 7

Political Inclusion and Representation of Afrodescendant Women in Latin America

MALA HTUN

INTRODUCTION

Women have gained access to elected office in record numbers in Latin America, and evidence suggests that they are acting to advance women's rights (see, e.g., Schwindt-Bayer 2006, 2009; Htun et al. 2013; Franceschet and Piscopo 2008; Taylor-Robinson and Heath 2003).[1] Yet not *all* women are present in power. Most of the women who occupy decision making positions are fair-skinned and Spanish speaking. Members of intersectionally disadvantaged sub-groups—particularly Afrodescendant[2] and indigenous women—are scarce. Though their numbers are growing, few have gained access to elected office, which is conspicuous in light of growing awareness of the racial and ethnic heterogeneity of the region.

The political exclusion of minority women raises several questions. How and through what means do women members of subordinate racial and ethnic groups gain access to power? What does it mean to represent intersectionally disadvantaged categories of women? How can the quality of representation offered by Afrodescendant women be assessed? Does their political presence affect democratic practices?

---

1. I am grateful for research assistance from Elvira Pichardo-Delacour, and comments and discussion from participants at the TAMU conference.

2. "Afrodescendant" has become the preferred way to refer to the collection of Latin Americans with some degree of African ancestry, largely replacing "Afro-Latin," "Afro-Brazilian," "negro," and so forth. It is both a noun and an adjective. In this chapter, "Afrodescendant" will be used interchangeably with "black" and "Afrodescendants" with "blacks."

This chapter poses some preliminary answers to these questions by focusing on the political inclusion and representation of Afrodescendant women in seven Latin American countries: Brazil, Colombia, Costa Rica, Ecuador, Peru, Uruguay, and Venezuela.[3] I show that Afrodescendant women tend to be under-represented relative to women as a whole, and to Afrodescendants as a whole, with the exception of Ecuador. Afrodescendants tend not to cluster in a particular party, but to get elected from parties on both sides of the partisan spectrum, though in Brazil black women are more likely to come from parties of the Left.

By identifying patterns of Afrodescendant women's presence in politics, this chapter considers the *who* question posed by this volume. Addressing the volume's other principal questions—namely, *what* interests they are representing and *how* this occurs—requires broader reflection on what it means to represent the interests of intersectionally disadvantaged sub-groups (and, indeed, whether we can attribute interests to them in the first place). With regard to Afrodescendant women, it is tempting to posit a list of their interests and then seek to match them against the behavior of elected officials. Taking theories of intersectionality seriously, however, cautions against such an approach. Intersectionality maintains that the effects of social structures are mutually constitutive and conditioning, not additive (Hancock, Chapter 3 of this volume and 2007; Weldon 2008; García Bedolla 2007). Afrodescendant women's interests cannot be derived from—or predicted by—women's interests or Afrodescendant interests.[4]

What matters most, I argue, is whether legislators are taking action to combat Afrodescendant women's disadvantage and exclusion. Though numbers are too small to permit systematic analysis, qualitative investigation of selected cases reveals that most, but not all, Afrodescendant women in office have taken initiatives to reverse the invisibility suffered by Afrodescendants in the region. Motivated by a concern for other members of their category as

3. These countries were chosen for the following reasons. First, Brazil, Colombia, Costa Rica, and Ecuador had, according to national census data available in the mid-2000s, the largest Afrodescendant populations in the region (with the exception of Cuba, with the third largest population, but where the lack of democratic politics preclude analysis of representation and inclusion) (del Popolo et al. 2009). Peru and Uruguay were also included since, though they lacked census data in the mid-2000s, survey estimates at the time revealed a sizable Afrodescendant presence. Both countries have Afrodescendants in the national legislature and civic associations organizing around Afrodescendant rights. Venezuela was included since scholarly observers had always estimated its Afrodescendant population to be large, though this was not confirmed through official data until 2011.

4. As I argue later, the interests of these groups cannot be posited *a priori* either. As Beckwith maintains in Chapter 2 of this volume, group interests ideally emerge from processes of democratic deliberation. Instead of talking about the representation of interests, it makes more sense to talk about whether legislators are taking action to combat structural disadvantages.

well as pressure from the international development community, they have raised awareness about racism and social exclusion. In this way, this chapter delves into the meaning of what other scholars call "substantive representation" and its connection to "descriptive" or "surrogate" representation as discussed by Dahlerup (Chapter 4 of this volume).

Following Mansbridge, I argue that Afrodescendant women in power offer surrogate representation. The quality of their representative behavior should be judged not on principal-agent terms but in terms of their contribution to democratic deliberation. They introduce new issues to national political agendas and compel others to adopt an intersectional perspective by serving as a reminder of the inherent heterogeneity of social groups and identities. Their political presence proves that the category "women" includes black women, Asian women, lesbian women, poor women, and more, and that the category "Afrodescendants" includes women as well as men. Merely by being present in power, they prevent people from ignoring or denying this inescapable reality of a diverse society and compel them to take it into account. This improves democratic representation and governance. In addition, my findings challenge the simple A → B expectation predicted by Implication 2.1 (see Chapter 1 of this volume)—that women in government will articulate women's interests more than men and, by extension, that Afrodescendant women will represent Afrodescendant women's interests. Yet this chapter offers evidence in support of Implication 2.2A: as the visibility of women (including Afrodescendant women) as a politically-relevant group and their access to government venues expands, a greater range of interests will be articulated.

AFRODESCENDANT WOMEN AND RACIAL FORMATION

Estimates suggest that Afrodescendants comprise around one-third of the population of Latin America, amounting to some 80 to 150 million people (del Popolo et al. 2009: 74).[5] These numbers are surprising because countries of the region—with few exceptions—have tended to portray themselves as largely white in the media and popular culture. George W. Bush's alleged question to Brazilian President Fernando Henrique Cardoso—"Do you have blacks too?"[6]—reflects the resulting ignorance of the region's heterogeneity.

Racial discourses espoused by Latin American elites are largely responsible for these impressions. In the late nineteenth and early twentieth centuries, nationalist elites—partially in response to scientific racism emanating from Europe—portrayed their countries as racially mixed and growing steadily

5. This section partially draws from Htun 2012.
6. Originally reported in *Der Spiegel* on May 19, 2002. See: http://www.spiegel.de/panorama/0,1518,196865,00.html (accessed February 13, 2012).

whiter (Skidmore 1993; Stepan 1996; Graham 1990). Countries such as Brazil, Colombia, and Venezuela—all with extremely large Afrodescendant populations—did not segregate and classify their citizenry along the US and South African models. They embraced a plurality of categories of color that were flexible, contextually defined, and transcendable (as in the adage, "money whitens") (Harris 1964; Degler 1986; Marx 1998). Intellectuals and political elites interpreted and framed social inequalities in terms of class, not race.

The state plays a singular role in "making" race by counting bodies in the census, allocating rights differentially, and segregating groups geographically (Marx 1998; Jung 2008; Htun 2004a). This raises the question of whether, in light of Latin American states' reluctance to count, classify, and segregate by race, "race" really exists there at all. Most white Brazilians—and Venezuelans and Colombians—historically denied that it did, and many still see the recent entrance of affirmative action and other racial discourses as marks of US imperialism (see also Bourdieu and Wacquant 1999). Yet it is undeniable that Latin American countries are stratified along color lines and that racism is pervasive. The darker one's skin, the lower one's life chances, social status, and economic opportunities tend to be (see, e.g., Reid Andrews 2004; Telles 2004; Wade 1997). Racially inflected terms to label and insult others proliferate in popular discourse, and racist behavior is widespread (see, e.g., Sheriff 2001).

The ambiguity of race in the region is reflected in the difficulty of acquiring statistical data on the social status and opportunities of Afrodescendants. Though many countries historically gathered information on indigenous populations, not until 2000 did Spanish-speaking countries collect data on race (with the exception of Cuba). In the early 2000s, only 9 of 19 Latin American countries collected data on Afrodescendant populations, and the criteria for counting differed across countries. By 2013, however, far more countries had gathered such data, though terms and criteria still differed.[7]

What is more, counting criteria tend systematically to underestimate the number of Afrodescendants. The internationally accepted standard for census counts is self-identification of racial and ethnic identity. All Latin American countries except for Cuba conform to this practice (Del Popolo et al. 2009: 63). Yet many people who are socially identified and treated as black are unwilling to self-identify this way because of racial stigmas and preferences for lighter skin. During their work on race and censuses in the region, "World Bank staff discovered that despite the quality of the questions asked, the level of technical support and the participation of Afro leaders, there was a low rate of self-identification as Afrodescendant" (Telles 2010: 8). This cross-national

---

7. Census results on the numbers of minority citizens vary depending on what categories are used (examples include: *Preto, Pardo, Moreno, Mulato, Afrocolombiano*) and how the question is worded.

variation precludes good comparisons of racial inequality and the design of policies to combat racism (Del Popolo et al. 2009: 62; Telles 2010).

With these caveats in mind, Table 7.1 presents available data on the size of the Afrodescendant group in Latin American countries.

Correlated with other social indicators, these data reveal significant racial differences in poverty levels, education, and wages. In Brazil, for example, 43% of blacks (*pretos* and *pardos*) lived below the poverty line in 2006, a decline of nine points from 54% in 1995. For whites, the figures were 22% and 28%, respectively. This implies a 21-point gap in the size of the black and white impoverished populations relative to their total numbers (Paixão and Carvano 2008: 121). Racial gaps persist in education. The average educational attainment of a black Brazilian in 2006 was 6.2 years (an increase from 4.3 years in 1995). For whites, the numbers are 8.0 and 6.4, respectively. This implies a gap of 1.8 years in 2006 (slightly smaller than 1995's gap of 2.1 years) (Paixão and Carvano 2008: 69). (For information on Colombia and the region generally, see Cruces et al. 2010; Atal et al. 2009.)

Table 7.1. AFRODESCENDANT POPULATION IN LATIN AMERICA (NUMBERS ARE ROUNDED OFF TO THE 1000S)

Countries	Total Population	Year	Afrodescendant Population	Percentage
Argentina	40,117,000	2010	150,000	0.4
Bolivia	10,027,000	2012	24,000	0.2
Brazil	190,733,000	2010	97,083,000	50.9
Chile	16,636,000	2012	97,000	0.6
Colombia	42,954,000	2005	4,274,000	10.5
Costa Rica	4,302,000	2011	334,000	7.8
Cuba	11,163,000	2012	3,885,000	34.8
Dominican Republic	9,445,000	2010	8,980,000	89.0
Ecuador	14,484,000	2010	1,043,000	7.2
El Salvador	5,744,000	2007	7,000	0.13
Guatemala	14,713,000	2011	5,000	0.0
Honduras	8,448,000	2011	59,000	1.0
Mexico	112,337,000	2010	2,366,000	2.2
Nicaragua	5,142,000	2005	23,000	0.4
Panama	3,454,000	2010	313,000	9.2
Paraguay	6,673,000	2012	234,000	3.5
Peru	27,412,000	2007	411,000	1.5
Uruguay	3,286,000	2011	255,000	7.8
Venezuela	27,228,000	2011	14,534,000	53.4

Source: Telles forthcoming. His data are from the latest round of national censuses. The Venezuela figure includes people who self-identify as "moreno."

Though the status of Afrodescendant women cannot be deduced merely by adding the effects of racial and gender hierarchies (Hancock 2007; Weldon 2008), data suggest that the combination, multiplication, and/or interaction of these two axes of disadvantage renders them vulnerable. Atal's study, for example, found that women members of subordinate ethnic and racial groups in Latin America have the lowest position in the labor market. The wage gap between white men and black and brown women is 60 points (though most of this can be explained by their differing educational levels, places of employment, and other variables) (Atal et al. 2009: 37).

ACCESS TO ELECTED OFFICE

Composing a picture of Afrodescendant representation required collecting original data. No country collects information on the race, color, or ethnicity of elected officials. Even in Brazil, where data are otherwise plentiful, scholars must estimate the racial composition of the legislature by classifying photos on file with the National Electoral Tribunal or relying on self-declaration in private surveys (Paixão and Carvano 2008). What is more, criteria for external classification and for self-declaration vary. In Brazil, for example, several self-declared Afrodescendant legislators have relatively fair skin color. In countries where race is less politicized and discourses of whitening more prevalent, it is possible that individuals with similar phenotype would be less likely to identify as Afrodescendant.

I estimated numbers of Afrodescendants in national legislatures crudely by classifying legislator photos available on congressional websites for every country except Brazil.[8] Ideally, it would be supplemented by two additional levels of measurement: (1) validation by the legislator in question that she or he identifies as Afrodescendant; and (2) intersubjective confirmation by legislative staff, political journalists, and others in the milieu that the legislator is "known as black." I have not yet had the resources to do this. Preliminary data are presented in Table 7.2.

In Brazil, the country for which data are most readily available, there were a total of 44 black federal deputies elected in 2010 (2010–14 mandate) out of 513, making up some nine percent of the total (see Table 7.2).[9] This included

8. This methodology is not unprecedented: it was used by Paixão and Carvano's team at the Federal University of Rio de Janeiro for the 2008–2009 report on Brazil's racial inequalities. The Brazil data in this chapter (for a more recent legislature than that studied by Paixão and Carvano) come from Universo Online's "Congreso em foco" (see Table 7.2).

9. For a count, see "Os deputados que se autodeclaram negros." Available at: http://congressoemfoco.uol.com.br/noticia.asp?cod_canal=21&cod_publicacao=36175 (accessed July 11, 2011). I added one person (Eliane Rolim—PT/RJ) to the list. As a *suplente*, she was not part of the original count.

Table 7.2. AFRODESCENDANTS IN NATIONAL LEGISLATURES IN SIX LATIN AMERICAN COUNTRIES, 2013

Country	Total blacks	Black women	Total # of legislators	Blacks as a % of total
Brazil				
Chamber	44	7	513	8.60%
Senate	1	0	81	1.20%
Colombia				
House	7	0	165	4.20%
Senate	2	0	102	2%
Costa Rica				
Unicameral	0	0	57	0%
Ecuador				
Unicameral	9	5	137	6.60%
Peru				
Unicameral	3	3	130	2.30%
Uruguay				
House	1	0	99	1%
Senate	0	0	31	0%
Venezuela	4	1	165	2.40%
Unicameral				

Source: Htun (forthcoming), based on her calculations of elected (titular) representatives.

seven Afrodescendant women. In 2006, there were 46 black deputies elected, but only three women (Paixão and Carvano 2008: 148).[10] As this suggests, the number of Afrodescendant women elected to the lower house of the Brazilian congress doubled from three to six deputies in one electoral cycle. In addition, one black female deputy assumed office as an alternate, bringing the total to seven. Overall numbers of women stayed the same (at 9%). No black women were elected to the Senate in 2006 or 2010, though the total number of women skyrocketed from four to 13.[11]

In both Brazilian chambers, black legislators as a whole do not concentrate ideologically: they were elected from parties across the political spectrum.

10. There is no official data on legislator race or ethnicity in Brazil, nor any opportunity for elected officials to declare their race or ethnicity. The 2006 data mentioned here are based on subjective classification of photos by the research team at LAESER (Laboratory for Statistical, Economic, and Social Analysis of Race Relations) in Rio de Janeiro (Paixão and Carvano 2008: 145).
11. In 2006, five of 81 senators were black men. Data for 2010 were not available. These numbers mark a dramatic improvement over previous decades. In the 1990s, for example, there were only about 15 black deputies in the lower house of congress (Johnson 2000). (The number of black women deputies is unknown.) Still, it is important to bear in mind that Afrodescendants make up over half of the Brazilian population.

In the Lower House in 2006, some 45% of black deputies were elected from leftist parties and some 55% from parties of the Center and Right (Paixão and Carvano 2008: 149–51).[12] Yet in 2010, six of seven black women in the Chamber of Deputies were from parties of the Left: four were elected by the PT, two by the PC do B. Only one deputy—Andreia Zito of the PSDB—came from a Center party. No black female deputies were elected from parties of the Right, suggesting that their path to power may be distinctive from those of Afrodescendant men.

In Colombia in 2013, Afrodescendants made up a mere 4% of the Chamber of Representatives (some seven of 165, including the deputies elected for the seats reserved for "black communities") and 2% of the Senate (two of 102). There were no women among them.[13] In the past, however, Colombia had elected black women to the lower house: at least two were elected in the seats reserved for "black communities" and one from the province of San Andrés and Providencia. As in Brazil, Afrodescendants in the Colombian congress are affiliated with a broad range of political parties (including two from the Liberal Party, two from the PIN, and one each from Afrovides, Movimiento Popular Unido, the Conservative Party and the Partido de la U).

Costa Rica did not have a single Afrodescendant man or woman in parliament in 2013, a significant break from past practice. From 1953 until his death in 1990, former president and chief political boss José Figueres used his power to guarantee the presence of at least one Afrodescendant member of the 57-person congress. He made sure the National Liberation Party (PLN, the dominant party) put an Afrodescendant candidate in an electable position on a party list, usually in Limón province. In total, there have been 17 Afrodescendant legislators elected via this route.[14]

In 2013, Ecuador was the only Latin American country where the presence of Afrodescendants in parliament was proportional to their population size. That year, the country had approximately nine black legislators, almost 7% of parliament. According to the census, Afrodescendants made up some 7% of the total population. Five of the nine legislators were women, and eight legislators came from President Rafael Correa's party (PAIS). In the previous legislature (2009–13), there were three Afrodescendant legislators, including one woman. In Peru, three Afrodescendant women held seats in congress. (There are no male Afrodescendant legislators.) All three black women in Peru's congress were former volleyball players, elected from different parties (Fuerza

12. Party affiliation data were not disaggregated by sex for the 2006 legislature.
13. These data are based on author's classification of legislator photos on the Congreso Visible website: http://www.congresovisible.org/congresistas/ (accessed June 23, 2011). The statutory size of the Chamber is 166, but just 165 members were elected.
14. Interview with Walter Robinson, July 26, 2011. Robinson was the 14th deputy elected this way and Epsy Campbell the 15th.

2011, Perú Posible, and Gana Perú). Of Venezuela's four Afrodescendant legislators, one was a woman.

In summary, these data show that Afrodescendant women held national elected office in only four of the seven countries analyzed. Afrodescendant men held seats in two more (Colombia and Uruguay). Only Costa Rica had no Afrodescendant representation, a break from its historical pattern. With the exceptions of Ecuador and Peru, Afrodescendant women were even more under-represented in national legislatures than the black group as a whole and than women as a whole. The challenges faced by women from subordinate racial and ethnic groups are not unique to Latin America. Based on her analysis of some 80 countries, Hughes (2011) finds that minority women's odds of getting elected to the national legislature are 1 in 14 compared to majority men, 1 in 2 compared to minority men, and 1 in 3 compared to majority women. In a different work, I analyze political interventions to boost their presence in elected office (Htun 2012) and conclude, following Hughes, that a combination of gender quotas and race-based group representation policies (tandem quotas) is the most promising strategy.

INTERSECTIONALITY AND REPRESENTATION

As Beckwith points out in Chapter 2 of this volume, social structures and institutions tend to position women at a disadvantage relative to men. (They also position whites more advantageously than blacks.) Women's disadvantageous structural position provokes episodes of collective action to improve their situation—episodes in which they articulate interests, introduce issues, and express preferences. To the extent that women have interests in common, it is by virtue of a shared social position, not a common identity. Interests arise situationally as groups—who may not reflect the broader category—mobilize to combat disadvantage. Many scholars refer to this process as the "substantive representation of women's interests" (but see Dahlerup, Chapter 4 of this volume). Resisting a preemptive definition of "women's interests," I prefer to speak in terms of advocacy and legislative behavior on behalf of women's rights (Htun et al. 2013).

What about the interests of sub-groups of women, such as Afrodescendant women, lesbian women, poor women, and so forth? We know from theories of intersectionality that social structures of gender, race, class, ethnicity, sexuality, among others, produce differences and hierarchies among women (see, e.g., Crenshaw 1991; Hancock 2007; Weldon 2008; García Bedolla 2007). Such theories argue that the effect of social structures is not additive, but mutually constitutive: race *conditions*, and *transforms*, the experience of sexist oppression. As a result, we cannot identify sub-group interests by adding

Afrodescendant interests to women's interests and then subtracting the male part (see Hancock, Chapter 3 of this volume). Afrodescendant women may have unique perspectives and face unique disadvantages that are not derivative of—or predicted by—the larger categories to which they belong. What is more, their perspectives may vary due to class, regional, religious, and, of course, individual differences.

As Beckwith notes, women's interests are ideally formulated during processes of democratic deliberation and decision making. This suggests that the identification of Afrodescendant women's interests should flow from their group-specific organization, articulation of perspectives, and formulation of positions. At the Fourth Regional Meeting of Afrodescendant Women, held in Costa Rica in 2011, participants emitted a Declaration that focused on combating the social exclusion produced by racism and sexism, with special mention of the need to analyze quota systems that would facilitate the election of minority women.[15] This suggests that Afrodescendant women have an interest in being full partners in society and in having a place in political decision making. To what extent are women in office taking action to combat the exclusions and disadvantages precluding such parity in participation (see Fraser 2007)?

ASSESSING AFRODESCENDANT WOMEN'S LEGISLATIVE BEHAVIOR

Though few Afrodescendant women have gained access to elected office, enough are present to engage in a preliminary analysis of their behavior. I will argue that the type of representation that Afrodescendant women offer differs from traditional, principal-agent models of representation: they are "surrogate" representatives. Measuring and evaluating surrogate representation involves different standards from those applied to traditional notions of representation (Mansbridge 2003).

Traditional Representation

The dominant understanding of representation in democratic theory revolves around "promissory" representation, or the principal-agent relationship between citizens and their elected representatives. In this model, citizens or voters select or authorize representatives to pursue their interests, instructions, and desires (Urbinati and Warren 2008; Mansbridge 2003; Przeworski

15. See text of the Declaration at: http://mujeresafrocostarricenses.blogspot.com/.

et al. 1999; Pitkin 1967). The quality of representation can therefore be judged by the extent to which the representative acted in line with voter preferences. Voters exercise quality control by virtue of their ability to hold representatives accountable at election time.

This notion of representation does not apply to the relationship between Afrodescendant women voters and female elected officials for the simple reason that Afrodescendant women do not constitute an electoral constituency. In every Latin American country, constituencies—understood as the group of voters that elects a representative—are defined by geography, not by social status.[16] Even in large multimember districts and permissive electoral systems where politicians are known to construct individual "bailiwicks" of voters from different residential areas, there is little evidence that race—or even gender—are consistently salient criteria.[17]

In certain regions where they are geographically concentrated—such as the Chocó in Colombia—Afrodescendants arguably constitute an electoral constituency. But *Afrodescendant women* are not a constituency since the districts include both male and female voters. What is more, studies show that voter motivations in the Chocó are largely distributional: they want their representatives to channel more national funding to their region. Very few Chocoano voters support candidates with platforms focused on ethnic and racial issues. This is evident in voting patterns for politicians contesting the country's reserved seats for "black communities." Most Chocoano voters have voted for candidates from the Liberal Party, not for those with platforms of "ethnic rights" (Agudelo 2000, 2002).

How do Afrodescendant women in elected office perform as agents responsive to the interests of their principals, the voters who elected them? Evidence suggests that they have taken action to benefit their communities. Zobeida Gudiño of Ecuador, reporting on her legislative activity to her district, said that she obtained important results in financing for the construction of schools, hospitals, and electrification, among other projects.[18] Leyla Chihuán Ramos of Peru emphasized her efforts to bring electrical power to a poor, isolated rural community to improve its prospects for economic

16. Colombia's reserved seats for indigenous peoples and "black communities" constitute an exception. Though only indigenous and Afrodescendant candidates can run for election in these seats, anyone can vote for them. At the time of voting, any voter can opt to cast their vote for one of the reserved seat candidates or to vote in the more general contest. Voters are not segregated by race or ethnicity. For more information, see Htun (forthcoming).

17. Ames argues, however, that politicians sometimes seek to aggregate votes of Japanese Brazilians across different geographical zones (1995: 328).

18. http://asambleanacional.gob.ec/201108186287/noticias/boletines/asambleista-zobeida-gudino-expone-principales-lineas-de-accion-de-su-gestion.html (accessed February 15, 2012).

development.[19] Janete Pietá of Brazil inaugurated public housing—financed by the federal government—in the Guarulhos area of São Paulo for former residents of favelas, and has sought the creation of an omnibus "social fund."[20]

These activities conform to the expectations of voters. According to Paula Moreno, former minister of culture of Colombia (and the country's first black female minister), representation means the provision of goods: "When you ask someone what representation means for them, and what matters, they say: "What have you done for Tolima [a Colombian department]?" Doing something for Tolima, in turn, means increasing its budget and raising its social status through symbolic gestures such as declaring and recognizing folk holidays.[21]

Is helping to advance the status of Afrodescendant women part of "doing something for Tolima?" Perhaps, but not explicitly. In fact, the dynamics of promissory representation—under which representatives are expected to deliver goods to a broad constituency—may conflict with overt activism to ameliorate the disadvantage of particular social groups. As one aspiring politician from Panama said in a group discussion: "[W]e are excluded because we are women and also because we are black. But if I actively assume the Afrodescendant label and identity, people think that I'm interested only in Afrodescendant issues. And that's limiting. I have to legislate for everyone. I have to represent everyone." Representative Zobeida Gudiño from Ecuador agreed: "I get elected by everyone."[22]

Surrogate Representation

Notwithstanding the perceived need to "represent everyone," there is evidence that some Afrodescendant women legislators have taken special action to advocate for the rights of women, Afrodescendants, and other marginalized groups. In addition, they contribute to democratic politics by their mere presence, reversing the historic invisibility of Afrodescendant peoples in sites of political power, evinced by the absence of any Afrodescendants among the portraits that cover the salons and corridors of Latin American government buildings.[23]

19. http://leylachihuan.pe/congresita-leyla-chihuan-ramos-intercede-a-favor-de-la-municipalidad-distrital-de-quinocay-yauyos-region-lima/#more-1189 (accessed February 15, 2012).

20. http://www.janeterochapieta.com.br/?p=3525

21. Interview, San José, Costa Rica, July 26, 2011.

22. Htun's notes from group discussion at the Fourth Regional Conference of Afrodescendant Women, San José, Costa Rica, July 27, 2011.

23. This reality promoted former Brazilian Minister for Racial Equality Matilde Ribeiro to declare, "I want to see photographs of black comrades [*companheiras negras e companheiros negros*] on the walls of these legislative chambers."

To assess linkages between Afrodescendant women voters and those in elected office, the "surrogate" model of representation is more useful than traditional notions. "Surrogates" provide representation to voters from different districts, particularly those with whom they share experiences in a way that the majority of the legislature does not (Mansbridge 2003: 523). This describes the relationship between Afrodescendant women officials and members of the broader category, whose perspectives they may feel compelled to represent for reasons "internal to their own convictions, consciences, and identities" (Mansbridge 2003: 524). The quality of surrogate representation cannot be evaluated by the same standards as promissory or principal-agent representation since surrogates represent constituencies that did not elect them, and cannot be held accountable in traditional ways. Mansbridge argues that the pertinent normative concern for surrogate representation is whether, in the aggregate: (1) the most conflictual interests in the polity are represented in rough proportions; and (2) all relevant perspectives are present in deliberation over key policy decisions. Assessing the quality of surrogate representation shifts our attention from the dyadic constituent-representative relationship to the *overall composition and behavior of the parliament* (Mansbridge 2003: 524–25, emphasis added).

Mansbridge's perspective implies that evaluating the representative contribution of Afrodescendant women (and other "surrogate" representatives) requires analysis not just of their own actions but of the deliberative practices and representational behavior of the *parliament as a whole*. What are the symbolic, behavioral, and discursive effects of the presence of Afrodescendant women legislators? How do others respond to them? Do their contributions transform parliamentary discourse? Mansbridge argues that surrogate representation has the potential to increase systemic democratic legitimacy. How does the political inclusion of Afrodecendant women affect the quality of democracy?

As this suggests, the important question is not whether Afrodescendant women in elected office are precisely channeling the perspectives of the broader category. To the extent that they are formulated during inclusive and democratic deliberation, Afrodescendant women's interests may vary from place to place and may be subject to change. Rather, the pertinent issue is whether Afrodescendant elected officials are taking action to combat the conditions that disadvantage women, Afrodescendants, Afrodescendant women, and other marginalized social groups, and whether these activities and the mere presence of Afrodescendant women representatives are shaping the overall legislative and political climate.

Janete Pietá of Brazil, for example, is one of the founders of the Workers' Party (PT) who was elected to the lower house of congress in 2006 after working in the PT's municipal administration in Guarulhos. She has long advocated Afrodescendant and women's rights, including anti-discrimination, protection from violence against women, prenatal care, breast cancer care, and the rights of residents of Quilombos (communities formed by runaway slaves). From 2006 to 2010, she coordinated the women's caucus and the black caucus within the PT, reminding both constituencies that the category "women" includes Afrodescendants and that the Afrodescendant category includes women. In the 2010–2014 legislature, she was vice-leader of the PT caucus and coordinated the interparty women's caucus.[24]

Representative Leyla Chichuán of Peru was the president of the congressional Afro Peruvian working group, whose work consisted primarily of sponsoring and supporting theater, artistic, and musical events to increase public appreciation of Afro-Peruvian contributions to history and culture.[25] She authored bills to promote the recognition of Afro-Peruvians and to combat discrimination, often in collaboration with the two other Afrodescendant women representatives. She was also active on women's rights and on issues pertaining to sports.

In Ecuador, Representative Zobeida Gudiño presented bills to recognize collective Afrodescendant rights and served as a spokeswoman for President Correa's anti-discrimination initiatives. Her goal was to see that the Afro-Ecuadorian sector is "taken into account in the laws that are approved by the National Assembly."[26]

Though no black women occupied seats in the Colombian congress in 2013, they have taken initiatives on behalf of both women and Afrodescendants in previous legislatures. Former Senator Piedad Córdoba served as a global spokesperson on these issues, as well as gay rights, during her many years in elected office (1992–2010). Former Deputy María Isabel Urrutia (2002–2006), though elected because of her gold medal in the Sydney Olympics, assumed a mandate to promote Afrodescendant rights once in office and sought to combat racism (Htun forthcoming).

Former Costa Rican representative Epsy Campbell Barr (2002–2006) acquired regional and international fame with her work on behalf of black rights and women's rights. A charismatic speaker, she called global attention to the low social status of Afrodescendants and mobilized the commitment of the international development community to social inclusion policies. In addition, Campbell Barr organized regional networks of Afrodescendant women, steering and participating in numerous groups including the Network of Afro-Latin American, Afro-Caribbean and Diaspora Women, the Black Parliament of the Americas, the Central American Black Organization, and the Alliance of Leaders of African Descent in Latin America and the

24. http://www.janeterochapieta.com.br/?p=2119.
25. http://leylachihuan.pe/category/mta/
26. Personal conversation, San José, Costa Rica, July 2011.

Caribbean. In addition, Campbell Barr serves as president of the Afro-Costa Rican Women's Center.[27]

Though serving as an alternate, not a titular deputy, Angélica Ferreira of Uruguay upheld a mandate to defend Afrodescendant and women's rights. She claimed that her placement on a party list—albeit as *suplente*—was the first for a black woman and that she strongly hoped that "more black women and black men will look at themselves and begin to occupy visible spaces in society without being afraid."[28] In congress, she gave speeches about the contributions made by Afrodescendants to Uruguayan history and also advocated women's rights.[29] She noted: "Looking at the books, we noticed the lack of Afro-Uruguayan history. We did not exist."[30]

These examples illustrate that Afrodescendant women from large and small parties, institutionalized and non-institutionalized party systems, programmatic and candidate-centered parties, and from the political Left and Center have advocated the interests of women and of Afrodescendants. This indicates support for Implication 2.2A and shows that surrogate representation has been occurring. Variations in how these Afrodescendant women were elected, through which parties and with what type of base, seemed to have little connection to differences in their legislative work (at least on these issues). Far more important was the growing awareness by national governments and the international community of racial inequality and mounting pressure to take action against it. International advocacy of Afrodescendant rights—exemplified by the Inter-American Development Bank's social inclusion programs, the World Bank's pressure for race data in national censuses, and the Ford Foundation's funding of movements demanding affirmative action in Brazil (Htun 2004a)—constitutes an important influence on legislative behavior. A small number of Afrodescendant women politicians have attained superstar status in local and global media and among the international development community. They are regular participants at conferences, frequently called upon as spokespeople for marginalized communities, and serve as symbols of global inclusivity. The fact that a growing number of legislators—not just Afrodescendant women—are taking action to promote their rights owes to international pressure as well as the mobilization of local constituencies.

27. While this chapter does not focus on strategizing to represent women's interests, Campbell Barr's work indicates that a multilevel strategy—national, regional, and even global—may be an important component of moving from articulation of interests to policy adoption and policy outcomes. This relates to Kang's findings (Chapter 8 of this volume) about abortion rights, and to Implication 3.1.

28. http://www.uruguayinforme.com/news/22102009/22102009_dornel_afro.php

29. http://www0.parlamento.gub.uy/forms2/fojaleg.asp?Legislaturas=47&Legislador=10015&QyBatch=n&FechaDesde=15022010&FechaHasta=17022012&FechaMin=15022010&FechaMax=17022012&Consultar=Consultar&Ini=Ini&Inf=Inf&Int=Int&Otr=Otr

30. http://fresaediciones-uruguay.blogspot.com/2010/04

CONCLUSION

Angélica Ferreira's statement, "we did not exist," points to what may be the singular democratic contribution of Afrodescendant women legislators: mere presence. Simply by being present in power, they render visible social identities and relationships long suppressed by racism and racialist ideology. There is some variation in their success. Janete Pietá rose to the rank of vice-leader of the PT in the Brazilian Chamber of Deputies; former Senator Marina Silva ran for president of Brazil in 2010 and received 19% of the vote. In spite of her global fame and nomination for the 2009 Nobel Peace Prize, Piedad Cordoba, of Colombia was twice removed from congress: she was forced out in 2005 under allegations of electoral fraud and in 2010, the Colombian inspector general removed her from congress and banned her from seeking public office for 18 years for alleged ties to paramilitary groups. Black women's political behavior mirrors the strengths and weaknesses of the broader political class.

Evidence suggests that many black women in elected office served as "surrogate representatives," acting to advance the rights of women, Afrodescendants, and other marginalized groups. Based on their common positioning as members of a subordinate group by virtue of racial and gender hierarchies, as well as international pressure and greater national awareness, they perceived a mandate to speak out and introduce policy initiatives on behalf of Afrodescendant and women's rights. In some countries, such as Peru, Ecuador, and Uruguay, these efforts are relatively new. Elsewhere, such as Brazil and Colombia, they followed in a longer tradition of social movement mobilization and growing public awareness of racial stratification.

These activities enhanced the quality of democratic representation by making sure that relevant perspectives were included in deliberation and decision making (evidence in support of Implication 2.2A). Speeches made and bills introduced by Afrodescendant women kept racial discrimination and inequality on political agendas. Regardless of whether one agrees with Brazil's Statute of Racial Equality, with proposals for racial quotas on party lists and affirmative action, or with granting collective rights to Afro-Peruvians, the insertion of these ideas into debates made it impossible to ignore the reality of racial inequality. Racism and inequality are pervasive in Latin America. Yet the historic absence of Afrodescendants from positions of power helped people get away with ignoring it.

Afrodescendant women added more still. They did not represent intersectionality in the legislature, at least no more than any other politician does. Intersectionality is a perspective, not a person. It is a vision of social groups as inevitably cross-cut by multiple axes of difference. Identities of the wealthy white people who historically occupied virtually all positions of power are intersectionally constituted. Their long hold on power, however, rendered "white" and "wealthy" normative and hid ongoing exclusion and marginalization from the purview of justice. Having Afrodescendant men in the legislature serves as a reminder of the multihued nature of Latin American societies and its oppressive racial order. The presence of Afrodescendant women provides a more profound safeguard against the sexism among Afrodescendants and the racism among women.

PART THREE

Representation: Securing Women's Interests in Policy

CHAPTER 8

How Civil Society Represents Women

Feminists, Catholics, and Mobilization Strategies in Africa

ALICE J. KANG

In recent years, civil society has risen to speak on behalf of underrepresented groups in Africa. In particular, civil society has advocated for the representation of women's interests (Tripp et al. 2008). Yet, relatively little is known about the full range of actors who seek the representation of women's interests, mobilize around women's issues, and articulate specific preferences.[1] Some of these actors include not only feminists, but also religious activists who may clash over women's issues. This gap in knowledge, moreover, extends to non-democratic countries. Who in civil society seeks to influence the representation of women's interests and how, in both democratic and authoritarian regimes? What impact do civil society groups have on specific policy outcomes?

This chapter contributes to the volume by addressing the *who* and *how* questions of women's representation. It identifies who in civil society can potentially mobilize for and against women's interests and how they try to hasten, or delay, policy outcomes. Focusing on the African Union's Maputo Protocol on the Rights of Women, I find that feminist groups and Catholic groups were central actors. These groups employed multilevel strategies to gain the government's attention. Both groups engaged in international networking and

---

1. Following Beckwith (Chapter 2 of this volume), women's interests are socially and politically constructed values. Issues are choices that emphasize components of interest as a policy initiative. Preferences are alternatives on a specific issue.

domestic lobbying, protesting, and consciousness-raising activities, though the strategies varied across democracies and autocracies. I then find that women's mobilization helped countries ratify the Protocol more quickly, in both democracies and autocracies, but find limited evidence that anti-Protocol mobilization slowed down the pace of ratification. Thus, this chapter explores Implications 3.1 and 3.2 from Chapter 1 regarding the importance of the venues in which women have representation.

WHO IN CIVIL SOCIETY CLAIMS TO REPRESENT WOMEN?

Though the scholarship on women and politics predominantly focuses on women's groups, they are not the only ones who care about how governments regulate women's and men's lives. Religious actors can also claim to represent women's interests. For instance, Sisters in Islam, an international women's group of Muslim women that advocates for women's rights, met in 2003 to reflect on the challenges that Muslim women's groups encounter "in the face of rising religious extremism" (Othman 2005: xiii). Women's activists from Egypt, Indonesia, Iran, Malaysia, and Morocco lamented that states were rejecting policies that would promote women's rights. Women's activists did not blame "Islam" writ large. This is an important point: Sisters in Islam was not struggling against religion per se. Rather, it identified specific Islamist political parties, politicians, and civil society groups that were mobilizing against proposed policies. Similarly, one study of Senegal argues that "the factor assumed here to be a, if not the, principal force restricting the political power of Senegalese women is the importance of Islamic institutions and leaders in Senegalese politics" (Creevey 2006: 154).

Opposition from civil society to pro-women policy is not limited to Muslim countries. One of the best-studied instances of anti-feminist mobilization took place in the United States, when conservative women activists mobilized against the Equal Rights Amendment (e.g., Mansbridge 1986; Soule and Olzak 2004). As Mazur finds, "[h]igher levels of feminist policy were achieved in countries where fundamentalist Christianity was less socially salient and politically influential" (2002: 189).

To better understand anti-feminist mobilization, scholars have considered the conditions under which anti-feminist actors succeed in influencing the state. One vein of theorizing focuses on pacts. Htun (2003a) compares women's rights policy making across Argentina, Brazil, and Chile under military and civilian rule in the 1970s through the 1990s. Htun finds that conflict between the state and the Catholic Church in authoritarian Brazil and democratic Argentina enabled politicians to vote against the Church's wishes and to legalize divorce. In authoritarian Brazil, the Catholic Church had joined the opposition. In Chile, however, state leaders hesitated to legalize divorce. Civilian rulers were loyal to the Church because the Church shielded them during the previous dictatorship.

Economic inequality might facilitate the success of conservative religious activism. Blofield (2006) analyzes divorce and abortion reform in Argentina, Chile, and Spain. She suggests that class divisions, rather than elite pacts, affect the representation of women's interests. Blofield suggests that in unequal societies, organizations like the Catholic Church have more financial resources than do women's organizations. Thus, politicians court the Church. For instance, Argentina's former President Carlos Menem sought out the Vatican's support by formulating an anti-abortion agenda. Moreover, in unequal societies, politicians use moral issues to deflect the poor's attention away from their economic woes. Finally, high levels of inequality undermine cross-class solidarity within women's movements. Blofield attributes the absence of legalized abortion in Argentina and Chile partly to the fact that middle- and upper-class women can afford to pay for medical abortions in private clinics, hence the lack of elite women's mobilization. In Spain, relative social equality meant that women's activists not only had access to the media and the political arena through a supportive left-wing party, but they also were able to mobilize a broad, multiclass support base to lobby for legal abortion.

A third vein of theorizing differentiates between doctrinal and non-doctrinal issues. Htun and Weldon's (2010) global study of women's rights policy suggests that religious leaders and civil society mobilize depending on the type of issue, along with other factors such as the political environment. Doctrinal issues, such as abortion, contraception, and family law, challenge the letter of religion. Non-doctrinal issues, such as maternity leave, workplace equality, gender quotas, violence against women, and constitutional equality, do not challenge the doctrine of organized religion. Htun and Weldon contend that if a women's issue is doctrinal, then religious actors will mobilize and challenge women's rights policy, but if the issue is non-doctrinal, then religious actors will not mobilize.

HOW CIVIL SOCIETY CLAIMS TO REPRESENT WOMEN

Civil society groups use several types of strategies to gain their government's attention and influence policy outcomes. These strategies are used singly. These strategies are also used in combination, including the combination of advocacy at the international level with advocacy at the domestic level.

International Strategies

An important aspect of women's mobilization for women's interests is its international character. In attending international conferences, workshops, and trainings, women from around the world make new friends, share ideas, and debate regarding what constitutes women's interests. Women in international arenas also identify and promote new international norms to promote women's interests. The creation of international norms can be effective. Scholars have found that governments respond to international norms because governments pay attention to what other countries do and fear being left out (Wotipka and Ramirez 2008). Additionally, scholars have found that governments try to keep up with international women's rights norms in the hopes of attracting foreign aid and favorable trade and lending agreements (Goodliffe and Hawkins 2006; Hathaway 2002).

Another strategy that civil society uses to gain government attention and influence policy outcomes is to use international law. International treaties can bind the hands of government actors and force them to reform domestic laws that undermine women's interests. Women's activists were instrumental in creating the United Nations Convention on the Elimination of All Forms of Discrimination Against Women (CEDAW) in 1979. Research suggests that governments that ratify CEDAW adopt more women's rights policies than governments that do not (Stetson 1995). Women's living conditions improve more in countries that have ratified CEDAW than in countries that have not (Gray et al. 2006). In her landmark study, Beth Simmons (2009) finds that, all else being equal, ratifying CEDAW decreases the gender gap in education and increases the likelihood that a government will adopt policies that will allow greater access to contraception.

Another strategy for civil society is to use international courts. Systematic study shows that through a long, incremental process of "judicial policy making," the European Court of Justice expanded the protection of women's pregnancy and maternity leave policy in European Union countries (Cichowski 2006). Representing a woman who had been enslaved most of her life, a coalition of international activists and Nigérien lawyers went to the Economic Community of West African States (ECOWAS) Court of Justice to enforce Niger's 2003 anti-slavery law. The international court fined the Nigérien government, and payment was accorded to the former slave (Duffy 2009). The ruling is now binding for ECOWAS's 15 member states.

Domestic Strategies

At home, civil society groups use several tactics to advocate for women's interests. Civil society groups can lobby government actors to build alliances. They can use newspapers, radio, and television to provide information to the public and mobilize public opinion. In the Republic of Niger, a coalition of women's activists used the media to call upon the constitutional court of Niger to reject political party candidate lists that violated Niger's gender quota in 2004. In that year and subsequent election years, the law on candidate lists was enforced (Kang, 2013). Civil society groups can also organize demonstrations, at times marching to sites of policy making to demand change (e.g., Fallon 2008; Weldon 2011b). In 2002, a coalition of women's activists, with support from UNICEF, marched to the seat of the national parliament in Benin. The demonstrators demanded that the parliament review a draft family code, which had been stalled for several years. The head of the parliament agreed to make family law reform a priority, and the reform was made into law in 2004 (Kang 2010).

THE MAPUTO PROTOCOL ON THE RIGHTS OF WOMEN

In July 2003, the African Union met in Maputo, Mozambique, and adopted the Protocol to the African Charter on Human and Peoples' Rights on the Rights of Women in Africa, hereafter the Maputo Protocol. The Maputo Protocol is a bold treaty. It identifies a wide variety of African women's concerns, from economic equality to reproductive rights to widow's rights. The Protocol further stipulates that women have the right to medical abortion in cases of assault, rape, incest, and the endangerment of the mother's health. It is the first international women's rights treaty to take such an explicit stance on abortion. Catholic civil society groups mobilized against the Maputo Protocol, specifically objecting to the abortion clause.

By the end of 2010, more than half of the countries in the African Union (29 out of 53) had ratified the Maputo Protocol (African Union 2011). Eight countries ratified the Protocol in 2004 and nine in 2005. Following the fifteenth ratification, the Protocol went into effect, in November 2005. The number of ratifications in subsequent years then tapered off: three in 2006, four in 2007, three in 2008, none in 2009, and two in 2010.

STRATEGIES USED TO ADVOCATE FOR THE MAPUTO PROTOCOL

Women's activists from across Africa came together early to push for the ratification of the Maputo Protocol. Activists employed a multilevel strategy, at the international and domestic levels, in democracies and autocracies. As will be shown below, the need for, and success of, a multilevel strategy is evidence in support of Implication 3.2 (see Chapter 1) regarding women having a voice in multiple venues.

One key strategy for proponents of the Maputo Protocol was to coordinate efforts and share ideas across borders. In 2004, four organizations (Equality Now, Fahamu, FEMNET, and Oxfam) created a network of supporters for the Maputo Protocol, called Solidarity for African Women's Rights (SOAWR). The purpose of SOAWR was to mobilize for the Protocol's ratification and implementation. SOAWR's 16 original organizations operated in 12 African countries (see Table 8.1).[2] Since 2004, SOAWR's membership has expanded to include 39 organizations.

Another network of African women's activists, Women in Law and Development in Africa (WiLDAF), led by women lawyers and judges, joined the movement for the Protocol's ratification. WiLDAF was created in 1990 "to promote the development of strategies that link law and development to empower women" (Hodgson 2002: 4). WiLDAF organizes legal education campaigns, provides legal advice to women, and lobbies governments to reform

Table 8.1. ORIGINAL MEMBERS OF SOLIDARITY FOR AFRICAN WOMEN'S RIGHTS (SOAWR), 2004

Organization	Country Headquarters
1. African Center for Democracy and Human Rights Studies (ACDHRS)	The Gambia
2. African Women's Development and Communication Network (FEMNET)	Kenya
3. Association des Juristes Maliennes (AJM)	Mali
4. Akina Mama wa Afrika (AMwA)	Uganda
5. Cellule de Coordination sur les Pratiques Traditionelles Affectant la Santé des Femmes et des Enfants (CPTAFE)	Guinea
6. Coalition on Violence Against Women (COVAW)	Kenya
7. Equality Now (the Secretariat of the Coalition)	UK, Kenya
8. Fahamu	Senegal
9. Federation of Women Lawyers Kenya (FIDA-K)	Kenya
10. Oxfam GB	UK
11. Sister Namibia	Namibia
12. Union Nationale des Femmes de Djibouti (UNFD)	Djibouti
13. University of Pretoria - Centre for Human Rights	South Africa
14. Voix de Femmes	Burkina Faso
15. Women in Law and Development in Africa (WiLDAF), Zambia	Zambia
16. Women's Rights Advancement and Protection Alternative (WRAPA)	Nigeria

Sources: E-mail correspondence between Equality Now and author (May 4, 2011) and websites of the organizations.

2. I thank Brenda Kombo of Equality Now for providing this information. E-mail correspondence with the author, May 4, 2011.

Table 8.2. COUNTRIES WITH A NATIONAL OFFICE OF WOMEN
IN LAW AND DEVELOPMENT IN AFRICA (WILDAF), 2003

1. Benin	13. Namibia
2. Botswana	14. Nigeria
3. Burkina Faso	15. Senegal
4. Cameroon	16. South Africa
5. Cote d'Ivoire	17. Sudan
6. Ghana	18. Swaziland
7. Guinea	19. Tanzania
8. Kenya	20. Togo
9. Lesotho	21. Uganda
10. Mali	22. Zambia
11. Mauritius	23. Zimbabwe
12. Mozambique	

Sources: Butegwa (1995), WiLDAF (2001).

laws, especially family law. Like SOAWR, WiLDAF brings together women's activists across African borders. It comprises country offices that accept applications for individual and group membership. Individual membership is open to people of any profession, though the majority of individual members are women lawyers and judges. Additionally, local groups may apply to be affiliated with a WiLDAF country office. These local groups vary in topical interest (e.g., Muslim women's empowerment, female photojournalists) and are not exclusive to women's organizations (e.g., development NGOs, human rights NGOs). By my count, WiLDAF had offices in 23 countries when the Protocol became open for ratification (see Table 8.2).

Together, SOAWR and WiLDAF spearheaded a serious continental movement for the ratification of the Maputo Protocol in democratic and authoritarian countries. In 2003, civil society groups in 25 countries belonged to SOAWR or had a national office for WiLDAF.[3] Eighteen of those countries were "free" or "partly free" according to Freedom House in 2003. Seven countries were authoritarian or "not free."

Lobbying

Activists mobilized for the ratification of the Maputo Protocol by lobbying key political actors. Activists in six countries used this type of strategy (see the quantitative section below for how I gathered this information). Pro-Protocol

3. Zimbabwe, which is one of the 25 countries, is not included in the quantitative analysis below due to missing data.

activists lobbied a wide range of political actors, from ministers to parliamentarians to ambassadors to the African Union to heads of state. Activists were reported to have lobbied their country's ministers for the ratification of the Protocol in Kenya, Mali, Tanzania, and Uganda. In Mauritania and Niger, activists were reported to have lobbied the president. Interestingly, I found relatively few reports of activists lobbying members of parliament, with the exception of Niger. This may be due to the relative strength of the executive branch over policy making in African countries whose parliaments are modeled on British or French parliaments rather than the US Congress. In some cases, activists met with multiple political actors to advocate for the Protocol's ratification. For instance, the Association of Malian Women Lawyers (an original member of SOAWR) and the minister for the promotion of women in Mali kept each other informed about their work on the Protocol. After the cabinet approved the decree for the Protocol's ratification in June 2004, the Association of Malian Women Lawyers then directed its efforts to lobbying parliamentarians so that the national assembly would approve the decree.[4] Mali ratified the Protocol in January 2005. In Tanzania, pro-Protocol activists lobbied two different ministers: the minister for justice and constitutional affairs and the minister for gender, children's affairs and community development.[5]

Lobbying was more commonly used in democratic and hybrid countries than in authoritarian countries. Kenya and Mali, which had reports of lobbying, were relatively stable democracies throughout the study period. Tanzania and Uganda, which are stable hybrid democracies, also had reports of lobbying. Niger saw lobbying and was a relatively stable democracy until 2009, when President Tandja vied for a third term and dissolved the Constitutional Court and National Assembly. I found one report of lobbying in authoritarian Mauritania, which was nonetheless transitioning toward more competitive rule during the study period. The lack of reports of lobbying in "not free" countries may stem from the relative lack of publicly available information about pro-Protocol mobilization in authoritarian states. It is plausible that activists in authoritarian states do have access to government officials; authoritarian ruling coalitions may seek to address activists' demands to promote the regime's legitimacy at home and abroad.

Women's activists used popular culture to help lobby key officials. Drawing on the colors of football penalty cards, SOAWR issued color-coded pieces of paper to government actors. Green cards signified that the country ratified the Protocol. Yellow cards meant that the country had signed but not ratified the

4. "Protocol on the Rights of Women in Africa: Update on Progress," *Pambazuka News* 165, July 15, 2004. Accessed at http://www.pambazuka.org/en/category/features/23224.

5. Joshua Ogada. "SOAWR Update on the Protocol on the Rights of Women in Africa," *Pambazuka News* 302, May 4, 2007. Accessed at http://www.pambazuka.org/en/category/wgender/41217.

treaty. Red cards, given to countries that had not signed the Protocol, read: "You have received a *red card* by the Solidarity for African Women's Rights, a coalition of organizations campaigning for the ratification of the Protocol on the Rights of Women."[6] At African Union summits, members of SOAWR issued the cards to country representatives, including ministers and heads of state. By 2007, the penalty card campaign became recognizable. When a minister from the Sahrawi Arab Democratic Republic received his country's card, he gladly announced that his country was now yellow and no longer red.[7] SOAWR mailed penalty cards as well. Following the August 3, 2005, *coup d'état* in Mauritania, Equality Now sent a letter to the newly installed president, with a red card.[8] Mauritania ratified the Protocol in September of that year. The ratification could have been used to improve the country's reputation internationally, including among the member states of the African Union following the *coup d'état*. While the president's concern about Mauritania's reputation may help account for the country's ratification of the Protocol, the timing of events suggests that lobbying may have been an effective tactic for pro-Protocol activists.

Consciousness-Raising Activities

To raise the public's awareness of the Maputo Protocol and to mobilize public opinion, activists organized a variety of consciousness-raising activities, from press conferences to workshops to documentary screenings, in both democratic and authoritarian states. Taking advantage of the widespread use of mobile phones, the campaign encouraged people to register support for the Protocol by sending text messages and to sign up for free alerts about the campaign's progress. As reported by one advocacy organization, SOAWR received approximately 1,000 requests for text message alerts in a six-month period (Fahamu 2005: 7).

Demonstrations

Finally, activists also created petitions and organized demonstrations to show that the Protocol had popular support. Reports of petitions and protests,

6. SOAWR Press Release, "Twelve African Leaders Receive Red Cards on Women's Rights at the African Union Summit in Khartoum, Sudan," January 20, 2006. Emphasis in the original.

7. Joshua Ogada. "Africa: SOAWR Update on the Protocol on the Rights of Women in Africa." *Pambazuka* 302, May 4, 2007. Accessed at http://www.pambazuka.org/en/category/wgender/41217.

8. "Women's Rights Protocol: Challenges of Domestication," *Pambazuka News* 222, September 20, 2005. Accessed at http://www.pambazuka.org/en/issue/222.

however, were relatively rare. Petitions and protests require the participation of greater numbers of people and special incentives or conditions to overcome the collective action problem. SOAWR organized an online petition. By their count, SOAWR had 3,849 signatures from individuals in nearly every African country (the exceptions are Chad, Gabon, Libya, Madagascar, and Sao Tome and Principe). Individuals signed the petition from other countries such as Canada, New Zealand, Pakistan, Turkey, Vietnam, the United Kingdom, and the United States.[9] In Djibouti, pro-Protocol activists in 2004 distributed a petition for the ratification of the Maputo Protocol and collected 383 signatures in the Protocol's favor.[10] I found reports of petitions or protests in three other countries: Republic of Congo, Uganda, and Zimbabwe. In the Republic of Congo, women's civil society groups held a march on International Women's Day in 2010 in which activists called for the Protocol's ratification.[11] In Zimbabwe, women's activists marched in the streets to call for the ratification of the Protocol in 2007.[12]

STRATEGIES USED TO OPPOSE THE MAPUTO PROTOCOL

Just as feminist civil society actors sought to advance women's interests by calling upon their governments to ratify the Maputo Protocol, others sought to advance women's interests by asking their government to *not* ratify the Protocol. Opponents of the Maputo Protocol used a multilevel strategy in their mobilization against the treaty in democracies and autocracies.

While some civil society groups opposed the Protocol, mobilization against the treaty was not as widespread as support in its favor (see Table 8.3). I found reports of public mobilization against the Protocol in nine countries: Burundi, Cameroon, Democratic Republic of the Congo, Ghana, Kenya, Madagascar, Niger, Tanzania, and Uganda. Public contestation over the Protocol was particularly rare in predominantly Muslim countries. Out of 18 predominantly Muslim countries in the African Union, I found reports of public opposition to the Protocol in one, the Republic of Niger.[13] This lack

9. "Petition Signatories." Accessed at http://www.pambazuka.org/en/petition/signatures.php.

10. "Campaign Update: What's Happening Around the Continent?" *Pambazuka* 190, January 20, 2005. Accessed at http://www.pambazuka.org/en/category/features/26462/print.

11. Lydie Gisèle Oko and Yvette Reine Nzaba. "Les Congolaises organisent une marche." *Dépêches de Brazzaville*, March 9, 2010. Accessed at www.brazzaville-adiac.com/medias/.../PDF942.pdf.

12. Nqobani Ndlovu. "Women Lawyers Protest over Protocol." *The Standard*, December 16, 2007. Accessed at: http://allafrica.com/stories/200712170538.html.

13. Predominantly Muslim countries are those where more than 50.1% of the population is Muslim. They are Algeria, Burkina Faso, Chad, Comoros, Djibouti, Egypt,

Table 8.3. COUNTRIES WITH REPORTS OF ANTI-PROTOCOL MOBILIZATION, 2003–2010 (MONTH AND YEAR OF FIRST INSTANCE)

1. Burundi (June 2007)
2. Cameroon (June 2009)
3. Democratic Republic of Congo (February 2007)
4. Ghana (April 2007)
5. Kenya (September 2004)
6. Madagascar (December 2007)
7. Niger (September 2006)
8. Tanzania (April 2007)
9. Uganda (January 2006)

Sources: AllAfrica.com and *Madagascar Tribune*.

of opposition surprised me because in previous research, I examined why women mobilized against the Protocol in Niger and found that they had rational reasons for doing so (Kang 2010). I expected other neighboring or predominantly Muslim countries to experience similar kinds of public contestation over the Protocol.

In the remaining eight of the nine countries, Catholic groups opposed the Protocol, but there is another surprise here. Opposition does not seem to correlate with the percentage of the population that is Catholic (see Table 8.4).

For one, opposition from Catholic groups emerged in countries where Catholics constitute a minority: Cameroon (39%), Ghana (10%), Kenya (30%), Madagascar (20%), and Uganda (35%) (Fox 2004).[14] In countries with similar proportions of Catholics, such as Benin, Zambia, Lesotho, and Swaziland, I did not find reports of anti-Protocol protests. Second, where Catholics constitute the majority, I found reports of anti-Protocol mobilization in two countries (Burundi and Democratic Republic of Congo) but not in the other two (Cape Verde and Rwanda). The lack of anti-Protocol mobilization in Cape Verde and Rwanda can be explained partly by timing: Cape Verde and Rwanda ratified the treaty quickly, in 2005 and 2004, respectively. Yet, Kenya saw anti-Protocol agitation as early as 2004. The connection between Catholicism and anti-Protocol activism is not as simple as one might think.

Networking across Borders

Anti-Protocol activists came together outside their countries, as did pro-Protocol activists. In March 2007, the Standing Committee of the

Gambia, Guinea, Libya, Mali, Mauritania, Niger, Nigeria, Senegal, Sierra Leone, Somalia, Sudan, and Tunisia (Pew Forum 2009).
14. Pew Forum (2011) is used to fill in missing information on Cameroon.

Table 8.4. COUNTRIES WITH CATHOLIC MINORITIES
AND MAJORITIES (ABOVE 10%)

Country	Percent Catholic
1. Cape Verde	90
2. Burundi	**60**
3. Rwanda	55
4. Democratic Republic of Congo	**50**
5. Congo	40
6. Cameroon	**39**
7. Angola	38
8. Lesotho	38
9. Uganda	**35**
10. Kenya	**30**
11. Zambia	28
12. Mauritius	26
13. Central African Republic	25
14. Tanzania	**24**
15. Benin	21
16. Madagascar	**20**
17. Togo	20
18. Malawi	20
19. Cote d'Ivoire	20
20. Namibia	18
21. Zimbabwe	16
22. Mozambique	16
23. Ghana	**10**
24. Swaziland	10

Note: Countries in bold saw anti-Protocol activism.
Sources: Fox (2004). For Cameroon: Pew Forum (2011).

Symposium of Episcopal Conferences of Africa and Madagascar (SECAM) met in Accra, Ghana. On their agenda was the Maputo Protocol.[15] Speaking in Ghana at a press briefing after the meeting, Cardinal Polycarp Pengo of Tanzania said, "we admire the efforts of some of the United Nations Committees, like the International Committee of the Convention for the Elimination of every type of Discrimination Against the Woman (CEDAW)," but "we equally denounce the unchallenged pressure they are exerting on Countries in Africa." Pengo asked African leaders to reconsider the Protocol: "We respectfully request all the Governments of Africa to remove from the Protocol Article 14 # 1, e and 2, c and

15. "Press Release," *Daily Mail*, March 27, 2007. Accessed at http://allafrica.com/stories/200703270231.html. "SECAM Committee Discusses Report on Evangelization," *Catholic Information Service for Africa*, March 27, 2007, http://allafrica.com/stories/200703270681.html.

so defend our African cultural and religious values with regard to the sacredness of life, before the final ratification of the Protocol."[16]

Archbishops and bishops from Burundi, Democratic Republic of Congo, and Rwanda reached a similar conclusion at a meeting of the Association of the Episcopal Conferences of Central Africa (ACEAC) in June 2007. Out of a concern for protecting "African family values" and "women as mothers and source of life," the ACEAC declared that it opposed the article granting African women the right to abortion.[17] International meetings provided a reason for Catholic leaders to come together and a space for them to identify their positions on the Maputo Protocol.

Lobbying, Consciousness-Raising, and Demonstrations

Anti-Protocol activists also mobilized on the ground in democracies and autocracies. Opponents of the Protocol lobbied political actors to sway the government from ratifying the treaty. In Niger, opponents asked the government and parliamentarians to refuse to ratify the Protocol. Opponents in Kenya met with President Kibaki to express their disapproval in June 2007. Anti-Protocol activists also sought to demonstrate that the public was on their side through petitions. In June 2009, activists organized a petition in Doula, Cameroon, against the Protocol for "legalizing homosexuality and abortion."[18] Finally, opponents took to the streets in protest against the Maputo Protocol. In July 2009, opponents organized a march of silence over Article 14 in Cameroon.[19] In Niger, dozens of women demonstrated against the Protocol in front of the National Assembly in September 2006.[20]

Civil society actors in Africa are mobilizing around women's interests. The question remains: Are women's activists and their opponents influencing whether governments represent women's interests? I address this question in the following section with an empirical test. This analysis directly addresses

16. Isabella Gyau Orhin, "Catholic Bishops Advocate Removal of Abortion Provisions in the African Charter," *Public Agenda*, April 16, 2007. Accessed at http://allafrica.com/stories/200704161064.html.

17. "Le droit à l'avortement de femmes en Afrique: Les Evêques du Burundi, RDC et Ruanda s'opposent au Protocole de Maputo," *La Prospérité,* June 21, 2007. Accessed at http://fr.allafrica.com/stories/200706210465.html.

18. Note that the Protocol does not make reference to homosexuality. Pierre-Marie Djongo. "De Maputo—Le rôle trouble de la France," *Le Messager*, July 1, 2009. Accessed at http://fr.allafrica.com/stories/200907010578.html.

19. Eric Vincent Fomo. "Avortement—Quand le protocole de Maputo anime le débat," *Cameroon Tribune*, July 13, 2009. Accessed at http://fr.allafrica.com/stories/200907130874.html.

20. Laoual Sallaou Ismaël. "Les femmes musulmanes interpellent le gouvernement," *Roue de l'histoire,* September 13, 2006.

Proposition 3, presented in Chapter 1, regarding the different and multiple venues in which policy is made by government.

DOES CIVIL SOCIETY INFLUENCE THE RATIFICATION OF THE MAPUTO PROTOCOL?

In this section, I analyze whether civil society groups affected the speed of the Protocol's ratification in 47 countries.[21] The dependent variable is the likelihood of country i ratifying the Maputo Protocol on the Rights of Women in year t (African Union 2011). The unit of observation is the country-year. In the data set, a country is included while it is "at risk" of experiencing the event. Once a country ratifies the Protocol, it exits the data set. All countries enter the data set in 2003, the year the Protocol first became open for ratification. The study period ends in 2010. I use Cox proportional hazard models, which allows me to estimate the effects of covariates on duration time without parameterizing time-dependency. Because Cox models assume that the effect of each covariate is constant, i.e., proportional, over time, I look for violations of the proportionality assumption by calculating scaled Schoenfeld residuals for each covariate.[22]

The central independent variables are mobilization for and mobilization against the Protocol. *Mobilization for the Protocol* equals 1 once a national newspaper or international news wire reports that a societal actor advocated for the ratification of the Maputo Protocol, and 0 otherwise. For instance, for Uganda, I marked that mobilization started in 2007. A Ugandan newspaper reported that Akina Mama wa Afrika said they discussed the Protocol's ratification with a gender minister.[23] I found reports by conducting a search on AllAfrica.com's database for the following combinations of keywords: < Protocol> <women> <rights>; < Charter> <women> <rights>; < Maputo> <women> <rights>. For countries with no national newspapers in AllAfrica.com's database, I searched national newspapers' websites by using the "Search within a site or domain" specification in Google's advanced search. The data collection included newspapers in English, French, Portuguese, and Spanish. Using this search method, I find reports of pro-Protocol mobilization in 23 countries between July 2003 and December 2010. Fifteen of the 23 ratified

21. Morocco is excluded from the study because it was not a member of the African Union during the study period. Libya, Sao Tome and Principe, Seychelles, Somalia, and Zimbabwe are excluded due to missing data. South Sudan was not a state until 2011 and is not included.

22. The results concerning mobilization remain substantively similar when using Weibull event history models.

23. Geresom Musamali. "Kadaga Appeals to Govt Over Women Rights Law." *New Vision*, August 9, 2007. Accessed at http://allafrica.com/stories/200708100088.html.

the Protocol. *Mobilization against the Protocol* equals 1 once a national newspaper or international news wire reports that a societal actor moved against the ratification of the Maputo Protocol, and 0 otherwise. I find reports of anti-Protocol mobilization in nine countries. Of those nine, five countries ratified the Protocol (Democratic Republic of Congo, Ghana, Kenya, Tanzania, Uganda).

Because measuring mobilization through newspapers has limitations (Earl et al. 2004), I also use an organization-based measure of mobilization as an alternative proxy. This measure follows Soule and Olzak (2004), who used the presence of an in-state chapter of the American Association of University Women, an organization that explicitly backed the ERA's ratification, as a proxy for pro-ERA mobilization. *SOAWR-WiLDAF* equals 1 if, in 2003, there was an in-country office of Solidarity for African Women's Rights (SOAWR) or of Women in Law and Development in Africa (WiLDAF), and 0 otherwise (Butegwa 1995; WiLDAF 2001; author communication with SOAWR). I chose to examine membership in SOAWR and WiLDAF in 2003 due to data availability. (Some countries did open an office later.) Twenty-four African countries had a national chapter of one or both of the pro-Protocol networks in 2003.

The models include six control variables. *Women in Parliament* is the percentage of women in the lower house of the national legislature or in the unicameral parliament (Inter-Parliamentary Union 2011). *Women in Parliament* ranges from 0 (Comoros in 2003) to 48.75 (Rwanda in 2004), with an average of 13.08%. Women in parliament may also represent women's interests (Escobar-Lemmon et al., Chapter 11 of this volume; Kittilson 2008; Reingold and Haynie, Chapter 10 of this volume; Schwindt-Bayer 2006; Swers, Chapter 9 of this volume). I expect that as the percentage of women in parliament increases, the speed of ratification increases.

Two controls take into account the country's political opportunity structure (see Beckwith, Chapter 2 of this volume). To control for regime type, I use *Level of Democracy* as measured by the Polity IV Project (Marshall and Jaggers 2010). Democracy ranges from -10 (full autocracy) to 10 (full democracy). In this study's sample, *Level of Democracy* ranges from -9 (Swaziland, all years) to 10 (Mauritius, all years). The average across all years and countries is 0.97. As *Level of Democracy* increases, I expect the pace of ratification to increase. This is because autocrats may support pro-women's rights in theory, but may undermine women's rights in practice. This false support for women's interests in autocracies is known as "First ladies syndrome," "wifeism," and "femocracy" (Abdullah 1995; Ibrahim 2004; Mama 1997; Okeke 1998; Tsikata 1998). Democracies, however, may be slow to ratify the Protocol as well. If the space for democratic debate is closed (Walsh 2010), then one would expect democratically elected governments to be slow at ratifying the Protocol. Further, the most organized and sustained anti-Protocol movements arose in the democracies of Kenya and Niger. Kenya ratified the Protocol relatively late, in 2010.

To control for regime ideology, *Left Leader or Government* equals 1 if the country's leader or ruling party is Left-leaning, and 0 otherwise (Beck et al. 2001). Out of 265 country years, a Left-leaning president or government was in power in 67 years. Countries that had leftist rule while they were at risk are Algeria, Angola, Cape Verde, Congo, Cote d'Ivoire, Lesotho, Libya, Mozambique, Namibia, Senegal, South Africa, Tanzania, Tunisia, and Zambia. Some countries become Left-leaning over time, such as Guinea-Bissau and Sierra Leone. I expect that ratification occurs more quickly when a Left-leaning government is in power. Scholars have shown that Left-leaning leaders in democracies and autocracies are more likely to adopt gender quotas and gender equality policies (Caul 2001; Charrad 2001; Htun 2003a; Tripp and Hughes n.d.), though Left party rule does not always translate into the adoption of other types of women-friendly policies (Htun and Power 2006; Kittilson 2008; Mazur 2002: 189, 197). I expect Left-leaning governments to ratify the Protocol more quickly in democracies and autocracies.

The fourth control variable addresses external incentives. *Foreign Aid* is the natural log of net official development assistance per capita in current US dollars in the previous year (World Bank 2011). *Foreign Aid* ranges from -2.30 to 6.00, with an average of 3.57. A government might ratify the Protocol to demonstrate to foreign governments and international organizations its commitment to liberalism. I expect ratification to happen more quickly when governments rely more on foreign aid. In alternative models not presented here, I include other proxies for foreign incentives, such as whether there is a liberalizing United Nations peacekeeping force in the country (Bush 2011).

Finally, I control for religious demographics and wealth. *Catholic* is the percentage of the country that is Catholic (Fox 2004; Pew Forum 2011). *Catholic* varies from 0 to 90, and the mean is 15.95. Alternative models examine the hypothesis that predominantly Muslim countries are less open to international women's rights norms (Fish 2002, 2011; Inglehart and Norris 2003; Poe et al. 1997). The percentage of Muslims in the country does not negatively influence the likelihood of ratification. *GDP per Capita* is the natural log of gross domestic product per capita of the previous year (World Bank 2011). The natural log of GDP per capita varies from 5.52 to 10.36, with an average of 7.46. Modernization theorists posit that post-industrial countries are more open toward norms of gender equality (Inglehart and Norris 2003). According to the modernization hypothesis, higher levels of wealth should have a positive influence on the ratification of the Protocol.

Table 8.5 reports the results in terms of hazard ratios. Hazard ratios estimate the change in odds of policy adoption given a one-unit change in the independent variable. When hazard ratios are greater than 1, this suggests a faster pace of ratification. Hazard ratios less than one indicate a slower pace of ratification. The results show that the mobilization of women's activists increases the pace at which the government ratifies the Maputo Protocol.

The baseline model in Table 8.5 does not include mobilization. The political opportunity structure seems to matter. The hazard ratio for *Women in Parliament* is greater than one, as expected. The higher the level of democracy, the faster the country is likely to ratify the Protocol. Countries appear to be at greater risk of ratifying the Protocol more quickly if there is a Left-leaning leader or government in power. Contrary to our expectations, higher levels of dependence on foreign aid does not correlate with a faster pace of ratifying the Protocol. Note as well that the percentage of the country that is Catholic and level of GDP per capita do not appear to influence the ratification of the Protocol.

Table 8.5. THE DETERMINANTS OF THE RATIFICATION OF THE AFRICAN UNION MAPUTO PROTOCOL, 2003–2010 (COX EVENT HISTORY ANALYSIS)

Variables	Baseline Model	Mobilization Model	Democracies Only Model	Autocracies Only Model
Mobilization for the		3.9910***	3.6480**	5.3687*
Protocol		(1.6395)	(2.2562)	(3.4840)
Mobilization against		1.7204	1.5607	2.2204
the Protocol		(1.3775)	(1.4390)	(1.9599)
Women in Parliament	1.0425*	1.0474*	.9683	1.0601
	(.0258)	(.0262)	(.0435)	(.0391)
Level of Democracy	1.1196**	1.0992**		
	(.0500)	(.0465)		
Left Leader or	1.9300*	1.6782	8.2457***	.7882
Government	(.7070)	(.7294)	(5.2831)	(.4306)
Foreign Aid	1.0031	1.1664		
	(.2639)	(.3636)		
Catholic	.9973	1.0008		
	(.0096)	(.0105)		
GDP per Capita	.8124	.8576		
	(.1483)	(.1471)		
Log pseudolikelihood	−84.3845	−78.4896	−22.9654	−37.0800
Number of countries	47	47	17	30
Number of failures	26	26	12	14
Observations	265	265	81	184

Note: Hazard ratios are estimated using the Efron method for ties. Robust standard errors, clustered by country, in parentheses. *$p < 0.10$, **$p < 0.05$, ***$p < 0.01$.

What happens when we include activism for and against the Protocol? I find a strong relationship between women's activism and the Protocol's ratification (Table 8.5, second column). When women's advocates publicly call on their governments to ratify the Maputo Protocol, governments are significantly faster to ratify the Protocol. Religious opposition to the Protocol, by contrast, does not appear to be effective. This may be due to the relatively late timing of opposition. The earliest instance of opposition against the Protocol I found was in a September 2004 speech at a seminar on women's rights in Nairobi. Mirugi Kariuki, assistant minister of foreign affairs, who would later become a parliamentarian and human rights advocate, "lamented that [Kenya] had not ratified the pact," which was "being criticized by religious organizations because it included abortion."[24] Kenya aside, the majority of anti-Protocol activity took place *after* the Protocol entered into force. In robustness tests, the variable for *Women in Parliament* does not consistently obtain significance at the .10 level. The degree to which a country is democratic is important for the pace of ratification.

The last two models split the countries into democracies and autocracies to examine whether pro- and anti-Protocol activism influences the speed of the Protocol's ratification under different regimes. Countries that scored a six or higher from the Polity IV Project in 2003, 2004, or 2005 were coded as democracies. The results in the last two columns should be interpreted with care, given the relatively small number of countries and observations in the models. Results for the first group, democracies, are shown in the third column of Table 8.5. The importance of women's activism on the pace of ratification remains strong. Mobilization against the Protocol does not appear to significantly affect the speed of ratification in democracies. Within democracies, countries with Left-leaning leaders and governments are significantly faster to ratify the Protocol. Contrary to my expectation, Left-leaning governments in autocratic regimes do not appear to be faster to ratify the Protocol. Among autocracies, governments are also quicker to ratify the Protocol when there is women's activism for the treaty, including in alternative models where I include foreign aid and GDP as control variables, neither of which are significantly related to the time it takes governments to ratify the Protocol. Again, the findings are preliminary, given the limited number of cases in the split samples.

Women's activism is the only explanatory variable in Table 8.5 that has a strong and consistent relationship across different models. This finding holds in a variety of robustness checks. The importance of women's activism holds when the models use an alternative measure of women's activism, *SOAWR-WiLDAF* (models not shown). The impact of women's mobilization on

24. "Equality Bill to Go Back to Parliament," *Daily Nation*, September 21, 2004. Accessed at http://allafrica.com/stories/200409210073.html.

the Maputo Protocol holds when the models replace a dichotomous measure of Muslim-majority population with a continuous variable (Pew Forum 2009). Different sources sometimes produce different lists of Muslim-majority countries, so I alternatively use Fish's (2002) and Fox's (2004) lists. Others have found that it is not religion per se, but state-church relations that influence women's rights reforms (Simmons 2009). Therefore, I include a measure of state religion (Fox 2004). To assess whether large oil rents create a structural impediment for the enjoyment of women's rights (Ross 2008), I add a variable measuring net oil and gas exports as a percentage of Gender-related Development Index (GDI) to the models (World Bank 2011). The central findings about the effect of pro-Protocol mobilization remain substantively similar.[25] Finally, leverage analysis suggested that Burkina Faso, Democratic Republic of Congo, Guinea-Bissau, and Mauritania are outliers. When these countries are excluded one at a time, pro-Protocol mobilization remains a positive and significant influence on the Protocol's ratification.

IMPLICATIONS OF THE STUDY

This chapter has provided an empirical analysis of who in civil society claims to represent women's interests and how civil society groups seek to influence policy outcomes. Civil society groups employ a variety of strategies over time and across the continent, which is evidence in support of Implication 3.2 from Chapter 1: success in realizing the translation of preferences into policy is greater when women have an influential voice in multiple venues.

Implications for *Who* Represents Women's Interests

One implication of this study is that a wide range of actors outside the state are actively involved in the representation of women's interests. I find that women's activism is the strongest determinant of the timing of ratification. Women's activism appears to matter more than the proportion of women in parliament, though in two out of the four models, *Women in Parliament* gains statistical significance. It is possible that this study's measure of women's representation does not adequately measure the substantive importance of female parliamentarians or female cabinet members, who may serve as crucial allies for women's groups.

Future work should examine not just the percentages of women in office or in cabinet, but whether and when women in office and in cabinet form alliances

25. Future research could examine why some countries ratified the Protocol with reservations, but the African Union has not released such information.

with women's groups. Dahlerup (Chapter 4 of this volume) argues that movements have to work to build a common ground, and makes a similar call for research that examines the conditions under which women from multiple venues form coalitions and work together. The anecdotal evidence suggests that these alliances matter. Indeed, many of the women's activists involved in promoting the Protocol were judges and ministers, who include women and men. As Maria Escobar-Lemmon et al. (Chapter 11 of this volume) find, male ministers do propose bills that seek to advance women's interests; male members of cabinet may serve as important allies for civil society. This analysis thus can be interpreted to provide support for Implication 3.1—access to the right venue is critical for the ability of representatives of women's interests to change policy—but it also indicates the need for more investigation of the factors that make a venue the "right venue." Only further research can tell us whether and under what conditions women in African parliaments and women in African cabinets are substantive representatives. Thus far, case study evidence goes in both directions (e.g., Beck 2003; Goetz and Hassim 2003; Hassim 2006; Tripp et al. 2008).

A second implication from this study is that civil society groups sometimes but not always conflict over women's issues. I was surprised by the relative lack of public debate over the issue of abortion and other potentially contentious issues, such as the age of marriage and polygamy, in the Maputo Protocol. Perhaps my surprise stems from the context in which I live, in the United States, where debates over abortion and contraception seem perennial. As Hancock (Chapter 3 of this volume) argues, race, ethnicity, gender, and other markers including religion are not static or homogenous categories. Let me be clear that I do not claim that African women enjoy free access to reproductive health; women face real hurdles in obtaining quality health care. Rather, I suggest that scholars further study the conditions in which opposing groups emerge. Africa provides a rich and diverse terrain in which to study the representation of women's interests—both who seeks to represent women's interests, and how they try to do so.

Implications for *How* the Representation of Women Occurs

A final implication from this study is that advocacy for women's interests is happening at multiple levels. Transnational networking is being employed by advocates and opponents. Advocates and opponents of the Maputo Protocol formulated and articulated their policy preferences in international arenas. Thus far, scholars have examined how transnational networking advances the representation of women's interests (e.g., Keck and Sikkink 1998; True and

Mintrom 2001). This chapter finds that much of the opposition to the Maputo Protocol came from groups in the transnational network of the Catholic Church. This suggests that the more conservative religious groups meet internationally, the more opportunities they have to discuss and claim to represent women's interests.

CHAPTER 9

Unpacking Women's Issues

Gender and Policymaking on Health Care, Education,

and Women's Health in the US Senate

MICHELE L. SWERS

Research on the US House of Representatives and state legislatures demonstrates that women are more active proponents of legislation concerning women's issues, variously defined. However, scholars generally do not unpack the universe of women's issues to determine if the influence of gender stems from activism on specific policy issues. Moreover, we lack a clear understanding of how gender and party reputations for policy expertise interact to create incentives for legislating on issues. Additionally, the political opportunity structure channels legislators' interests as issues arise in the public consciousness, and institutional dynamics encourage activity on specific policies. Focusing on the US Senate, an institution in which members have more freedom to pursue their policy priorities, I analyze gender differences in the activism of senators on health care and education, two prominent components of social welfare policy. I also examine senators' engagement of women's health, a policy domain directly connected to women's rights. Thus, health care, education, and women's health constitute the *what interests* analyzed in this chapter, and senators are the *who* that are representing these interests. The analysis incorporates the agenda-setting activities of sponsorship and cosponsorship in the 107th and 108th Congresses (2001–2004) as well as amending activity on two major initiatives, the No Child Left Behind education law in the 107th Congress and the Medicare Prescription Drug law in the 108th Congress.

I demonstrate that gender is an important predictor of activism on health care, an area that dominates the congressional agenda and consumes a large portion of the federal budget. However, gender has little impact on engagement of education once one accounts for other influences on senators' legislative activity, including party, ideology, constituency demand, and committee position. Thus, this chapter adds nuance to Implication 2.1 presented in Chapter 1, which expected that women in government will articulate women's issues more than men.

In addition to a political opportunity structure that has focused congressional attention on health care, senators also develop their priorities with an eye to party reputations. The association of the Democratic Party with social welfare issues like health care and education makes it easier for Democrats to promote these initiatives. Indeed, Democrats offered more proposals on health, education, and women's health issues across both Congresses. Furthermore, the importance of women's groups and women voters to the Democratic coalition encourages Democratic women to champion women's health bills. By contrast, for Republican women, proposals related to safeguarding reproductive rights can alienate the core Republican constituency of social conservatives creating a more complicated calculation for Republican women.

Reflecting Implication 2.2A, this chapter demonstrates that as more women enter government, they will express divergent preferences regarding the articulation of women's interests. Moreover, Implication 1.2 indicates that senators are constrained by the existing power structure. The ability of women to pursue their preferences is limited by what policies powerful interests within their party can support, a significant constraint for Republican women seeking to accommodate conservative interests and powerbrokers.

GENDER DIFFERENCES AND LEGISLATING ON WOMEN'S ISSUES

There is a significant body of research highlighting gender differences in activity on women's issues. While scholars vary in their definitions, the set of legislation incorporating women's issues includes some combination of social welfare policies regarding health care, education, and welfare that constitute the social safety net and are associated with women's traditional role as caregiver, as well as feminist policies concerning the advancement of women's rights such as family leave, sexual harassment, and reproductive rights (Dodson and Carroll 1991; Thomas 1994; Rosenthal 1998; Bratton and Haynie 1999; Reingold 2000; Swers 2002, 2013; Dodson 2006; Osborn 2012). These differences hold, even after accounting for other influences on legislative behavior, including party, ideology, and constituency characteristics.

Yet scholars also find that advocacy of women's issues is both facilitated and constrained by legislators' partisanship, institutional position, and other political context factors. For example, Reignold (2000) finds that partisanship often overwhelms the importance of gender as a predictor of activism on women's issues. Osborn (2012) maintains that party identity shapes female legislators' perception of women's policy problems and the solutions they offer. Focusing on the interaction between partisanship, electoral coalitions, and institutional position, Swers (2002) demonstrates that women in the House of Representatives became more active on social welfare issues when they were in the majority party, indicating that when they have access to the congressional agenda, women increase their participation on the social welfare policies that have constituted a fundamental cleavage between the parties since the New Deal. Moreover, Republican women shifted away from feminist issues when they advanced to the majority because they feared alienating the party's social conservative base.

Given the importance of partisanship and institutional position as guides to how members structure their agendas, it is essential to further examine the influence of institutional structures, party reputations, and electoral dynamics on legislators' decisions to champion specific policies. In this research, I examine senators' activism on three issues that are central components of the broad array of women's issues: general health care, education, and women's health. To date, few scholars have examined gender differences in senators' legislative activity (for exceptions, see Frederick 2010, 2011; Swers 2007, 2008, 2013). I pay particular attention to how features of the political opportunity structure—including party reputations for policy expertise, the elevation of issues on the public agenda, and partisan competition for policy advantage—channel senators' policy preferences into decisions to focus on specific issues.

The Senate is an ideal setting for studying activism in multiple policy areas because the rules of the Senate favor individual and minority party rights, making it easier for senators to insert themselves into multiple policy areas regardless of seniority and committee position. In comparison to House members, whose impact is largely confined to the issues within their committee jurisdictions, senators receive multiple committee assignments (Sinclair 1989; Evans 1991). Because they represent an entire state, senators are expected to engage multiple policy areas, and they oversee large staffs to facilitate activism on a wide range of issues (Schiller 2000; Baker 2001). Finally, in contrast to the House, permissive floor rules allow senators to speak on any topic and offer amendments to legislation, regardless of whether they are germane. Furthermore, senators who are intensely committed to an issue can threaten filibusters (Sinclair 1989, 2009; Binder and Smith 1997; Koger 2010). As a result, all senators have an opportunity to legislate on issues related to general health care, education, and women's health if they so choose. The wide-ranging influence of senators reinforces Implication 3.1, which emphasizes that access to the right venue to achieve policy change is critical for representatives of women's interests. The Senate is a powerful venue, but, as the chapter will show, multiple factors structure the incentives for individual women senators to prioritize some women's interests over others.

A THEORY OF GENDER, POLICY PREFERENCES, AND THE POLITICAL OPPORTUNITY STRUCTURE

I assert that gender is a fundamental identity that interacts with traditional influences on legislative behavior, such as partisanship and constituent interests, to shape senators' priorities. Representation theorists point to patterns of gender role socialization, the history of women's integration into politics, and differences in women's economic standing and opinion on issues to support the idea that women have distinctive if not universally agreed-upon interests (Beckwith, Chapter 2 of this volume; Mansbridge 1999; Sapiro 1981; Phillips 1998). For example, sociological research notes women's role as primary caregivers for children and elderly relatives and tracks the impact on women's career choices and economic standing, including the feminization of poverty, sex segregation of jobs, the wage gap, and retirement insecurity (Conway et al. 2005; Blau and Kahn 2007).

Moreover, scholars find gender differences in public opinion on social welfare policy. In comparison to men, women are more supportive of social welfare spending and they favor a more activist role for government in assisting the poor and guaranteeing a standard of living (Box-Steffensmeier et al. 2004; Norrander 2008). While women's rights issues do not drive the gender gap, abortion is more salient for women, and women are more likely to hold extreme positions on the issue, favoring or opposing abortion in all circumstances (Norrander 2008; Kaufmann 2002; Jelen and Wilcox 2005). Similarly, research on voter stereotypes demonstrates that voters prefer women candidates to handle social welfare issues, including health and education, and they perceive female candidates as more compassionate (Huddy and Terkildsen 1993; Sanbonmatsu 2002a; Dolan 2004; Fridkin and Kenney 2009). Given this evidence, I expect that shared identity will impact women's policy priorities. In line with Implication 2.1 regarding women's greater commitment to women's issues, female senators will be more inclined to activism on issues related to general health care, education, and women's health.

At the same time, candidates run as members of political parties, and their electoral fortunes are shaped by the reputations of the parties. Perceptions about gender interact with party priorities and reputations for issue ownership to structure senators' incentives to focus on specific policy areas. Studies of issue ownership demonstrate that voters trust Democrats more than Republicans to handle social welfare issues like health care and education (Petrocik 1996; Petrocik et al. 2003; Sellers 2010). These social welfare issues are a key driver of the gender gap in recent elections, in which women voters favor the Democratic Party (Schaffner 2005; Norrander 2008; Carroll 2010). Moreover, women's rights issues like abortion are top priorities for the feminist organizations that raise money and mobilize the vote for Democratic candidates (Wolbrecht 2000; Sanbonmatsu 2002b). Indeed, women's groups are particularly supportive of Democratic women candidates, as organizations like EMILY's List donate money and get out the vote for pro-choice female Democratic candidates. Because of the Democratic Party's strong association with social welfare issues and the status of women's groups as central to the Democratic electoral coalition, Democrats, both male and female, should be the most active proponents of bills on health, education, and women's health. Democratic women should be the most active proponents of these issues as voter stereotypes about gender and issue expertise align with the issue strengths of the Democratic Party and female Democrats often benefit from the strong support of women's organizations.

By contrast, social welfare issues like health care and education are not central to the Republican message of lower taxes, less government spending, and reducing regulation on business (Petrocik 1996; Sellers 2010). Therefore, Republicans should be less active than Democrats on these issues. However, for Republican women, the party and gender cues provide conflicting information to voters. Gender-based preferences and voter expectations about women's policy expertise should encourage Republican women to be more active on social welfare issues than Republican men. Yet Republican women must be cautious about engaging these gender-based preferences because voter perceptions that women are more liberal can hurt Republican women with increasingly conservative primary voters (Koch 1999; King and Matland 2003; Sanbonmatsu and Dolan 2009). In line with Implication 1.2, Republican women will be particularly cautious about pursuing women's health concerns like abortion because engagement of these issues will alienate the social conservative base of the party.

Finally, when constructing their agendas, senators respond to the political opportunity structure. One of the most prominent features of contemporary politics is the increasing polarization of the parties in conjunction with a competitive electoral environment. As a result, senators pursue their policy goals in an ideologically polarized atmosphere in which senators are expected to act as members of partisan teams (Lee 2009; Poole and Rosenthal 1997, 2007). To improve the party brand with voters, party leaders develop messaging strategies to sell party policies and attract voters. While voters may favor Democrats to handle health care, the issue is a central concern of voters, and both parties shape their proposals and message campaigns to compete for policy advantage (Sellers 2010). As they work to persuade the public, the parties may be more inclined to turn to women to sell their message in an effort to capitalize on voters' association of women with social welfare issues. Similarly, women may become more active on these issues in order to help their party attract more women voters. While the gender gap favors Democrats, both parties target sub-groups of women voters. Thus, Democrats work to increase turnout among single women and Republicans seek to mobilize white suburban married women (Norrander 2008; Carroll 2010).

As health care and reproductive rights become more central to the competition between the parties, Democratic women will perceive more opportunities to raise their profile and gain action on issues that reflect their policy priorities and are attractive to the base of Democratic voters and donors. By contrast, the ideological polarization and heighted competition surrounding these issues create conflicting pressures for Republican women. As Democrats work to portray Republican policies as anti-women, party leaders will increasingly turn to Republican women to defend the party and to reach out to women voters who favor Republicans, including suburban married women and evangelical women. More conservative Republican women will need to balance the increased demand for public defense of the party against their desire to achieve action on their larger policy agenda. More moderate Republican women who do not agree with the party on issues like abortion and contraception will be placed in an increasingly difficult position as they seek to represent their own views and the views of their constituency without harming the party.

In addition to polarization and electoral competition, senators' priorities are shaped by other aspects of the political opportunity structure, including the agenda of the president and the level of federal involvement in the issue. If the public considers an issue a high priority and/or the president is focused on an issue, more senators will offer policy proposals in that area. Thus, it is likely that more senators offered bills on education when President Bush was pursuing his No Child Left Behind education initiative. The heightened focus on health care from the plight of the uninsured to rising costs means that more senators will get involved in health care debates. When debates recur year after year, senators will gain more experience with the issue, creating more incentives for senators outside the committee of jurisdiction to develop policy proposals. Similarly, when a policy constitutes a larger part of the federal budget, more senators will want to engage the issue. Comparing health and education spending in fiscal year 2013, Medicare, Medicaid, and other health spending constituted 25% ($877 billion) of federal budget outlays, while only 2% ($71 billion) of the federal budget was spent on education (http://concordcoalition.org/federal-government-spending). Therefore, I expect more senators to engage health care than education because health care programs occupy a much larger share of the federal budget.

ANALYZING SENATORS' POLICY PRIORITIES ON HEALTH CARE, EDUCATION, AND WOMEN'S HEALTH

To examine whether women are more active advocates for policies related to health care, education, and women's health, I analyze senators' sponsorship and cosponsorship activity on these issues in the 107th (2001–2002) and 108th (2003–2004) Congresses. Women constituted 13% of senators in the 107th Congress and 14% of senators in the 108th Congress. Democrats gained the majority in the 107th Congress after Jim Jeffords (VT) left the Republican Party to caucus with the Democrats in May 2001. Republicans regained the majority in the 108th Congress. While the number of women in the Senate is proportionately equivalent to their representation in the House, because there are only 100 senators, gender differences among Republicans must be interpreted with caution. There were only three Republican women serving in the 107th Congress and five in the 108th Congress. There are four Republican women in the current 113th Congress (Center for the American Woman and Politics 2013). To identify the legislation, I read summaries of each senator's bills on THOMAS, the legislative information website of the Library of Congress. I also examine senators' participation in the major debates on health care and education during these Congresses by analyzing their sponsorship and cosponsorship of amendments to the No Child Left Behind Education bill in the 107th Congress and the Medicare Prescription Drug Act in the 108th Congress. Both initiatives were priorities of Republican President George W. Bush, and both were passed into law.

Sponsorship and cosponsorship of bills and amendments are good indicators of senators' interest in issues, as senators use these tools to stake their claim to policy areas and establish their expertise. Sponsoring and cosponsorsing legislation helps members serve both electoral and policy goals. Through sponsorship and cosponsorship, members can support policies that are closer to their preferences and build coalitions in favor of those policies. Senators can also inoculate themselves against criticism from electoral opponents and interest groups by pointing to alternative proposals they have sponsored or cosponsored (Schiller 1995; Koger 2003; Woon 2009; Harward and Moffett 2010).

Turning first to senators' sponsorship and cosponsorship of bills related to general health care, education, and women's health, Table 9.1 indicates that across the 107th and 108th Congresses, senators focused the greatest attention on health care. This greater focus on health care is likely a response to the overall political opportunity structure. Medicare and Medicaid comprise a significant proportion of the federal budget, and the costs of these programs and other federal health initiatives continue to expand as health care costs rise. The public routinely cites health care as among the most important problems facing the country. The failure of President Clinton's national health insurance program catapulted health care to the forefront of the public agenda and intensified the struggle between the parties over the issue. Indeed, after the demise of Clinton's health care plan, Congress created SCHIP to insure more low-income children, the parties battled over a Patients' Bill of Rights, and George W. Bush and the Republican majority pushed through a Medicare prescription drug bill in the 108th Congress (Jacobs and Skocpol 2011). Most recently Congress and President Obama passed the Affordable Care Act, an effort to expand and reform the provision of health insurance coverage. This constant activity on health care means that senators feel they need to develop health care proposals to represent their constituents' interests and influence policy. Once a senator offers a bill on health care, he or she begins to develop expertise to offer more proposals in the area. Moreover, given the long time frame of health debates, the same initiatives can be offered in multiple years.

While Table 9.1 indicates that senators devoted less attention to education, a majority of senators did offer education bills. The slight decrease in the number of education bills offered between the 107th and 108th Congress likely reflects the fact that senators in the 107th Congress increased their activity on education in response to President Bush's focus on his No Child Left Behind education plan. By contrast, only one-third of senators, 37 in the 107th Congress and 27 in the 108th Congress, offered bills on women's health. These issues included efforts to expand health services for pregnant women, funding for research on diseases that predominantly affect women, expansion of coverage for preventive services such as mammograms and pap smears, and bills related to abortion and contraception. Among the 126 women's health bills offered across the two Congresses, there were 22 bills sponsored by Republican men that sought to restrict abortion or impose bans on human cloning and stem cell research.

Table 9.1. SPONSORSHIP AND COSPONSORSHIP: HEALTH CARE, EDUCATION, AND WOMEN'S HEALTH BILLS

	Total Bills	No. Members Sponsor	Mean Bills Sponsored	No. Members Cosponsor	Mean Bills Cosponsored
107th					
Health Care	503	83	5	100	34.2
Education	244	73	2.4	99	11.8
Women's Health	73	37	0.7	92	5.5
108th					
Health Care	515	93	5.2	100	34.2
Education	200	66	2	100	9.5
Women's Health	53	27	0.5	97	5.7

To evaluate partisan and gender differences in senators' policy focus, I divided senators' sponsorship and cosponsorship activity by gender and party (results not shown). Across all issues, Democrats are more likely than Republicans to sponsor and cosponsor health care, education, and women's health bills, reflecting patterns of issue ownership in which the public associates social welfare and women's rights issues with the Democratic Party (Petrocik 1996; Sellers 2010). The one exception is cosponsorship of women's health issues in the 108th Congress, when Republicans and Democrats cosponsored an equivalent number of women's health bills. However, during the 108th Congress, the Republican Party pushed through several initiatives to restrict abortion rights, including the Partial Birth Abortion Ban and the Unborn Victims of Violence Act, a bill that pro-choice groups feared would set a precedent for giving rights to the fetus by creating a separate offense for killing an unborn child in a federal crime. Almost the entire Republican caucus cosponsored these two bills. When bills restricting abortion are removed from the sample, Republicans cosponsor a mean of 3.3 women's health bills and Democrats cosponsor a mean of 5.7 women's health bills.[1]

Turning to gender differences, male and female partisans sponsor similar amounts of legislation on health care and education, with Republican women sponsoring the greatest mean number of health and education bills in the 107th Congress, likely reflecting the activism of the two moderate women from Maine, Olympia Snowe and Susan Collins. The greatest gender differences emerge in cosponsorship. Through cosponsorship senators can express preferences on issues regardless of their level of seniority or institutional position. Women clearly used their cosponsorhip activity to reinforce their commitment to health care (and to a lesser extent education) with voters and to signal other legislators about the saliency of these issues to their agendas. Gender differences are most striking on health care. Democratic women cosponsor the largest number of health care bills across the two Congresses. In comparison to Democratic men, Democratic women cosponsored on average 20 more health bills in the 107th Congress (62.7 v. 42.4) and 28 more health bills in the 108th Congress (71.8 v. 43.4). Republican women cosponsor a mean of 35 more health bills than Republican men in the 107th Congress (54.3 v. 19.4)

1. Because only one-third of members sponsor a women's health bill, I do not include a table for women's health bill sponsorship. In the 107th Congress, 37 members sponsored women's health bills including 12 (29%) Democratic men, 8 (80%) Democratic women, 14 (30%) Republican men, and 3 (100%) Republican women. If bills restricting abortion or contraception are removed, there are 6 (13%) Republican men who sponsored women's health bills. Similarly, in the 108th Congress, 27 senators sponsored women's health bills including 9 Democratic men (23%), 7 (70%) Democratic women, 10 (22%) Republican men, and 1 (20%) Republican woman. When bills restricting reproductive rights are dropped from the sample, 5 (11%) Republican men sponsor women's health bills.

and 16 more health bills than their male partisans in the 108th Congress (34.6 v. 18.8). These patterns suggest that women exhibit gender-based preferences in favor of activism on health care (supporting Implication 2.1), and this tendency to activism is reinforced by the political opportunity structure, as the large number of health bills offered provides more opportunities for women to pursue their commitment to these issues.

Finally, patterns of cosponsorship on women's health support the idea that Democratic women will be more committed to advancing women's health bills because their policy goals on these issues align with the views of Democratic voters and activists who strongly support women's health. Indeed, Democratic women cosponsored twice as many women's health bills as Democratic men in the 107th Congress (14.2 v. 6.1) and three times as many women's health bills as Democratic men in the 108th Congress (12 v. 4.4). Republican women cosponsored approximately the same amount of women's health bills as Democratic men (7.3 v. 6.1, 107th Congress and 4.8 v. 4.4 108th Congress). However, pursuing women's health legislation can bring Republican women into conflict with the socially conservative base of the party. Therefore, these women must be more cautious than Democratic women when deciding which policies to support.[2]

To fully examine the impact of gender on senators' choices, I utilize regression analysis to test whether gender remains a significant influence on senators' policy activities once we account for other predictors of behavior. These influences include partisanship, ideology, constituency interests, and the senators' institutional resources such as his or her committee position.

The negative binomial models in Tables 9.2–9.5 are event count models that allow one to estimate the number of bills that a member with a given set of characteristics will sponsor in a set period of time.[3] The dependent variable is a count of the number of bills/amendments that a senator sponsored or cosponsored in the 107th and 108th Congresses. The independent variables draw on the literature concerning the factors that motivate legislators' policy decisions. Since party affiliation is one of the most reliable guides to senators'

2. In the 108th Congress, when bills that restrict access to abortion and contraception are dropped from the sample, Republican men cosponsor a mean of 3.2 women's health bills and Republican women cosponsor a mean of 4 women's health bills.

3. The most common event count model is the Poisson regression model. This model assumes that the probability of an event occurring at any given time is constant within a specified period and independent of all previous events. However, members who sponsor/cosponsor one health bill may be more likely to sponsor/cosponsor additional health bills, thus violating the assumption of independence. The negative binomial model accounts for this dependence through the dispersion parameter. A dispersion parameter of zero indicates an absence of dispersion and independence of events while a dispersion parameter greater than zero indicates over-dispersion (King 1989). While the dispersion parameters are small and statistically insignificant, I use the negative binomial for theoretical reasons.

Table 9.2. HEALTH SPONSORSHIP AND COSPONSORSHIP MODELS
(Standard Errors in Parentheses)

Independent Variables	107th Sponsor	108th Sponsor	107th Cosponsor	108th Cosponsor
Republican Women	.662^	.594	.316^	.801***
	(.385)	(.466)	(.174)	(.2)
Democratic Women	.047	.021	.256**	.161
	(.229)	(.221)	(.096)	(.109)
Republican Men	.467	.632	.11	.606**
	(.386)	(.43)	(.147)	(.192)
Ideology	−1.15**	−1.4*	−.295^	−.995***
	(.432)	(.556)	(.17)	(.266)
First Term Senator	.285	−.213	−.018	.018
	(.237)	(.284)	(.092)	(.111)
Retiring Senator	−1.49*	−.224	−.328^	.022
	(.649)	(.305)	(.176)	(.152)
State Vote for Bush	.014	.033*	−.003	.003
	(.015)	(.014)	(.006)	(.006)
African American Population	−.047***	−.017	−.009^	.004
	(.015)	(.013)	(.005)	(.005)
Hispanic Population	−.011	.002	−.006	−.002
	(.011)	(.011)	(.005)	(.005)
Median Household Income	−.159	.255	.009	−.067
	(.231)	(.222)	(.09)	(.1)
Urban Population	.014^	−.001	.002	.004
	(.008)	(.009)	(.004)	(.004)
Elderly Population	.083	.154**	.035	.042
	(.058)	(.06)	(.023)	(.026)
Proportion Receiving Public Assistance	.111	.048	.087	.098
	(.073)	(.067)	(.076)	(.086)
Southern State	.752**	.239	.273*	.131
	(.292)	(.285)	(.115)	(.133)
Up for Re-election	.138	−.019	−.03	.092
	(.139)	(.148)	(.06)	(.076)
HELP	.325*	.414*	.075	.076
	(.158)	(.163)	(.072)	(.087)
Finance	.149	.013	.054	.107
	(.179)	(.175)	(.076)	(.08)
Veterans' Affairs	−.176	.142	.135^	.16^
	(.199)	(.184)	(.079)	(.091)
Special Aging	.204	.009	−.034	.054
	(.167)	(.16)	(.068)	(.075)

(Continued)

TABLE 9.2. CONTINUED
(Standard Errors in Parentheses)

Independent Variables	107th Sponsor	108th Sponsor	107th Cosponsor	108th Cosponsor
Appropriations Labor, Health and Human Services, and Education Subcommittee	.136 (.215)	.066 (.191)	.103 (.086)	.055 (.094)
Health Committee Chair	−.129 (.307)	−.007 (.344)	−.007 (.145)	−.316 (.201)
Health Committee Ranking Member	.194 (.359)	−.238 (.297)	−.127 (.166)	−.117 (.154)
Health Subcommittee Chair	.652* (.288)	.398 (.277)	.097 (.13)	−.038 (.157)
Health Subcommittee Ranking Member	.177 (.273)	.414 (.258)	.135 (.123)	−.018 (.134)
Same−State Senator's Health Bills	−.018 (.014)	−.024 (.016)	−.012^ (.006)	−.004 (.007)
Total Bills Sponsored	.032*** (.005)	.027*** (.005)	.008*** (.001)	.007*** (.001)
Constant	−2.25 (2.25)	−4.41* (2.04)	1.69* (.794)	.988 (.823)
Dispersion Parameter	.083 (.045)	.085 (.044)	.026 (.01)	.04 (.011)
Log Likelihood	−209.21	−220.77	−343.8	−344.81
Log Likelihood Ratio Chi Square	123.27	98.41	196.4	199.16
Psuedo−R2	.228	.182	.222	.224
N	100	100	100	100

^p<=.1 *p<=.05 **p<=.01 ***p<=.001.

Note: Health Committee chair and ranking members were the chairs and ranking members of HELP, Finance, Special Committee on Aging, Veterans' Affairs, and the Appropriations Subcommittee on Labor, Health and Human Services, and Education. Health Subcommittee chairs and ranking members were the chairs and ranking members of the subcommittees of the HELP Committee and the Finance Committee's subcommittees on Health and Social Security and Family Policy. The Veterans' Affairs and Special Committee on Aging do not have subcommittees.

policy choices, I created dummy variables for Republican men and women and Democratic women. Democratic men are the comparison category. By examining the interplay between gender and party, I can test, for example, whether assumptions about Democratic Party issue ownership of health care and education and voter perceptions about women's policy expertise lead Democratic women to greater activism on health and education. Thus, a positive and significant coefficient for Democratic women would indicate that relative to Democratic men, being a Democratic woman exerts an even more important

Table 9.3. 107TH AND 108TH EDUCATION SPONSORSHIP AND
COSPONSORSHIP MODELS
(Standard Errors in Parentheses)

Independent Variables	107th Sponsor	108th Sponsor	107th Cosponsor	108th Cosponsor
Republican Women	.86*	–.829	.067	.472^
	(.381)	(.589)	(.221)	(.286)
Democratic Women	–.299	.205	–.038	–.109
	(.268)	(.245)	(.12)	(.144)
Republican Men	.122	–1.13*	.116	.264
	(.398)	(.553)	(.191)	(.279)
Ideology	–.367	.669	–.346	–.748*
	(.455)	(.688)	(.229)	(.377)
First Term Senator	–.368	–.033	–.013	–.024
	(.329)	(.417)	(.119)	(.16)
Retiring Senator	–1.17^	.29	–.277	–.039
	(.622)	(.332)	(.243)	(.211)
State Vote for Bush	.008	.025	–.003	–.004
	(.017)	(.02)	(.009)	(.01)
African American Population	–.023^	–.03^	.009	.001
	(.013)	(.017)	(.008)	(.009)
Hispanic Population	–.019	–.033*	.0003	–.006
	(.013)	(.015)	(.007)	(.008)
Median Household Income	.238	.131	–.033	–.123
	(.231)	(.249)	(.113)	(.142)
Urban Population	.008	.021*	–.001	.003
	(.009)	(.011)	(.004)	(.005)
Youth Population (under 18)	.03	–.081	–.042	.028
	(.072)	(.077)	(.036)	(.043)
Proportion without a High School Diploma	.097**	.037	–.004	–.009
	(.033)	(.038)	(.018)	(.022)
Southern State	...	...	.162	.16
			(.152)	(.196)
Small State	...	...	.211*	.064
			(.1)	(.126)
Up for Re–election	.362*	–.065	.061	–.163
	(.153)	(.213)	(.08)	(.122)
HELP	.576**	.729***	.307***	.369**
	(.196)	(.228)	(.094)	(.125)
Appropriations Labor, Health and Human Services, and Education Subcommittee	.504*	.013	.303**	.039
	(.213)	(.232)	(.104)	(.125)

(Continued)

TABLE 9.3. CONTINUED
(Standard Errors in Parentheses)

Independent Variables	107th Sponsor	108th Sponsor	107th Cosponsor	108th Cosponsor
Education Committee Chair	−.125	1.3**	−.328	−.341
	(.335)	(.468)	(.217)	(.442)
Education Committee Ranking Member	−.0003	−.459	−.229	−.241
	(.551)	(.475)	(.296)	(.258)
HELP Subcommittee Chair	.468	.485	.266	.202
	(.309)	(.389)	(.169)	(.244)
HELP Subcommittee Ranking Member	.271	.532	.207	.201
	(.352)	(.39)	(.198)	(.227)
Same–State Senator's Education Bills	.042	−.004	.004	−.008
	(.034)	(.043)	(.016)	(.02)
Total Bills Sponsored	.025***	.036***	.006***	.007***
	(.005)	(.006)	(.001)	(.001)
Constant	−4.72*	−1.79	2.48*	.641
	(2.2)	(2.03)	(1.04)	(1.24)
Dispersion Parameter	0	0	.011	.028
	(0)	(0)	(.014)	(.022)
Log Likelihood	−162.5	−146.87	−262.46	−249.67
Log Likelihood Ratio Chi Square	88.82	87.97	147.95	149.33
Psuedo–R2	.215	.231	.22	.23
N	100	100	100	100

^p<=.1 *p<=.05 **p<=.01 ***p<=.001.
Note: The Education Committee chairs and ranking members were the chairs and ranking members of the HELP Committee and the Appropriations Subcommittee on Labor, Health and Human Services, and Education. The Education Subcommittee chairs and ranking members are the chairs and ranking members of the HELP subcommittees.

influence on the decision to sponsor/cosponsor a health (or education or women's health) bill.

I utilize Poole and Rosenthal's DW-NOMINATE scores as an indicator of senators' ideology (Poole and Rosenthal 1997).[4] The scores range from -1, most liberal, to +1, most conservative. Therefore, an expected negative relationship between ideology and sponsorship would indicate that more liberal members promote health, education, and women's health initiatives. These scores allow me to capture intraparty differences in priorities among liberal and conservative Democrats and moderate and conservative Republicans.[5]

4. The DW-NOMINATE data can be accessed at http://voteview.com/index.asp.
5. Party affiliation and ideology are highly correlated, with a correlation coefficient of .91 in the 107th Congress and .93 in the 108th Congress. This high level of correlation creates problems of multicolinearity. However, the fact that the gender-party variables are often significant even after accounting for ideology indicates that the

Table 9.4. WOMEN'S HEALTH COSPONSORSHIP MODELS
(Standard Errors in Parentheses)

Independent Variables	107th	108th
Republican Women	−.357	.017
	(.352)	(.358)
Democratic Women	.701***	.705***
	(.149)	(.184)
Republican Men	−.128	.021
	(.282)	(.333)
Ideology	.361	1.53***
	(.324)	(.455)
First Term Senator	−.004	.088
	(.15)	(.167)
Retiring Senator	.211	.024
	(.311)	(.258)
State Vote for Bush	−.012	.004
	(.01)	(.011)
African American Population	.016^	.016^
	(.008)	(.009)
Hispanic Population	.007	.008
	(.008)	(.009)
Median Household Income	.344*	.384*
	(.146)	(.173)
Urban Population	−.008	−.001
	(.006)	(.007)
Elderly Population	.07	.072
	(.043)	(.046)
Southern State	−.265	−.37^
	(.213)	(.225)
Small State	.169	−.094
	(.144)	(.155)
Up for Re-election	−.103	.156
	(.111)	(.133)
HELP	.184	.161
	(.118)	(.139)
Finance	.118	.161
	(.133)	(.134)
Appropriations Labor, Health and Human Services, and Education Subcommittee	.353*	.1
	(.149)	(.156)
Women's Health Committee Chair	.535*	−.298
	(.233)	(.34)

(Continued)

TABLE 9.4. CONTINUED
(Standard Errors in Parentheses)

Independent Variables	107th	108th
Women's Health Committee Ranking Member	−.528 (.38)	.37 (.313)
Women's Health Subcommittee Chair	−.219 (.213)	−.025 (.215)
Women's Health Subcommittee Ranking Member	.232 (.238)	−.326 (.244)
Same–State Senator's Women's Health Bills	.059^ (.034)	.025 (.047)
Total Bills Cosponsored	.007*** (.001)	.007*** (.001)
Constant	−1.07 (1.32)	−2.53^ (1.49)
Dispersion Parameter	0 (0)	.024 (.026)
Log Likelihood	−207.43	−218.52
Log Likelihood Ratio Chi Square	137.92	102.29
Psuedo–R2	.25	.19
N	100	100

^p<=.1 *p<=.05 **p<=.01 ***p<=.001.
Note: Women's Health Committee chairs and ranking members are the chairs and ranking members of HELP, Finance, and the Appropriations Subcommittee on Labor, Health and Human Services, and Education. The Women's Health Subcommittee chairs and ranking members are the chairs and ranking members of HELP and the Finance Committee's Subcommittees on Health and Social Security and Family Policy.

To assess constituent demand for legislation on health care, education, and women's health, I include census data measuring characteristics of each state: median household income, urban population, African American population, Hispanic population, the state's elderly population (over 65), the school age population, the proportion of state residents without a high school degree, and the proportion of residents receiving public assistance. State vote for President Bush in 2000 captures the ideology of the district. I also include a variable measuring whether the senator represents a Southern state. A variable for small states (states with 3 or fewer congressional districts) draws on the insights of Lee and

inclusion of both sets of variables allows me to capture the intraparty differences in activity among liberals and conservatives within the two parties. The ideology scores are also correlated with some of the constituency variables, particularly the state vote for President Bush. Therefore, the impact of some of the constituency variables may be reduced. However, since gender is the main variable of interest, I include the ideology and multiple constituency variables to ensure that differences attributed to gender are not masking differences attributed to ideology or other constituency factors.

Independent Variables	NCLB Sponsored Amendment	NCLB Cosponosred Amendment	Medicare Sponsored Amendment	Medicare Cosponsor Amendment
Republican Women	−.223	.944^	1.02^	.506
	(.535)	(.491)	(.54)	(.537)
Democratic Women	.371	−.42	.59*	.64*
	(.323)	(.289)	(.291)	(.266)
Republican Men	−.618	.536	−.403	.643
	(.535)	(.434)	(.581)	(.517)
Ideology	.441	−1.22*	−.759	−1.63*
	(.604)	(.521)	(.722)	(.694)
First Term Senator	−.091	.483^	−.408	.205
	(.321)	(.251)	(.364)	(.305)
Retiring Senator	−.712	−.837	−1.05^	.491
	(.601)	(.766)	(.571)	(.373)
State Vote for Bush	−.021	−.026	.033^	−.012
	(.02)	(.019)	(.018)	(.016)
African American Population	−.052**	.043**	−.008	.022
	(.019)	(.016)	(.016)	(.014)
Hispanic Population	.011	.011	−.001	.006
	(.015)	(.013)	(.015)	(.013)
Median Household Income	.508^	−.444^	.13	.065
	(.274)	(.26)	(.308)	(.259)
Urban Population	−.001	.012	.004	−.012
	(.01)	(.01)	(.013)	(.01)
Elderly Population	...	...	.043	−.032
			(.082)	(.068)
Youth Population (% under 18)	.112	.051	...	...
	(.084)	(.076)		
Proportion without High School Diploma	.129***	−.037	...	...
	(.04)	(.042)		
Southern State	.304	−.324	−.135	−.455
	(.399)	(.365)	(.39)	(.369)
Small State	.446^	.647**	−.513^	.219
	(.24)	(.21)	(.264)	(.226)
Up for Re-election	.539**	.302^	−.172	−.062
	(.185)	(.174)	(.202)	(.213)
HELP	.764**	.486*	.606*	.23
	(.259)	(.223)	(.242)	(.228)

(Continued)

TABLE 9.5. CONTINUED
(Standard Errors in Parentheses)

Independent Variables	NCLB Sponsored Amendment	NCLB Cosponosred Amendment	Medicare Sponsored Amendment	Medicare Cosponsor Amendment
Finance	...	...	.631**	.354
			(.221)	(.222)
Special Aging	...	...	.064	.189
			(.2)	(.192)
Veterans;' Affairs	...	...	.226	.023
			(.252)	(.252)
Appropriations	−.032	.512*	−.436	.189
Labor, Health and	(.272)	(.227)	(.301)	(.244)
Human Services,				
and Education				
Subcommittee				
Education/Health	−.46	−.46	1.2**	−1.33^
Committee Chair	(.563)	(.563)	(.47)	(.797)
Education/Health	.638	.638	−.949^	.068
Committee Ranking	(.707)	(.707)	(.525)	(.368)
Member				
Education/Health	.383	.383	.824*	−.314
Subcommittee Chair	(.406)	(.406)	(.36)	(.495)
Education/Health	−.327	−.327	−.289	.165
Subcommittee	(.467)	(.467)	(.382)	(.328)
Ranking Member				
Same−StateSenator's	−.067^	−.067^	.042	.079^
Amendments	(.04)	(.04)	(.049)	(.043)
Constant	−5.16*	−5.16*	−2.5	1.32
	(2.28)	(2.28)	(2.52)	(2.13)
Dispersion	.138	.138	.03	.097
Parameter	(.081)	(.081)	(.079)	(.075)
Log Likelihood	−174.88	−174.88	−155.36	−175.32
Log Likelihood	67.34	67.34	50.7	59.18
Ratio Chi Square				
Psuedo−R2	.161	.161	.14	.144
N	100	100	100	100

^p<=.1 *p<=.05 **p<=.01 ***p<=.001.
Note: Health Committee chair and ranking members were the chairs and ranking members of HELP, Finance, Special Committee on Aging, Veterans' Affairs, and the Appropriations Subcommittee on Labor, Health and Human Services, and Education. Health Subcommittee chairs and ranking members were the chairs and ranking members of the subcommittees of the HELP Committee and the Finance Committee's subcommittees on Health and Social Security and Family Policy. The Veterans' Affairs and Special Committee on Aging do not have subcommittees. The Education Committee chairs and ranking members were the chairs and ranking members of the HELP Committee and the Appropriations Subcommittee on Labor, Health and Human Services, and Education. The Education Subcommittee chairs and ranking members are the chairs and ranking members of the HELP subcommittees.

Oppenheimer (1999) who find that small state senators have qualitatively different relationships with their constituents than large state senators. A measure indicating whether the senator is up for re-election captures the political imperatives of senators who might increase their activism in an election year.

Finally, a senator's position within the institution impacts his or her decision to pursue legislation. I include variables that capture whether senators are retiring, are in the first two years of their freshman term, and senators' committee positions. While the expansive floor rights granted to individuals reduce the gatekeeping power of Senate committees, their entrepreneurial role in drafting legislation influences bill sponsorship and cosponsorship (Evans 1991). Using information on bill referral and jurisdiction (King 1997), I include measures that capture membership on the following committees: Health, Education, Labor, and Pensions (HELP); Finance; Special Committee on Aging; Veterans' Affairs; and the Appropriations Committee's Subcommittee on Labor, Health and Human Services, and Education. I also include variables for the committee (and relevant subcommittee) chairs and ranking members. A variable measuring the number of education (health/women's health) bills offered by a senator's same-state colleague accounts for the calculations that senators make about how to navigate the policy reputation of their same-state colleague (Schiller 2000). Variables measuring the total number of bills sponsored and cosponsored account for the fact that the more bills a member sponsors/cosponsors the higher the probability that one of these bills will be on a given issue.

Looking first at sponsorship and cosponsorship of bills, the regression models in Tables 9.2, 9.3, and 9.4 demonstrate that gender does matter as an influence on senators' choices. However, activism on issues varies by party. Both Democratic and Republican women were strong proponents of health care legislation. However, only Republican women were significantly more active advocates of education bills, and Democratic but not Republican women were more likely than their male colleagues to pursue women's health initiatives.

The strongest gender differences emerge in cosponsorship. Cosponsorship can be seen as loud voting, where senators sign on to proposals to signal their preferences to voters, interest groups, and other legislators (Swers 2002; Koger 2003). Both Democratic and Republican women were more active cosponsors of health care legislation than the comparison category, Democratic men. The strong commitment of Democratic and Republican women to health care is reinforced by the dominance of health care on senators' agendas (see Table 9.1).

Looking at sponsorship and cosponsorship of education bills, Democratic women are no more likely than Democratic men to engage education, while Republican women were more active sponsors of education bills in the 107th Congress, when Republican President Bush's No Child Left Behind act was considered, and Republican women were more likely than Democratic men to cosponsor education bills in the 108th Congress. Thus, the Democratic Party's strong association with social welfare issues provides incentives for all Democrats to support education initiatives, and there are no additional gender effects found in this area. By contrast, since social welfare issues are not central to the message of the Republican Party, gender-based preferences may provide additional incentives for Republican women to focus on health care and education.

Focusing on the ideological, constituency, and institutional variables indicates that senators confront a different political opportunity structure when legislating on health care and education. These political and institutional dynamics encourage greater activism on health and therefore provide women with more incentives to pursue their interest in health. First, the models demonstrate that ideology is an important determinant of which senators engage health policy, as liberal senators are the most active sponsors and cosponsors of health care legislation. However, ideology is not an important predictor of which senators sponsor education bills and it only exerts an important influence on cosponsorship of education bills in the 108th Congress. The centrality of liberal ideology to engagement of health care reflects the fact that amid rising ideological polarization in Congress, health care has become one of the central battlegrounds between the parties. Since the failure of Clinton's health reform, the parties have battled over initiatives ranging from a Patients' Bill of Rights to Obama's health care overhaul. This repeated contestation creates incentives for senators to offer more health bills, as they know these issues will be prominent on the Senate agenda. Senators who offer health bills work to maximize the cosponsors on their legislation to demonstrate support for their initiatives. If women are perceived as more interested in health, bill sponsors will look to them as likely supporters of their bills. These additional cosponsorship opportunities will encourage women to become even more active on health.

In addition to these partisan and ideological incentives, the political opportunity structure favors activism on health. First, the size of the federal budget devoted to health spending far outpaces the proportion of the budget devoted to education; therefore senators will focus more attention on health issues. Moreover, committee jurisdiction on health issues is more broadly distributed across the Senate, with more committees having a stake in these issues. As a result, committee position is a very important predictor of which senators sponsor and cosponsor education bills, while holding a seat on a particular committee is not as strong a factor in the decision to sponsor or cosponsor health bills. The reduced importance of committee seats leaves more room for senators to act on gender-based preferences.

Finally, the analysis of cosponsorship of women's health bills indicates that gender differences in activism on these issues are mediated by party. Democratic women are significantly more likely than Democratic men to cosponsor women's health bills in both the 107th and 108th Congresses.[6]

6. The significance levels of the gender coefficients remain the same when the bills restricting abortion are dropped from the dependent variable. In the 108th

However, among Republicans, gender had no impact on the decision to cosponsor women's health bills. For Democrats, the policy preferences of Democratic women on women's health issues align with the views of Democratic voters. Furthermore, women's health issues from reproductive rights to disease research and insurance coverage of women's health services mobilize the Democratic base and are priorities of women's groups. Female Democratic senators can claim expertise and moral authority as women on these issues, making it more likely that the party will turn to them for leadership and to serve as party spokespersons on these issues (Swers 2013).

By contrast, focusing on women's health is not universally positive for Republican women. Both Republican men and women are supportive of proposals related to breast cancer and other diseases that impact women. Indeed, support for women's health research may help pro-life Republicans reach out to women voters. Activism on more controversial women's health issues of reproductive rights creates conflict for moderate Republican women as cosponsorship of Democratic bills expanding contraception or abortion rights will alienate the social conservative base of the party. For conservative women, activism on abortion brings heightened media scrutiny of their positions and pressures from party leaders to defend the party against Democratic criticism that Republican policies are anti-women, making them more careful about how much of their agenda they want to devote to the issue (Swers 2013).

In sum, gender clearly influences the priorities of female senators. However, the impact of gender is mediated by party dynamics and institutional incentives. To highlight the relative influence of gender on senators' policy activity, I calculated predicted probabilities to assess the mean number of bills the models predict a senator with a given set of characteristics, such as gender, party affiliation, and ideology would cosponsor.[7] Figure 9.1 demonstrates that Democratic women are predicted to cosponsor a mean of 7 more health bills than Democratic men in the 107th Congress and 5 more health bills in the 108th Congress. Thus, for example, a liberal Democratic woman is predicted to cosponsor 34 health bills in the 107th Congress, while a liberal Democratic man would cosponsor a mean of 27 bills. Similarly, moderate and conservative Republican women are predicted to cosponsor approximately 5 more health bills than their male Republican counterparts in the 107th and 108th Congresses. On women's health, where Democratic women exhibit significant activism, a liberal Democratic woman serving in the 107th Congress is predicted to cosponsor 3.5 more women's health bills than a liberal male Democrat (6.8 v. 3.3) (results not shown).

Congress, conservative ideology is no longer significant in the model without the anti-abortion bills.

7. To generate predicted probabilities, I utilize *Clarify* (Tomz et al. 2003).

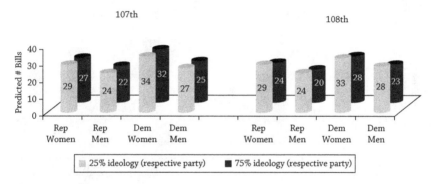

107th

108th

| | Rep Women | Rep Men | Dem Women | Dem Men | | Rep Women | Rep Men | Dem Women | Dem Men |

25% ideology (respective party)   ■ 75% ideology (respective party)

Figure 9.1
General Health Bill Cosponsorship
Note: DW-NOMINATE ideology scores are set at the 25% and 75% levels within each party to capture most liberal and conservative senators in each party. All other dichotomous variables are set at the mode of 0 and continuous variables are set at their means.

Do these patterns of gender- and party-based preferences persist beyond sponsorship and cosponsorship to consideration of major legislation on the floor? In the 107th and 108th Congresses, legislators passed major initiatives on health care and education into law. The No Child Left Behind Act (NCLB) was a bipartisan education reform law passed in the 107th Congress. The Medicare Prescription Drug bill began as a bipartisan effort that passed the Senate 76–21, but the ultimate legislation was engulfed in partisan warfare and passed on a party line vote, 54–44 (CQ Almanac 2003). I analyzed the number of amendments that senators sponsored and cosponsored to each of these bills. Using THOMAS and the text of the Congressional Record, I coded the number of amendments that senators filed to the legislation and offered on the floor to create dependent variables measuring the total number of amendments senators proposed to the NCLB and Medicare bills and the total number of amendments senators cosponsored.[8] Seventy-two senators drafted 182 amendments to the Medicare Prescription Drug bill. These amendments were cosponsored by 77 senators. Seventy-eight senators sponsored 249 amendments to the NCLB. These amendments were cosponsored by 80 senators.

The negative binomial regressions in Table 9.5 show very similar gender patterns to the results of the bill sponsorship and cosponsorship analyses. Both Democratic and Republican women are more active sponsors of amendments to the Medicare Prescription Drug bill than are their male partisan

8. To have their amendments considered on the floor, senators must first file their amendments and the text is recorded in the Congressional Record. Not all amendments are ultimately considered on the floor as senators negotiate and party leaders devise unanimous consent agreements to allow specific amendments to be considered. To measure senators' interest in health and education, the dependent variables account for all amendments that were either filed or considered on the floor. I eliminated duplicate amendments.

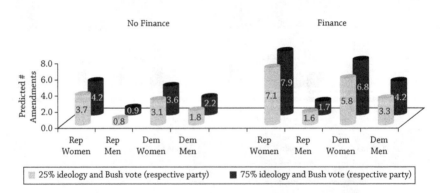

Figure 9.2
Medicare Prescription Drug Amendment Sponsorship
Note: DW-NOMINATE ideology and state vote for President Bush are set at the 25% and 75% levels within
each party to capture most liberal and conservative senators in each party. Finance committee membership is
varied from 0 to 1 indicating a seat on the committee. All other dichotomous variables are set at mode of 0 and
continuous variables are set at their means.

colleagues, indicating greater engagement of health care. Democratic women
are also more likely to cosponsor amendments to the Medicare bill. By contrast, there are no gender differences in sponsorship activity on the education
bill, NCLB. Only Republican women are more likely to cosponsor amendments
to the NCLB. To more closely examine the influence of gender on senators'
decisions to offer amendments to the Medicare bill, the predicted probabilities in Figure 9.2 indicate the mean number of amendments a senator with a
given set of characteristics is expected to offer.

Republican women are expected to offer on average approximately 3 more
amendments than Republican men (4.2 v 0.9 among conservatives, 3.7 v. 0.8
among moderates). Democratic women are predicted to sponsor on average
almost 1.5 more amendments than Democratic men (3.1 v. 1.8 among liberals, 3.6 v. 2.2 among conservatives). These are meaningful differences when one
considers that the average senator offered a mean of 1.8 amendments to the
Medicare legislation. If a hypothetical senator is given a seat on the committee
with jurisdiction over the bill, the Finance committee, Republican women are predicted to sponsor a mean of 5 more bills than Republican men, and Democratic
women are predicted to sponsor a mean of almost 3 more bills than Democratic
men. Clearly, the ascension of more women to these key committees could have
a significant impact on the level of attention devoted to health care, reinforcing
Implication 3.1 concerning women's access to the right venue to change policy.

CONCLUSION

Aggregate indexes of women's issues tend to obscure differences in policy
focus among women and the varying incentives provided by the political

opportunity structure. The analysis of senators' policy activity on health care, education, and women's health issues, as well as the examination of senators' amendments to the Medicare Prescription Drug bill and the No Child Left Behind Act demonstrates that gender is an important influence on senators' priorities. However, there are important partisan differences among women. Party reputations for issue ownership and electoral coalitions combine with senators' preferences to incentivize senators' choices. Thus, the association of health care, education, and women's health with the Democratic Party makes it easier for all Democrats to offer legislation on these issues. Because the gender gap favors Democrats on these issues and women's groups are central to the Democratic coalition, Democrats and female Democrats in particular will offer legislation on health care and women's health. Among Republicans, social welfare issues are not a core feature of the Republican Party message, and women's health proposals on contraception and abortion can alienate social conservatives. Reflecting Implication 1.2, Republican women avoid engagement of issues that conflict with key party constituencies and may give rise to primary challengers. Therefore, Republican women focus more on the social welfare policies of health and education that can win partisan support.

The political opportunity structure also helps to channel legislators' priorities. Ideological polarization is a persistent feature of the contemporary Congress and health care is wrapped up in partisan warfare. A key concern to voters and a frequent presidential priority, the recurring nature of health care battles encourages senators to expend resources developing health policy expertise. The importance of health issues to constituents means that both parties want to utilize their female senators to reach out to segments of voters who might favor their party. The size of the federal budget devoted to health care and the importance of the issue to constituents also means that more members will want to exercise influence over health policy, reducing the relevance of committee positions and providing more opportunities for women and other senators with strong preferences on health to engage the debate. By contrast, the more limited federal role in education means that contestation of education policy is more sporadic and concentrated in the committees of jurisdiction, thereby reducing the importance of gender as a predictor of participation.

In sum, this research demonstrates that senators begin with a set of policy preferences and that gender does impact this basic set of preferences. However, the influence of gender on senators' agendas is channeled by constituent needs, party priorities, and other features of the political context in a way that incentivizes senators to pursue some policies over others. Unpacking the concept of women's issues and examining the interaction of policy areas with party reputations for policy expertise and the overarching political opportunity structure can illuminate the paths through which gender influences legislative behavior. Addressing the *who* question, this analysis shows that the incentives to represent women's interests vary across the definition of women's interest used, across the party of the official, and with the political and institutional context factors that constitute the political opportunity structure.

CHAPTER 10

Representing Women's Interests and Intersections of Gender, Race, and Ethnicity in US State Legislatures

BETH REINGOLD AND KERRY L. HAYNIE

Decades of research on the impact of women in elective office have demonstrated quite forcefully that representation in the United States is gendered.[1] Throughout the policymaking process—and beyond—female officeholders are often more likely than their male colleagues to act for women or women's interests.[2] In terms of the relationship between descriptive and substantive representation, public officials who "stand for" women are more likely to "act for" women (Pitkin 1967).[3] Nowhere is this link between gender identity and representation more clearly and consistently demonstrated than in the research on legislators' policy leadership.

Across time, office, and political parties, legislative women, compared to their male counterparts, care more about, know more about, and do more about "women's issues" (and the more general interests from which they are

1. The authors are deeply grateful for the research assistance generously provided by Emily Calvert, Ly Ngoc Le, and Yaesul Park, all of Emory University. We also thank Kathleen Bratton and the many research assistants (too numerous to name) who have worked diligently over the years to build the data sets we use here. This research is funded in part by the National Science Foundation (SES-0618368) and the Institute for Advanced Policy Solutions, the Provost's Strategic Fund, and the University Research Committee at Emory University.
2. For a review of this literature, see Reingold (2008).
3. In Dahlerup's terms (Chapter 4 of this volume), the bulk of this research, with its focus on gender differences in the behavior of individual policy makers, adopts a "classic narrow understanding" of women's substantive representation as the relationship between voters and representatives.

derived).[4] In interviews, surveys, press releases, and newsletters, women officeholders are more likely to express concern about such issues and claim them as their own (Barrett 1995; Boles 2001; Diamond 1977; Dolan and Kropf 2004; Fridkin and Woodall 2005; Garcia Bedolla et al. 2005; Reingold 2000). They are more likely to serve on committees relevant to women's interests (Carroll 2008; Diamond 1977; Reingold 2000; Thomas 1994; Thomas and Welch 1991). And, perhaps most important, they are more likely to introduce or sponsor legislation addressing such interests (Bratton 2002, 2005; Bratton and Haynie 1999; Bratton et al. 2006; Carroll 2001; Dodson and Carroll 1991; Osborn 2012; Reingold 2000; Saint-Germain 1989; Swers 2002; Tamerius 1995; Thomas 1994; Thomas and Welch 1991; Wolbrecht 2002).[5]

These studies employ a variety of conceptual and operational definitions of women's issues or interests. For example, while most scholars broadly conceive of women's issues as those particularly salient to women (Carroll 1994), they differ on how directly salient those issues are. Some issues are salient because they primarily or most directly concern or affect women as women, while others are salient because they reflect the more "traditional" concerns that women as primary caretakers presumably have about others, especially children and those in need. Accordingly, some studies distinguish "women's" issues like abortion, domestic violence, sexual harassment, and child care from more general social welfare issues, such as education, health care, and poverty assistance (e.g., Reingold 2000; Saint-Germain 1989; Osborn 2012; Swers 2002; Thomas 1994). Similarly, researchers differ in whether they draw ideological lines, especially when dealing with issues more directly salient to women. Some studies distinguish and compare leadership on feminist initiatives that promote women's rights or equality and more general, liberal *or* conservative, social welfare issues (e.g., Saint-Germain 1989; Swers 2002). Others, like Dahlerup (Chapter 4 of this volume), restrict women's issues to only those that are feminist (and women-centered), or at least not anti-feminist (e.g., Bratton 2002; Bratton and Haynie 1999; Dodson and Carroll 1991; Wolbrecht 2002). Still others impose no ideological restrictions (e.g., Thomas 1994; Osborn 2012; Reingold 2000).[6] Remarkably, however, gender gaps in policy leadership appear across all these definitions of women's issues/interests.

4. We use the terms "women's issues" and "women's interests" in this chapter as Beckwith (Chapter 2 of this volume) defines them. Thus, we are careful to distinguish the more general and abstract "interests" or concerns of women from the more specific, empirically manifested "issues" that address or articulate them. When the distinction is blurred or both terms seem applicable, we often use terms like "interests/issues."

5. Some studies also report that male legislators are more active on "men's issues" such as fiscal affairs or commerce (Diamond 1977; Dodson and Carroll 1991; Thomas and Welch 1991; Thomas 1994; Reingold 2000; Fridkin and Woodall 2005).

6. Swers (2002; Swers and Larson 2005) is the only one, to our knowledge, who examines legislative activity on anti-feminist measures specifically.

A few studies have noted that the size of the gender gap, or the strength of the relationship between identity and representational leadership, may vary across different types of women's issues (Osborn 2012; Reingold 2000; Swers 2002; Thomas 1994). Swers's (2002) study of the 103rd and 104th Congresses, for example, finds that gender differences in policy leadership were more pronounced on feminist issues than on social welfare issues. And a few studies have examined variation across different types of women in public office, most notably differences related to partisanship (Osborn 2012; Swers 2002) and race (Bratton and Haynie 1999; Bratton et al. 2006; Orey et al. 2006). These studies raise important questions about the generalizability and reliability of this extensive body of research across differences in measurement and differences in representatives. Others have rightly cautioned, moreover, that these differences may be interdependent; different women may have different conceptions of women's issues/interests. Dodson (1998: 148), for example, argues that women in Congress "differ in the solutions they see to the problems women face, they differ in the kinds of women they represent, and they differ in the extent to which these concerns are salient." As a result, Carroll (2002, 66–67) adds, "even when women members of Congress act in ways that they perceive as representing women, their actions may not always look the same" (see also, Reingold 2000). This is precisely what Osborn (2012) finds to be the case among Democratic and Republican women in state legislatures. Yet no one, to our knowledge, has investigated the possibility that the *who* and *what* of women's representation are linked according to race/ethnicity.

If different women have different conceptions of women's interests, then it is entirely possible that researchers' decisions about how to define and measure those interests will have significant effects on who appears more or less willing to act for women. To what extent, then, do our conclusions about the relationship between women's descriptive and substantive representation depend on how we define women's interests? In this chapter, we are particularly interested in whether and how definitions of women's interests affect the conclusions we draw about women of color in US state legislatures. Are legislative women, regardless of race and ethnicity, equally likely to take the lead on women's issues, regardless of how they (or their corresponding interests) are defined? Or is women's substantive representation—in theory (or by definition) and practice—gendered and raced? Thus this chapter examines Implications 2.1 and 2.2A, proposed in Chapter 1, that women (all women and regardless of venue) will articulate women's interests more than will male elected officials, and that as women in government become more diverse, more diverse interests will be articulated.

Intersectionality, as both a normative theory and a research paradigm (Hancock, Chapter 3 of this volume, 2007), cautions against generalizing about women's representation across race and ethnicity (or any other salient categorical difference) and suggests that any "single-axis" conception of women's interests risks excluding or obscuring the representational advocacy provided by women of color, while privileging that provided by white women (Crenshaw 1989). To test this proposition, we examine the agenda-setting behavior (i.e., bill introductions) of state legislators—female and male; Latino/a, African American, and white—serving in the lower chambers of six states, in 1997. The dependent variables are the number of bills legislators introduce that address women's interests, variously defined. The main independent variables capture both the gender and race/ethnicity of state legislators. To maximize variation in legislators' race/ethnicity and gender, we selected six states with some of the highest numbers of African American women and Latinas serving in the lower chamber of the legislature.

To maximize variation in our dependent variables, particularly those based on more "cross-cutting" or intersectional conceptions of women's interests (Cohen 1999), we examine legislative activity in 1997, the year in which all states were engaged in major welfare reform efforts. Welfare policy making in the states peaked in the immediate aftermath of the 1996 Personal Responsibility and Work Opportunity Reconciliation Act (PRWORA), which gave states unprecedented discretion in shaping the contours of the new Temporary Assistance to Needy Families (TANF) program and the demise of welfare "as we know it" (Reingold and Smith 2012). Since then, states have made very few changes to their welfare policies. Given the significance of those welfare reform efforts and the distinctive impact of legislative women of color on the outcomes (Reingold and Smith 2012), we believe that welfare policy making is a crucial dimension of our inquiry. Welfare is also one of the few policy arenas widely recognized for its deeply cross-cutting, raced-gendered-classed past, present, and future (Abramovitz 1996; Collins 2000; Gordon 1994; Hancock 2004; Hawkesworth 2003; Mink 1995; Neubeck and Cazenave 2001; Roberts 1997; Sparks 2003).

DEFINITIONS OF WOMEN'S INTERESTS AND INTERSECTIONS OF GENDER, RACE, AND ETHNICITY

As numerous critiques of feminist politics and scholarship offered by women of color attest, "[t]heories advanced as being universally applicable to women as a group upon closer examination appear greatly limited by the White, middle-class, and Western origins of their proponents" (Collins 2000: 5–6). The same might be said of definitions of women's issues/interests employed in studies of women's representation that, with too few exceptions, have had little to say about the politics of race and ethnicity, the intersections of race, ethnicity, and gender, or the perspectives of women of color. Indeed, while almost every study cited above acknowledges at least the potential signifi-cance of partisan and ideological differences among legislative women, very few have recognized the potential significance of racial and ethnic diversity. As a result, the experiences of women of color and questions about *their* representation are too often ignored and/or marginalized; and what we think we know about "women" in public office may be applicable only to the majority of white, non-Hispanic women.[7] To what degree, then, have the various definitions of women's interests effectively privileged the needs, concerns, and activities of some and obscured those of others?

Theories of intersectionality and secondary marginalization (Cohen 1999) suggest that any attempt to identify or construct common group interests, especially among marginalized groups, will reflect intragroup power differentials (Hancock, Chapter 3 of this volume). The interests of those who are subject to multiple, overlapping, intersecting, interlocking, and compounding axes of inequality and subordination will differ from—and perhaps even be at cross-purposes with—the interests of those who are privileged but for their disadvantaged location on one, single axis (Crenshaw 1989, 1991; Dovi 2002; Glenn 1992; Haynie 2011; hooks 2000; King 1988). Indeed, the privileges of one sub-group may even depend on the marginalization and deprivations of another (Glenn 1992; Cohen 1999). At the very least, group members who are relatively privileged may have the luxury of being unaware of such conflicting interests, while those who are "multiply burdened" (Crenshaw 1989) may be all too aware (Collins 2000). Thus, to the degree to which we as researchers rely on dominant, single-axis conceptions of women's interests, our definitions will be more likely to capture the representational commitments of white women than those of women of color. As Hancock (Chapter 3 of this volume) suggests, this would be the analytic or epistemological equivalent of Crenshaw's "political intersectionality"—a representational failure in its own right.

The few studies that do provide valuable insight into the legislative priorities of African American women and Latinas, however, suggest that it would be a mistake to assume that women of color do not share a commitment to women's issues and interests. Carroll (2002: 57) notes that, in interviews with female members of Congress, the commitment to representing women was widely shared, though the congresswomen of color "talked in somewhat different ways" about that responsibility. Some "expressed the inseparability of their identities as, and their responsibilities to, people of color and women"; others expressed a particularly strong sense of responsibility to poor and working class women, or to women outside the United States (see also Garcia Bedolla et al. 2005; Htun, Chapter 7 of this volume). Reviewing the research literature on "Latinas as advocates and Representatives," García et al.

---

7. This may be especially characteristic of and problematic for the more quantitative studies that rely heavily, if not exclusively, on (male vs. female) group averages and central tendencies.

(2008: 30) theorize that "Latinas, like most women, will demonstrate a propensity to advocate for women and families. But, different from most women, Latinas will also advocate for issues affecting the Latino community."

Closer examination of the behavior of legislative women of color largely confirms the expectation that they will take a "both/and" rather than an "either/or" approach to addressing the multiple, intersecting concerns of gender and race/ethnicity. Takash's (1997) survey of Latina public officials in California led her to conclude that "the majority of Latina officeholders support feminist agendas and may be expected to promote legislation on women's rights," but they "express more concern with issues facing the Latino community as a whole, such as employment, access to education and retention, and safe neighborhoods" (p. 429). Bratton et al. (2006) find that African American female lawmakers are uniquely responsive to both black interests and women's interests—narrowly defined as measures "that directly address and seek to improve [each group's] economic, political, and social status" (pp. 79–80). They sponsor just as many black interest measures as do African American men, and just as many women's interest measures as do non-black women; and they are more likely than any others to sponsor at least one black interest and one women's interest bill. Using similar definitions of group interests, Orey et al. (2006) find that, in the Mississippi legislature, African American women are *more* likely than any of their other colleagues to introduce "progressive" women's interest bills, as well as progressive measures addressing black interests, welfare, and children.

Other studies report that legislative women of color are just as, if not more committed to, issues that address both gender and racial/ethnic interests more broadly conceived. Comparing the three "public policy issues that are of greatest concern" to the black and white, male and female Democratic legislators in her survey, Barrett (1995: 226) finds that "the greatest difference is not in the issues per se, but rather in the level of agreement among black female legislators" (pp. 233–34). Thus, while education and health care issues were the most frequently cited priorities among all four groups of legislators, black women were more likely than any others to mention them. Fraga et al. (2008) asked a very similar question in their 2004 survey of Latino state legislators. Again, education and health care were at the top of the list for both Latino men and Latinas, with nearly identical percentages ranking each as either their most important issue or among the their top three (see also García et al. 2008).

Together, the empirical research and theories of intersectionality reinforce Smooth's (2011) argument that the more narrowly defined, single-axis conceptions of women's issues/interests may be the most problematic—precisely because they neglect "cross-cutting," "multifaceted" issues that address "the material consequences of race, class, and sexual identities" as well as gender (p. 437). As outlined above, operational definitions that identify issues or bills directly salient to women as women (e.g., abortion, domestic violence, sexual harassment, child care) come closest to this more "narrow" or single-axis conception of women's interests. Thus, we hypothesize that these more narrow, women-centered definitions of women's interests will be most likely to underestimate the representational leadership of women of color and overestimate that of white women. These patterns may be even stronger when the definition of women's interests is *not* ideologically restricted to only feminist initiatives (e.g., Osborn 2012; Reingold 2000; Thomas 1994). Such definitions are more likely to include the activities of conservative, white female (or male) lawmakers as well as more liberal or feminist ones, thus maximizing the level of activity for white women (or white men) as a group. Including conservative, even anti-feminist, measures in the definition should not have similar effects for African American female or Latina state legislators (or their male counterparts), hardly any of whom are conservative Republicans.

More capacious, social welfare–oriented definitions of women's interests, however, are expected to have the opposite effects. Precisely because they overlap and intersect with purported interests of African Americans and/or Latinos (Bratton 2006; Bratton and Haynie 1999; Canon 1999; Casellas 2011; Griffin and Newman 2008; Haynie 2001; Martinez-Ebers et al. 2000), conceptions of women's interests that include education, health care, and welfare/poverty policy will be more likely to capture the representational efforts of women of color. We hypothesize, therefore, that African American female and Latina legislators' efforts to address women's interests will more likely be manifested in the introduction of education, health, and welfare bills than in the introduction of bills specific to or directly salient for women. Thus, when women's substantive representation is defined broadly to include both women-specific measures and measures dealing with education, health care, and/or welfare, legislative women of color should appear just as, if not more, committed to representing women than their white female colleagues.

DATA, MEASURES, AND MODELS

To test these hypotheses, we draw from two inter-related databases created by and for a larger, collaborative project on identity and representation in US state legislatures: one on individual state legislators and their constituencies, and the other on bills introduced by those legislators.[8] We restrict our analysis of identity and women's substantive representation to a cross-section of lower-chamber members of six of the most racially and ethnically diverse state legislatures: Arizona, Florida, Mississippi, New Mexico, Tennessee, and

8. National Science Foundation SES #0618368; Kathleen A. Bratton, Kerry L. Haynie, and Beth Reingold, Principal Investigators.

Texas. This maximizes variation in our key independent variables, the race/ethnic and gender identities of individual legislators. Our sample (N = 612) includes 87 white women, 29 African American women, 17 Latinas, 52 African American men, and 47 Latino men. We study the 1997 regular legislative sessions, as mentioned earlier, to maximize variation on one of our key dependent variables, welfare- or poverty-related legislative activity.

Working with numerous research assistants, we identified the gender, racial, and ethnic identity of all state legislators in our sample of state-years. Our determination of gender was based primarily on pictures in state legislative directories or websites, along with names and/or pronouns used. To identify the racial/ethnic identity of legislators, we used a variety of information including: pictures and organizational affiliations, such as ethnic/racial caucuses or Historically Black Colleges and Universities, available in directories and/or webpages of individual legislators; lists of African American or Latino representatives published on state webpages or other state documents; and explicit references to the racial/ethnic identity of legislators found in newspaper (Lexis/Nexis) and/or Google searches (e.g., "Representative XX is the first Latino to be elected to the YY state legislature").[9] On the basis of this information, we measure the intersecting gender and racial/ethnic identities of the state legislators with a series of five dummy variables that indicate whether the legislator is a Latina, an African American woman, a white woman, a Latino, or an African American man. The omitted reference category, therefore, is white men.

In operationalizing our key independent variables in this fashion, we do not mean to suggest or assume that these intersecting identities are static, essential ones, as Hancock's (Chapter 3 of this volume) critique of dummy variables might imply. Rather, our coding protocol is meant to capture legislators' contemporaneous, publicly acknowledged identities—the sort of socially constructed and recognized identities that give meaning to the concept of descriptive representation. Furthermore, we measure legislator identity in this dummy-variable fashion in order to critically evaluate the more reductive "identity politics" assumptions and expectations that often surround the politics and political science of descriptive representation and group interests. Although it is not our intention or goal to "fully operationalize intersectionality" (Hancock, Chapter 3 of this volume) with these (or any other) variables, our measurement strategies, analytic choices, and research questions are all

9. To the best of our ability, we identified all African American, Latino, Asian American, and Native American legislators. There are too few Asian American (N = 1) or Native American (N = 8) legislators in our 1997 sample of six lower chambers to analyze them as separate categories. Rather than group them with white, African American, or Latino legislators, we exclude them from the analysis. We do include two legislators who are identified as both Native American and Latino/a; they are coded as Latino/a.

animated by the concerns of intersectionality, as articulated by Hancock and others.

Teams of research assistants also enabled us to code the primary sponsors, committee referrals, final disposition, and issue content of all bills introduced during the regular session of each state-year lower chamber.[10] With these data, we construct our dependent variables: the number of women's interest bills—variously defined—introduced by each legislator as primary sponsor. Primary sponsors were distinguished from co-sponsors according to standard operating procedures in each state. Some states (AZ and FL) allow for multiple primary sponsors who, on paper at least, are equally responsible and accountable, though most states allow for only one (MS and NM) or bestow gatekeeping powers upon only one primary sponsor (TN and TX). Thus, in AZ and FL (only), multiple legislators could get "credit" for introducing the same bill as primary sponsors.

Content codes were organized under 12 general headings: health; education; groups; civil rights and liberties; social welfare; family; crime; business, commerce and labor; agriculture, environment, and transportation; campaigns, voting, and elections; immigration, military, and foreign affairs; and general government.[11] Coders were instructed to select as many content codes as necessary to capture the substance of the bill accurately; when in doubt, they were advised, more is better and redundancy is all right. These content codes were used to identify and classify bills into the following categories or types of women's interests and issues: Women-Specific; Health; Education; Welfare/Poverty; and All Women's Issues.[12] Table 10.1 lists the codes selected for (or associated with) each type.

As Table 10.1 shows, some content codes are associated with multiple categories of women's issues/interests. Similarly, any particular bill could be classified and included in multiple women's issue/interest categories. For example, a measure requiring health care insurers to cover breast reconstructive surgery (TN HB517) counts as both a Women-Specific bill and a Health bill. Given this overlap, our measure of bill activity across All categories of

10. Only regular/general bills were coded; resolutions, memorials, and such were not. In Florida, "local" bills were excluded from the analysis, for they did not have any designated sponsors. The New Mexico and Tennessee legislatures permit "placeholder" or "caption" bills—empty vessels waiting to be amended with "real" proposals when needed, usually after the deadline for bill introductions. Such bills, when left un-amended, were excluded from the analysis.

11. A full list of content codes is available from the authors upon request.

12. Whenever possible, content codes were based upon the bill as introduced. Coders read summaries of bill proposals, usually captured in either the bill's caption (a.k.a., long title) or in an official synopsis provided at the beginning of the bill text. Full text was consulted in very few cases in which such summaries were either unavailable or prohibitively vague.

Table 10.1. BILL CONTENT CODES FOR WOMEN'S ISSUES/INTERESTS

<u>Women-Specific Codes</u>

Health Policy:

Reproductive Health, Birth Control: *NOT including abortion*

Abortion, Fetal Rights Protection: *including clinic access, emergency contraception*

Sex Ed—Abstinence Only (*IF specific to issues of birth control and/or teen pregnancy; also available under Education Policy*)

Sex Ed—Other (*IF specific to issues of birth control and/or teen pregnancy; also available under Education Policy*)

Groups:

All, General Women

Pregnant Women, Mothers

African American Women

Latina Women

Native American Women

Other women of color: *e.g., Asian American women*

Civil Rights and Liberties:

Discrimination, Civil Rights: *including sexual harassment (IF it includes reference to sex/gender/women)*

Affirmative Action (*IF targeted groups or categories include women*)

Hate Crimes (*IF targeted groups or categories include women; also available under Crime*)

Family Policy:

Child Custody: *including issues re visitation, foster care, and/or guardianship*

Child Support

Other Divorce/alimony

Marriage: *NOT including same-sex marriage*

Day Care: *including child care and elder care*

Family Leave

Surrogacy

Other family policy (*IF specific to paternity, fathers' "rights," teen pregnancy, abortion, or marriage; not including general issues of parental notification or liability*)

Crime:

Harassment, Stalking

Prostitution

Sex Offenses: *NOT including sex offenses against children or trafficking in pornography or prostitution*

Domestic Violence: *including shelters and other victim support services*

Hate Crimes (*IF targeted groups or categories include women; also available under Civil Rights and Liberties*)

<u>Health Codes</u>

Health Policy:

Mental Health

Sex Ed—Abstinence Only (*also available under Education Policy*)

Sex Ed—Other (*also available under Education Policy*)

Reproductive Health, Birth Control: *NOT including abortion*

(Continued)

TABLE 10.1. CONTINUED

HIV and AIDS

Occupational Health and Safety

Disaster Relief: *specific to health and public safety; including preparedness measures, emergency procedures, evacuation, shelters, search and rescue*

Drug or alcohol treatment, prevention: *including educational efforts (also available under Crime)*

Biomedical ethics, euthanasia, cloning, genetic screening

Other, General Health: *public health and safety; restrictions on smoking in public places; in-home support services; nursing homes; long-term care; general health care reform; medical liability; health promotion and prevention*

Education Codes

Education Policy:

Pre-K thru 12, Administration and Management: *issues re educational infrastructure (e.g., facilities maintenance, school finance, teacher salary/benefits) or the safety of children and staff at/in schools*

Pre-K thru 12, Curriculum and Programs: *issues re the quality and/or equity of education or instruction, including teacher credentials and training*

Higher Ed, Administration and Management: *colleges, universities, and vocational schools; including general budget and expenditures, facilities maintenance (including student housing); student loans, financial aid*

Higher Ed, Curriculum and Programs: *colleges, universities, and vocational schools; including faculty hiring and promotion, research support/infrastructure*

Adult literacy

Sex Ed—Abstinence Only *(also available under Health Policy)*

Sex Ed—Other *(also available under Health Policy)*

Bilingual Education: *including ESL instruction; for adults and/or children; NOT including foreign language instruction or promotion*

Multicultural Education: *including diversity training, tolerance curricula; in schools or workplace*

Workforce Training

Other Education: *including anything not related to administration/management or curriculum/ programs (in Pre-K thru 12, or Higher Ed)*

Welfare/Poverty Codes

Groups:

Poor Individuals, Economically Disadvantaged

Social Welfare Policy:

Homeless: *restrictions on panhandling; provision, regulation of shelters*

Low-income Housing: *provision and regulation*

Welfare Reform: *"workfare" or work/job training requirements; family caps; time limitations; paternity identification; etc.*

Other, general poverty policy: *aid for the economically disadvantaged; means-tested programs; income support, food subsidies, etc.*

All Women's Issues

Any of the content codes listed above

Women's Issues is the number of bills a legislator introduces that fall into *at least* one category of women's issues/interests.

Women-Specific codes were selected to replicate as closely as possible the more narrow conceptions of women's interests that capture only those directly salient issues that most directly or most disproportionately concern or affect women as women (e.g., Bratton 2002; Reingold 2000; Swers 2002). No attempt is made to identify and exclude anti-feminist measures.[13] Our operational definitions of Education and Health bills are more inclusive. All education-related content codes are designated indicators of Education bills and education-related legislative activity; and all health-related content codes—with the one exception of "abortion, fetal rights protection"—are designated indicators of Health bills and health-related legislative activity. Striking a sort of middle ground, our Welfare/Poverty category does not include all codes in the "social welfare" rubric; nor is it limited to the very specific "welfare reform" code. Instead, Welfare/Poverty codes reflect a more general concern with government assistance for poor, homeless, or low-income individuals and families. Again, no ideological filters were used for any of our dependent variable bill counts.

To gauge the effects of legislator identity on bill introduction, we control for a number of possible confounding factors that previous research suggests can influence policy leadership on women's issues/interests (see especially: Bratton 2002; Bratton and Haynie 1999; Bratton et al. 2006; Swers 2002). We control for several constituency characteristics, including racial and ethnic composition (percentages of constituents who are African American and Latino); socioeconomic status (average household income and percentage of constituents who are college-educated); and population density (percentage of constituents residing in urban areas).[14] All district demographic data are taken from Congressional Quarterly's *State Legislative Elections* almanac (Barone et al. 1998), and are derived from the 1990 US Census.

We also control for legislators' party affiliation (coded 1 if Democrat, 0 otherwise) and seniority (number of consecutive years served in lower chamber).[15] Additionally, we take into account whether the legislator chaired a

13. In Beckwith's terms, excluding anti-feminist bills would limit our analysis of women's interest representation to only some "preference alternatives" (Chapter 2 of this volume).

14. Average household income and college education measures are highly correlated (Pearson's r = .8237), indicating potential multicollinearity problems. Preliminary bivariate analysis also reveals that average household income is related only to welfare/poverty-related legislative activity, while college education is associated with both women-specific and health related bill activity. Thus, to avoid multicollinearity problems, we include only the college education measure in all models except those of welfare/poverty activity, in which we use the measure of average household income only.

15. Preliminary bivariate analysis indicates that party leadership bears no relation to bill activity in any of our designated women's issue areas. Thus, it is not included in our multivariate models.

"relevant committee"—one to which the women's interest bills under consideration were referred on a regular basis.[16] Information regarding legislator characteristics was obtained from state-published directories or the *State Yellowbook* (Spring 1997 edition). Finally, we control for the legislator's overall level of policy-making activity (total number of bills introduced as primary sponsor) and include fixed effects for the six states.

Given that our dependent variables are event counts restricted to positive integers, ordinary least squares (OLS) regression is inappropriate for our multivariate analysis. Poisson regression is often recommended as an alternative for event count models (King 1988), but it rests on the assumption that distinct events are statistically independent, which is highly unlikely in the case of content-specific bill introductions. A legislator who introduces one women's issue bill likely has an increased probability of introducing more. In such instances of over-dispersion, negative binomial regression is the most appropriate model—and the one employed here.

Because bill activity on Women-Specific and Welfare/Poverty issues was rather limited in the six chambers examined (even in 1997), we also employ supplementary logistic regression analysis to model the probability of a legislator introducing *any* bills in those areas, as well as in Health and Education.[17] On the other hand, almost all legislators in our sample (89%) introduced at least one bill that met our criteria for a Women-Specific, Health, Education, *or* Welfare/Poverty measure. Thus, our analysis of All Women's Issues bill activity relies exclusively on negative binomial regression models of bill counts.

RESULTS

To gauge the effects of changing definitions of women's issues/interests on the relationship between women's descriptive and substantive representation across race/ethnicity, we examine our results one issue-area at a time—beginning with the most narrowly defined Women-Specific issues, proceeding with broader Health, Education, and Welfare issues, and ending with the broadest, most inclusive definition, All Women's Issues. Our expectation is that as we move toward broader definitions of women's interests, which overlap with conceptions of black and Latino/a group interests, legislative women of color will become increasingly more active as agenda-setters and policy leaders vis-à-vis their white female colleagues. We also expect, given the extant

16. A standing committee is defined as "relevant" when at least 10% of the bills in the designated policy area are referred to it. A full list of relevant committees for each definition of women's issues is available from the authors upon request.

17. Less than half (43%) of the legislators introduced at least one Women-Specific bill, and only 27% introduced at least one Welfare/Poverty bill. In contrast, 67% introduced at least one Health bill and 72% introduced at least one Education bill.

research on racial/ethnic representation, that legislative *men* of color will become increasingly more active. Thus, gender differences in policy leadership among African American and Latino/a legislators may diminish as the definition and measurement of women's issues/interests broadens. Gender differences among white legislators, however, are expected to remain significant across all definitions.

Beginning with Women-Specific issues, the figures in Table 10.2 show that policy leadership in this more narrowly construed area of women's substantive representation is strongly gendered, regardless of legislator race/ethnicity. Among white, black, and Latino legislators alike, women introduce significantly more Women-Specific bills and are more likely to introduce at least one, compared to their male counterparts. Racial/ethnic differences among female legislators (and among male legislators), however, are more complex and unexpected. Most important, there is no indication that legislative women of color are any less active on these issues than are white women. Rather, Latinas are the most involved, followed closely by white women and African American women, who are equally active. A similar pattern is apparent among the male legislators: Latinos are more active than their white and African American counterparts. In fact, Latino involvement in women-specific policy making is comparable to that of black and white women, but still falls below that of their Latina colleagues.

Gender differences in legislative leadership on Health issues, according to Table 10.3, remain, though they are not always statistically significant (at p≤.10). As predicted by the negative binomial regression model, white female legislators introduce on average 0.87 more Health measures than their white male counterparts do (p = .000); Latinas introduce an average of 1.55 more Health bills than do their Latino counterparts (p = .030); and black female legislators introduce 0.66 more bills than black male legislators do (p = .175). There are no statistically significant differences among the legislative women (or the men), though Latinas are again a bit more active than other women. The results of the logistic regression analysis, which distinguishes any activity from no activity, tells a somewhat different story, however. Here, black women—who the predicted probabilities suggest are almost guaranteed to introduce at least one Health measure—stand out as significantly more involved than all other legislators, female and male. Plus, gender differences vary by race/ethnicity. Legislative women of color are more likely than their male counterparts to sponsor at least one Health bill (though the difference among Latina/os is not statistically significant), but white women and men are equally likely. Overall, however, the results of Table 10.3 (Health bills) compared to those of Table 10.2 (Women-Specific bills) do not provide much support for our hypotheses. There is no clear or consistent evidence of increased involvement in Health policy making on the part of women of color (vis-à-vis white women) or of men of color (vis-à-vis women of color).

Table 10.2. LEGISLATIVE LEADERSHIP ON WOMEN-SPECIFIC BILLS

AZ, FL, MS, NM, TN, and TX Representatives (1997 Regular Session)

Independent Variable	Number of Bills Introduced (Negative Binomial Regression)		One or More Bills Introduced (Logistic Regression)	
	Coef.	Std. Err.	Coef.	Std. Err.
White female	1.005075	.1646015***	1.385722	.2905741***
Black female	.7482336	.3621965**	.9817135	.6446666
Black male	−.002574	.3610704	−.4205072	.6371601
Latina	1.578038	.3744735***	2.642935	.718689***
Latino	.72591	.3532494**	1.61141	.572387***
Democrat	.1032413	.1557574	.3982097	.240156*
Seniority	−.0316595	.0111437***	−.0511635	.0179818***
Chair W–Spec	.7515064	.2308707***	.8801815	.5143221*
Dist %Black	.0027836	.0068254	−.0069548	.011575
Dist %Hisp	−.0067972	.005712	−.014122	.0090174
Dist %Urban	.0031953	.0019263*	.0066135	.0031982**
Dist %Col Ed	.0044703	.0068041	.0044611	.0113179
Total Bills Introduced	.0565602	.0050312***	.0897322	.0105624***
_constant	−1.722631	.3004785***	−2.075947	.4928812***
	N = 612		N = 612	
	LR chi²(18) = 242.02***		LR chi²(18) = 188.60***	
	Pseudo R² = 0.1513		Pseudo R² = 0.2258	

Predicted Counts [95% Confidence Intervals]			Predicted Probabilities [95% Confidence Intervals]		
Bl male	.45	[.16, .73]	Bl male	0.24	[0.03, 0.44]
Wh male	.45	[.36, .54]	Wh male	0.32	[0.26, 0.39]
La male	.92	[.34, 1.51]	Bl female	0.56	[0.28, 0.84]
Bl female	.95	[.34, 1.55]	Wh female	0.66	[0.54, 0.77]
Wh female	1.22	[.88, 1.56]	La male	0.71	[0.49, 0.92]
La female	2.17	[.71, 3.62]	La female	0.87	[0.72, 1.02]

*** p ≤ .01 ** p ≤ .05 * p ≤ .10 (2-tailed tests).
State fixed effects not shown.
Difference in negative binomial coefficients for black female and black male legislators is statistically significant (p≤.0154), as is that for Latina and Latino legislators (p≤.0152) and for black female and Latina legislators (p≤.0873).
Difference in logit coefficients for black female and black male legislators is statistically significant (p≤.0146), as is that for white female and Latina legislators (p≤.0883), and for black female and Latina legislators (p≤.0700).

The gender and racial/ethnic differences in Education policy leadership revealed in Table 10.4 are more congruent with many of our expectations. Whether it be the number of Education bills introduced or the likelihood of introducing at least one, legislative women of color are at least as active as their white female colleagues, if not more so (differences are not statistically

Table 10.3. LEGISLATIVE LEADERSHIP ON HEALTH BILLS

AZ, FL, MS, NM, TN, and TX Representatives (1997 Regular Session)

Independent Variable	Number of Bills Introduced (Negative Binomial Regression)		One or More Bills Introduced (Logistic Regression)	
	Coef.	Std. Err.	Coef.	Std. Err.
White female	.4580359	.1281015***	.4246526	.3028083
Black female	.4268811	.2912782	1.663595	.7185365**
Black male	.0880936	.261198	.507979	.6304554
Latina	.8121552	.3016364***	−.0235092	.739952
Latino	.2019184	.2500925	−.9859581	.6209004
Democrat	−.0017077	.1093353	.0893023	.2450284
Seniority	.003968	.0076474	.0207873	.0174095
Chair Health	.7910169	.2020789***	.6956289	.8053854
Dist %Black	−.0029023	.0050551	−.023425	.0120912*
Dist %Hisp	−.0013394	.0040696	.0163806	.0096258*
Dist %Urban	.0018253	.0014327	.0019223	.0032593
Dist %Col Ed	−.0013322	.0051707	−.0042078	.0116637
Total Bills Introduced	.0508775	.0039575***	.1174012	.0139623***
_constant	−.6456055	.22187***	−1.752599	.5238747***

N = 612
LR chi²(18) = 274.10***
Pseudo R² = 0.1114

N = 612
LR chi²(18) = 146.10***
Pseudo R² = 0.1885

Predicted Counts [95% Confidence Intervals]			**Predicted Probabilities** [95% Confidence Intervals]		
Wh male	1.50	[1.30, 1.71]	La male	0.50	[0.22, 0.77]
Bl male	1.64	[0.89, 2.39]	La female	0.72	[0.44, 1.00]
La male	1.84	[1.01, 2.67]	Wh male	0.72	[0.66, 0.79]
Bl female	2.30	[1.11, 3.50]	Wh female	0.80	[0.71, 0.89]
Wh female	2.38	[1.84, 2.91]	Bl male	0.81	[0.65, 0.98]
La female	3.39	[1.50, 5.27]	Bl female	0.93	[0.85, 1.01]

*** p ≤.01 ** p ≤.05 * p ≤.10 (2-tailed tests).
State fixed effects not shown.
Difference in negative binomial coefficients for Latina and Latino legislators is statistically significant (p≤.0305).
Difference in logit coefficients for white female and black female legislators is statistically significant (p≤.0979), as is that for black female and Latina (p≤.0867) and that for black female and black male legislators (p≤.0482).

significant). Legislative men of color are significantly more active on Education issues than are white men; in fact, they are just as involved as their female counterparts are. Thus, on this broader dimension of women's interests, both women and men of color provide more substantive representation of women than their white male colleagues do. Our expectation that significant gender differences

Table 10.4. LEGISLATIVE LEADERSHIP ON EDUCATION BILLS

AZ, FL, MS, NM, TN, and TX Representatives (1997 Regular Session)

Independent Variable	Number of Bills Introduced (Negative Binomial Regression)		One or More Bills Introduced (Logistic Regression)	
	Coef.	Std. Err.	Coef.	Std. Err.
White female	.1513155	.1255872	.3569655	.3126811
Black female	.5912034	.2779511**	1.369128	.7120551*
Black male	.6509055	.2627141**	1.204758	.6296838*
Latina	.5432242	.280874*	1.638582	.892213*
Latino	.4502444	.2239802**	1.694035	.8052641**
Democrat	.0004808	.1057848	−.1208532	.2513573
Seniority	−.0124348	.0069942*	−.0263479	.0172109
Chair Educ	1.031818	.2094342***	1.888581	1.063601*
Dist %Black	−.0065546	.0050609	−.0148336	.0119465
Dist %Hisp	−.0032521	.0036777	−.0071895	.0105797
Dist %Urban	.0003772	.0013605	.0011956	.0034092
Dist %Col Ed	−.0001139	.0048275	−.0015486	.0121383
Total Bills Introduced	.0405637	.0036071***	.1005789	.013868***
_constant	.0480361	.2078035	−.5392567	.525871
	N = 612		N = 612	
	LR chi^2(18) = 237.78***		LR chi^2(18) = 125.78***	
	Pseudo R^2 = 0.0935		Pseudo R^2 = 0.1735	
	Predicted Counts **[95% Confidence Intervals]**		**Predicted Probabilities** **[95% Confidence Intervals]**	
	Wh male	1.69 [1.47, 1.91]	Wh male	0.73 [0.66, 0.79]
	Wh female	1.97 [1.52, 2.41]	Wh female	0.79 [0.69, 0.89]
	La male	2.65 [1.59, 3.72]	Bl male	0.90 [0.79, 1.00]
	La female	2.91 [1.39, 4.43]	Bl female	0.91 [0.81, 1.02]
	Bl female	3.05 [1.55, 4.56]	La female	0.93 [0.82, 1.04]
	Bl male	3.24 [1.76, 4.72]	La male	0.93 [0.84, 1.03]

*** p ≤.01 ** p ≤.05 * p ≤.10 (2-tailed tests).
State fixed effects not shown.

among white legislators remain across all dimensions of women's interests is the only one not confirmed by the figures reported in Table 10.4: here for the first time white women appear no more involved than white men.[18]

We see yet another pattern in the relationship between intersecting gender-race identities and women's substantive representation in Table 10.5's

18. This pattern of gender differences in state legislative leadership on Health matters but not on Education policy is similar to that found in Swers's (Chapter 9 of this volume) analysis of legislative activity in the US Senate. However, unlike Swers, we

Table 10.5. LEGISLATIVE LEADERSHIP ON WELFARE/POVERTY BILLS

AZ, FL, MS, NM, TN, and TX Representatives (1997 Regular Session)

Independent Variable	Number of Bills Introduced (Negative Binomial Regression)		One or More Bills Introduced (Logistic Regression)	
	Coef.	Std. Err.	Coef.	Std. Err.
White female	.5439098	.2377651**	.4082197	.2973246
Black female	.4797264	.5305094	.6456689	.6346749
Black male	.3007554	.474983	.1241167	.613771
Latina	1.631033	.4947395***	1.877994	.6479675***
Latino	1.233404	.42972***	1.154303	.5511882**
Democrat	−.1377452	.2156229	.2489576	.2632073
Seniority	−.0078726	.0142348	−.0215278	.0179998
Chr Welfare	.5785781	.3195799*	.8613972	.4764196*
Dist %Black	.0062828	.0096964	.0052812	.0117582
Dist %Hisp	−.0099692	.0072517	−.0155597	.0090277*
Dist %Urban	.0008763	.0023963	.0014635	.0030681
Dist Ave Inc	−.0000145	.0000121	−9.09e−06	.0000141
Total Bills Introduced	.0494601	.0063806***	.0631964	.0093841***
_constant	−1.461042	.5674455***	−2.049174	.6878461***

N = 612	N = 612
LR chi²(18) = 131.39***	LR chi²(18) = 102.46***
Pseudo R² = 0.1126	Pseudo R² = 0.1432

Predicted Counts [95% Confidence Intervals]			Predicted Probabilities [95% Confidence Intervals]		
Wh male	.28	[.20, .35]	Wh male	0.20	[0.15, 0.25]
Bl male	.37	[.06, .68]	Bl male	0.22	[0.03, 0.41]
Bl female	.45	[.03, .87]	Wh female	0.27	[0.17, 0.38]
Wh female	.48	[.28, .67]	Bl female	0.32	[0.08, 0.57]
La male	.95	[.23, 1.67]	La male	0.44	[0.20, 0.69]
La female	1.41	[.15, 2.67]	La female	0.62	[0.34, 0.90]

*** p ≤.01 ** p ≤.05 * p ≤.10 (2-tailed tests).
State fixed effects not shown.
Difference in negative binomial coefficients for white female and Latina legislators is statistically significant (p≤.0312), as is that for black female and Latina legislators (p≤.0896).
Difference in logit coefficients for white female and Latina legislators is statistically significant (p≤.0290).

analysis of Welfare and Poverty policy leadership. Here, as with Women-Specific issues, Latina lawmakers stand out as the most actively involved: they introduce significantly more Welfare/Poverty bills than anyone else, and they are more likely than anyone else to introduce at least one such bill (though the

find that partisanship has little or no effect on bill sponsorship in state legislatures (see Tables 10.2–10.6). Indeed, our results (not shown) are quite similar, even when we restrict the analysis to Democrats only.

differences between Latinas and Latinos are not statistically significant). Black female legislators, on the other hand, introduce just as few Welfare/Poverty bills as their white female colleagues do and are equally unlikely to introduce at least one. Meanwhile, significant gender differences are few, even among white legislators. Latinos appear less active than Latinas, but the differences are not statistically significant. By all measures, African American men and women are equally inactive—no more active, in fact, than white men. White legislative women introduce significantly more Welfare/Poverty bills on average than do white men, but the two groups are equally unlikely (or reluctant) to introduce any such measures. Few of these patterns are congruent with our hypotheses.

Table 10.6's analysis of legislative leadership on All Women's Issues provides some support for our expectation that the broadest conception of women's interests would best capture African American and Latina women's commitment to women's substantive representation. While almost all legislators introduce at least one bill that qualifies as Women-Specific, Health-, Education-, or Welfare/Poverty-related, there are significant differences in degree or level of involvement. Latina lawmakers again stand out as the most active leaders on women's interest legislation (by this measure), introducing significantly more bills than anyone else. Black female legislators rank second, with white female and Latino legislators following close behind. White male legislators, meanwhile, lag behind all others; only the difference between them and their black male colleagues fails to meet conventional levels ($p \le .10$) of statistical significance. It is the case, then, that when women's substantive representation is defined broadly to include both women-specific measures and measures dealing with education, health care, and/or welfare, legislative women of color appear just as, and sometimes more committed to, representing women as their white female colleagues. Moreover, by this all-inclusive measure, white women, African American women, and Latinas alike provide more substantive representation of women's interests than do their male counterparts. Yet these results are not much different from those obtained with our most selective, Women-Specific measure of substantive representation.

DISCUSSION AND CONCLUSIONS

This chapter's exploration of Implications 2.1 and 2.2A from Chapter 1 indicates that the relationship between women's descriptive and substantive representation is not a simple one. As our results illustrate, it depends in no small part on which women (and men) and which definition of women's interests one considers.[19] But do some definitions of women's interests spotlight

19. No doubt the relationship between women's descriptive and substantive representation also depends on which legislative body(ies) and which year(s) one examines.

Table 10.6. LEGISLATIVE LEADERSHIP ON ALL WOMEN'S
ISSUE BILLS

AZ, FL, MS, NM, TN, and TX Representatives (1997 Regular Session)

Independent Variable	Number of Bills Introduced (Negative Binomial Regression)	
	Coef.	Std. Err.
White female	.3664003	.0797568***
Black female	.4373839	.1779619**
Black male	.1924536	.1639498
Latina	.8420836	.1799056***
Latino	.3366151	.1479942**
Democrat	.0097036	.0686606
Seniority	-.0034628	.0046668
Chair Any	.4011875	.0913663***
Dist %Black	-.0018202	.003171
Dist %Hisp	-.0028953	.0024246
Dist %Urban	.0010311	.0008829
Dist %Col Ed	.0004916	.003164
Total Bills Introduced	.0464845	.0023952***
_constant	.5049359	.1355467***

N = 612

LR chi^2(18) = 501.98***

Pseudo R^2 = 0.1471

Predicted Counts

[95% Confidence Intervals]

Wh male	3.79	[3.48, 4.10]
Bl male	4.59	[3.27, 5.91]
La male	5.31	[3.89, 6.72]
Wh female	5.47	[4.69, 6.24]
Bl female	5.87	[4.01, 7.23]
La female	8.80	[5.88, 11.72]

*** p ≤.01 ** p ≤.05 * p ≤.10 (2-tailed tests).
State fixed effects not shown.
Difference in coefficients for white female and Latina legislators is statistically
significant (p≤.0111), as is that for black female and Latina legislators (p≤.0945), and
for Latina and Latino legislators (p≤.0027).

the representational leadership of some women while obscuring that of others? More specifically, are definitions of women's interests and measures of women's substantive representation racially or ethnically biased? This chapter explores that possibility by examining systematically how varying definitions of women's interests—the *what*—affect the *who* in analyses of US state legislative agenda-setting behavior.

Relying on the theory and epistemology of intersectionality, as well as the extant research on Latina and African American women in public office, we speculated that such a racial/ethnic bias would be more likely to occur when women's interests are defined more narrowly in terms of issues that affect women most directly and primarily. Gauging legislative leadership on such women-specific issues (only), we hypothesized, may overestimate the representational commitments of white women and underestimate those of women of color. In contrast, broader definitions of women's interests, which overlap and intersect with definitions of African American and Latino interests, might capture the representational activities of legislative women of color more accurately, revealing a stronger commitment than we might otherwise observe. Our analyses do not uncover consistent or clearly egregious patterns of racial/ethnic bias, but they do suggest that some conceptual and measurement strategies might be preferable to others.

It is important—methodologically, empirically, and normatively—to highlight what is our most consistent finding: no matter what definition of women's interests we employ, legislative women of color never appear disengaged from or significantly less committed to women's substantive representation than anyone else. Thus, our findings corroborate Implication 2.1 that women in government articulate women's issues more than men do, and that is true for ethnically and racially diverse women, not just for white women only. When legislative women of color are distinguished, it is because they provide *higher* levels of leadership on women's issues—and this is the case regardless of how narrowly or broadly those issues or interests are defined. Indeed, Latinas stand out as the most active group of legislators on the most narrowly defined, Women-Specific issues *and* on the broadest, All Women's Issues measures. Latina legislators also introduce more Welfare/Poverty bills than anyone else and, unlike any other group, they are more likely than not to sponsor at least one such measure. Similarly, black women are significantly more likely than any other group of legislators to introduce as least one Health-related measure. As these results indicate, we must also recognize that African American women and Latinas do not always pursue the same paths to women's substantive representation, as the "women of color" moniker often implies. Thus, our findings also indicate support for Implication 2.2A that the incorporation of more diverse women in government leads to articulation of more diverse preferences and priorities.

Moreover, there is no clear, consistent pattern of increasing legislative activity among women and men of color as the definition of women's interests gets broader, as we hypothesized. Nor is there any consistent tendency for Latino and African American male lawmakers to match the advocacy levels of their female counterparts across issues of health, education, and welfare. Similarly, there is no clear indication that white women's leadership on behalf of women's interests wanes as the definition broadens. Only on Education issues does white women's leadership fall behind that of both black women and Latinas. Nor do gender differences among white legislators remain constant across issue-areas, as we expected. We thus return full circle to the conclusion that the relationship between legislator identity and women's substantive representation is a complex and contingent one.

But, to paraphrase Smooth (2006a), this is a mess worth capturing in our research designs. If our findings are any indication, no simple, single-axis, single-shot, or one-size-fits-all approach to defining and measuring women's political interests will do justice to the very complexity of the phenomena we hope to understand. Different definitions can and do yield different results. Allowing for and even embracing such complexity is, of course, especially valuable and appropriate for an intersectional approach to political representation (Hancock, Chapter 3 of this volume, 2007; McCall 2005). It also recognizes the complexity and contingency of the very political, socially constructed nature of women's political interests themselves (Htun this volume; Reingold and Swers 2011). Perhaps, then, the best strategy is to maintain the one we developed for this study: identify multiple definitions of women's interests; theorize about the meaningful conceptual and empirical differences (and similarities) between them; and empirically test propositions derived from such theorizing.

CHAPTER 11

Representing Women

Empirical Insights from Legislatures and

Cabinets in Latin America

MARIA C. ESCOBAR-LEMMON,
LESLIE A. SCHWINDT-BAYER, AND
MICHELLE M. TAYLOR-ROBINSON

A key argument for why women need to be represented in government is that women will bring different issues to the policy agenda, and in particular, that women will represent women (Sinkkonen and Haavio-Mannila 1981; Skjeie 1991).[1] Descriptive representation has value in its own right, but whether it also produces substantive representation merits empirical investigation because there has long been debate about whether descriptive representation will produce representation of a specific group's interests (see Pitkin 1967; Sapiro 1981). This is particularly important in the context of the concept stretching that Dahlerup (Chapter 4 of this volume) described related to substantive representation.

This chapter articulates specific hypotheses and provides empirical support for several of the propositions outlined in Chapter 1. First, we expect that women in government will articulate women's issues more often than will male officials (Implication 2.1 from Chapter 1). A goal of this chapter is to test if evidence corroborates this expectation, particularly across different government policy-making venues, and to test how that varies across definitions of women's interests. We also address Implications 2.2B and 3.2, arguing

1. We thank Eduardo Alemán, Lee Ann Banaszak, and Mariana Caminotti for comments on earlier versions of this chapter.

that the presence of women in more venues will lead to more articulation of women's interests.

We begin by grappling with *what* types of legislation should be coded as "women's issue" bills, moving from a narrow definition of women's rights and equality to a broader coding of children's and family issues, and then anti-poverty legislation. We then assess how our answer to the questions "Do women represent women's interests? Do men?" changes as we vary our measure. Examining legislative behavior in Colombia and Costa Rica by both members of congress and the president's cabinet, we find that different definitions yield different answers to the question of *who* represents women's interests, *where* representation of women occurs (how it varies across venues and countries), and *when* (i.e., how it changes over time). Representation of women's interests is highly dependent upon how women's issues are measured.

DIFFERENT MEASURES OF "WOMEN'S INTERESTS"

As discussed in Chapter 1 of this book, conceptualizations of how to measure women's interests are varied and often controversial. At one extreme, scholars sometimes use a very narrow definition that derives from women's long-time subordination in society and focuses on concerns with equality (e.g., Beckwith and Cowell-Myers 2007; Bratton 2005; Swers 2002). This categorization incorporates issues such as violence against women, equal pay, and equal treatment in the workplace. Yet, this view has been criticized as *too* narrow because of the heterogeneity of women as a social group and because of the Western bias inherent in that definition. What one woman (or researcher) might call discrimination, another might call treating women with respect.

At the other end of the spectrum, scholars characterize women's interests very broadly as those dealing with a host of issues deriving from women's traditional roles in the private sphere. This usually includes issue areas such as education, health care, and poverty. Although broader, it too has been criticized for being too traditional, not representing concerns of women in the twenty-first century, and for reinforcing traditional gender stereotypes and marginalization of women because it implies that men do not have to focus on these issues (Baldez 2012 makes this point). As this brief review shows, no single definition of women's interests encompasses all perspectives. This underscores the need to examine women's representation across a broad spectrum of women's issue definitions.

Do findings about who represents women and where representation occurs change if we adopt a broader conceptualization of "women's issues?" We view it as unsatisfying to stop analysis of who represents women's interests with the small number of issues associated with what Beckwith

(Chapter 2 of this volume) refers to as the meta-interest of access to political power and voice. Interviews consistently find that women legislators consider women and women's groups to be a special or important constituency that they represent (see Mansbridge 1999, 2003; Reingold 2000; Carroll 2002; Trembley 2003; Childs 2004; Franceschet and Piscopo 2008; Saint-Germain and Chavez Metoyer 2008; Schwindt-Bayer 2010: 69), and they may view themselves as representing women by focusing on other issues (see Smooth 2011 for an excellent illustration). Some studies found that many men also say that women are a constituency they represent (see Thomas 1994; Schwindt-Bayer 2010). Thus, we conceive of and code legislation in several ways.[2]

Women's Interests Manifested as Women's Rights/Equality Issues

In general, these are bills that fit under a feminist rubric. We based this coding on Dodson and Carroll (1991: 38), who consider women's rights bills to be those "that dealt specifically with issues of direct concern to women generally (e.g., legislation concerning rape, teen pregnancy, or women's health) or in terms of their special concerns as wage earners (e.g., pay equity), others balancing home and work (e.g., maternity leave, day care) or marital partners (e.g., domestic violence, spousal retirement benefits, division of property in divorce)." Bratton (2005: 107) describes women's equality issues as those "that directly address and seek to improve women's economic, political, and social status."[3] This concept of women's interests has been used extensively in studies on the United States (see Dodson and Carroll 1991; Thomas 1994; Reingold 2000; Swers 2002) and a more limited number of studies in Latin America (e.g., Chaney 1979; Molyneux 1985; Craske 1999, 2003; Htun 2003b; Schwindt-Bayer 2006, 2010). Many female politicians in Latin America resist the label "feminist," however, making this a narrow definition for a study of representation in Latin American cases.

2. Owing to the origins of these data sets, there are some discrepancies across the two sets of analyses for how bills were coded and years covered, but because of some unique variables included, it was not possible to obtain additional data allowing identical coding or time coverage. The most salient implication of this is that in the legislator data set, but not the cabinet minister data set, women's issue bill categories are mutually exclusive. A few bills in Colombia were co-sponsored by a minister and one or more legislators.

3. See Beckwith and Cowell-Meyers (2007: 556) for a comprehensive list of the types of policy issues that fall into this category.

Women's Interests Manifested as Children and Family Issues

Our second category is less feminist, making it perhaps more applicable to Latin America, but also more traditional, which has its own shortcomings. It builds from studies that have found that female legislators are more likely than their male colleagues to initiate or pass children or families bills (Schwindt-Bayer 2006, 2010; O'Regan 2000; Kittilson 2008). Such bills include: treaties to found the Iberoamerican Youth Organization, regulation of housing costs, creating funds for providing poor families with potable water, regulating child labor, creating a national center for attention to minors with drug addictions. While this "traditional" definition may be a broader conceptualization of women's issues than equality bills, children/ family legislation may not represent the interests of all women, particularly women without children.

Women's Interests Manifested as Pro-poor Issues

Empirically, more women than men are poor, particularly women heads of household.[4] In addition, female politicians may focus on welfare topics because of the disadvantage women historically faced in the labor market and because social welfare policy areas have historically been open to women, whereas fields such as defense, economics, and foreign affairs have not. Building on older literature that emphasized social issues as women's issues, we expect that women may initiate more pro-poor legislation than do men (Chaney 1979; Dodson and Carroll 1991; Thomas 1994; Schwindt-Bayer 2006). Who represents a "pro-poor" conception of women's issues is particularly noteworthy because most top-level politicians are well off, prompting the question of whether they will represent issues of concern to poor people (see Hancock, Chapter 3 of this volume; Weldon 2011b). Our uncertainty about whether elite women in government will initiate more pro-poor legislation than their male colleagues is increased by Reingold and Smith's (2012) finding that it is women of color, not white women, in US state legislatures who are most often proponents of broader social welfare coverage. Bills coded as pro-poor include: loans to build a hospital or school; extending provision of clean water; limitations on child labor; programs for treating drug addiction (but not criminalization); bills that target resources at micro-, small- and medium-sized

---

4. According to Beckwith (Chapter 2 of this volume), "If women are the major disputants in an issue contest, this is probably a strong signal that a women's *interest* is involved; in fact, that the interest of concern is a women's interest."

producers; legislation to stabilize prices (bus fare, basic foods); regulating working conditions and union rights.[5]

WHY STUDY BILL INITIATION

We focus on who puts women's interests on the government's agenda, and how the answer to that question varies as we change our definition of women's issues. All members of the congress and all cabinet ministers can initiate legislation, so our question is, do they choose to spend at least part of the scarce time they can devote to legislating initiating bills on women's issue topics? There are other ways that officials can work for (and receive credit for working on) women's issues, such as amending bills, lobbying for funding, engaging in program oversight, and appointing managers who will work aggressively on projects. But, we explore bill initiation directly to engage a well-established literature that studies the topic this way. Also, because we are concerned with the empirical analysis of interests and issues, we think it important to examine an area where empirical (and quantitative) data exist and are frequently used.

CASE SELECTION

We want to explore *who* represents women's interests, depending on how women's issues are defined, and *where* representation occurs across venues within government, across countries, or over time. Legislatures are the classical venue for studying representation, because the legislature is supposed to be the representative branch of government. Yet in Latin America, the executive is generally viewed as the leader in policy making, with the congress reacting to the executive's initiatives. Thus, it is important to explore who represents women's interests within the legislature, but also whether the executive branch is a venue for representation of women's interests. The latter can be studied directly in Latin America because the executive can initiate bills, and a cabinet minister(s) signs the bill as the author. Another reason to include cabinet ministers in our analysis is that women are often over-represented on committees whose policy purview falls into a stereotypically "feminine" policy domain (e.g., women's issues committee, family issues, education, health) (Heath et al. 2005; Schwindt-Bayer 2010). However, women in Latin American cabinets hold diverse posts (Escobar-Lemmon and

5. Of course, we acknowledge that a politician may still be interested in an issue even if she does not view it as a women's issue, or she may know it is of great importance to her constituents and thus propose legislation on the topic.

Taylor-Robinson 2009). These broader postings are a sign of greater integration of women in government (Borrelli 2010), but they bring up the question of whether women holding such posts legislate for women.

Studying two branches of government and two countries allows us to explore how differences in the political opportunity structure influence the propensity of women and men in government to represent women. As Swers (Chapter 9 of this volume) explains, legislators from Left-leaning parties may expect greater rewards from their partisans for sponsoring women's equality, children/family, or pro-poor bills, while legislators from conservative parties might expect to be punished for proposing what could be branded as "liberal" bills, but they may build links to party constituents with "children/family" bills. However, this may mean that legislators from both sides initiate bills on the same issue, but have different preferences about how to address it (consistent with Beckwith's [Chapter 2 of this volume] predictions). In addition to party influences on their legislative agendas, legislators may be constrained by the policy purview of their committee assignments, and district demographics may shape constituent pressure to introduce pro-poor bills. Cabinet ministers should also consider career benefits and risks, but the "constituents" to whom they owe their loyalty may be different from those for elected officials. Cabinet ministers serve at the pleasure of the president, and can be dismissed if they pursue legislation that is contrary to the president's agenda. They also face norms of legislating only on topics within the purview of their ministry. Department constituents may pressure a minister to initiate bills to defend or promote their interests. These constraints may limit differences in the legislative agendas of male and female ministers. Some ministers have links to women's organizations, and they may benefit from or be expected to represent those groups. Our three different categories of women's issues make it possible to explore whether institutional constraints predict who represents women.

Latin America provides an intriguing context for exploring who represents women's interests because of the region's traditionally *machista* culture, and because it is "a region that traditionally has lagged far behind others in gender equality policies" (Schwindt-Bayer 2010: 84; also Htun 2003b). Recently, however, Latin America has surpassed much of the rest of the world in terms of numerical representation of women, including electing women presidents.[6] In this chapter we compare two Latin American countries: Colombia and Costa Rica.

The countries are similar in their long history of democratic government (at least compared to most other countries in the region). During the years we cover, both countries had centrist, or Center-Right party systems, and neither country was governed by a Left-leaning party or president, which unfortunately means that they do not permit a strong test of how party ideology

6. Laura Chinchilla was elected president in Costa Rica *after* the period covered by either dataset.

impacts the political opportunity structure of legislating on topics that may be defined as women's issues.[7] Both Colombia and Costa Rica have gender quotas, but Costa Rica's quota is for the Legislative Assembly, while Colombia's applies to the executive branch, and a much larger percentage of women have been elected to the legislature in Costa Rica than Colombia.

The legislative data set (covering the 1994–98 and 1998–2002 legislative sessions) includes 304 representatives and 181 senators in Colombia and 114 deputies in Costa Rica's unicameral legislature, who sponsored at least one bill, with 12%, 11%, and 18% women, respectively.[8] It includes all legislators whether or not they served the entire term. The executive datasets (covering the cabinets of the 1998–2002, 2002–2006, and 2006–2010 presidential administrations) include 83 ministers in Colombia and 97 in Costa Rica, with 24% and 25% women, respectively.[9] We include all initial and replacement ministers of full cabinet rank. Rules for initiating bills in the two countries are similar. There are no limits on the number of co-sponsors a bill can have, and we consider all signers equal supporters of the bill.

Tables 11.1 and 11.2 provide descriptive information on the numbers of bills sponsored by legislators and cabinet ministers, respectively. Legislators sponsored over 2,000 bills in each country, with the vast majority of these being single-authored bills (Table 11.1). Legislators also sponsored comparable numbers of women's equality, children/family, and pro-poor bills in each country (Table 11.1). The total number of bills sponsored by cabinet ministers was smaller, but still, a total of 476 bills in Colombia and 630 in Costa Rica were sponsored by ministers (Table 11.2). In Colombia, only one of those bills was a women's equality bill. In Costa Rica, 13 were. Ministers sponsored more children/family bills and pro-poor bills in each country.

WHO REPRESENTS WOMEN'S INTERESTS IN THE LEGISLATURE?

Data

We use the legislator as the unit of analysis and the dependent variable is the number of bills that a legislator sponsors.[10] The total number of bills initiated

7. Costa Rica had a prominent left-of-center party in the Assembly during the 2002–2006 and 2006–2010 administrations, the PAC, but the PAC did not have any seats in the cabinet. In Colombia, leftist parties held some seats in the Congress and no posts in the cabinet.

8. The total number of legislators and the number who sponsored bills do not match in Colombia because some legislators never sponsor a bill.

9. Two Colombian ministers are dropped from the analysis because of missing data on the experience variable (both are men from the Pastrana administration).

10. This dependent variable includes individually sponsored and co-sponsored legislation. We tested alternative specifications of the dependent variable, including a

Table 11.1. NUMBER OF BILLS SPONSORED BY LEGISLATORS IN
COLOMBIA AND COSTA RICA

	Colombia Chamber 1994–1998 1998–2002	Colombia Senate 1994–1998 1998–2002	Costa Rica 1994–1998 1998–2002
Total Bills	1,252	1,134	2,112
Single-sponsored Bills	1,031	956	1,579
Co-sponsored Bills	221	178	533
Women's Equality Bills	32	34	58
Single-sponsored	27	32	40
Co-sponsored	5	2	18
Children/Family Bills	20	31	52
Single-sponsored	20	31	39
Co-sponsored	0	0	13
Pro-poor Bills	91	64	233
Single-sponsored	84	58	197
Co-sponsored	7	6	36

Table 11.2. NUMBER OF BILLS SPONSORED BY CABINET
MINISTERS IN COLOMBIA AND COSTA RICA

	Colombia 1998–2002 2002–2006 2006–2010	Costa Rica 1998–2002 2002–2006 2006–2010
Total Bills	476	630
Single-sponsored Bills	341	565
Co-sponsored Bills	135	65
Women's Equality Bills	1	13
Single-sponsored	1	11
Co-sponsored	0	2
Children/Family Bills	16	28
Single-sponsored	11	24
Co-sponsored	5	4
Pro-poor Bills	45	50
Single-sponsored	33	37
Co-sponsored	12	13

by legislators varied widely. In Colombia, some legislators (8%) sponsored
only one bill, while three sponsored over 100 bills, with the median being 5
in the Chamber and 8 in the Senate. Legislators in the smaller (57-member)
Costa Rica Assembly sponsor many bills—the median legislator sponsored 39

bills, the smallest number of bills sponsored was 14. The variation carries over into the different subject areas.

The primary explanatory variable in the analyses of legislative bill sponsorship is the gender of the legislator (coded "1" for female).[11] We include a series of control variables to isolate the effect of gender. We account for the legislator's ideology because legislators whose party is on the Left of the ideological spectrum may benefit more politically from sponsoring bills in all three categories of women's issue bills than those from parties on the Right. We measure legislators' ideology based on where their party falls on a 5-point ordinal scale from Left to Right (Alcántara 2006; Coppedge 1997; Rosas 2005).

We include a variable for a legislator's committee membership to account for whether or not a legislator served on a standing committee that deals with topics related to women's issues. This ensures that gender is not picking up the fact that women might be disproportionately situated on women's issue committees, or the fact that legislators may be more likely to sponsor bills that deal with topics related to their committee assignment. In Colombia and Costa Rica, the chambers have seven and six standing committees, respectively, and neither country has a standing committee for "women's issues." Therefore, we use a dichotomous variable for whether the legislator sits on the social issues committee.[12]

Senior members have greater experience and knowledge about the chamber and they may initiate more bills than junior legislators, so we control for the number of terms the legislator has served.[13] We control for whether the legislator is a member of the largest party in the chamber,[14] because the

dichotomous measure of whether or not the legislator sponsored at least one bill in the issue area and a continuous measure of the priority that legislators place on different types of bills measured as the percentage of the bills a legislator sponsors that fall into each thematic area. These specifications yielded comparable results.

11. We do not control for race or ethnicity of legislators because of lack of variance.

12. In Colombia, a floor vote determines who sits on the seven permanent committees for the duration of the four-year congress and each legislator gets one assignment. In Costa Rica, the chamber president makes committees assignments annually, with many deputies changing committees, so we code legislators as sitting on a relevant committee if he or she did so in any of the four years of the congress. The Costa Rican Assembly's ad hoc committees are not included in this coding.

13. In Colombia, one legislator was in his eighth term, but most legislators were in their first or second term. In Costa Rica, 88% of deputies were in their first term. The prohibition against immediate reelection in Costa Rica deters many legislators from seeking additional terms after sitting out four years. Average number of terms is 1.8 for Colombian senators and representatives and 1.2 terms for Costa Rican deputies.

14. In both chambers and congresses in Colombia, the Liberals were the largest party and held a majority in all congresses except 1998–2002 in the Senate where they held 48% of the seats. In Costa Rica, the PLN and PUSC alternated as the largest party with the PLN holding 49% of seats in 1994–98 and the PUSC with 51% of the seats in 1998–2002.

largest party can set the legislative agenda and is better positioned to move legislation through the policy process.[15] As a result, legislators from the largest party might be more likely to sponsor bills, in general, and in thematic areas the party sees as important. We control for whether the legislator served as president of the chamber at any point during the congress. Chamber presidents have numerous responsibilities that detract from the time they can spend sponsoring legislation. Consequently, they should sponsor fewer bills than other legislators.

To account for the influence that a legislator's electoral district may have over his or her bill sponsorship behavior, we use a dichotomous measure of whether the legislator's district is urban (higher population density than the country average, coded "1") or rural. This correlates highly with other measures of district demographics such as literacy and unemployment rates. We also include dummy variables to control for legislative term in both countries (1998–2002 coded "1") and chamber in Colombia (upper house coded "1"). Finally, we control for the total number of bills a legislator initiates during the congress.

Multivariate Analysis Findings

We use negative binomial regression for the analysis because the dependent variable is a count of the number of bills a legislator sponsors. This analysis allows us to draw two overarching conclusions. First, coding women's issues in different ways does indeed produce different results. Second, who represents women's issues in the legislature differs across countries (see Table 11.3). With respect to Implication 2.1, women legislators, at least in Costa Rica, do not always initiate more women's interest bills than do men.

In Colombia, female legislators are significantly more likely than male legislators to sponsor women's equality, children/family, and pro-poor legislation. The substantive effect of gender on the likelihood of sponsoring different kinds of legislation also varies. Figure 11.1 shows the predicted probabilities that women and men will sponsor one or more bills in each of the categories of women's issues, setting other variables at their means or modes.[16] The probability that women will sponsor one or more women's equality

---

15. In Costa Rica the capacity of the largest party to control the Assembly's agenda has decreased as rules changes have empowered small parties, but that occurred after the time period included in this analysis (see Alemán 2006; Taylor-Robinson and Ross 2011).

16. We are estimating the predicted probabilities for male and female legislators in the Colombian Chamber in the 1998–2002 term who are centrist (ideology set at its

Table 11.3. LEGISLATOR BILL INITIATION (DEPENDENT VARIABLE = NUMBER OF BILLS SPONSORED BY A LEGISLATOR)

	Colombia			Costa Rica		
	Women's Equality	Children/ Family	Pro–poor Bills	Women's Equality	Children/ Family	Pro–poor Bills
Gender	1.78***	0.95**	0.54***	1.13***	0.31	0.13
	(0.41)	(0.40)	(0.21)	(0.20)	(0.22)	(0.13)
Ideology	−1.30**	−1.87**	0.05	0.00	0.41**	0.03
	(0.65)	(0.78)	(0.38)	(0.23)	(0.18)	(0.13)
Related committee	0.66	0.92**	0.20	0.23	0.27	0.20
	(0.50)	(0.39)	(0.19)	(0.19)	(0.19)	(0.12)
Experience	−0.11	0.10	−0.11	0.16	0.07	0.22**
	(0.21)	(0.14)	(0.07)	(0.15)	(0.15)	(0.10)
Urban district	15.13***	−1.07	0.43	0.31	0.95***	−0.08
	(0.47)	(0.68)	(0.34)	(0.20)	(0.28)	(0.12)
Largest party	0.17	−0.76*	−0.08	−0.37	−0.18	−0.02
	(0.41)	(0.44)	(0.21)	(0.23)	(0.21)	(0.12)
Chamber president	0.26	−0.36	−0.64	0.36	−0.00	0.15
	(0.70)	(0.68)	(0.70)	(0.28)	(0.29)	(0.18)
Legislative term	−1.09***	−1.38***	−0.68***	0.35*	−0.08	−0.31**
	(0.35)	(0.40)	(0.18)	(0.20)	(0.20)	(0.12)
Legislative chamber	0.15	0.66	−0.41**	–	–	–
	(0.45)	(0.48)	(0.20)			
Total bills sponsored	0.11***	0.06***	0.10***	0.02***	0.02***	0.03***
	(0.02)	(0.02)	(0.01)	(0.01)	(0.00)	(0.01)
Constant	−18.32***	−1.74**	−1.85***	−1.52***	−1.89***	−0.22
	(0.51)	(0.76)	(0.40)	(0.42)	(0.44)	(0.30)
N	485	485	485	114	114	114
Log pseudolikelihood	−146.87	−133.34	−338.02	−148.15	−122.52	−221.16
X^2	2722.57	35.52	133.07	86.91	54.94	42.28
A	3.23	5.27	0.77	0.10	0.00	0.08

* $p<0.05$, ** $p<0.01$, *** $p<0.001$.
Table presents negative binomial estimates with robust standard errors clustered around the legislator in parentheses.

bills is 0.13 compared to 0.03 for men. In other words, nearly 13% of female representatives would sponsor women's equality bills compared to only 3% of male representatives, all else being equal. For children/family bills, the probabilities are 0.01 and 0.03 for men and women, respectively. These smaller probabilities for both men and women reflect the relatively small numbers of children/family bills sponsored. The *difference* between men and women is still evident, however. For pro-poor legislation, the statistical models estimate that 29% of female

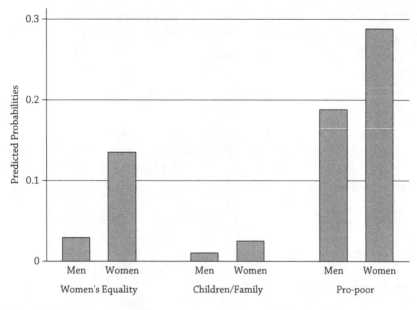

Figure 11.1
Predicted Probabilities of Initiating One or More Women's Interest Bills in Colombia

representatives will sponsor one or more pro-poor bills compared to only 19% of male representatives, all else held constant—a substantively large difference between men and women.

In Costa Rica's Assembly, gender differences in bill sponsorship appear only for women's equality bills. Figure 11.2 shows the predicted probabilities that women and men will sponsor varying numbers of women's equality bills, ranging from 0 to 9—the actual values for the number of women's equality bills that any legislator sponsored.[17] The figure shows that men are more likely than women to have sponsored no women's equality bills or only 1. Women, however, have a significantly higher probability than men

mean, which is close to 0), do not sit on a social committee, have been in office for one term only, are from urban districts, are members of the largest political party in the chamber, are not the chamber president, and sponsored the average number of bills, which was 8.3. Importantly, the statistical model estimates the effect of gender on the *number* of bills sponsored and allows us to predict the probability that men and women will sponsor zero, one, two, three, etc., bills. For ease of presentation in the figure, we add together the predicted probabilities for all numbers of bills sponsored that are greater than 0. In most cases, the probability of sponsoring more than one bill was infinitely small.

17. We also set the control variables at their means and modes to calculate the predicted probabilities for Costa Rica: male and female legislators in the 1998–2002 term who are Center-Right (ideology set at its mean, which is -.40), do not sit on the social issues committee, have been in office for one term only, are from urban districts, are

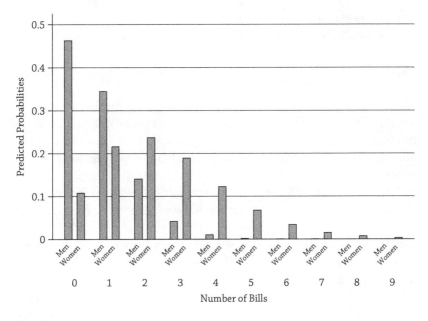

Figure 11.2
Predicted Probabilities of Initiating Varying Numbers of Women's Equality Bills in Costa Rica

of sponsoring two or more bills. The predicted percentage of women who sponsor two bills is 24% compared to only 14% for men. We expect 19% of women and only 4% of men to sponsor three or more bills. The larger predicted probabilities of sponsoring a women's equality bill in Costa Rica than in Colombia for both women and men reflect the fact that the average legislator in Costa Rica sponsors more bills (44 bills compared to only 8 in Colombia).

We find little evidence that committee assignments, district demographic characteristics, or ideology affect initiation of women's issue bills. We expected that legislators assigned to social issues committees would have more opportunity to initiate women's issue bills, but only find evidence to support this expectation for children/family bills in Colombia's Congress. Regarding incentives created by district demographics, we would expect legislators from rural districts to initiate more pro-poor bills. However, there is no statistical support for that expectation; legislators from urban districts initiate more women's equality bills in Colombia, and more children/family bills in Costa Rica. Ideology's impact differs across our two countries' legislatures. Conservative deputies in Costa Rica initiate more children/family bills (which may reflect a similar political opportunity structure to what Swers [Chapter 9 of this volume] finds in the US Senate), while in Colombia, liberal legislators initiate more women's equality and children/family bills.

WHO REPRESENTS WOMEN'S INTERESTS
IN THE EXECUTIVE BRANCH?

Data

We use the minister as the unit of analysis,[18] and the dependent variable is whether a minister sponsors or co-sponsors a women's equality, children and family, or pro-poor bill. In Colombia, 73 ministers (88%) sponsored at least one bill, and 72 (or 74%) did so in Costa Rica, but the number initiated varied widely, ranging from 0 to 46 bills in Colombia (mean of 7.3) and 0 to 84 bills in Costa Rica (mean 6.6). Most ministers initiated no bills that fit under any of the three definitions of women's issues (99% and 91% in Colombia and Costa Rica, respectively, under the narrowest definition, and 65% and 63% under the pro-poor definition). Moreover, among those who did initiate women's issue bills, very few initiated more than one, leading us to use a dichotomous measure in the analysis.[19]

The primary variable of interest is the gender of the minister (coded "1" for female).[20] We include a series of control variables to isolate the effect of gender. To ensure that gender is not picking up the fact that women might be disproportionately situated in portfolios in a stereotypically feminine policy domain, we include a variable for a minister's post. Rather than add dummy variables for specific portfolios, we created a "social welfare portfolios" category (Education, Health, Housing and Urbanization, Labor and Social Security, Culture, Women's Issues) (see Keman 1991). This strategy is also useful because Costa Rica had a "women's affairs" ministry from 1998 to 2006, but Colombia does not have a women's affairs ministry. "Social welfare portfolio" allows us to test how the policy domain of the minister's post affects the initiation of this type of legislation, regardless of sex.

To take into account that some ministers have greater experience related to their portfolio, which may lead them to initiate more bills, we control

members of the largest political party, are not the chamber president, and sponsored the average number of bills, which was 44.

18. We record each post a minister held and each presidential administration they served in as separate observations. An individual who switched posts during a term contributes two observations, as does a minister who served in multiple terms. Roughly 20% of the data in both countries is non-unique observations.

19. Of the 9 ministers who initiated women's equality bills in Costa Rica, 4 initiated one, 4 initiated two, and one initiated three. Of the 14 ministers who initiated children/family bills, 9 initiated only one, with the remaining 5 initiating 2–7 bills, and of the 36 ministers who sponsored pro-poor bills, 22 wrote only one. In Colombia, of the 16 ministers who authored children/family bills, 13 sponsored only one; of the 29 who sponsored pro-poor legislation, 18 did so only once.

20. We do not control for race or ethnicity because there is almost no variance in our data set.

for experience with a dummy variable measuring whether the minister had education or work experience relevant to that ministry. We control for the total number of bills a minister initiates because some ministers are "super-initiators," but we include all ministers, even those who do not initiate any bills. We include a dummy variable controlling for the number of days a minister stayed in office since more time in post gives them more opportunities to legislate.[21] We also include dummy variables for presidential administration, with Pastrana's 1998–2002 administration as the comparison category in Colombia, and Pacheco's 2002–2006 administration as the comparison category in Costa Rica. Both presidents faced challenges in dealing with the legislature owing to the party situation, making them a comparable baseline. However, as mentioned above, all the presidents in our study were ideologically centrist or somewhat right of center, so they do not create an ideal opportunity for exploring the impact of ideology on representation of women's issues.

Multivariate Analysis Findings

Table 11.4 presents the findings for minister bill sponsorship. Given our dichotomous dependent variable, we estimate the model via logistic regression. We do not include a model of women's equality bills in Colombia because there was only one bill in that category. This analysis leads to three important conclusions. First, in contradiction to the expectation of Implication 2.2B, substantial representation of women in the cabinet does *not* lead to a legislative agenda that represents women's issues, but it does illustrate the importance of having access to multiple venues because not all may be equally good. Second, coding women's issues in different ways produces slightly different results. Third, who represents women's issues in the cabinet differs across countries.

Cabinet ministers (women or men) are *not* representing women's issues when they are narrowly defined as women's equality bills. However, ministers are active legislators when we adopt broader conceptualizations of "women's issue" bills. Yet gender has a different impact in our two countries, making conclusions regarding Implication 2.1 less clear.

In Colombia, female cabinet ministers are not sponsoring women's equality or children/family bills at all. The only women's equality bill initiated by a minister during this 12-year period was a bill to increase advantages for rural women in the agricultural sector, initiated by a male minister of agriculture.

---

21. In both countries, the number of days a minister spends in post is a significant (at the .001 level) predictor of the number of bills the minister writes, but by itself explains only about 12% of the variance in Colombia and 15% in Costa Rica.

Table 11.4. CABINET MINISTER BILL INITIATION (DEPENDENT VARIABLE = WHETHER A MINISTER SPONSORED A BILL)

	Colombia			Costa Rica		
	Women's Equality	Children/ Family	Pro–poor Bills	Women's Equality	Children/ Family	Pro–poor Bills
Gender		n/a [a]	−1.64*	2.29	0.06	0.13
			(0.80)	(1.37)	(0.87)	(0.66)
Social welfare portfolio		0.23	1.39*	1.80	1.72	0.87
		(0.77)	(0.67)	(1.15)	(0.97)	(0.63)
Experience		−0.91	0.19	3.35*	−0.17	0.15
		(0.78)	(0.96)	(1.62)	(0.91)	(0.62)
Total bills sponsored		0.15***	0.13**	0.12*	0.26**	0.42***
		(0.04)	(0.05)	(0.05)	(0.09)	(0.13)
Days in post		−0.0004	−0.0003	0.001	−0.001	−0.00003
		(0.0009)	(0.0007)	(0.001)	(0.0008)	(0.0007)
Uribe I		−0.40	1.53*			
		(0.95)	(0.75)			
Uribe II		−0.09	0.77			
		(0.91)	(0.75)			
Arias II				−0.39	−6.32*	−1.08
				(1.51)	(2.69)	(0.85)
Rodríguez				1.70	0.38	0.29
				(1.04)	(0.83)	(0.64)
Constant		−1.72	−2.27**	−10.67***	−3.34*	−2.61**
		(0.88)	(0.82)	(2.55)	(1.37)	(0.86)
N		79	79	97	97	97
Log pseudolikelihood		−30.19	−38.09	−14.99	−19.72	−38.20
X^2		19.38	18.63	23.28	15.00	23.80
Pseudo R–square		.24	.26	.50	.51	.40

* $p<0.05$, ** $p<0.01$, *** $p<0.001$.
Table presents logistic regression coefficients with robust standard errors in parentheses.
[a] Being a woman is a perfect predictor of not initiating any children/family bills. To avoid dropping all the women from the analysis, the model reported in this column is estimated without including the gender variable.

This one bill is additionally noteworthy, because it shows that women's equality bills can come out of unexpected portfolios. None of the 16 children/family bills was authored by women.[22] The negative effect of gender is substantively

22. The fact that women did not sponsor any of the children/family bills in Colombia meant that gender was a perfect predictor. In order to test our hypothesis about the

and statistically significant for pro-poor legislation, as being a woman decreased the odds of sponsoring pro-poor legislation by 81%. Colombia's female cabinet ministers are not initiating bills to advance women's interests, at least as manifested through these three issue categories. Thus, at least in Colombia we do not find evidence in support of Implication 2.2B or 3.2—more women with an influential voice in multiple policy venues is not enhancing the articulation of women's interests, or substantive representation, at least as measured by bill initiation.

In Colombia, only two female ministers were known to have links to women's groups.[23] However, neither of these women sponsored any women's equality, children/family, or pro-poor legislation, even though we expected connections to women's groups to increase the benefit to a politician of initiating such bills. Cabinet portfolio had a mixed effect. Ministers holding social welfare posts in Colombia initiated more pro-poor bills (400% increase in the odds), but the type of post had no effect on children/family legislation. Male ministers holding those portfolios may be representing ministry constituents with women's issue bills, or may be pursuing a party agenda to attract women's votes.

In Costa Rica, female ministers are no more likely than male to sponsor women's equality, children/family, or pro-poor legislation, although all coefficients are in the expected direction. Thus, in Costa Rica's cabinet we do not find support for Implication 2.1, that women will articulate women's interests more than men. Three of the four female ministers in Costa Rica who were known to have ties to women's groups were appointed to head the Ministry of Women's Affairs, yet only one of them sponsored bills in any women's issue categories (two women's equality, one children/family, one pro-poor). The fourth—appointed to Science and Technology—also authored none. Again, our expectation that ministers with connections to women's groups would have more incentive then their colleagues to initiate bills to represent women is not supported by their actions. Interestingly, in Costa Rica holding a social welfare portfolio is not associated with initiation of women's equality, children/family, or pro-poor bills. This may mean that despite norms for ministers to limit their legislation to the policy purview of their portfolios, with broader conceptualizations of women's issues such policy can be pursued in a broad range of portfolios.

political opportunity structure, however, we did not want to drop the women from the data set. Thus, the model we report in Table 11.4 does not include a gender variable. Estimating the model without the women yields substantively similar results.

23. Because of the limited variation, we did not include links to women's groups in the statistical model.

IMPLICATIONS OF OUR STUDY

One overall finding of this study is that while in most, but not all cases, women are more likely to sponsor women's issue bills than are men in the legislature, this is categorically not true in the executive, providing direct evidence against Implication 2.1. A second overall finding is that representation behavior with respect to different women's issues varies across countries and over time. Our findings suggest that all venues are not equally good for the representation of women's interests. This speaks to Implication 2.2B. Even with substantial numbers of women in the cabinet and women holding diverse cabinet posts, the presence of women in more venues is not associated with more articulation of women's interests, at least not in Costa Rica and Colombia.

Implications for *Who* Represents Women's Interests

In Colombia's Congress, women are more likely to sponsor women's issue bills than are men, but the size of this difference is not uniform. The differences in the predicted percentage of women who sponsor women's equality bills and pro-poor legislation is 10%, all else being equal, but it is only 2% for children/family bills. This suggests that women in Colombia are not much more active than their male colleagues in initiating bills on children/family issues. Costa Rican female deputies are more likely than male deputies to sponsor women's equality issue bills, but are no more likely to sponsor bills in any of the other categories of women's issue legislation. With respect to Implication 2.1, this underscores that whether women legislators are more likely than men to represent "women's issues" depends on how we define "women's issues."

Regardless of how women's issues are measured, female cabinet members are not more likely than men to initiate women's issue legislation in Costa Rica, and in Colombia, and the limited evidence we have suggests that they are less likely to do so. It is important to note that across all issue categories, women's issue bills remain a small part of any individual minister's agenda. Ministers—female or male—hardly ever initiate women's equality bills (they constitute only 11% of the legislative agenda for the most active author of women's equality bills, Danilo Chaverri, Minister of the Presidency for President Rodríguez of Costa Rica). For Roberto Rojas Lopez, Minister of Foreign Affairs for President Rodríguez, who authored seven children/family bills (the most we observe), they represent only 8% of his overall bill sponsorship. Why ministers in general do not advance women's issues through legislation is one avenue for future work. This is important because we would expect that more women in more venues would enhance the articulation of women's interests and also movement from interest articulation to policy change. Another area where further research is needed is to examine differences among male and female ministers who occupy the same post within a country to determine if women holding traditionally male posts break with tradition and initiate more women's issue legislation or not.

Implications for *Where* Representation of Women Occurs

The second important conclusion is that there are differences in *where* representation of women's issues takes place, suggesting that not all venues within government are equally valuable to women. In Colombia's Congress, female legislators are more likely than male legislators to sponsor women's interest bills—they do so in all of the categories of women's issues. In Costa Rica's Assembly, however, female deputies are only more likely than men to sponsor bills in one issue category—women's equality. Female ministers in Costa Rica are no more likely than men to sponsor women's issue bills. Possibly this is a result of Costa Rica having implemented an active welfare state decades ago, so welfare programs are mainstream issues for both parties, and are not solely "women's issues."[24] In Colombia's cabinet, female ministers are less likely than their male colleagues to sponsor bills of any women's issue category. What "women's issues" are being represented primarily by female politicians, in comparison to male politicians, clearly varies across countries. In sum, the congress appears (at least in these two countries) to be a more promising venue than the executive for representation of women's issues.

Additional differences exist across the two legislative chambers within Colombia. Disaggregated analyses (not shown) reveal differences between the Colombian Chamber and the Senate. Women are more likely than men to sponsor women's equality issues in both legislative chambers, but in the lower house, women are also significantly more likely to sponsor bills about children/family issues than men, whereas in the upper house, women are significantly more likely to sponsor pro-poor legislation than men.

Among cabinet ministers, the nature of the post they hold may affect representation of women's issues,[25] yet portfolio is not the rigid constraint on representation of women's issues that might be expected, since only in Colombia, and only for pro-poor bills, do ministers in social welfare posts propose more

24. We thank Drude Dahlerup for making this suggestion.

25. Elsewhere we show that women are more likely than men to be appointed to stereotypically feminine policy domain posts (Escobar-Lemmon and Taylor-Robinson 2009) but they are not exclusively appointed to these posts, nor are these posts held exclusively by women. In Colombia, 45% of women are appointed to "social welfare posts," but only 40% of "social welfare posts" are held by women. In Costa Rica, 54% of female ministers hold a "social welfare post," but only 38% of ministers in "social welfare posts" are female.

women's issue legislation. It is ministers of agriculture, in Colombia, and ministers of health, labor, justice, foreign relations, and presidency as well as women's affairs in Costa Rica who are initiating women's equality bills, and many of those ministers are male. Even as ministers restrict their legislation to the policy purview of their portfolio, some are clearly working to advance women's issues as related to their policy domain. Similarly, being assigned to a "social issues" committee in the legislature does not appear to promote representation of women's interests, as this variable is significant (and positive) only for children/family bills and only in the Colombian Congress. It again appears that many policy areas can be used to represent women's interests, and structural constraints are not limiting the capacity of ministers or legislators for representing. These findings speak to the need for nuanced analysis of the meaning of venue, as well as unpacking of the constraints versus opportunities that different venues can create for politicians—both women and men—to articulate women's interests and to transform preferences into policy.

These cross-chamber and cross-branch differences underscore the oft-noted point that generating a single, generalizable classification of women's interests that is applicable across both space and time is inappropriate (Celis et al. 2008; Mackay 2008). Our analysis shows that *who* represents women's issues varies. It also underscores the importance of exercising care in deciding what issues one will use to measure women's interests. More expansive definitions certainly yield more observations, which is helpful for statistical analysis, but may yield different results, underscoring that the choice of operationalization should be driven by theory, not methodological convenience.

Finally, women's equality bills are always a topic for which women in congress are more active than men, but that is not true for women in cabinets (at least not in these two countries), and the cabinet minister analysis suggests that men can be at least as active as women in advancing women's issues via the legislation they initiate. These findings indicate that women's groups that want to promote specific types of issues should choose with care *where* they lobby for their issue, and that the most likely venue will vary across place and across time within a country.

PART FOUR

Representation: Women and Beyond

CHAPTER 12

Does Presence Produce Representation of Interests?

MARIA C. ESCOBAR-LEMMON AND
MICHELLE M. TAYLOR-ROBINSON

In 2011 the Nobel Committee made a deliberate decision to draw attention to women's issues and the status of women by jointly honoring three women—Ellen Johnson Sirleaf, Leymah Gbowee, and Tawakkul Karman—"for their non-violent struggle for the safety of women and for women's rights to full participation in peace-building work" with the Nobel Peace Prize. Liberian President Johnson Sirleaf, Africa's first female president, was honored for her efforts to bring peace, to promote social and economic development, and to improve the status of women. Her fellow countrywoman, Leymah Gbowee, worked to organize women across traditional divides in support of peace and participation in elections. Tawakkul Karman of Yemen organized others to demand peace, democracy, and the rights of women including an end to child marriage. In selecting these three women, the committee stated in its press release: "It is the Norwegian Nobel Committee's hope that the prize to Ellen Johnson Sirleaf, Leymah Gbowee and Tawakkul Karman will help to bring an end to the suppression of women that still occurs in many countries, and to realise the great potential for democracy and peace that women can represent. We cannot achieve democracy and lasting peace in the world unless women obtain the same opportunities as men to influence developments at all levels of society."

The 2011 Nobel Peace Prize was not the first time an international body sought to draw attention to the status of women; it is simply a recent and highly visible example. Certainly the series of United Nations World Conferences for Women, beginning in 1975, and the Convention on Eliminating All Forms of

Discrimination Against Women (CEDAW) also served this role. Similarly, the adoption of Resolution 1325 by the UN Security Council in 2000, which made violence against women in armed conflict an international security issue, also underlined the need for women to participate in aspects of political life from which they have traditionally been excluded and yet which affect them profoundly.

The Nobel Committee's statements represent lofty goals regarding the political inclusion of women. Similarly the goal of CEDAW – eliminating all forms of discrimination against women – also reflects the ambition of gender equality. Both remind us that while much has been accomplished, there is still much to be done before women achieve equal footing with men, and raise questions about whether the presence of women in government can be assumed to produce representation of women's interests in all their diversity. In honoring these women, the Nobel Committee highlights the numerous issues on which and different contexts in which activists and female government officials have worked. The breadth of issues (e.g. protection from sexual violence and sexual harassment, ending war and its related atrocities, social equality, ensuring access to political power) encompassed by the activities of Johnson Sirleaf, Gbowee, and Karman make it clear that women have an appropriate role and a stake in all facets of economic, social, and political life.

As the contributors to this volume show, there are multiple ways to conceive of women's interests[1] and to measure them, and there are also diverse venues where representation may occur. The diversity of definitions, measurement strategies, and observational strategies has hindered the accumulation of knowledge about substantive representation of women, making it difficult for us to understand what it means to represent women's interests and who does the representing. In particular, this research field confronts the ongoing debate over whether *all action* on women's interest topics—including "acting for" by conservative women—constitutes representation, or if action requires a feminist perspective to represent women (see Dahlerup [Chapter 4 of this volume]; Piscopo 2011). Yet the chapters in this volume clearly indicate that these choices about definition and research design affect findings about *who* represents women, on *what issues, where, when,* and *how.*

In this chapter we return to the propositions in Chapter 1 which argue that representation is a multistage process, which can be stalled or derailed due to competing interests, descriptive representation in only some venues, unequal power structures and access, or contradictory political incentive structures. We assess what the empirical chapters, with their diverse research projects, find with regard to the propositions, and we draw conclusions about how the meaning and measurement of representation and of women's interests impact

---

1. Childs and Krook (2009: 133) offer a useful review of different categories of ways "women's issues" have been defined.

the accumulation of knowledge in the field of women and politics. We also suggest directions for future research about representation. Our conclusions in this volume are based on the study of women, yet the lessons learned should be applicable to the study of representation of historically under-represented groups more generally. We return explicitly in the latter half of this chapter to the way these conclusions can be generalized.

How can we best study what those expected to be "group representatives" do once they are in government? Who do women in government, and increasingly diverse women, represent, and when will they do so? How can we determine if female officials provide different forms of representation, or representation of different interests and issues than the dominant group (typically white men) has historically offered? Do women in government become "critical actors," which Childs and Krook (2009: 138) define as "legislators who initiate policy proposals on their own and/or embolden others to take steps to promote policies for women, regardless of the number of female representatives"? This volume indicates that critical actors may operate in multiple venues. Work by critical actors for women's interests may also prompt backlash from other groups. How, where, and when (inside and outside government) does representation of women and their interests occur? What might the findings presented in this book that address questions of *who, where, how, when,* and *what* mean for groups outside government that are lobbying to improve the quality of life of women, or of other historically under-represented groups (even when competing groups may have different preferences about the policies they want government to adopt)? We start addressing these questions by drawing conclusions building from the propositions advanced in Chapter 1.

CONCLUSION 1: CONDITIONS THAT PROMOTE WOMEN'S PRESENCE IN GOVERNMENT AND WOMEN ACTING AS SPOKESPEOPLE FOR WOMEN'S INTERESTS ARE HIGHLY CONTINGENT

In many countries, the number of women holding posts in government—often in diverse government venues—is increasing. But numerical representation of women is uneven across venues and over time within countries, and across countries. In addition, within a policy-making venue, numerical representation of women and the *incentives* to incorporate women into politics ebb and flow as: (1) the organizational strength and unity of women demanding representation fluctuates, and (2) women's interests clash with the interests of groups with long-established political power (see Proposition 1, Chapter 1, also Hancock, Chapter 3, in this volume). Implication 1.1 predicted that "[w]omen's access to decision-making venues increases as women as a group become organized and demand voice and participation." If this is true, we expected the contributors to find evidence that women's mobilization led to increased numerical representation, which led to more articulation of women's interests. But Implication 1.2 predicted backlash; specifically, "[w]omen's access to decision-making venues will decrease if women's issues threaten the power of groups with long-established power." Evidence in support of Implication 1.2 could be fewer women elected or appointed to government posts over time, or that women in government are allowed to have less real influence over policy, or possibly even less opportunity to articulate their views (see Walsh 2012).

Matland and Lilliefeld (Chapter 5) show that parties promote the presence of women, but where representation of women is not a primary concern of party voters, the parties may find their voters selecting male candidates over women, and when women are selected they may be expected to represent other interests. Hoekstra et al. (Chapter 6) show that the presence of more women in the legislature can be an important catalyst for increasing nomination of women to the high court. These chapters present nuanced ideas about when women becoming organized will lead to women having increased, or possibly decreased, access to decision-making venues, and raise important questions about the diffusion of egalitarian representation.

Htun (Chapter 7) reminds researchers of the ongoing importance of the politics of presence (Phillips 1995), even when numerical representation is very limited. She explains that the presence of one or more Afrodescendant women in a legislature in Latin America makes it impossible for male or white legislators to ignore that there is diversity in society—both ethnic and gender diversity. Afrodescendant women legislators speak out for their ethnic group, for women, and for women Afrodescendants. It is not their legislative record, so much as their opportunity to have a voice in deliberations in the chamber, often as surrogate representatives, that is crucial, at least at present in these legislatures. Dahlerup (Chapter 4) also points out the cross-pressures faced by officials and by voters, reminding us that ignoring women's intersectional identities also means that we ignore some of the cross-pressures representatives face. Dahlerup reminds researchers studying representation that "[a]n important criterion of success for the efforts to change women's historical under-representation is whether increasing the number of women in political institutions leads to the representation of a diversity of women and that different voices of women are being heard."

In sum, a first conclusion that can be drawn from this edited volume is that incentives to incorporate new groups into politics (be they women or other groups that have historically been excluded) are complex and contingent. The ability of organized women to obtain presence in government is shaped or limited by the design of institutions (e.g., electoral rules, nomination procedures, where the center of real policy-making power is found) and is something about which a well-developed literature exists. The ability of a historically under-represented group to obtain presence *and* an effective voice in government is also dependent on the organization and political weight of other, often long-established interests, and whether those established groups have interests that dove-tail with, or conflict with, the demands of the newer group. Thus, women's presence and influence (of women as a group or of sub-groups of women) are likely to ebb and flow. This means that even while women's descriptive representation in government has increased, we still have more to learn about descriptive representation.

CONCLUSION 2: WHAT INTERESTS ARE DEFINED, BY RESEARCHERS OR BY POLITICS, AS WOMEN'S INTERESTS INFLUENCE ANSWERS ABOUT WHO REPRESENTS WOMEN

As Beckwith outlines in Chapter 2, there is great diversity in what women want from government and society. There are interests that most women would agree are matters of concern to women, particularly meta-interests such as the right to representation and to participate in politics. But soon thereafter the agreement breaks down, as women or groups of women organize around different issues that are of concern to them and which they want placed on the government's policy agenda. There is even more disagreement about the preferred policy for resolving any specific issue about which women are concerned. It is useful to think of representation of women in terms of this hierarchy of *interests, issues*, and *preferences*. This hierarchical concept of what women want from government, with increasing diversity of what an individual woman or women's group would consider to be "representation" as we move down the ladder, indicates the complexity of studying representation of women. It also underscores differences in preferences, for example between feminists and conservative women, of actors claiming to speak for women. Such complexity is likely to exist in studying representation of other historically under-represented groups as well, since even if there is agreement on their interests, they can define concrete manifestations of that interest as different issues and likely have dissimilar preferences over policy options. Distinguishing interests from preferences may explain why the answers we find in research projects about *who* represents women, *when, where* and *how* are likely to vary when researchers adopt different definitions of women's issues in their studies. The women or women's groups, as well as other groups in a society that are activated by issue X, may be quite different from those who are activated by issue Y, and the same is true for the women (and men) in government who have the capacity and career incentives to act on issue X or Y.

Scholars studying substantive representation often design a research project to examine how a particular issue develops and is addressed by government (e.g., reproductive rights, a welfare program, policies to protect vulnerable people from violence). As such, the study can make a valuable contribution to our understanding about how representation of women occurs: by whom, when, where, or why an attempt at representation is foiled. Yet this volume shows that we need to be cautious about drawing *general* conclusions about *how* representation of women occurs and *by whom* and *where* from the study of a single issue or country. Several of the chapters in this volume explicitly adopt multiple definitions of "women's issues" and demonstrate that *who* represents women changes as the measure (*what interests*) varies.[2]

Proposition 2 underlined how group member agreement on a common interest can be accompanied by disagreement about issues or policy preferences. Implication 2.1 predicted that "[w]omen in government (regardless of venue) will articulate women's issues more than men." Implication 2.2 expects that more women in government, and in more venues, will present more divergent preferences. Findings from the empirical chapters indicate that, while the general impression is that female officials are more active representatives of women than their male colleagues, activity by women officials is only actually seen on some issues and in some venues. More women are found to be associated with more divergent policy preferences, but getting women into more venues of government is not consistently associated with more interest articulation.

Reingold and Haynie in Chapter 10 show that all types of women in six US state legislatures engage in legislative work about women's issues both when narrowly defined with a more feminist definition, and when more broadly defined as welfare policy, and that women are more active than their male colleagues, but minority women, particularly Latina representatives, are frequently the most active representatives, particularly when the definition of women's issues focuses on welfare policy. Swers in Chapter 9 shows that in the US Senate, women are more likely than men to legislate on women's issues, but Republican women are more active on topics related to education, while Democratic women are more active on health care issues, particularly women's health. Escobar-Lemmon et al. in Chapter 11 show that women members of the legislature in Colombia and Costa Rica are active legislators on women's rights, but only in Colombia were women more active legislators than men when women's issues were defined as "children/family bills" or "pro-poor bills," while in Costa Rica there was no evidence of difference in representative behavior between men and women legislators when those definitions were used. Female cabinet ministers in Colombia are not even participants in representation of women's issues (by any definition) when the measure of activity is bill introduction, while in Costa Rica both women and men in the cabinet initiate all types of women's issues bills, though they offer a small number

2. See the Critical Perspectives symposium about the meaning and measurement of women's interests in *Politics and Gender* (2011 volume 3) for more possible definitions.

compared to legislators. The relative inactivity of cabinet ministers as representatives of women (at least in the form of bill introduction) needs to be explored in more countries.

These differing findings about who represents women—which women in government, which men, and in which government venues—indicate that it is necessary to develop systematic, testable theory about when it is logical for career-minded politicians (both group members and non-members) to engage in representation of interests of historically under-represented groups. Theory also needs to address how and when incentives vary across political parties and types of political career aspirations to better specify the context(s) where representation should be expected to occur. We take steps in this direction in the final section of the chapter.

This volume also shows that it is imperative to be aware of the cross-pressures faced by government officials. An official whom scholars "count" as another woman in government—and expect to act for women—may see herself as a representative of women, of her ethnic or racial group, of her party, of the constituents in her district, or as a representative of some or all of the above, at all times, or depending on the bill on the agenda for debate (see Htun, Chapter 7 of this volume). The fluid identities that elected representatives adopt may influence whether, when, and how they represent women and on which issues. Hancock in Chapter 3 reminds us that there are many subtleties to the groups of which people perceive themselves to be members, and thus to the representational hats that government officials wear. We cannot just assume that the government official in a study sees her- or himself as wearing the hat that the research is interested in, or at least not only that hat. Barring the possibility of obtaining interview data to determine which representational hat an official considers herself to be wearing (most of the time or when specific issues are on the agenda), it might be possible to conduct statistical checks of whether empirical findings about representational behavior change when we parse a group (e.g., women) into different sub-categories (à la Reingold and Haynie's analysis in Chapter 10). Though an admittedly crude method, such parsing could provide more traction about when representatives of a large and diverse group such as women are likely to wear different sub-group hats, or hats that make them representatives of other groups (e.g., partisan hats).

Also speaking to definitional challenges, Dahlerup in Chapter 4 reminds us that the meaning of substantive representation is contentious. She explains that "different evaluations of the effects of increases in women's representation, the effects of various quota systems, as well as disagreements in the evaluation of the performance and effectiveness of women politicians in the scientific literature derive often...from lack of clear criteria for evaluation." This is in part due to stretching of Pitkin's concept of "substantive representation" where representation is "acting for...in the interest of" (Pitkin 1967: 111–13, 209 from Dahlerup, Chapter 4 of this volume).

CONCLUSION 3: NOT ALL GOVERNMENT VENUES ARE EQUALLY USEFUL FOR OBTAINING SUBSTANTIVE REPRESENTATION, AND NOT ALL THE ACTION THAT PRODUCES REPRESENTATION OCCURS INSIDE GOVERNMENT

Laurel Weldon (2002b), and Htun and Weldon (2010) argue that representation occurs outside government, and that the number of women in government is not the most important predictor of when progress representing women's issues will be made. Kang's study in Chapter 8 of this volume provides broad cross-national evidence from Africa that clearly illustrates both that civil society groups are active players in calling attention to women's issues, and that there are divergent policy preferences among groups claiming to represent women. Kang studies the Maputo Protocol on the Rights of Women, specifically the part of the Protocol that guarantees women the right to medical abortion, and she shows that civil society groups—both pro- and anti-abortion rights—mobilized over whether the Protocol should be ratified (with both types of groups calling themselves representatives of women). Civil society groups worked with and lobbied different types of government officials to obtain their preferred policy outcome. In the case of ratification of the Maputo Protocol, both supporters and opponents put pressure on government officials and worked with government officials—often women officials in the legislature and the cabinet. It is interesting to note, however, that Kang's statistical findings parallel Weldon's (2002b), as the percentage of women in parliament is not significant. Yet Kang concludes that "[f]uture work should examine not just the percentages of women in office or in cabinet, but whether and when women in office and in cabinet form alliances with women's groups.... The anecdotal evidence suggests that these alliances matter. Indeed, many of the women's activists involved in promoting the Protocol were judges and ministers...." Kang's analysis points to the specific mechanism through which women's representation in one part of government can spill over into other branches of government. Hoekstra et al. in Chapter 6 find evidence that diffusion and spill-over matter in increasing women's numerical representation on high courts. They speculate that this is because women in the legislature recognize that the courts can play an important role in whether women's issue policies, once adopted as laws, are sustained and enforced.

Although spill-over can occur across venues, that does not make all venues equally good for representation. When studying less divisive issues than abortion rights, such as children/family legislation, or pro-poor legislation, Escobar-Lemmon et al. in Chapter 11 find that the cabinet is not a likely venue for representation of these types of women's issues, while the legislature provides more fertile ground, at least in terms of initiating bills. That study, which utilizes data from Colombia and Costa Rica, does not account for pressure from civil society, so it is possible that civil society groups that care about children/family issues or welfare policies are only actively pressuring members of the legislature, not cabinet ministers. Maybe civil society groups lack access to cabinet ministers. Or maybe cabinet ministers in those countries during the presidential administrations studied were occupied pursuing presidents' agendas that did not include children/family or pro-poor policies. Regardless of the cause, the cabinet did not appear to be a prime venue for representing women's issues, even though a substantial percentage of ministers holding diverse portfolios were women. However, legislatures (in Latin America, as well as the US Senate and US state legislatures) are rather consistently found by several chapters in this volume to be active venues for representation of women's issues in the form of bill initiation and amendments, as well as surrogate representation through participation in debates.

As Proposition 3 in Chapter 1 explains, preferences can be articulated in one governmental, or nongovernmental venue, and policy can be made in other government venues. Where a group has descriptive representation could influence the venues that are likely to respond to group demands for representation. Implication 3.1 states that "[a]ccess to the right venue is critical for the ability of representatives of women's interests to change policy." Implication 3.2 predicts that women will have greater success in transforming their preferences into policy when they have an influential voice in multiple venues. Kang's analysis in Chapter 8 provides support for both these implications, but Escobar-Lemmon et al.'s findings in Chapter 11 call into question Implication 3.2—that more women in more places will produce more women's representation. This suggests that overall the key is having access to "the right" venue at the right time, and that because "the right venue" can be contingent and context or issue dependent, having access to more venues is helpful for expanding representation of the interests of historically under-represented groups.

Chapters 9, 10, and 11 (by Swers; Reingold and Haynie; and Escobar-Lemmon et al.) all engage in coding bills that are initiated by legislators, and two of the three chapters examine the United States. And yet across the three chapters the authors do not find consistent results. In part this difference is due, as discussed above, to the deliberately different ways the authors have chosen to operationalize women's issues in their coding schemes. But this also suggests that not all venues are equally responsive. Venues closer to voters (state legislatures) may be more easily penetrated by a diversity of interest groups and, especially if they are descriptively representative, they may be more responsive to the representation of women's interests in myriad ways. As we move upward toward the apex of power (in presidential systems, the president and their cabinet) the number of decision makers narrows. This may make it harder for groups without significant resources to gain access to decision makers and thus, their interests may not be represented, at least not through legislation. Certainly, cabinet secretaries may choose to advance the interests of women in other ways (e.g., budget expenditures, regulations), but may not expend the political capital to do so via legislation, making venues closer to constituents the places *where* articulation of interests is more likely to take place. This compliments Celis et al.'s (2008: 103) point that there are "multiple potential sites of substantive representation, which may substitute, work together, or even potentially compete with one another to promote women's policy concerns" and that "it is crucial to consider the opportunities and constraints presented by multiple possible sites of representation..." (p. 105).

This volume also reminds researchers that new venues may be arising, or becoming more propitious for representation of women as the number of women present increases. Hoekstra et al. in Chapter 6 show that seats held by women on high courts are increasing in a number of European countries, though the expansion is slow and often non-linear. They also show that there is a link between women's presence in the legislature, the appointment mechanism used to select judges, and the selection of more women for the court. High courts have been an important venue for obtaining rights for historically under-represented groups (e.g., the landmark case of *Brown v. the Board of Education of Topeka, Kansas* [1954] that led to the integration of schools in the United States) or preventing the loss of rights. Future research will need to explore whether women appointed to high courts are more active defenders of women's interests than male judges in general or on different types of women's issues.

In sum, proponents of a women's issue often need to work in multiple venues to obtain representation in the form of policy outcomes, not just articulation of concerns or adoption of new policies. Not only does the presence of women matter, but having women present in many venues across government, and in positions where they have the capacity to have an influential voice, can determine whether representation occurs.

CONCLUSION 4: WHOM YOU KNOW IS NOT ENOUGH— REPRESENTATIVES NEED TO BE IN THE RIGHT PLACE AND HAVE AN INCENTIVE TO WORK ON YOUR POLICY PREFERENCE

Building a body of knowledge about representation of women, or other historically under-represented groups, also requires consideration of the strategy of representation—*when* and *how* it occurs. For example, as we improve our understanding of the political opportunity structure different kinds of officials face (i.e., in different institutions and levels of government, from different parties, and standing for different or multiple groups in society), this can feed into the study of interest groups and civil society organizations who want representation, and the strategies they pursue to obtain the policy outcomes they desire. What do groups know about the venues where the issue they care about can be addressed, or are likely to be addressed? Are those groups more successful at getting their preferred policy enacted if there are more group members present in the appropriate venue in government (Implication 2.2A)? Do more women in more places in government create better opportunities for groups organized around women's interests to obtain the representation they want (Implication 2.2B)? Might there be a strategic advantage to framing an issue as broader than a group-specific interest (Proposition 3)?

Answers to questions such as those posited above are likely to depend on how a researcher defines and measures women's interests and representation, such as whether a desired policy bill is proposed versus whether it becomes law, or receives adequate appropriations to be implemented, and if there is aggressive enforcement. This acknowledges that there is a difference between getting an issue on the agenda (which might be helpful in raising awareness) and passing policy that can affect outcomes. As Childs (2006: 9) writes, there is a difference between "feminization of the political agenda (where women's concerns and perspectives are articulated) and a feminization of legislation (where output has been transformed)." To date, scholars have found that more women in the legislature seem to correlate with more bills (an expanded agenda), but that those bills do not always pass. (See, for instance, Devlin and Elgie 2008 on Rwanda or Francheschet and Piscopo 2008 on Argentina.)

If groups seeking representation of their policy concerns simply contact government officials with whom they have prior contacts (e.g., a legislator or cabinet minister who is affiliated with the group), they may be given an appointment. However, ultimately the group may be frustrated because the official lacks the power to help them achieve their preferences or perceives that he or she will damage their own political career for the future if they work on the group's issues and policy preferences because party leaders do not see that issue as compatible with the party's platform or the president/prime minister does not see it as an important part of the administration's agenda. The political opportunity structure may also be biased against the representation of women's issues because they may not have the high profile or high payoff to enable an ambitious politician to use them to move upward. Several studies in this volume indicate that interest group strategy to obtain women's interest policies should plan beyond utilizing group contacts in government to also consider the political opportunity structure faced by career-seeking politicians (see Chapters 5, 8, 9, 11 [Matland and Lilliefeldt; Kang; Swers; Escobar-Lemmon et al.]).[3] Implication 3.1 predicted that "access to the right

---

3. Childs and Krook (2009: 139) also point to the importance of studying the strategy used to obtain representation in research looking to identify critical actors. Annesley and Gains (2010) also consider how the opportunity for representation can be constrained by the institution where actors are located. They argue that "to understand whether, when and how gender policy change can be achieved it is crucial to identify first the appropriate institutional venue for policy change and to assess the resources of and constraints on feminist actors operating in that site" (p. 925).

venue is critical for the ability of representatives of women's interests to change policy." This suggests that groups may be able to exploit the political opportunity structure to their advantage in some instances by using openings and contacts in one branch to put pressure on policy makers in another (who might have greater power over the issue at hand). However, it also indicates that if the political opportunity structure in a country is consistently structured in a way that is gendered, getting more women into the legislature will not be sufficient to change outcomes; broader representation in more venues may be needed.

Future research needs to take seriously the way that women's issues are perceived because this will influence which issues politicians take up if they want to advance their careers (i.e., what issues and who they have an incentive to represent). Rosemary Whip (1991: 18) found that among female legislators in Australia there was a possible tension between serving their gender and their career. "[M]ost women who saw themselves representing women and/or who concerned themselves with matters of interest to women were much more overt about the conflicts involved in taking this stand, recognizing that the pursuit of women's interests could be a real threat to their political careers." If the risk of being a single-issue politician (where that issue is women's interests) is too great, female legislators may choose not to represent women's interests (Whip 1991). As detailed in Proposition 3, policy opponents can mobilize to prevent adoption of a policy, or to prevent implementation after the policy is adopted (Kang in Chapter 8 showed that after-policy-adoption mobilization occurs). Women's interests also may not be taken into account because no one is willing to serve as their champion. This indicates that women need representatives willing to champion their cause in many and diverse venues of government (from elected to bureaucratic venues) in order to actually see their interests and policy preferences become policy outcomes and change. In sum, presence facilitates representation of women's interests if interest articulation occurs. Yet how effective that representation will be at changing policy outcomes is mediated by the political opportunity structures for career-seeking politicians (both female and male), whether they are present in the right venues to actually take effective action, and whether the representational hat they are wearing leads them to represent that perspective.

PROPOSALS FOR A RESEARCH AGENDA TO MOVE TOWARD A GENERALIZABLE UNDERSTANDING OF SUBSTANTIVE REPRESENTATION OF HISTORICALLY UNDER-REPRESENTED GROUPS

This volume underscores that representation is a complex, contingent, multi-stage process, even after members of a historically under-represented group have obtained some presence in government. The diverse works presented here, both theoretical and empirical, point to the need to take theory development and testing forward in several directions in order to advance our understanding of how representation works—for women in all their diversity, and for other groups.

A Research Agenda on Inclusive versus Exclusive Representation

One area that merits systematic study is how inclusive or exclusive is the representation that actually occurs. Some kinds of representation reflect a broad array of viewpoints, while others may seem broad on the surface, but in reality only reflect the views of some groups (likely groups who have long controlled the reins of political power in a society). Table 12.1 provides examples of how representation can be arrayed from "inclusive" to "exclusive" on the *who, what, where, when*, and *how* dimensions highlighted throughout this volume.

Inclusive representation would be expected where formal institutions, such as legislatures, have provisions for actors outside the legislature to propose legislation (e.g., individual citizens, diverse interest groups, NGOs) and where bureaucratic agencies have effective provisions for citizen consultation about policy changes or diverse membership mandated on their boards. Courts that are accessible to diverse groups in society, both to express their opinions and to fight for their rights, would also facilitate inclusive representation. Candidate nomination procedures (formal or informal), electoral rules, and norms for appointment of officials that make it possible for groups outside established power networks to gain seats in government can promote inclusive representation. Where representation is inclusive we should see diverse actors speaking out on issue X or Y, and diverse sectors within a party or the legislature calling for action on their preferences and also being able to affect the government's policy agenda and policy outputs. For groups who are still underdogs in politics (i.e., numerically under-represented and typically lacking seats in the inner circles of power, or when they have seats they are compelled to conform to the norms of traditionally dominant groups in order to succeed), institutions that promote inclusive representation in politics should facilitate representation of their interests.

Exclusive representation would be expected where only a small sector, or traditionally powerful groups in society, have access to the venues where policy decisions are really made (e.g., agency boards composed of only the power elite, an executive branch that sends policy to the legislature with a norm of no prior consultation or post–bill initiation amendment, where justices are descriptively representative of only the traditional power elite of society). Where representation is exclusive we should see only a few legislators, or one party (or party faction) speaking out on the floor or in standing committees,

Table 12.1. EXAMINING WHETHER REPRESENTATION IS INCLUSIVE OR EXCLUSIVE

	Inclusive Representation	Exclusive Representation
Who	• Social movements • Diverse interest groups • NGOs • Legislators • Political parties	• Judges • Appointed bureaucrats • Agency directors • Cabinet secretaries • Presidents • Supreme Court Judges
What	• Meta-interests • Interests	• Issues • Preferences
Where	• The nation writ large • The streets • Internet campaigns • The media • UN conferences • Political parties • Women's policy agencies	• Legislatures • Interest groups • Bureaucratic agencies • Cabinets • High Courts • Policy decided "behind closed doors"
When	• Diverse actors speak out on interest X • Sectors or groups within a party call for action	• Individual legislators speak out on the floor • Single powerful actor makes a priority
How	• Process open to penetration: referenda, initiatives • Popular mobilization, protests • Nomination of candidates through primaries, open caucuses • Nomination of candidates though party closed-caucuses • Speaking in legislatures	• Introduction of bills • Party adopts voluntary gender quota • Issuing rulings that enforce laws upholding women's rights • Behind closed door processes • Executive decrees • Government appointments • Striking down laws as unconstitutional • Top party leaders select candidates

or a single powerful actor making policy (e.g., executive decrees, agencies issuing rulings without mandatory consulting periods), with most meaningful decision making occurring behind closed doors. Exclusive representation may avoid policy stagnation due to the lack of veto players in the policy process, but it is unlikely to promote representation of historically under-represented groups unless those groups succeed in ousting the former power holders.

At its heart, inclusive representation involves active participation from many people and organized groups, allows the expression of multiple viewpoints, and with regard to process, it offers multiple chances for the articulation of different and varied interests. Going back to Figure 1.1 in Chapter 1, inclusive representation activates many of the arrows in that figure, with many groups having access to parties and to government institutions. Since policy making is a multistage process, inclusion of diverse groups can occur at various stages of the policy process, or in the iterative back-and-forth of policy evolution as policy losers (and winners) fight to gain (or maintain) their preferred policy. At the other end of the spectrum is exclusive representation, which means that representation reflects the articulation of interests from fewer groups, or even just a few individuals, in a process that may be less transparent and more opaque. Where representation is exclusive, many of the groups depicted in Figure 1.1 would not have arrows connecting them to parties or government.

The very nature of inclusive representation makes the articulation of diverse interests more likely and should better reflect and respect, for example, the diversity among women, or within ethnic, racial, religious, or linguistic minorities. Inclusive representation makes the understanding of interests much less monolithic. Instead, the interests of black women, Hispanic women, poor women, Asian women, etc., all can have a voice at the policy table. Intersectional concerns can be taken more seriously, as inclusive representation means, for example, that a woman of color is not forced to choose whether to speak as a woman or as a person of color—she may speak as a woman of color. Choices are not necessary because, while representing her fully intersectional identity, "women" are still covered because others are representing other intersections within the diverse group "women." Inclusive representation should also facilitate representation by surrogates.

Exclusive representation often makes women chose whether they will speak for women, or for their other more powerful identity groups (e.g., party), and this is also true for members of other historically under-represented groups who obtain public office. It can dampen the representation capacity of surrogates, or runs the risk that privileged women (or minorities) will claim to speak for all women, when they actually only speak for the part of women reflected by their own intersectional identity.

Institutions can be designed to promote inclusive or exclusive representation (e.g., election laws, how justices or agency boards of directors are nominated and selected, whether women's policy agencies have the legal right and capacity to mainstream gendered aspects of policies). Where we find inclusive representation, we would expect that society not only allows, but listens to and acts, on representation of its diverse members; representation is more than just having a seat at the policy deliberation table (Mansbridge 2003). Where representation is more exclusive, diverse groups and sub-groups that historically have not been parties to deliberation find their voices muted, or not heard where it really matters—where policy gets made, budgeted, implemented and enforced; or their policy victories at early stages of the multistage policy process are quickly overturned at later stages. Some institutions within a country may be more inclusive, while others are more exclusive. In a country (or province, municipality, or international organization) representation might be inclusive on some issues, but not on others.

These are all empirically testable questions, and future research should test hypothesis about how elements of institutional structure contribute to inclusive or exclusive representation, both of women and other historically under-represented groups. Additionally, research will need to empirically assess whether, as we expect, inclusive representation better respects intersectionality by allowing for more diverse issues and preferences among women.

A Research Agenda Incorporating Political Opportunity Structures and Diversity Within Groups

Another area where richer theory is needed is how political opportunity structures and diversity within groups incentivize representation by descriptive representatives of a group, and by non-group members. For example, should all women in government represent women's interests? Should all minority group descriptive representatives in government represent minority interests? Is it rational for them to do so if they wish to build a political career and move into top leadership positions, or is it expected but unrewarded work? Will their party reward or punish them? What about voters, or campaign contributors? If a female or minority official opts to focus on topics other than those of special concern to their descriptive group, will they be castigated for letting their group down (see Dahlerup, Chapter 4 of this volume)? There is a significant body of literature that explores the way institutions create incentives for representatives to behave in particular ways, for instance for legislators to seek personal votes. We might expect that electoral laws that promote personal vote seeking may be most advantageous to the representation of group interests because they allow ambitious politicians to build a power base and reputation independent of their party. However, research to test this hypothesis is needed.

Greater understanding is also needed about the linkages between groups working from outside government to obtain representation and actors working from within government (elected, appointed, career bureaucrats). We know that work for representation occurs both outside and within government, but is representation of the interests of historically under-represented groups more likely to occur when there is a cooperative effort by actors outside and inside government, or when they can work tag-team through the multiple stages of the policy process? Issue-specific research has already proven useful, providing stimulating findings about when progress is made on specific issues (e.g., policies to criminalize violence against women). But issue-specific research that addresses questions of *who* represents, *where*, *when*, and *how* would aid aggregation of findings across studies. Issue-specific research should also include conscious discussion of the conditions under which policy debate is inclusive or exclusive as another potential way to aggregate findings and accumulate knowledge.

Issue-specific research can also facilitate a deliberate focus on intersectional identities, particularly the nuanced aspects of intersectional identity discussed by Hancock (Chapter 3 of this volume), and development and testing of theory about when representatives are likely to wear which of their various identity hats. Issues where group identities would seem to be in conflict (e.g., where women might have to choose a women's issue perspective or, for example, an ethnic group perspective) would be most useful in understanding when and how the two are pursued. We might predict that the issues of the larger (more numerous) group will triumph, but this is an empirically testable proposition, and the answer may vary across different institutional settings and vote aggregation rules.

An issue specific focus also invites bringing in different preferences over the same issue (e.g., women arguing that both pro-life and pro-choice views reflected women's interest as African countries considered whether to ratify, and then to implement the Maputo Protocol [Kang, Chapter 8 of this volume]). Do different groups of women with different policy preferences strategize differently about how to obtain their preferred policy? Do they work with different sets of government officials, in different venues? A focus on individual issues may allow for better identification of relevant actors and a more in-depth tracing of the process to better understand *how* representation occurs and why particular actors choose to work on representing group X on issue Y at that particular point in time. Yet a goal of such work should be a more generalizable understanding of which types of groups work with the legislature versus cabinet ministers or bureaucratic agencies or through the courts. In particular, studies that examine issue-specific representation *across venues* should do more to advance our understanding of how and where issues and groups have access and may shed light on the way the political opportunity structure rewards behaviors in some venues but not others.

A Research Agenda about the Dynamics of Representation

There need to be more studies with a dynamic research design. Dahlerup overtly makes this call in the section of Chapter 4 titled "Representation Seen as a Process." She asks, "Do we see representation, not as an act of giving voice to fixed and well-defined interests or identities, but as a demand to be included in a dynamic process and interaction between the represented and the representatives?" Hancock (Chapter 3 of this volume) also criticizes the static nature of most operationalizations of intersectionality. This volume does a better job of addressing *who, what,* and *where* questions about representation of women than it does with the *how* question, though Alice Kang's Chapter 8 is an exception with its explicit focus on how competing groups worked to gain representation of their policy preference.

A challenge at present for addressing *how* women's interests are represented is that how is a process; and much work on substantive representation of women is static, based on cross-sectional analysis, which is often ill-suited to studying processes. Concern with process and how representation of group interests proceeds over time is not limited to representation of women, but also applies to representation of other historically under-represented groups. *How* representation occurs can refer to bill initiation (possibly with the bills becoming laws), court rulings, treaties, and budget allocations. *How* also refers to the process of policy negotiation. Thus, another fruitful avenue for future research is dynamic work with research designed specifically to address the multistage aspect of how women's interests obtain representation, or how other historically under-represented groups gain representation. Needed are both methodological advances and wider adoption of statistical methodologies better suited to the use of data to study dynamic processes. This would permit testing hypotheses regarding where in the process of articulation to implementation the representational links are broken. We predict that representation not only becomes less inclusive, but that as the number of decision makers narrows, certain groups find it harder to get their issues and preferences heard. Future work needs to test this prediction, and also to explore whether the higher one moves in the political structure the more the incentives to represent women (and other historically under-represented groups) decrease.

Enhanced understanding of the dynamics of moving from interest articulation to getting on the government's agenda, to policy making and implementation will not only improve understanding of when representation of women and other historically under-represented groups occurs, but will also point to potential roadblocks in this multistage process. Research designs that capture the dynamic aspect of representation can shed light on how or why historically under-represented groups' interests are not obtaining representation. This could be because, at some stage during the process, groups or government officials pressing for representation of their interests get ignored, because officials do not follow through on promises to address those issues, or because groups with conflicting interests enter the fray to regain representation of their own policy goals. Greater insight about the political opportunity structure (as discussed above) will facilitate understanding the dynamic mechanisms by which interest articulation is, or it not, transformed into policy outcomes. A full test would mean testing all the arrows and relationships captured in Figure 1.1 (from Chapter 1) and would enable modeling the political system as a full system.

CHANGING POLITICS, CHANGING RESEARCH?

Women are one of many identifiable groups that historically have been excluded from access to power, and whose interests have not been represented in government. Ethnic, racial, religious, and linguistic minority groups have often been left out of the political process, even in otherwise democratic regimes, as have people of low socioeconomic status. In some authoritarian regimes, even majority groups are excluded from real political power, as an ethnic, racial, or religious minority holds on to power and monopolizes the benefits produced by the public sector. But "times are a-changing" and many historically under-represented groups are becoming more important players in politics, with increasing numbers of group members holding posts inside government, more political parties and interest groups emerging to represent specific racial, ethnic, or religious groups, and increased activity by nongovernmental organizations who speak on behalf of these groups to put pressure on government. Descriptive representation has increased dramatically in many countries, even if historically under-represented groups still have fewer representatives than the size of their group would merit based on proportional representation.

There is still much to be learned about the factors that promote or inhibit descriptive representation. Yet with increased descriptive representation, scholarly research—as well as the assessments of political pundits and possibly also of the mass public—can turn to questions of substantive representation of the interests of historically under-represented groups. Are group members' issues and preferences receiving increased representation in policy debates as they acquire more descriptive representatives of their group in government? Are the descriptive representatives the ones providing the substantive representation of their group? If yes, of what group interests and of which sub-groups? If no, why not? Do increased numbers of diverse descriptive representatives prompt government officials not from those groups to take up issues of concern to historically under-represented groups, or does their presence produce backlash? Answering such questions is an important part of building a richer understanding of representation. This means moving beyond conceptualizations of representation that ask whether Representative X from Group Z speaks/acts on behalf of Group Z. Instead, it requires the empirical investigation of more complex forms of representation, such as: In what venues and under what conditions does Representative X from Group Z speak/act on behalf of Group Z, and when does she choose to represent Group B? When does Representative Y who is not a descriptive member of Group Z have an incentive to speak/act for Group Z? How does competition across group interests, issues, and preferences impact the behavior of Representatives X and Y?

This volume has provided theoretical and empirical studies of representation, focused on representation of women. Theory chapters grapple with the challenges of defining "women's interests" as well as the different sub-groups within the large and diverse group "women." Empirical chapters explore different definitions and measures of women's issues, and where representation is occurring, by which types of government officials, and what role is played by parties and interest groups in the representation process. Lessons learned in this volume about the importance of how women's interests are defined and measured, that representation occurs on different women's issues in different venues and by different strategies, can provide a useful base for the study of representation of other historically under-represented groups. The propositions and implications laid out in Chapter 1 and the complex process portrayed in Figure 1.1 regarding representation of women's interests should also apply to representation of other groups that historically have been excluded from power. Table 12.1 and the expectations generated above about when representation will be inclusive or exclusive should also be applicable beyond the case of women. But these ideas need to be empirically tested with regard to other historically under-represented groups, since the process of and constraints on group representation could be different for groups that are numerical minorities in society, or that are geographically concentrated.

As stated in Chapter 1 of this volume, "Representation of historically under-represented groups has long been a rallying cry for improving the quality of democracy." It is a task for political science to explore when that representation is likely to occur, by whom, for whom, and of what types of interests. We hope that this volume provides a useful set of insights for how to take this field of study to the next stage to build a broader and generalizable understanding of representation of groups and their interests that have historically been excluded from or marginalized in politics.

As the study of representation advances it becomes time for scholars to look beyond traditional and/or narrow, pre-conceived definitions of women's interests to embrace and include the many issues that women around the world are fighting for, and which they define as women's interests, sometimes based on context-specific needs, as demonstrated by the work of Johnson Sirleaf, Gbowee, and Karman. Access to political power and political voice (which Beckwith [Chapter 2 this volume] defines as a meta-interest) clearly remains important, but other issues and interests, which vary across time and countries, also merit study. Beyond a doubt, in terms of descriptive representation women have made giant strides. The contributors to our volume suggest that this has been accompanied by what can at least be called baby steps in enhanced substantive representation, although there may be bigger steps in some venues and on some issues than others. Arguing for the need to include women's voices in the political process, the Argentine Network of Political Women noted, "With few women in politics, it's the women who change. With many women in politics, politics changes" (Marx et al. 2007: 61, cited in Franceschet and Piscopo 2008: 407). Optimistically, then, future research may need to cast the net more broadly to capture not simply change in policy, but institutional transformation.

REFERENCES

Aars, Jacob. 2001. "Rekrutteringsveier i norske kommuner." Sluttrapport.
SEFOS-notat 6-2001. Bergen, Norway: Senter for samfunnsforskning.

Abdullah, Hussaina. 1995. "Wifeism and Activism: The Nigerian Women's
Movement." In *The Challenge of Local Feminisms: Women's Movements in Global
Perspectives*, ed. Amrita Basu. Boulder, CO: Westview, 209-25.

Abramovitz, Mimi. 1996. *Regulating the Lives of Women: Social Welfare Policy from
Colonial Times to the Present* (rev. ed.). Boston, MA: South End Press.

African Union. 2011. "List of Countries Which Have Signed, Ratified/Acceded to the
Protocol to the African Charter on Human and People's Rights on the Rights of
Women in Africa." July 22. http://www.africa-union.org (April 1, 2011).

Agudelo, Carlos Efrén. 2002. *"Etnicidad negra y elecciones en Colombia." Journal of Latin
American Anthropology*, 7 (2): 168-97.

Agudelo, Carlos Efrén. 2000. *"Comportamiento electoral en poblaciones negras: Algunos
elementos para el análisis." Documento de Trabajo*, 50 (Julio).

Alcántara Saez, Manuel. 2006. *Datos de Opinión: Elites Parlamentarias
Latinoamericanas*. Salamanca, Spain: Instituto Interuniversitario de
Iberoamérica de la Universidad de Salamanca.

Alemán, Eduardo. 2006. *"Policy Gatekeepers in Latin American Legislatures." Latin
American Politics and Society*, 48 (3): 125-55.

Alexander-Floyd, Nikol. 2012. *"Disappearing Acts: Reclaiming Intersectionality in the
Social Sciences in a Post-Black Feminist Era." Feminist Formations*, 24 (1): 1-25.

Annesley, Claire. 2010. *"Gender, Politics and Policy Change: The Case of Welfare Reform
Under New Labour." Government and Opposition*, 45 (1): 50-72.

Annesley, Claire, and Francesca Gains. 2010. *"The Core Executive: Gender, Power and
Change." Political Studies*, 58: 909-29.

Atal, Juan Pablo, Hugo Ñopo, and Natalia Winder. 2009. "New Century, Old
Disparities: Gender and Ethnic Wage Gaps in Latin America." IDB Working
Paper 109.

Atchison, Amy, and Ian Down. 2009. *"Women Cabinet Members and Female-Friendly
Social Policy." Poverty and Public Policy*, 1 (2): 1-23.

Bachrach, Peter, and Morton S. Baratz. 1970. *Power and Poverty: Theory and Practice*.
New York: Oxford University Press.

Baer, Judith A., and Leslie Friedman Goldstein, eds. 2006. *The Constitutional and
Legal Rights of Women* (3rd ed.). Los Angeles, CA: Roxbury.

Baker, Carrie. 2008. *The Women's Movement Against Sexual Harassment*.
Cambridge: Cambridge University Press.

Baker, Ross K. 2001. *House and Senate* (3rd ed.). New York: W.W. Norton.

Baldez, Lisa. 2011. *"The UN Convention to Eliminate All Forms of Discrimination Against Women (CEDAW): A New Way to Measure Women's Interests." Politics & Gender,* 7 (3): 419–23.

Baldez, Lisa. 2002. *Why Women Protest.* Cambridge: Cambridge University Press.

Banaszak, Lee Ann. 2010. *The Women's Movement Inside and Outside the State.* Cambridge: Cambridge University Press.

Banaszak, Lee Ann. 1996. *Why Movements Succeed or Fail: Opportunity, Culture, and the Struggle for Woman Suffrage.* Princeton, NJ: Princeton University Press.

Barone, Michael, William Lilley III, and Laurence J. DeFranco. 1998. *State Legislative Elections: Voting Patterns and Demographics.* Washington, DC: CQ Press.

Barrett, Edith J. 1997. *"Gender and Race in the State House: The Legislative Experience." Social Science Journal,* 34 (2): 131–44.

Barrett, Edith J. 1995. *"The Policy Priorities of African American Women in State Legislatures." Legislative Studies Quarterly,* 20 (2): 223–47.

Bauer, Gretchen. 2008. *"Electoral Gender Quotas for Parliament in East and Southern Africa." International Feminist Journal of Politics,* 10 (3): 348–68.

Beauvoir, Simone de. [1949] 1953. *The Second Sex.* London: Alfred Knoph.

Beck, Linda. 2003. *"Democratization and the Hidden Public: The Impact of Patronage Networks on Senegalese Women." Comparative Politics,* 35 (2): 147–69.

Beck, Thorsten, George Clarke, Alberto Groff, Philip Keefer, and Patrick Walsh. 2001. *"New Tools in Comparative Political Economy: The Database of Political Institutions." World Bank Economic Review,* 15 (1): 165–76.

Beckwith, Karen. 2011. *"Interests, Issues and Preferences: Women's Interests and Epiphenomena of Activism," Politics & Gender,* 7 (3): 424–29.

Beckwith, Karen. 2007. *"Numbers and Newness: The Descriptive and Substantive Representation of Women." Canadian Journal of Political Science,* 40 (1): 27–49.

Beckwith, Karen. 2005. *"A Common Language of Gender?" Politics & Gender,* I (1): 128–37.

Beckwith, Karen. 1987. "Response to Feminism in the Italian Parliament: Divorce, Abortion and Sexual Violence Legislation." In *The Women's Movements of the United States and Western Europe*, eds. Mary Fainsod Katzenstein and Carol McClurg Mueller. Philadelphia: Temple University Press, 153–71.

Beckwith, Karen, and Kimberly Cowell-Meyers. 2007. *"Sheer Numbers: Critical Representation Thresholds and Women's Political Representation." Perspectives on Politics,* 5 (3): 553–65.

Binder, Sarah A., and Steven Smith. 1997. *Politics or Principle: Filibustering in the United States Senate.* Washington, DC: Brookings Institution Press.

Birch, Sarah. 2003. "Women and Political Representation in Contemporary Ukraine." In *Women's Access to Political Power in Post-Communist Europe*, eds. Richard E. Matland and Kathleen A. Montgomery. Oxford: Oxford University Press, 130–52.

Black, J. H., and Lynda Erickson. 2003. *"Women Candidates and Voter Bias: Do Women Politicians Need to Be Better?" Electoral Studies,* 22 (1): 81–100.

Blau, Francine D., and Lawrence M. Kahn. 2007. *"The Gender Pay Gap." The Economists' Voice,* 4 (4) Article 5.

Blofield, Merike. 2006. *The Politics of Moral Sin: Abortion and Divorce in Spain, Chile and Argentina.* New York: Routledge.

Boles, Janet K. 2001. "Local Elected Women and Policy-Making: Movement Delegates or Feminist Trustees?" In *The Impact of Women in Public Office*, ed. Susan J. Carroll. Bloomington: Indiana University Press, 68–88.

Borrelli, MaryAnne. 2010. *"Gender Desegregation and Gender Integration in the President's Cabinet, 1933–2010." Presidential Studies Quarterly*, 49 (4): 734–49.

"The Boston Pill Trials." N.d. http://www.pbs.org/wgbh/amex/pill/peopleevents/e_boston.html (Accessed January 9, 2012).

Bourdieu, Pierre, and Loïc Wacquant. 1999. *"On the Cunning of Imperialist Reason." Theory, Culture, and Society*, 16 (1): 41–58.

Box-Steffensmeier, Janet M., Suzanna DeBoef, and Tse-Min Lin. 2004. *"The Dynamics of the Partisan Gender Gap." American Political Science Review*, 98 (3): 515–528.

Bratton, Kathleen A. 2006. *"The Behavior and Success of Latino Legislators: Evidence from the States." Social Science Quarterly*, 87(5): 1136–57.

Bratton, Kathleen A. 2005. *"Critical Mass Theory Revisited: The Behavior and Success of Token Women in State Legislatures." Politics & Gender*, 1 (1): 97–125.

Bratton, Kathleen A. 2002. *"The Effect of Legislative Diversity on Agenda Setting: Evidence from Six State Legislatures." American Politics Research*, 30 (2): 115–42.

Bratton, Kathleen A., and Kerry L. Haynie. 1999. *"Agenda-Setting and Legislative Success in State Legislatures: The Effects of Gender and Race." Journal of Politics*, 61 (3): 658–79.

Bratton, Kathleen A., Kerry L. Haynie, and Beth Reingold. 2006. *"Agenda Setting and African American Women in State Legislatures." Journal of Women, Politics & Policy*, 28 (3–4): 71–96.

Bratton, Kathleen A., and Leonard P. Ray. 2002. *"Descriptive Representation, Policy Outcomes and Municipal Day-Care Coverage in Norway." American Journal of Political Science*, 46 (2): 428–37.

Bratton, Kathleen A., and Rorie L. Spill. 2002. *"Existing Diversity and Judicial Selection: The Role of the Appointment Method in Establishing Gender Diversity in State Supreme Courts." Social Science Quarterly*, 83 (2): 504–18.

Brown, Nadia. 2012. "Representation for Whom? Identity Politics and Marginalized Women." Unpublished Manuscript.

Bush, Sarah Sunn. 2011. *"International Politics and the Spread of Quotas for Women in Legislatures." International Organization*, 65 (1): 103–37.

Butegwa, Florence. 1995. "The Human Rights of Women in Conflict Situations in Africa: A Key Concern for WiLDAF." Paper presented at the UNIFEM-AFWIC Conference on Women in Conflict Situations in Africa, August 1–4, 1995, Addis Ababa, Ethiopia.

Butler, Judith. 1999. *Gender Trouble: Feminism and the Subversion of Identity*. New York: Routledge.

Butler, Judith. 1990. *Gender Trouble: Feminism and the Subversion of Identity*. New York: Routledge.

"Campaign Update: What's Happening Around the Continent?" *Pambazuka* 190, January 20, 2005. http://www.pambazuka.org/en/category/features/26462/print (Accessed July 25, 2013).

Campbell Barr, Epsy. 2007. *Liderazgo y participación política para las mujeres afrodescendientes*. Prepared for Women in the Americas. Paths to Political Power. Washington, DC: Inter-American Development Bank.

Canon, David T. 1999. *Race, Redistricting, and Representation: The Unintended Consequences of Black Majority Districts*. Chicago: University of Chicago Press.

Caraway, Teri L. 2004. *"Inclusion and Democratization: Class, Gender, Race and the Extension of Suffrage." Comparative Politics*, 36 (4): 443–60.

Carbado, Devon and Mitu Gulati. 2013. *Acting White? Rethinking Race in Postracial America*. New York: Oxford University Press.

Carroll, Susan. 2010. "Voting Choices: The Politics of the Gender Gap." In *Gender and Elections: Shaping the Future of American Politics* (2nd ed.), eds. Susan Carroll and Richard Logan Fox. New York: Cambridge University Press, 117–43.

Carroll, Susan J. 2008. "Committee Assignments: Discrimination of Choice?" In *Legislating Women: Getting Elected, Getting Ahead*, ed. Beth Reingold. Boulder, CO: Lynne Rienner, 135–56.

Carroll, Susan J. 2002. "Representing Women: Congresswomen's Perceptions of Their Representational Roles." In *Women Transforming Congress*, ed. Cindy Simon Rosenthal. Norman: University of Oklahoma Press, 50–68.

Carroll, Susan J. 2001. "Representing Women: Women State Legislators as Agents of Policy-Related Change." In *The Impact of Women in Public Office*, ed. Susan J. Carroll. Bloomington: Indiana University Press, 3–21.

Carroll, Susan J. 1994. *Women as Candidates in American Politics*. Bloomington: Indiana University Press.

Casellas, Jason P. 2011. *Latino Representation in State Houses and Congress*. New York: Cambridge University Press.

Caul, Miki. 2001. *"Political Parties and the Adoption of Candidate Gender Quotas: A Cross-National Analysis." Journal of Politics*, 63 (4): 1214–29.

Celis, Karen. 2008. "Gendering Representation." In *Politics, Gender and Concepts: Theory and Methodology*, eds. Gary Goertz and Amy Mazur. New York: Cambridge University Press, 71–93.

Celis, Karen. 2006. *"Substantive Representation of Women: The Representation of Women's Interest and the Impact of Descriptive Representation in the Belgian Parliament (1900–1979)." Journal of Women, Politics and Policy*, 28 (2): 85–114.

Celis, Karen, Sarah Childs, Johanna Kantola, and Mona Lena Krook. 2008. *"Rethinking Women's Substantive Representation." Representation*, 44 (2): 99–110.

Center for the American Woman and Politics. 2013. *"Fact Sheet: Women in the U.S. Congress 2013."* New Brunswick: Eagleton Institute of Politics, Rutgers, The State University of New Jersey.

Chae, David, Amani Nuru-Jeter, Karen D. Lincoln, and Darlene D. Francis. 2011. *"Conceptual Approaches to Disparities in Health: Advancement of a Socio-Psychobiological Approach." Du Bois Review*, 8 (1): 63–77.

Chafetz, Janet Salzman, Anthony Gary Dworkin, and Stephanie Swanson. 1990. "Social Change and Social Activism: First-Wave Women's Movements Around the World." In *Women and Social Protest*, eds. Guida West and Rhonda Lois Blumberg. Oxford: Oxford University Press, 302–20.

Chaney, Elsa M. 1979. *Supermadre: Women in Politics in Latin America*. Austin: University of Texas Press.

Chang, Robert S., and Jerome McCristal Culp. 2002. *"After Intersectionality." University of Missouri Kansas City Law Review*, 71: 485.

Charrad, Mounira. 2001. *States and Women's Rights: The Making of Postcolonial Tunisia, Algeria, and Morocco*. Berkeley: University of California Press.

Childs, Sarah. 2008. *Women and British Party Politics: Descriptive, Substantive and Symbolic Representation*. London & New York: Routledge.

Childs, Sarah. 2006. *"The Complicated Relationship Between Sex, Gender and the Substantive Representation of Women." European Journal of Women's Studies*, 13 (1): 7–21.

Childs, Sarah. 2004. *New Labour's Women MPs: Women Representing Women*. London and New York: Routledge.

Childs, Sarah, and Paul Webb. 2012. *Women and the Conservative Party*. Palgrave.

Childs, Sarah, and Mona Lena Krook. 2009. *"Analysing Women's Substantive Representation: From Critical Mass to Critical Actors."* Government and Opposition, 44 (2): 125–45.

Choo, Hae Yeon, and Myra Marx Ferree. 2010. *"Practicing Intersectionality in Sociological Research: A Critical Analysis of Inclusions, Interactions, and Institutions in the Study of Inequality."* Sociological Theory, 28 (2): 129–49.

Christiansen, Dag Arne, Tor Midtbø, Hans-Erik Ringkjøb, and Jacob Aars. 2008. *To valg med ny personvalgordning—Kontinuitet eller endring?* Bergen, Norway: Rokkansenteret, Rapport 2008: 8.

Christiansen, Dag Arne, Tor Midtbø, Hans-Erik Ringkjøb, Lars Svåsand, and Jacob Aars. 2004. *Ny personvalgordning og hva så? En analyse av kommune og fylkestingsvalget i* 2003. Bergen, Norway: Rokkansenteret, Rapport 2004: 8.

Cichowski, Rachel. 2006. *The European Court, Civil Society and European Integration.* Cambridge: Cambridge University Press.

Cohen, Cathy J. 1999. *The Boundaries of Blackness: AIDS and the Breakdown of Black Politics.* Chicago: University of Chicago Press.

Collins, Patricia Hill. 2000. *Black Feminist Thought: Knowledge, Consciousness, and the Politics of Empowerment* (2nd ed.). New York: Routledge.

Condon, Stephanie. 2010. "Number of Millionaires in Congress: 261." November 17. http://www.cbsnews.com/8301-503544_162-20023147-503544.html (Accessed January 5, 2012).

Conway, M. Margaret, David W. Ahern, and Gertrude A. Steurnagel. 2005. *Women and Public Policy: A Revolution in Progress* (3rd ed.). Washington, DC: CQ Press.

Coppedge, Michael. 1997. "A Classification of Latin American Political Parties." Kellogg Institute Working Paper 244, University of Notre Dame.

Cott, Nancy F. 1987. *The Grounding of Modern Feminism.* New Haven, CT: Yale University Press.

CQ. 2003. "Medicare Overhaul Provisions." In *CQ Almanac* 2003 (59th ed.). 11-8-11-13. Washington, DC: Congressional Quarterly, 2004.

Craske, Nikki. 2003. "Gender, Politics, and Legislation," In *Gender in Latin America,* eds. Sylvia Chant and Nikki Craske. New Brunswick, NJ: Rutgers University Press, 19–45.

Craske, Nikki. 1999. *Women and Politics in Latin America.* New Brunswick, NJ: Rutgers University Press.

Creevey, Lucy. 2006. "Senegal: Contending with Religious Constraints." In *Women in African Parliaments,* eds. Gretchen Bauer and Hannah Britton. Boulder, CO: Lynne Rienner.

Crenshaw, Kimberle. 1991. *"Mapping the Margins: Intersectionality, Identity Politics, and Violence Against Women of Color."* Stanford Law Review, 43 (6): 1241–99.

Crenshaw, Kimberle. 1989. *"Demarginalizing the Intersection of Race and Sex: A Black Feminist Critique of Antidiscrimination Doctrine, Feminist Theory, and Antiracist Politics."* The University of Chicago Legal Forum, 139: 139–67.

Cruces, Guillermo, Leonardo Gasparini, and Fedora Carbajal. 2010. *Situación socio-económica de la población afrocolombiana en el marco de los Objetivos del Desarrollo del Milenio.* Panamá: PNUD.

CSB. 2011. "Members Elected to the Saeima by Sex." http://www.csb.gov.lv/en/members-elected-saeima-sex (Accessed February 21, 2012).

CSB. 2010. "PR10. Elected Local Government Members of the Republic of Latvia by Age, Sex, Ethnicity and Education Qualification." http://www.csb.gov.lv/ (Accessed February 3, 2011).

Curtin, Jennifer. 2008. *"Women, Political Leadership and Substantive Representation: The Case of New Zealand." Parliamentary Affairs*, 61 (3): 490–504.

Curtin, Jennifer. 2006. "Conclusion: Gendering Political Representation in the Old and New Worlds of Westminster." In *Representing Women in Parliament*, eds. Marian Sawer, Manon Tremblay, and Linda Trimble. London and New York: Routledge, 236–51.

CVK. 2011 *11. Saeimas vēlēšanas*. Central Election Commission of Latvia. www.cvk.lv (Accessed February 22, 2012).

CVK. 2010. *10. Saeimas vēlēšanas*. Central Election Commission of Latvia. www.cvk.lv (Accessed February 21, 2012).

Dahlerup, Drude. 2013a "Disruption, Continuity and Waves in the Feminist Movement." In *The Women's Movement in Protest, Institutions and the Internet*, eds. Sarah Maddison and Marian Sawer. Routledge, 20-36.

Dahlerup, Drude. 2013b. "Denmark: High Representation of Women Without Gender Quotas." In *Breaking Male Dominance in Old Democracies*, eds. Drude Dahlerup and Monique Leyenaar. Oxford: Oxford University Press, 146–71.

Dahlerup, Drude. 2011. "Engendering Representative Democracy." In *The Future of Representative Democracy*, eds. Sonia Alonso, John Keane, and Wolfgang Merkel. Cambridge: Cambridge University Press, 144–68.

Dahlerup, Drude. 2009. *"Women in Arab Parliaments: Can Gender Quotas Contribute to Democratization?" al-raida*, 126–127 (Summer/Fall): 28–38.

Dahlerup, Drude, ed. 2006a. *Women, Quotas and Politics*. New York and London: Routledge.

Dahlerup, Drude. 2006b. *"The Story of the Theory of Critical Mass." Politics & Gender*, 2 (4): 511–22.

Dahlerup, Drude, and Lenita Freidenvall. 2010. *"Judging Gender Quotas: Predictions and Result." Policy & Politics*, 38 (3): 407–25.

Dahlerup, Drude, and Monique Leyenaar, eds. 2013. *Breaking Male Dominance in Old Democracies*. Oxford: Oxford University Press.

Darcy, R., Susan Welch, and Janet Clark. 1994. *Women, Elections, and Representation* (2nd ed.). Lincoln: University of Nebraska Press.

Davis, Rebecca Howard. 1997. *Women and Power in Parliamentary Democracies*. Lincoln: University of Nebraska of Nebraska Press.

Degler, Carl N. 1986. *Neither Black nor White: Slavery and Race Relations in Brazil and the United States*. Madison: University of Wisconsin Press.

Del Popolo, Fabiana, Ana María Oyarce, Susana Schkolnik, and Fernanda Velasco. 2009. La inclusión del enfoque étnico en los censos de población de América Latina. *Censos 2010 y la inclusión del enfoque étnico: Hacía una construcción participativa con pueblos indígenas y afrodescendientes de América Latina*. CEPAL Serie seminarios y conferencias no. 57. Santiago de Chile: Septiembre.

De Queiroz, Mario. 2007. "Legal Abortion after Decades of Struggle." Inter Press Service News Agency. February 12. http://ipsnews.net/news.asp?idnews=36534 (Accessed January 9, 2012).

Devlin, Claire, and Robert Elgie. 2008. *"The Effect of Increased Women's Representation in Parliament: The Case of Rwanda." Parliamentary Affairs*, 61 (2): 237–54.

Dhamoon, Rita. 2011. *"Considerations on Mainstreaming Intersectionality," Political Research Quarterly*, 64 (1): 230–43.

Dhamoon, Rita. 2009. *Identity/Difference Politics: How Difference Is Produced and Why It Matters*. Vancouver: University of British Columbia Press.

Diamond, Irene. 1977. *Sex Roles in the State House*. New Haven, CT: Yale University Press.

Diamond, Irene, and Nancy Hartsock. 1981. *"Beyond Interests in Politics: A Comment on Virginia Sapiro's 'When Are Interests Interesting? The Problem of Political Representation of Women.'"* American Political Science Review, 5 (3): 717–21.

Diascro, Jennifer Segal, and Rorie Spill Solberg. 2009. *"George W. Bush's Legacy on the Federal Bench: Policy in the Face of Diversity."* Judicature, 92: 289–301.

Diaz, Mercedes Mateo. 2005. *Representing Women? Female Legislators in West European Parliaments*. Essex: University of Essex, European Consortium for Political Research Monographs.

Disch, Lisa. 2011. *"Toward a Mobilization Conception of Democratic Representation."* American Political Science Review, 105 (1): 100–14.

Djongo, Pierre-Marie. *"De Maputo: Le rôle trouble de la France."* Le Messager, July 1, 2009. http://fr.allafrica.com/stories/200907010578.html.

Dodson, Debra L. 2006. *The Impact of Women in Congress*. Oxford: Oxford University Press.

Dodson, Debra L. 1998. "Representing Women's Interests in the U.S. House of Representatives." In *Women and Elective Office: Past, Present, and Future* (1st ed.), eds. Sue Thomas and Clyde Wilcox. New York: Oxford University Press, 130–49.

Dodson, Debra L., and Susan Carroll. 1991. *Reshaping the Agenda: Women in State Legislatures*. New Brunswick: Center for the American Woman and Politics, Rutgers, The State University of New Jersey.

Dolan, Julie, and Jonathan S. Kropf. 2004. *"Credit Claiming from the U.S. House: Gendered Communication Styles?"* Harvard International Journal of Press/Politics, 9 (1): 41–59.

Dolan, Kathleen A. 2004. *Voting for Women: How the Public Evaluates Women Candidates*. Boulder, CO: Westview.

Dovi, Suzanne. 2006. "Political Representation." *Stanford Encyclopedia of Philosophy*. http://plato.stanford.edu/entries/political-representation.

Dovi, Suzanne. 2002. *"Preferable Descriptive Representatives: Will Just Any Woman, Black, or Latino Do?"* American Political Science Review, 96 (4): 729–43.

Dryzek, John S., and Simon Niemeyer. 2008. "Discursive Representation." *American Political Science Review*, 102 (4): 481–93.

Dubrow, Joshua Kjerulf. 2008. *"How Can We Account for Intersectionality in Quantitative Analysis of Survey Data? Empirical Illustration for Central and Eastern Europe."* Ask: Research and Methods, 17 (1): 85–100.

Duffy, Helen. 2009. *"Hadijatou Mani Koroua v Niger: Slavery Unveiled by the ECOWAS Court."* Human Rights Law Review, 9 (1): 151–70.

Duverger, Maurice 1955. *The Political Role of Women*. Paris: UNESCO.

Earl, Jennifer, Andrew Martin, John D. McCarthy, and Sarah Soule. 2004. *"The Use of Newspaper Data in the Study of Collective Action."* Annual Review of Sociology, 30: 65–80.

Elman, R. Amy. 2003. "Refuge in Reconfigured States: Shelter Movements in the United States, Britain, and Sweden." In *Women's Movements Facing the Reconfigured State*, eds. Lee Ann Banaszak, Karen Beckwith, and Dieter Rucht. Cambridge: Cambridge University Press, 94–113.

"Equality Bill to Go Back to Parliament," *Daily Nation*, September 21, 2004. http://allafrica.com/stories/200409210073.html.

Escobar-Lemmon, Maria C., and Michelle M. Taylor-Robinson. 2009. *"Getting to the Top: Career Paths of Women in Latin American Cabinets."* Political Research Quarterly, 62 (4): 685–99.

Escobar-Lemmon, Maria C. and Michelle M. Taylor-Robinson. 2005. *"Women Ministers in Latin American Government: When, Where, and Why?"* American Journal of Political Science, 49 (4): 829–44.

Evans, C. Lawrence. 1991. *Leadership in Committee: A Comparative Analysis of Leadership Behavior in the U.S. Senate*. Ann Arbor: University of Michigan Press.

Fahamu. 2005. "Annual Report 2004/2005." http://unpan1.un.org/intradoc/groups/public/documents/other/unpan025352.pdf.

Fallon, Kathleen. 2008. *Democracy and the Rise of Women's Movements in Sub-Saharan Africa*. Baltimore, MD: Johns Hopkins University Press.

Fidler, Laura. 2005. "A Minority of the Majority: The Curious Place of Women's Political Parties in Electoral Systems." Paper presented at the annual meeting of the American Political Science Association, Washington, DC.

Fish, M. Steven. 2011. *Are Muslims Distinctive? A Look at the Evidence*. Oxford: Oxford University Press.

Fish, M. Steven. 2002. *"Islam and Authoritarianism." World Politics*, 55 (1): 4–37.

Fogg-Davis, Hawley. 2008. *"Theorizing Black Lesbianism within Black Feminism: A Critique of Same Race Street Harassment." Politics & Gender*, 2 (1): 57–76.

Fomo, Eric Vincent. "Avortement: Quand le protocole de Maputo anime le débat." *Cameroon Tribune*, July 13, 2009. http://fr.allafrica.com/stories/200907130874.html.

Fox, Jonathan. 2004. *"Religion and State Failure: An Examination of the Extent and Magnitude of Religious Conflict from 1950 to 1996." International Political Science Review*, 25 (1): 55–76.

Fraga, Lius Ricardo, Valerie Martinez-Ebers, Linda Lopez, and Ricardo Ramírez. 2008. "Representing Gender and Ethnicity: Strategic Intersectionality." In *Legislative Women: Getting Elected, Getting Ahead*, ed. Beth Reingold. Boulder, CO: Lynne Rienner, 157–74.

Fraga, Luis Ricardo, Valerie Martinez-Ebers, Linda Lopez, and Ricardo Ramirez. 2007. *"Gender and Ethnicity: Patterns of Electoral Success and Legislative Advocacy among Latina and Latino State Officials in Four States." Journal of Women, Politics & Policy*, 28 (3–4): 121–45.

Franceschet, Susan, and Jennifer M. Piscopo. 2008. *"Gender Quotas and Women's Substantive Representation: Lessons from Argentina." Politics & Gender*, 4 (3): 393–425.

Franzese, Robert J. 2009. "Multicausality, Context-Conditionality, and Endogeneity." In *The Oxford Handbook of Comparative Politics*, eds. Carles Boix and Susan C. Stokes. New York: Oxford University Press, 27–72.

Fraser, Nancy. 2007. *"Feminist Politics in the Age of Recognition: A Two-Dimensional Approach to Gender Justice." Studies in Social Justice*, 1 (1): 23–35.

Frederick, Brian. 2011. *"Gender Turnover and Roll Call Voting in the US Senate." Journal of Women, Politics & Policy*, 32 (3): 193–210.

Frederick, Brian. 2010. *"Gender and Patterns of Roll-Call Voting in the Senate." Congress and the Presidency*, 37 (2): 103–24.

Freidenvall, Lenita. 2013. "Sweden: Step by step—Women's inroads into parliamentary politics." In *Breaking Male Dominance in Old Democracies*, eds. Drude Dahlerup and Monique Leyenaar. Oxford: Oxford University Press, 97–123.

Fridkin, Kim L., and Patrick J. Kenney. 2009. *"The Role of Gender Stereotypes in U.S. Senate Campaigns." Politics & Gender*, 5 (3): 301–24.

Fridkin, Kim L., and Gina Serignese Woodall. 2005. "Different Portraits, Different Leaders? Gender Differences in U.S. Senators' Presentation of Self." In *Women and Elective Office: Past, Present, and Future* (2nd ed.), eds. Sue Thomas and Clyde Wilcox. New York: Oxford University Press, 81–93.

Galligan, Yvonne. 2007. "Theorizing Political Representation." In *Gender Politics and Democracy in Post-Socialist Europe,* eds. Yvonne Galligan, Sara Clavero, and Marina Calloni. Opladen and Farmington Hills: Barbara Budrich Publishers, 35–52.

García, Sonia R., Valerie Martinez-Ebers, Irasema Coronado, Sharon A. Navarro, and Patricia A. Jaramillo. 2008. *Políticas: Latina Public Officials in Texas.* Austin: University of Texas Press.

Garcia Bedolla, Lisa. 2007. "Intersections of Inequality: Understanding Marginalization and Privilege in the Post-Civil Rights Era." *Politics & Gender,* 3 (2): 232–48.

Garcia Bedolla, Lisa, Katherine Tate, and Janelle Wong. 2005. "Indelible Effects: The Impact of Women of Color in the U.S. Congress." In *Women and Elective Office: Past, Present, and Future* (2nd ed.), eds. Sue Thomas and Clyde Wilcox. New York: Oxford University Press, 152–75.

Gerber, Elizabeth R., and John E. Jackson. 1993. *"Endogenous Preferences and the Study of Institutions." American Political Science Review,* 87 (3): 639–56.

Giele, Janet Zollinger, and Audrey Chapman Smock, eds. 1977. *Women: Roles and Status in Eight Countries.* New York: Wiley.

Gill, Rebecca. 2012. "A Framework for Comparative Judicial Selection Research with an Application to Gender Diversity on High Courts". Presented at the 2012 Annual Meeting of the Southern Political Science Association. New Orleans, LA.

Glenn, Evelyn Nakano. 1992. *"From Servitude to Service Work: Historical Continuities in the Racial Division of Paid Reproductive Labor." Signs,* 18 (1): 1–43.

Goertz, Gary, and Amy Mazur. 2008. "Mapping Gender and Politics Concepts: Ten Guidelines." In *Politics, Gender and Concepts: Theory and Methodology,* eds. Gary Goertz and Amy Mazur. New York: Cambridge University Press, 14–45.

Goetz, Anne Marie, and Shireen Hassim, eds. 2003. *No Shortcuts to Power: African Women in Politics and Policy Making.* London and New York: Zed Books; Cape Town: David Philip.

Goodliffe, Jay, and Darren Hawkins. 2006. *"Explaining Commitment: States and the Convention against Torture." Journal of Politics,* 68 (2): 358–71.

Gordon, Linda. 1994. *Pitied But Not Entitled: Single Mothers and the History of Welfare, 1890–1935.* New York: Free Press.

Graham, Richard, ed. 1990. *The Idea of Race in Latin America, 1870–1940.* Austin: University of Texas Press.

Gray, Mark, Miki Caul Kittilson, and Wayne Sandholtz. 2006. *"Women and Globalization: A Study of 180 Countries, 1975–2000." International Organization,* 60 (2): 293–333.

Greenwood, Ronni Michelle. 2008. *"Intersectional Political Consciousness: Appreciation for Intra-group Differences and Solidarity in Diverse Groups." Psychology of Women Quarterly,* 32: 36–47.

Greenwood, Ronni Michelle, and Aidan Christian. 2008. *"What Happens When We Unpack the Invisible Knapsack? Intersectional Political Consciousness and Intergroup Appraisals." Sex Roles,* 59 (5–6): 404–17.

Griffin, John D., and Brian Newman. 2008. *Minority Report: Evaluating Political Equality in America.* Chicago: University of Chicago Press.

Halsaa, Beatrice. 1987. *"Har kvinnor gemensamma intressen?" Kvinnovetenskaplig tidskrift,* 4 (8): 42–56.

Hancock, Ange-Marie. 2013. "Empirical Intersectionality: Two Approaches." *University of California, Irvine Law Review,* 8 (2): 259–96.

Hancock, Ange-Marie. 2011. *Solidarity Politics for Millennials: A Guide to Ending the Oppression Olympics*. New York: Palgrave Macmillan.

Hancock, Ange-Marie. 2007. *"When Multiplication Doesn't Equal Quick Addition: Examining Intersectionality as a Research Paradigm." Perspectives on Politics*, 5 (1): 63–79.

Hancock, Ange-Marie. 2004. *The Politics of Disgust: The Public Identity of the Welfare Queen*. New York: New York University Press.

Harris, Marvin. 1964. *Patterns of Race in the Americas*. New York: Walker.

Harward, Brian M., and Kenneth W. Moffett. 2010. *"The Calculus of Cosponsorship in the U.S. Senate." Legislative Studies Quarterly*, 35 (1): 117–43.

Hassim, Shireen. 2006. *Women's Organizations and Democracy in South Africa: Contesting Authority*. Madison: University of Wisconsin Press.

Hathaway, Oona. 2002. *"Do Human Rights Treaties Make a Difference?" Yale Law Journal*, 111: 1935.

Hawkesworth, Mary. 2003. *"Congressional Enactments of Race–Gender: Toward a Theory of Raced–Gendered Institutions." American Political Science Review*, 97 (4): 529–50.

Haynie, Kerry L. 2011. "Comprendre les minorities visibles en politiqu au-dela des axes unique de la race et du genre." In *Minorities visible en politique*, ed. Estjer Benbassa. Paris, France: CNRS Editions, 191–201.

Haynie, Kerry L. 2001. *African American Legislators in the American States*. New York: Columbia University Press.

Hazan, Reuven, and Gideon Rahat. 2010. *Democracy within Parties: Candidate Selection Methods and Their Political Consequences*. New York: Oxford University Press.

Heath, Roseanna, Leslie Schwindt-Bayer, and Michelle M. Taylor-Robinson. 2005. *"Women on the Sidelines: The Rationality of Isolating Tokens." American Journal of Political Science*, 49 (2): 420–36.

Hellevik, Ottar, and Tor Bjoerklund. 1995. "Velgerne og Kvinnereprenstasjon." In *Kjønn og Politikk*, ed. Nina Cecelia Raaum. Oslo: Tano, 113–29.

Hellevik, Ottar, and Toril Skard. 1985. *Norsk kommunestyrer – Plass for kvinner?* Oslo, Norway: Universitetsforlaget.

Hill, Lisa, and Louise Chappell. 2006. "Introduction: The Politics of Women's Interests." In *The Politics of Women's Interests: New Comparative Perspectives*, eds. Louise Chappell and Lisa Hill. Abingdon: Routledge, 1–4.

Hodgson, Dorothy. 2002. *"Women's Rights as Human Rights: Women in Law and Development in Africa (WiLDAF)." Africa Today*, 49 (2): 3–28.

Hoekstra, Valerie J. 2010. *"Increasing the Gender Diversity of High Courts: A Comparative View." Politics & Gender*, 6 (3): 474–84.

Hoekstra, Valerie, and Elizabeth Andrews. 2010. "Promoting Diversity on the Bench: A Comparative Approach." Presented at the annual meeting of the Southern Political Science Association, New Orleans, LA.

hooks, bell. 2000. *Feminist Theory: From Margin to Center* (2nd ed.). Cambridge, MA: South End Press.

Htun, Mala. Forthcoming. *Politics of Inclusion: Gender Quotas and Ethnic Reservations in Latin America*. Unpublished manuscript under contract with Cambridge University Press.

Htun, Mala. 2012. *Intersectional Disadvantage and Political Inclusion: Getting More Afrodescendant Women into Elected Office in Latin America*. Washington, DC: Inter-American Development Bank.

Htun, Mala. 2005a. *"What It Means to Study Gender and the State." Politics & Gender*, 1 (1): 157–66.

Htun, Mala. 2005b. "Women, Political Parties and Electoral Systems in Latin America." In *Women in Parliament: Beyond Numbers. A New Edition*, eds. Julie Ballington and Azza Karam. Stockholm: International IDEA, 112–21.

Htun, Mala. 2004a. *"From 'Racial Democracy' to Affirmative Action: Changing State Policy on Race in Brazil." Latin American Research Review*, 39 (1): 60–89.

Htun, Mala. 2004b. *"Is Gender Like Ethnicity? The Political Representation of Identity Groups." Perspectives on Politics*, 2 (3): 39–58.

Htun, Mala. 2003a. *Sex and the State: Abortion, Divorce, and the Family under Latin American Dictatorships and Democracies*. Cambridge: Cambridge University Press.

Htun, Mala. 2003b. "Women's Leadership in Latin America: Trends and Challenges." In *Politics Matters: A Dialogue of Women Political Leaders*. Washington, DC: Inter-American Development Bank, Inter-American Dialogue, and International Center for Research on Women, 13–26.

Htun, Mala, Marina Lacalle, and Juan Pablo Micozzi. 2013. *"Does Women's Presence Change Legislative Behavior? Evidence from Argentina, 1983–2007." Journal of Politics in Latin America*, 2 (1): 95–125.

Htun, Mala, and Timothy Power. 2006. *"Gender, Parties, and Support for Equal Rights in the Brazilian Congress." Latin American Politics and Society*, 48 (4): 83–104.

Htun, Mala, and S. Laurel Weldon. 2012. *"The Civic Origins of Progressive Policy Change: Combatting Violence against Women in Global Perspective, 1975–2005." American Political Science Review*, 106 (3): 548–69.

Htun, Mala, and S. Laurel Weldon. 2010. *"When Do Governments Promote Women's Rights? A Framework for the Comparative Analysis of Sex Equality Policy." Perspectives on Politics*, 8 (1): 207–16.

Huddy, Leonie, and Nayda Terkildsen. 1993. *"Gender Stereotypes and the Perception of Male and Female Candidates." American Journal of Political Science*, 37 (1): 119–47.

Hughes, Melanie. 2011. *"Intersectionality, Quotas, and Minority Women's Political Representation Worldwide." American Political Science Review*, 105 (3): 604–20.

Ibrahim, Jibrin. 2004. "The First Lady Syndrome and the Marginalisation of Women from Power: Opportunities or Compromises for Gender Equality?" *Feminist Africa* 3. http://www.feministafrica.org/index.php/first-lady-syndrome (Accessed June 5, 2009).

Ikstens, Janis. 2013. "This Is a Man's World: Effects of Preferential Voting on Women's Representation in Latvia." Paper presented at ECPR Joint Sessions, March 11–16, 2013.

Inglehart, Ronald, and Pippa Norris. 2003. *Rising Tide: Gender Equality and Cultural Change Around the World*. Cambridge: Cambridge University Press.

Inter-Parliamentary Union. 2011. "Parline Database on National Parliaments." http://www.ipu.org/parline-e/parlinesearch.asp (Accessed May 2, 2011).

Ismaël, Laoual Sallaou. "Les femmes musulmanes interpellent le gouvernement." *Roue de l'histoire*, September 13, 2006.

Jacobs, Lawrence R., and Theda Skocpol. 2010. *Health Care Reform and American Politics: What Everyone Needs to Know*. New York: Oxford University Press.

Jelen, Ted G., and Clyde Wilcox. 2005. *"Attitudes toward Abortion in Poland and the U.S." Politics & Gender*, 1 (2): 297–317.

Jónasdóttir, Anna G. 1991. *Love Power and Political Interests*. Örebro University: Örebro Studies 7.

Jónasdóttir, Anna G., and Kathleen B. Jones. 2009. "The Political Interests of Gender Revisited: Reconstructing Feminist Theory and Political Research." In *The*

Political Interests of Gender Revisited, eds. Anna G. Jónasdóttir and Kathleen B. Jones. Manchester: Manchester University Press, 1–16.

Jung, Courtney. 2008. *The Moral Force of Indigenous Politics: Critical Liberalism and the Zapatistas*. Cambridge and New York: Cambridge University Press.

Kang, Alice. 2013. "The Effect of Gender Quota Laws on the Election of Women: Lessons from Niger." *Women's Studies International Forum*, 41 (2): 94–102.

Kang, Alice. 2010. *Bargaining with Islam: Of Rule, Religion, and Women in Niger*. Ph.D. Dissertation, University of Wisconsin-Madison.

Kantola, Johanna. 2006. *Feminists Theorize the State*. Palgrave Macmillan.

Karpowitz, Christopher F., Tali Mendelberg, and Lee Shaker. 2012. "Gender Inequality in Deliberative Participation." *American Political Science Review*, 106 (3): 533–47.

Karvonen, Lauri. 2004. "Preferential Voting: Incidence and Effects." *International Political Science Review*, 25 (2): 203–26.

Katz, Richard. 1986. "Intraparty Preference Voting." In *Electoral Laws and Their Political Consequences*, eds. Bernard N. Grofman and Arend Lijphart. New York: Algora Publishing, 85–103.

Kaufmann, Karen M. 2002. "Culture Wars, Secular Realignment, and the Gender Gap in Party Identification." *Political Behavior*, 24 (3): 283–307.

Keck, Margaret, and Kathryn Sikkink. 1998. *Activists Without Borders: Advocacy Networks in International Politics*. Ithaca, NY: Cornell University Press.

Keman, Hans. 1991. "Ministers and Ministries." In *The Profession of Government Minister in Western Europe*. eds. Jean Blondel and Jean-Louis Thiébault. New York: St. Martins Press, 99–118.

Kenney, Sally J. 2008. "Thinking about Gender and Judging." *International Journal of the Legal Profession*, 15: 87–110.

King, David. 1997. *Turf Wars: How Congressional Committees Claim Jurisdiction*. Chicago: University of Chicago Press.

King, David C., and Richard E. Matland. 2003. "Sex and the Grand Old Party: An Experimental Investigation of the Effect of Candidate Sex on Support for a Republican Candidate." *American Politics Research*, 31 (6): 595–612.

King, Deborah K. 1988. "Multiple Jeopardy, Multiple Consciousness: The Context of a Black Feminist Ideology." *Signs*, 14 (1): 42–72.

King, Gary. 1989. "Variance Specification in Event Count Models: From Restrictive Assumptions to a Generalized Estimator." *American Journal of Political Science*, 33 (3): 762–84.

King, Gary. 1988. "Statistical Models for Political Science Even Counts: Bias in Conventional Procedures and Evidence for the Exponential Poisson Regression Model." *American Journal of Political Science*, 32 (3): 838–63.

Kingdon, John. 1995. *Agendas, Alternatives and Public Policies*. Boston, MA: Little, Brown.

Kittilson, Miki Caul. 2008. "Representing Women: The Adoption of Family Leave in Comparative Perspective." *Journal of Politics*, 70 (2): 323–34.

Kittilson, Miki Caul. 2006. *Challenging Parties, Changing Parliaments: Women and Elected Office in Contemporary Western Europe*. Columbus: Ohio State University Press.

Knapp, Gudrun-Axeli. 2005. "Race, Class, Gender: Reclaiming Baggage in Fast Traveling Theories." *European Journal of Women's Studies*, 12 (3): 249–65.

Koch, Jeffrey W. 2002. "Gender Stereotypes and Citizens' Impressions of House Candidates' Ideological Orientations." *American Journal of Political Science*, 46 (2): 453–62.

Koch, Jeffrey W. 2000. *"Do Citizens Apply Gender Stereotypes to Infer Candidates' Ideological Orientations?" Journal of Politics*, 62 (2): 414–29.

Koch, Jeffrey W. 1999. *"Candidate Gender and Assessments of Senate Candidates." Social Science Quarterly*, 80 (1): 84–96.

Koger, Gregory. 2010. *Filibustering: A Political History of Obstruction in the House and Senate*. Chicago: University of Chicago Press.

Koger, Gregory. 2003. *"Position Taking and Cosponsorship in the U.S. House." Legislative Studies Quarterly*, 28 (2): 225–46.

Krook, Mona Lena. 2010. *"Women's Representation in Parliament: A Qualitative Comparative Analysis." Political Studies*, 58 (5): 886–908.

Krook, Mona Lena. 2009. *Quotas for Women in Politics: Gender and Candidate Selection Reform Worldwide*. Oxford: Oxford University Press.

Krook, Mona Lena. 2006. *"Reforming Representation: The Diffusion of Candidate Gender Quotas Worldwide." Politics & Gender*, 2 (3): 303–27.

Kunovich, Sherri. 2012. *"Unexpected Winners: The Significance of an Open-List System on Women's Representation in Poland." Politics & Gender*, 8 (2): 153–77.

Label, Richard, and Philip S. C. Lewis. 1996. *Lawyers in Society: An Overview*. Berkeley: University of California Press.

"Le droit à l'avortement de femmes en Afrique: Les Evêques du Burundi, RDC et Ruanda s'opposent au Protocole de Maputo." La Prosperité, June 21, 2007. http://fr.allafrica.com/stories/200706210465.html.

LeDuc, Lawrence, Richard G. Niemi and Pippa Norris. 2010. *Comparing Democracies 3: Elections and Voting in the 21st Century*. New York: Sage.

Lee, Frances. 2009. *Beyond Ideology: Politics, Principles, and Partisanship in the U.S. Senate* Chicago: University of Chicago Press.

Lee, Frances E., and Bruce I. Oppenheimer. 1999. *Sizing Up the Senate: The Unequal Consequences of Equal Representation*. Chicago: University of Chicago Press.

Lee, Taeku. 2007. *"From Shared Demographic Categories to Common Political Destinies: Immigration and the Link from Racial Identity to Group Politics." Du Bois Review*, 4 (2): 433–56.

Lépinard, Eléonore. 2007. *"The Contentious Subject of Feminism: Defining Women in France from the Second Wave to Parity." Signs*, 32 (2): 375–403.

Lichtblau, Eric. 2011. "Economic Downturn Took a Detour at Capitol Hill," *New York Times*, December 26. http://www.nytimes.com/2011/12/27/us/politics/economic-slide-took-a-detour-at-capitol-hill.html?_r=1&ref=ericlichtblau (Accessed January 5, 2012).

Lilliefeldt, Emelie. 2011. "European Party Politics and Gender: Configuring Gender-Balanced Parliamentary Presence." Stockholm: Ph.D. Diss., Department of Political Science, Stockholm University. Available at http://urn.kb.se/resolve?urn=urn:nbn:se:su:diva-63628.

Listhaug, Ola, Beate Huseby, and Richard E. Matland. 1995. "Valgatferd blant kvinner og menn: 1957–1993 [The Gender Gap in Norwegian Voting: 1957–1993]." In *Kjønn og Politikk* [Gender and Politics], ed. Nina Raaum. Oslo: Tano Publishing.

Lopez, Iris. 1993. *"Agency and Constraint: Sterilization and Reproductive Freedom among Puerto Rican Women in New York City." Urban Anthropology and Studies of Cultural Systems and World Economic Development*, 22 (3–4): 299–323.

Lovenduski, Joni, ed. 2005. *State Feminism and Political Representation*. Cambridge: Cambridge University Press.

Lovenduski, Joni, and Pippa Norris. 1993. *Gender and Party Politics*. London: Sage.

Lublin, David. 2013. *"The 2012 Latvia Language Referendum." Electoral Studies*, 32(2): 385–87.

Luker, Kristin. 1984. *Abortion and the Politics of Motherhood*. Berkeley and Los Angeles: University of California Press.

Lukes, Steven. 1984. *Power: A Radical View*. London and Basingstoke: Macmillan.

Mackay, Fiona. 2008. *"'Thick' Conceptions of Substantive Representation: Women, Gender, and Political Institutions." Representation*, 44 (2): 125–40.

Mackay, Fiona. 2001. *Love and Politics: Women Politicians and the Ethics of Care*. London and New York: Continuum.

Mama, Amina. 1997. "Feminism or Femocracy? State Feminism and Democratization" In *The Expansion of Democratic Space in Nigeria*, ed. Jibrin Ibrahim. Dakar, Senegal: CODESRIA, 37–58.

Mansbridge, Jane. 2011. "Clarifying the Concept of Representation." *American Political Science Review*, 105 (3): 621–30.

Mansbridge, Jane. 2005. "Quota Problems: Combating the Dangers of Essentialism." *Politics & Gender*, 1 (4): 622–38.

Mansbridge, Jane. 2003. "Rethinking Representation." *American Political Science Review*, 97 (4): 515–28.

Mansbridge, Jane. 1999. "Should Blacks Represent Blacks and Women Represent Women? A Contingent 'Yes.'" *Journal of Politics*, 61 (3): 628–57.

Mansbridge, Jane. 1986. *Why We Lost the ERA*. Chicago: University of Chicago Press.

Marshall, Monty, and Keith Jaggers. 2010. "Polity IV Project: Political Regime Characteristics and Transitions, 1800–2009." College Park: University of Maryland.

Martinez-Ebers, Valerie, Luis Fraga, Linda Lopez, and Arturo Vega. 2000. *"Latino Interests in Education, Health, and Criminal Justice Policy." PS: Political Science and Politics*, 33 (3): 547–54.

Marx, Anthony W. 1998. *Making Race and Nation: A Comparison of South Africa, the United States, and Brazil*. Cambridge and New York: Cambridge University Press.

Marx, Jutta, Jutta Borner, and Mariana Caminotti. 2007. *Las Legisladoras: Cupos de Género y Política en Argentina y Brasil*. Buenos Aires: Siglo XXI.

Mateo Diaz, Mercedes. 2005. *Representing Women? Female Legislators in West European Parliaments*. Colchester, England: ECPR Press.

Matland, Richard E. 1998. *"Women's Representation in National Legislatures: Developed and Developing Countries." Legislative Studies Quarterly*, 23 (1): 109–25.

Matland, Richard E. 1994. *"Putting Scandinavian Equality to the Test: An Experimental Evaluation of Gender Stereotyping of Political Candidates in a Sample of Norwegian Voters." British Journal of Political Science*, 24 (2): 273–92.

Matland, Richard E. 1993. *"Institutional Variables Affecting Female Representation in National Legislatures: The Case of Norway." Journal of Politics*, 55 (3): 737–55.

Matland, Richard E., and David C. King. 2002. "Women as Candidates in Congressional Elections." In *Women Transforming Congress*, ed. Cindy Simon Rosenthal. Norman: University of Oklahoma Press, 119–45.

Matland, Richard E., and Kathleen Montgomery. 2003a. "Recruiting Women to National Legislatures: A General Framework with Applications to Post-Communist Democracies." In *Women's Access to Political Power in Post-Communist Europe*, eds. Richard E. Matland and Kathleen Montgomery. Oxford: Oxford University Press, 19–42.

Matland, Richard E., and Kathleen Montgomery, eds. 2003b. *Women's Access to Political Power in Post-Communist Europe*. Oxford: Oxford University Press.

Matland, Richard E., and Donley T. Studlar. 1996. *"The Contagion of Women Candidates in Single and Multimember District Systems: Canada and Norway." Journal of Politics*, 58 (3): 707–33.

Matland, Richard E., and Gunes Tezcur. 2011. *"Women as Candidates: An Experimental Study in Turkey." Politics & Gender,* 7 (3): 365–90.

Mazur, Amy. 2002. *Theorizing Feminist Policy.* New York: Oxford University Press.

McCall, Leslie. 2005. *"The Complexity of Intersectionality." Signs: Journal of Women in Culture and Society,* 30 (3): 1771–800.

McCall, Leslie. 2001. *Complex Inequality: Gender, Class and Race in the New Economy.* London: Routledge.

McDermott, Monica L. 1997. *"Voting Cues in Low-Information Elections: Candidate Gender as a Social Information Variable in Contemporary United States Elections." American Journal of Political Science,* 41 (1): 270–83.

McElroy, Gail, and Michael Marsh. 2010. *"Candidate Gender and Vote Choice: Analysis from a Multimember Preferential Voting System." Political Research Quarterly,* 63 (4): 822–33.

Mink, Gwendolyn. 1995. *The Wages of Motherhood: Inequality in the Welfare State,* 1917–1942. Ithaca, NY: Cornell University Press.

Molyneux, Maxine. 1985. *"Mobilization Without Emancipation? Women's Interests, State, and Revolution in Nicaragua. Feminist Studies,* 11 (2): 227–54.

Moore, Mignon. 2011. *Invisible Families: Gay Identities, Relationships, and Motherhood among Black Women.* Berkeley: University of California Press.

Moser, Robert A. 2003. "Electoral Systems and Women's Representation: The Strange Case of Russia." In *Women's Access to Political Power in Post-Communist Europe,* eds. Richard E. Matland and Kathleen Montgomery. Oxford: Oxford University Press, 153–72.

Musamali, Geresom. *"Kadaga Appeals to Govt over Women Rights Law." New Vision,* August 9, 2007. http://allafrica.com/stories/printable/200708100088.html.

Nelson, Jennifer. 2003. *Women of Color and the Reproductive Rights Movement.* New York and London: New York University Press.

Neubeck, Kenneth J., and Noel A. Cazenave. 2001. *Welfare Racism: Playing the Race Card Against America's Poor.* New York: Routledge.

Nikoukari, Mondana. 2001. *"Gradations of Coercion: The Plight of Women of Color and Their Informed Consent in the Sterilization Debate." Connecticut Public Interest Law Journal,* 1: 49–76.

Norrander, Barbara. 2008. "The History of the Gender Gaps." In *Voting the Gender Gap.* ed. Lois Duke Whitaker. Urbana and Chicago: University of Illinois Press, 9–32.

Norris, Pippa. 1997. *Passages to Power: Legislative Recruitment in Advanced Democracies.* Cambridge: Cambridge University Press.

Norris, Pippa, and Joni Lovenduski. 1995. *Political Recruitment.* Cambridge: Cambridge University Press.

Novikova, I. 2006. "Gender Equality in Latvia: Achievements and Challenges." In *Women and Citizenship in Central and Eastern Europe,* eds. Jasmina Lukic, Joanna Regulska and Darja Zavirsek. Aldershot: Ashgate, 101–20.

Nqobani Ndlovu. "Women Lawyers Protest over Protocol." *The Standard,* December 16, 2007. http://allafrica.com/stories/200712170538.html.

Ogada, Joshua. "Africa: SOAWR Update on the Protocol on the Rights of Women in Africa." *Pambazuka* 302, May 4, 2007. http://www.pambazuka.org/en/category/wgender/41217.

Okeke, Phil. 1998. *"First Lady Syndrome: The (En)Gendering of Bureaucratic Corruption in Nigeria." CODESRIA Bulletin,* 3 & 4: 16–19.

Oko, Lydie Gisèle, and Yvette Reine Nzaba. "Les Congolaises organisent une marche." *Dépêches de Brazzaville.* March 9, 2010. www.brazzaville-adiac.com/medias/.../PDF942.pdf.

Omi, Michael, and Howard Winant. 1994. *Racial Formations in the United States: From the 1960s to the 1990s*. New York: Routledge.

O'Regan, Valerie R. 2000. *Gender Matters: Female Policymakers' Influence in Industrialized Nations*. Westport, CT: Praeger.

Orey, Byron D'Andra, Wendy Smooth, Kimberly Adams, Kish Harris-Clark. 2006. "Race and Gender Matter: Refining Models of Legislative Policy Making in State Legislatures." *Journal of Women, Politics, and Policy,* 28 (3–4): 97–119.

Orhin, Isabella Gyau. 2007. "Catholic Bishops Advocate Removal of Abortion Provisions in the African Charter," *Public Agenda,* April 16, 2007. http://allafrica.com/stories/200704161064.html.

Osborn, Tracy L. 2012. *How Women Represent Women: Political Parties, Gender, and Representation in State Legislatures*. New York: Oxford University Press.

Othman, Norani, ed. 2005. *Muslim Women and the Challenge of Islamic Extremism*. Petaling Jaya, Malaysia: Sisters in Islam.

Paixão, Marcelo, and Luis M. Carvano. 2008. *Relatório Anual das Desigualdades Raciais no Brasil, 2007–2008* [Annual Report on Racial Inequality in Brazil, 2007–2008]. Rio de Janeiro: Laboratório de Analise Econômicas, Sociais e Estatísticas em Relações Raciais (LAESER) at the Federal University of Rio de Janeiro.

Palici di Suni, Elisabetta. 2012. "Gender Parity and Quotas in Italy: A Convoluted Reform Process." *West European Politics,* 35(2): 380–94.

Pastor, Manuel, Chris Benner, and Martha Matsuoka. 2009. *This Could Be the Start of Something Big: Social Movements for Regional Equity are Reshaping Metropolitan America*. Ithaca, NY: Cornell University Press.

Paxton, Pamela, and Melanie M. Hughes. 2007. *Women, Politics and Power: A Global Perspective*. Los Angeles: Pine Forge Press.

"Petition Signatories." http://www.pambazuka.org/en/petition/signatures.php.

Petrocik, John R. 1996. "Issue Ownership in Presidential Elections, with a 1980 Case Study." *American Journal of Political Science,* 40 (3): 825–50.

Petrocik, John R., William L. Benoit, and Glenn J. Hansen. 2003. "Issue Ownership and Presidential Campaigning." *Political Science Quarterly,* 118 (4): 599–626.

Pew Forum. 2011. *Christian Population as a Percentage of Total Population by Country.* http://features.pewforum.org/global-christianity/total-population-percentage. php.

Pew Forum. 2009. *Mapping the Global Muslim Population: A Report on the Size and Distribution of the World's Muslim Population*. Washington, DC: Pew Research Center.

Phillips, Anne. 1998. "Democracy and Representation: Or, Why Should It Matter Who Our Representatives Are?" In *Feminism and Politics*, ed. Anne Phillips. New York: Oxford University Press, 224–40.

Phillips, Anne. 1995. *The Politics of Presence*. Oxford: Clarendon Press.

Piscopo, Jennifer M. 2011. "Rethinking Descriptive Representation: Rendering Women in Legislative Debates." *Parliamentary Affairs* 64 (3): 338–72.

Pitkin, Hanna. 1967. *The Concept of Representation*. Berkeley: University of California Press.

"Platform for Action." 1995. The United Nations Fourth World Conference on Women. Beijing, China. September. http://www.un.org/womenwatch/daw/beijing/platform/decision.htm (Accessed 5 January 2012).

Poe, Steven, Dierdre Wendel-Blunt, and Karl Ho. 1997. "Global Patterns in the Achievement of Women's Human Rights to Equality." *Human Rights Quarterly,* 19 (4): 813–35.

Poole, Keith T., and Howard Rosenthal. 2007. *Ideology and Congress*. Piscataway, NJ: Transaction Publishers.

Poole, Keith T., and Howard Rosenthal. 1997. *Congress: A Political-Economic History of Roll Call Voting*. New York: Oxford University Press.

"Portugal Ratifies Law Allowing Abortions." 2007. *The Guardian*, April 10. http://www.guardian.co.uk/world/2007/apr/10/1 (Accessed January 9, 2012).

Powell, G. Bingham, Jr. 2009. "Aggregating and Representing Political Preferences." In *The Oxford Handbook of Comparative Politics*, eds. Carles Boix and Susan C. Stokes. Oxford: Oxford University Press, 653–77.

"Press Release." *Daily Mail*, March 27, 2007. http://allafrica.com/stories/200703270231.html.

"Protocol on the Rights of Women in Africa: Update on Progress." 2004. *Pambazuka News* 165, July 15, 2004. http://www.pambazuka.org/en/category/features/23224.

Przeworski, Adam, Susan C. Stokes, and Bernard Manin. 1999. *Democracy, Accountability, and Representation*. Cambridge and New York: Cambridge University Press.

Quintanilla, Ray. 2004. "Anger At Island's 'Pill' Test Lingers: Some Women Were Unwitting Subjects of Birth Control in 1950s and '60s Puerto Rico." *Orlando Sentinel*, April 5. http://www.puertorico-herald.org/issues/2004/vol8n27/AngerPill.html (Accessed January 9, 2012).

Ragin, Charles. 2008. *Redesigning Social Inquiry: Fuzzy Sets and Beyond*. Chicago: University of Chicago Press.

Ragin, Charles. 2000. *Fuzzy-Set Social Science*. Chicago: University of Chicago Press.

Rai, S. M., Bari, F., Mahtab, N. and Mohanty, B. 2006. "South Asia: Gender quotas and the Politics of Empowerment—A Comparative Study", In *Women, Quotas and Politics,* ed. Drude Dahlerup. New York/London: Routledge, 222–45.

Reed, Adolph. 2002. *"Unraveling the Relation of Race and Class in American Politics." Political Power and Social Theory*, 15: 265–74.

Rehfeld, Andrew. 2011. *"The Concept of Representation." American Political Science Review,* 105 (3): 631–41.

Rehfeld, Andrew. 2009. *"Representation Rethought: On Trustees, Delegates, and Gyroscopes in the Study of Representation and Democracy." American Political Science Review,* 103 (2): 214–30.

Reid Andrews, George. 2004. *Afro-Latin America, 1800–2000*. New York: Oxford University Press.

Reingold, Beth. 2008. "Women as Office Holders: Linking Descriptive and Substantive Representation." In *Political Women and American Democracy*, eds. Christina Wolbrecht, Karen Beckwith, and Lisa Baldez. New York: Cambridge University Press, 128–47.

Reingold, Beth. 2000. *Representing Women: Sex Gender, and Legislative Behavior in Arizona and California*. Chapel Hill: The University of North Carolina Press.

Reingold, Beth, and Adrienne R. Smith. 2012. *"Welfare Policymaking and Intersections of Race, Ethnicity, and Gender in U.S. State Legislatures." American Journal of Political Science*, 56 (1): 131–47.

Reingold, Beth, and Michele Swers. 2011. *"An Endogenous Approach to Women's Interests: When Interests Are Interesting in and of Themselves." Politics & Gender,* 7 (3): 429–35.

Rekkas, Marie. 2008. *"Gender and Elections: An Examination of the 2006 Canadian Federal Election." Canadian Journal of Political Science,* 41 (4): 987–1001.

Roberts, Dorothy E. 1997. *Killing the Black Body: Race, Reproduction, and the Meaning of Liberty*. New York: Pantheon Books.

Rodríguez Ruiz, Blanca, and Ruth Rubio-Marin. 2008. *"The Gender of Representation: On Democracy, Equality, and Parity."* International Journal of Constitutional Law, 6 (2): 287–316.

Rosas, Guillermo. 2005. *"The Ideological Organization of Latin American Legislative Parties: An Empirical Analysis of Elite Policy Preferences."* Comparative Political Studies, 38 (7): 824–49.

Rose, Richard, and Neil Munro. 2009. *Parties and Elections in New European Democracies.* Colchester: ECPR.

Rosenthal, Cindy Simon. 1998. *When Women Lead: Integrative Leadership in State Legislatures.* NewYork: Oxford University Press.

Ross, Michael. 2008. *"Oil, Islam, and Women."* American Political Science Review, 102 (1): 107–23.

Rubenstein, Jennifer. 2007. *"Accountability in an Unequal World."* Journal of Politics, 69 (3): 616–32.

Rule, Wilma. 1987. *"Electoral Systems, Contextual Factors and Women's Opportunity for Election to Parliament in Twenty-Three Democracies."* Western Political Quarterly, 40 (3): 477–98.

Rule, Wilma, and Matthew Shugart. 1995. *"The Preference Vote and Election of Women: Women Win More Votes in Open List PR."* In *Voting and Democracy Report* 1995. Washington, DC: The Center for Voting and Democracy, 177–78.

Saint-Germain, Michelle A. 1989. *"Does Their Difference Make a Difference? The Impact of Women on Public Policy in the Arizona Legislature."* Social Science Quarterly, 70 (4): 956–68.

Saint-Germain, Michelle A. and Cynthia Chavez Metoyer. 2008. *Women Legislators in Central America: Politics, Democracy, and Policy.* Austin: University of Texas Press.

Sanbonmatsu, Kira. 2002a. *"Gender Stereotypes and Vote Choice."* American Journal of Political Science, 46 (1): 20–34.

Sanbonmatsu, Kira. 2002b. *Gender Equality, Political Parties, and the Politics of Women's Place.* Ann Arbor: University of Michigan Press.

Sanbonmatsu, Kira, and Kathleen Dolan. 2009. *"Do Gender Stereotypes Transcend Party?"* Political Research Quarterly, 62 (3): 485–94.

Sapiro, Virginia. 1981. *"When Are Interests Interesting? The Problem of Political Representation of Women."* American Political Science Review, 75 (3): 701–16.

Saward, Michael. 2010. *The Representative Claim.* Oxford: Oxford University Press.

Sawer, Marion, Manon Trimbley, and Linda Trimble. 2006. *Representing Women in Parliament. A Comparative Study.* London and New York: Routledge.

Schaffner, Brian F. 2005. *"Priming Gender: Campaigning on Women's Issues in U.S. Senate Elections."* American Journal of Political Science, 49 (4): 803–17.

Schattschneider, E. E. 2009 (originally published 1942). *Party Government: American Government in Action.* New Brunswick, NJ: Transaction.

Schiller, Wendy. 2000. *Partners and Rivals: Representation in U.S. Senate Delegations.* Princeton, NJ: Princeton University Press.

Schiller, Wendy. 1995. *"Senators as Political Entrepreneurs: Using Bill Sponsorship to Shape Legislative Agendas."* American Journal of Political Science, 39 (1): 186–203.

Schmidt, Gregory D., and Kyle L. Saunders. 2004. *"Effective Quotas, Relative Party Magnitude, and the Success of Female Candidates in Peruvian Municipal Elections in Comparative Perspective."* Comparative Political Studies, 37 (6): 704–34.

Schwindt-Bayer, Leslie A. 2010. *Political Power and Women's Representation in Latin America.* Oxford and New York: Oxford University Press.

Schwindt-Bayer, Leslie. 2009. *"Making Quotas Work: The Effect of Gender Quota Laws on the Election of Women." Legislative Studies Quarterly,* 34 (1): 5–28.

Schwindt-Bayer, Leslie A. 2006. *"Still Supermadres? Gender and the Policy Priorities of Latin American Legislators." American Journal of Political Science,* 50 (3): 570–85.

Schwindt-Bayer, Leslie, and William Mishler. 2005. *"An Integrated Model of Women's Representation." Journal of Politics,* 67 (2): 407–28.

"SECAM Committee Discusses Report on Evangelization." *Catholic Information Service for Africa,* March 27, 2007. http://allafrica.com/stories/200703270681.html.

Segal, Jennifer A. 2000. *"Representative Decision Making on the Federal Bench: Clinton's District Court Appointees." Political Research Quarterly,* 53 (1): 137–50.

Sellers, Patrick. 2010. *Cycles of Spin: Strategic Communication in the U.S. Congress.* New York: Cambridge University Press.

Seltzer, Richard, Jody Newman, and Melissa Voorhees Leighton. 1997. *Sex as a Political Variable: Women as Candidates and Voters in U.S. Elections.* Boulder, CO: Lynne Rienner.

Sen, Amartya. 1999. *Development as Freedom.* New York: Knopf.

Shaffer, William R., Gunnar Grenstad, and Eric N.Waltenberg. 2011. "Policy Making by Appointment: The Composition of the Norwegian Supreme Court 1945–2009." Paper presented at the Faculty of Law, University of Oslo, May 12.

Shaw, Ulrike, and Gisela Schultz. 2003. *Women in the Judiciary.* London: Routledge.

Sheriff, Robin E. 2001. *Dreaming Equality: Color, Race, and Racism in Urban Brazil.* New Brunswick, NJ: Rutgers University Press.

Sieminenska, Renata. 2003. "Women in the Polish Sejm: Political Culture and Party Policies versus Electoral Rules." In *Women's Access to Political Power in Post-Communist Europe,* eds. Richard E. Matland and Kathleen Montgomery. Oxford: Oxford University Press, 217–44.

Simien, Evelyn M., and Rosalee A. Clawson. 2004. *"The Intersection of Race and Gender: An Examination of Black Feminist Consciousness, Race Consciousness, and Policy Attitudes." Social Science Quarterly,* 85 (3): 793–810.

Simmons, Beth. 2009. *Mobilizing for Human Rights: International Law in Domestic Politics.* Cambridge: Cambridge University Press.

Sinclair, Barbara. 2009. "The New World of US Senators." In *Congress Reconsidered* (9th ed.), eds. Lawrence C. Dodd and Bruce I. Oppenheimer. Washington, DC: CQ Press, 1–22.

Sinclair, Barbara. 1989. *The Transformation of the U.S. Senate.* Baltimore, MD: Johns Hopkins University Press.

Sinkkonen, Sirkka, and Elina Haavio-Mannila. 1981. "The Impact of the Women's Movement and Legislative Activity of Women MPs on Social Development." In *Women, Power and Political Systems,* eds. Margherita Rendel. London: Croom Helm, 195–215.

Skidmore, Thomas E. 1993. *Black into White: Race and Nationality in Brazilian Thought.* Durham, NC: Duke University Press.

Skjeie, Hege. 1991. *"The Rhetoric of Difference: On Women's Inclusion into Political Elites." Politics and Society,* 19 (2): 233–63.

Smooth, Wendy. 2011. *"Standing for Women? Which Women? The Substantive Representation of Women's Interests and the Research Imperative of Intersectionality." Politics & Gender,* 7 (3): 436–41.

Smooth, Wendy. 2006a. *"Intersectionality in Electoral Politics: A Mess Worth Making." Politics & Gender,* 2 (3): 400–14.

Smooth, Wendy. 2006b. "African American Women and Electoral Politics: Journeying from the Shadows to the Spotlight." *In Gender and Elections: Shaping the Future of American Politics*, eds. Susan J. Carroll and Richard L. Fox. Cambridge: Cambridge University Press, 117–42.

Smooth, Wendy. 2001. *African American Women State Legislators and the Politics of Legislative Incorporation*. New Brunswick, NJ: Center for the American Woman in Politics Rutgers University.

SOAWR Press Release. 2006. "Twelve African Leaders Receive Red Cards on Women's Rights at the African Union Summit in Khartoum, Sudan." January 20, 2006. http://www.pambazuka.org/aumonitor/images/uploads/soawr_press_release_200106.pdf.

Soule, Sarah, and Susan Olzak. 2004. *"When Do Social Movements Matter? The Politics of Contingency and the Equal Rights Amendment." American Sociological Review*, 69 (4): 473–97.

Sparks, Holloway. 2003. "Queens, Teens, and Model Mothers." In *Race and the Politics of Welfare Reform*, eds. Sanford F. Schram, Joe Soss, and Richard C. Fording. Ann Arbor: University of Michigan Press, 171–95.

Staggenborg, Suzanne. 1991. *The Pro-Choice Movement: Organization and Activism in the Abortion Conflict*. New York: Oxford University Press.

Stepan, Nancy. 1996. *"The Hour of Eugenics": Race, Gender, and Nation in Latin America*. Ithaca, NY: Cornell University Press.

Stetson, Dorothy McBride, and Amy Mazur, eds. 1995. *Comparative State Feminism*. Thousand Oaks, CA: Sage.

Strolovitch, Dara Z. 2007. *Affirmative Advocacy: Race, Class, and Gender in Interest Group Politics*. Chicago: University of Chicago Press.

Strolovitch, Dara Z. 2006. *"Do Interest Groups Represent the Disadvantaged? Advocacy at the Intersections of Race, Class, and Gender." Journal of Politics*, 68 (4): 893–908.

"Summary of Abortion Laws Around the World." N.d. http://www.pregnantpause.org/lex/world02.jsp (Accessed January 9, 2012).

Swers, Michele. 2013. *Making Policy in the New Senate Club: Women and Representation in the U.S. Senate*. Chicago: University of Chicago Press.

Swers, Michele. 2008. "Policy Leadership Beyond 'Women's' Issues." In *Legislative Women: Getting Elected, Getting Ahead*, ed. Beth Reingold. Boulder, CO: Lynne Rienner, 117–34.

Swers, Michele. 2007. *"Building a Reputation on National Security: The Impact of Stereotypes Related to Gender and Military Experience." Legislative Studies Quarterly*, 32 (4): 559–95.

Swers, Michele L. 2002. *The Difference Women Make: The Policy Impact of Women in Congress*. Chicago: University of Chicago Press.

Swers, Michele L., and Carin Larson. 2005. "Women in Congress: Do They Act as Advocates for Women' Issues?" In *Women and Elective Office: Past, Present, and Future* (2nd ed.), eds. Sue Thomas and Clyde Wilcox. New York: Oxford University Press, 110–28.

Takash, Paule Cruz. 1997. "Breaking Barriers to Representation: Chicana/Latina Elected Officials in California." In *Women Transforming Politics: An Alternative Reader*, eds. Cathy J. Cohen, Kathleen B. Jones, and Joan C. Tronto. New York: New York University Press, 412–34.

Tamerius, Karin L. 1995. "Sex, Gender, and Leadership in the Representation of Women." In *Gender Power, Leadership, and Governance*, eds. Georgia

Duerst-Lahti and Rita Mae Kelly. Ann Arbor: University of Michigan Press, 93–112.

Taylor-Robinson, Michelle M., and Roseanna Michelle Heath. 2003. *"Do Women Legislators Have Different Policy Priorities than Their Male Colleagues?"* Women & Politics, 24 (4): 77–101.

Taylor-Robinson, Michelle M., and Ashley Ross. 2011. *"Can Formal Rules of Order Be Used as an Accurate Proxy for Behavior Internal to a Legislature? Evidence from Costa Rica."* Journal of Legislative Studies, 17 (4): 479–500.

Telles, Edward. Forthcoming. "Introduction." In *Pigmentocracies: Ethnicity, Race, and Color in Latin America,* ed. Edward Telles and the Project on Ethnicity and Race in Latin America. Durham: University of North Carolina Press.

Telles, Edward. 2010. "A Review of Social Inequality and Millennium Development Goals in Latin America and Caribbean (LAC) Region." Consultancy Report Prepared for Dr. Naila Kabeer, Institute of Development Studies.

Telles, Edward. 2004. *Race in Another America: The Significance of Skin Color in Brazil.* Princeton, NJ: Princeton University Press.

Thames, Frank, and Margaret Williams. 2010. *"Incentives for Personal Votes and Women's Representation in Legislatures."* Comparative Political Studies, 43 (12): 1575–1600.

Thomas, Sue. 1994. *How Women Legislate.* New York: Oxford University Press.

Thomas, Sue, and Susan Welch. 1991. *"The Impact of Gender on Activities and Priorities of State Legislators."* Western Political Quarterly, 44 (2): 445–56.

Threlfall, Monica. 2007. *"Explaining Gender Parity Representation in Spain: The Internal Dynamics of Parties."* West European Politics, 30 (5): 1068–95.

Threlfall, Monica, Lenita Freidenvall, Malgorzata Furzara and Drude Dahlerup. 2012. "Remaking Political Citizenship in Multicultural Europe: Addressing Citizenship Deficits in the Formal Political Representation System." In *Remaking Citizenship in Multicultural Europe,* eds. Beatrice Halsaa, Sasha Roseneil and Sevil Sümer. The FEMCIT-project. London: Palgrave, 141–65.

Tomz, Michael, Jason Wittenberg, and Gary King. 2003. CLARIFY: Software for Interpreting and Presenting Statistical Results. Version 2.1. Stanford University, University of Wisconsin, and Harvard University. January 5. http://gking.harvard.edu/.

Townsend-Bell, Erica. 2011. *"What Is Relevance? Defining Intersectional Praxis in Uruguay."* Political Research Quarterly, 64: (1): 187–99.

Trahan, Adam. 2011. *"Qualitative Research and Intersectionality."* Critical Criminology, 19 (1): 1–14.

Tremblay, M. 2007. *"Electoral Systems and Substantive Representation of Women: A Comparison of Australia, Canada and New Zealand."* Commonwealth & Comparative Politics, 45 (3): 278–302.

Trembley, Manon. 2003. *"Women's Representational Role in Australia and Canada: The Impact of Political Context."* Australian Journal of Political Science, 38 (2): 215–39.

Tripp, Aili Mari, and Melanie Hughes. N.d. "Women, Civil War, and Political Representation in Africa."

Tripp, Aili Mari, Isabel Casimiro, Joy Kwesiga, and Alice Mungwa. 2008. *African Women's Movements: Transforming Political Landscapes.* Cambridge: Cambridge University Press.

True, Jacqui, and Michael Mintrom. 2001. *"Transnational Networks and Policy Diffusion: The Case of Gender Mainstreaming."* International Studies Quarterly, 45 (1): 27–57.

Truman, David B. 1951. *The Governmental Process: Political Interests and Public Opinion.* New York: Knopf.

Tsikata, Dzodzi. 1998. "The First Lady Syndrome." *Public Agenda*, January 19.

United Nations Development Program. 2011. "Table 4: Gender Inequality Index and Related Indicators." http://hdr.undp.org/en/media/HDR_2011_EN_Table4.pdf.

Urbinati, Nadia, and Mark Warren. 2008. *"The Concept of Representation in Contemporary Democratic Theory."* Annual Review of Political Science 11: 387–412.

Valdini, Melody Ellis. 2012. *"A Deterrent to Diversity: The Conditional Effect of Electoral Rules on the Nomination of Women Candidates."* Electoral Studies, 41 (4): 740–49.

Vickers, Jill. 2006. "The Problem with Interests: Making Political Claims for Women." In *The Politics of Women's Interests: New Comparative Perspectives*, eds. Louise Chappell and Lisa Hill. London and New York: Routledge, 5–38.

Wade, Peter. 1997. *Race and Ethnicity in Latin America*. London; Chicago: Pluto Press.

Wadsworth, Nancy. 2011. "Intersectionality in California's Same-Sex Marriage Battles: A Complex Proposition." *Political Research Quarterly*, 64 (1): 200–16.

Walsh, Denise. 2012. "Party Centralization and Debate Conditions in South Africa." In *The Impact of Quota Laws*, eds. Susan Franceschet, Mona Lena Krook, and Jennifer M. Piscopo. New York: Oxford University Press, 119–35.

Walsh, Denise. 2010. *Women's Rights in Democratizing States: Just Debate and Gender Justice in the Public Sphere*. Cambridge: Cambridge University Press.

Wängnerud, Lena. 2009. *"Women in Parliaments: Descriptive and Substantive Representation."* Annual Review of Political Science, 12: 51–69.

Wängnerud, Lena. 2000. "Representing Women." In *Beyond Westminster and Congress: The Nordic Experience*, eds. Peter Esaisson and Knut Heidar. Columbus: Ohio State University Press, 132–54.

Welch, Susan, and Donley T. Studlar. 1986. *"British Public Opinion toward Women in Politics: A Comparative Perspective."* Western Political Quarterly, 39 (1): 138–52.

Weldon, S. Laurel. 2011a. *"Perspectives Against Interests: Sketch of a Feminist Political Theory of 'Women.'"* Politics & Gender, 7 (3): 441–46.

Weldon, S. Laurel. 2011b. *When Protest Makes Policy: How Social Movements Represent Disadvantaged Groups*. Ann Arbor: University of Michigan Press.

Weldon, Laurel. 2008. "Intersectionality." In *Politics, Gender and Concepts*, eds. Gary Goertz and Amy G. Mazur. Cambridge: Cambridge University Press, 193–218.

Weldon, S. Laurel. 2002a. *Protest, Policy, and the Problem of Violence Against Women*. Pittsburgh, PA: University of Pittsburgh Press.

Weldon, S. Laurel. 2002b. "Beyond Bodies: Institutional Sources of Representation for Women in Democratic Policymaking." *Journal of Politics*, 64 (4): 1153–74.

Whip, Rosemary. 1991. *"Representing Women: Australian Female Parliamentarians on the Horns of a Dilemma."* Women and Politics, 11 (3): 1–22.

WILDAF. 2001. "List of Offices." http://membres.multimania.fr/cyberlys/wildaf/html/eng.html (Accessed April 3, 2012).

Wiliarty, Sarah Elise. 2010. *The CDU and the Politics of Gender in Germany*. Cambridge: Cambridge University Press.

Williams, Margaret. 2007. *"Women's Representation on State Trial and Appellate Courts."* Social Science Quarterly, 88 (5): 1192–204.

Williams, Margaret S. and Frank C. Thames. 2008. *"Women's Representation on High Courts."* Politics & Gender, 4 (3): 451–71.

Winker, Gabriele, and Nina Degele. 2011. *"Intersectionality as Multi-Level Analysis: Dealing with Social Inequality."* European Journal of Women's Studies, 18 (1): 51–66.

Wolbrecht, Christina. 2002. "Female Legislators and the Women's Rights Agenda: From Feminine Mystique to Feminist Era." In *Women Transforming Congress*, ed. Cindy Simon Rosenthal. Norman: University of Oklahoma Press, 170–239.

Wolbrecht, Christina. 2000. *The Politics of Women's Rights: Parties, Positions, and Change*. Princeton, NJ: Princeton University Press.

"Women's Rights Protocol: Challenges of Domestication," *Pambazuka News* 222, September 20, 2005. http://www.pambazuka.org/en/issue/222.

Woon, Jonathan. 2009. *"Issue Attention and Legislative Proposals in the U.S. Senate." Legislative Studies Quarterly,* 34 (1): 29–54.

World Bank. 2011. *World Development Indicators.* http://data.worldbank.org/data-catalog/world-development-indicators (Accessed May 4, 2011).

Wotipka, Christine Min, and Francisco Ramirez. 2008. "World Society and Human Rights: An Event History Analysis of the Convention on the Elimination of All Forms of Discrimination Against Women." In *The Global Diffusion of Markets and Democracy*, eds. Beth Simmons, Frank Dobbin, and Geoffrey Garrett. Cambridge: Cambridge University Press, 303–43.

Young, Iris Marion. 2002. *"Lived Body versus Gender: Reflections on Social Structure and Subjectivity." Ratio,* 15 (4): 410–28.

Young, Iris Marion. 2000. *Inclusion and Democracy.* Oxford and New York: Oxford University Press.

Yuval-Davis, Nira. 2006. *"Intersectionality and Feminist Politics." European Journal of Women's Studies,* 13 (3): 193–209.

Zetterberg, Pär. 2009. "Engendering Equality? Assessing the Multiple Impacts of Electoral Gender Quotas." Ph.D. dissertation. Uppsala University. Dept. of Political Science.

INDEX

Bettiol, Guiseppe, 103
Biden, Joe, 46
bill content codes, 191–94,
  192–93t, 207–9
bill sponsorship: abortion, partisan
  differences in, 165, 166, 178; by
  cabinet ministers, 211, 212t,
  218–21, 220t, 222–24, 232–33; committee position as predictor of, 160,
  167, 177, 180, 194–95; on education
  policy, 164, 165–66, 165t, 170–71t;
  gender differences in, 214–17,
  216–17f, 219–21, 222–24, 232–33;
  on healthcare policy, 164–65, 165t,
  166–67, 168–69t; by legislators,
  211–17, 212t, 215t, 216f, 222,
  223, 232; political opportunity structure influencing, 210; on women's
  health policy, 164, 165–66, 165t,
  167, 172–73t; on women's interests,
  209, 210
birth control methods, access to,
  30, 30n22
Bjørklund, Tor, 80
Blofield, Merike, 139
Bond, Elizabeth Andrews, 13
Borrelli, MaryAnne, 210
Bratton, Kathleen A., 44, 102, 188, 207
Brazil: disparities in education and poverty, 122; legalization of divorce in,
  138–39; racial classification in, 121;
  representation of Afrodescendant
  women in, 119, 123–25, 124t,
  129, 130–31
breast cancer movement, 41
Brinker, Roberta, 57
Brown, Nadia, 44
Butler, Judith, 59, 68

cabinet ministers: bill sponsorship by,
  211, 212t, 218–21, 220t, 222–24,
  232–33; political opportunity
  structure and, 210; as venues of
  representation, 34, 144, 155, 223–24,
  234–35; women members in Latin
  America, 209–10
Campbell Barr, Epsy, 131–32
Canada, reproductive rights in, 30
candidate lists, 79, 141
Carroll, Susan J., 185, 187, 207

categories of difference, approaches to
  conceptualizing, 49–50, 49t
Catholic groups, mobilization of,
  137–39, 141, 147, 148t
CEDAW (Convention on the Elimination
  of All Forms of Discrimination Against
  Women), 11, 140, 227–28
Celis, Karen, 2, 6, 9, 11, 16, 34,
  64–65, 236
Center Party (Norway), 83, 84, 85, 88, 92
Chihuán Ramos, Leyla, 128–29, 131
children and family issues, as women's
  interests, 208
Childs, Sarah, 2, 229, 237
Chile, abortion laws in, 30n23, 139
Choo, Hae Yeon, 44, 47, 51
Christian Democratic party
  (Germany), 107
Christian's People's Party (Norway), 83,
  84, 85, 88, 90, 92, 94
civil society organizations, 137–57;
  actors involved in, 138–39; advocacy strategies of, 137–38, 141–46;
  alliances formed by, 155–56;
  anti-feminist mobilization and, 138–
  39; conflict within, 156; directions
  for future research, 155–56; domestic
  strategies of, 140–41; influence on ratification of Maputo Protocol, 137–38,
  141–55, 147t, 153t, 234; international
  strategies of, 140; lobbying by, 140–
  41; opposition strategies of, 137–38,
  146–50, 147t; policy outcomes and,
  137, 139, 140, 155, 234, 236
claims-making, 32
closed list systems, 79
Cohen, Cathy, 43
Colombia: cabinet minister-sponsored
  bills in, 211, 212t, 218, 219–21, 220t,
  222–24, 232; gender differences in
  bill sponsorship in, 214–16, 216f,
  219–21, 222–24, 232; gender quotas
  in, 211; legislator-sponsored bills in,
  211–13, 212t, 214–17, 215t, 216f,
  222–23, 232; party system in, 210;
  racial classification in, 121; representation of Afrodescendant women
  in, 119, 124t, 125, 131; substantive
  representation in, 15–16; voter motivations in, 128

committee leadership by women, 71

committee position, as predictor of bill sponsorship, 160, 167, 177, 180, 194–95

competing policy demands, 7, 19, 23, 228, 244

complex causality, 48

concept stretching, 62, 65, 233

Congress, U.S.: constraints facing female members of, 33; House of Representatives, 158, 160; income of members, 23n8; race of members, 23n7. *see also* Senate, U.S.

Conservative Party (Great Britain), 107

Conservative Party (Norway), 83, 84, 85, 88, 92, 93

constituency: legislative influence of, 101, 173; relationship with representatives, 63

constitutional courts: appointment of women to, 13; cross-national dynamics in, 109–16, 110t, 112t, 115f; as venues of representation, 34–35

contraceptives, access to, 30, 30n22

Convention on the Elimination of All Forms of Discrimination Against Women (CEDAW), 11, 140, 227–28

Córdoba, Piedad, 131, 133

corporate gender quotas, 115, 116

Costa Rica: cabinet minister-sponsored bills in, 211, 212t, 218, 220t, 221, 222–23, 232–33; gender differences in bill sponsorship in, 216–17, 217f, 221, 222–24, 232–33; gender quotas in, 211; legislator-sponsored bills in, 211–13, 212t, 216–17, 222, 223, 232; party system in, 210; representation of Afrodescendant women in, 119, 124t, 125, 131–32; substantive representation in, 15–16

courts. *see* constitutional courts; high courts

Crenshaw, Kimberle Williams, 43, 44, 45, 46, 47, 48, 187

critical actors, 229

Dahlerup, Drude: on changes in women's political representation, 72; on concept stretching, 12; ideological restrictions on women's issues, 184; on representation as dynamic process, 104, 244; substantive representation, lack of criteria for evaluating, 61, 69, 230, 233; on women's movements, 156

Day O'Connor, Sandra, 107

deliberative democracy, 21, 42

Democratic Party (U.S.), 107, 159, 161–62, 166, 176, 177–78, 181

Denmark, national legislature and high court in, 109, 110t, 111, 112t, 113

descriptive representation: defined, 3; growth of, 245, 247; policy outcomes and, 6; preferential voting, impact on, 101–2; significance of, 3–4; substantive representation resulting from, 4–5, 183, 205

developing countries, women's interests in, 10–11

Dhamoon, Rita, 52

Diaz, Mercedes Mateo, 67

difference fallacy, 72n4

doctrinal vs. non-doctrinal issues, 139

Dodson, Debra L., 33, 185, 207

Dubrow, Joshua Kjerulf, 47–48

Eastern Europe, lack of gender bias in, 82

Economic Community of West African States (ECOWAS) Court of Justice, 140

Ecuador, representation of Afrodescendant women in, 119, 124t, 125, 128, 131

education policy: bill content codes for, 194; constituent demand influencing legislation on, 173; gender as predictor of activism on, 159, 160, 176; partisanship as predictor of activism on, 160, 161–62, 176, 181; political opportunity structure shaping, 176–77; Senate sponsorship of, 164, 165–66, 165t, 170–71t; state legislatures, (race, ethnicity, gender) leadership on, 197–99, 199t, 203–4

electoral gender quotas, 64, 72

electoral incentives, 2, 2n1, 242

electoral institutions, 80, 102

electoral rules, 80, 92

Goertz, Gary, 46, 56
Goetz, Anne Marie, 64
Government of India Act, 28
Great Britain, advancement of women in, 106, 107
Greenwood, Ronnie, 46
Griswold v. Connecticut (1965), 30*n*22
group interests, defined, 12
Gudiño, Zobeida, 128, 129, 131

Halsaa, Beatrice, 66
Hancock, Ange-Marie: on operationalization of intersectionality, 12, 49, 55, 156, 187, 244; on privileged sub-groups, 7; on representational identities, 233
Handel, Karen, 42, 53
Harmony Centre party (Latvia), 96, 97, 100
Hassim, Shireen, 64
Hawkesworth, Mary, 44
Haynie, Kerry L., 15, 232
healthcare policy: bill content codes for, 194; constituent demand influencing legislation on, 173; gender as predictor of activism on, 158–59, 160, 176; partisanship as predictor of activism on, 160, 161–62, 176, 181; political opportunity structure shaping, 176–77; Senate sponsorship of, 164–65, 165*t*, 166–67, 168–69*t*; state legislatures, (race, ethnic, gender), leadership on, 196, 198*t*, 203
Hellevik, Ottar, 80
hierarchies of power, 20*n*2
high courts, 103–17; appointment methods for, 106–7, 108–9, 113; cross-national dynamics in, 109–16, 110*t*, 112*t*, 115*f*; executive appointments to, 106–7, 109; explanations for gender inclusiveness on, 105–9; gender equality on, 104, 105–9, 114, 115–16; ideology of appointer impacting, 107, 108, 113; legislative gender balance promoting change in, 13, 105, 106, 107–8, 108*f*, 116–17; representation of women, importance of, 103–4, 116–17, 236; as venues of representation, 236, 239, 240*t*
HIV/AIDS, 43

Hoekstra, Valerie, 13, 230, 234, 236
House of Representatives, U.S., 158, 160
Htun, Mala: on anticipatory representation, 4; comparison of women's rights policy making, 138–39; on defining women's interests, 20*n*2; on electoral incentives, 2*n*1; future research directions of, 70; on political advancement of women, 107; on representation of Afrodescendant women, 14, 230; on venues of representation, 234
Hughes, Melanie, 2*n*1, 126

IDEA (Institute for Democracy and Electoral Assistance), 28
identity politics, 44, 45, 59, 190
inclusive representation, 239–42, 240*t*
incremental track changes, 72
India, gender quotas in, 28
industrialized democracies, women's interests in, 10
Inglehart, Ronald, 96
Institute for Democracy and Electoral Assistance (IDEA), 28
Inter-American Development Bank, 132
interest groups, 36, 43, 176, 235, 237
interests: defined, 11–12, 20; issues and preferences vs., 12, 23–26, 25*f*, 231; power shaping, 21; social construction of, 21. *see also* women's interests
intersectional identity, 11, 12
intersectionality, 41–57; Afrodescendant women and, 126–27, 133–34; categories of difference, approaches to conceptualizing, 49–50, 49*t*; diversity within groups and, 23, 26, 39–40, 54–55, 243; embodied approach to, 44–47, 51, 56; inclusive representation and, 241, 242; Komen Foundation–Planned Parenthood case study, 41–42, 44, 45–46, 52–54, 57; operationalizing, challenges of, 12, 42–44, 56, 244; paradigm, 12, 50–55, 57; political, 43, 45, 187; privileged sub-groups and, 43, 44, 46; quantitative and qualitative dimensions of, 43, 44, 47–48, 51, 54–55; representational, 45; reproductive rights and, 30; state legislatures and, 187; strategic, 44, 46, 56;

workers, shaping forces on,
20–21
Workers' Party (Brazil), 130–31
World Bank, 121, 132
World Conferences for Women (UN),
227–28

xenophobic parties, 73

Young, Iris Marion, 67

Zito, Andreia, 125
ZZS party (Latvia), 96, 97, 100